The Street Railways of
Grand Rapids

Horsecars • Cable Cars
Steam Dummies • Electric Streetcars

by Carl Bajema and Tom Maas

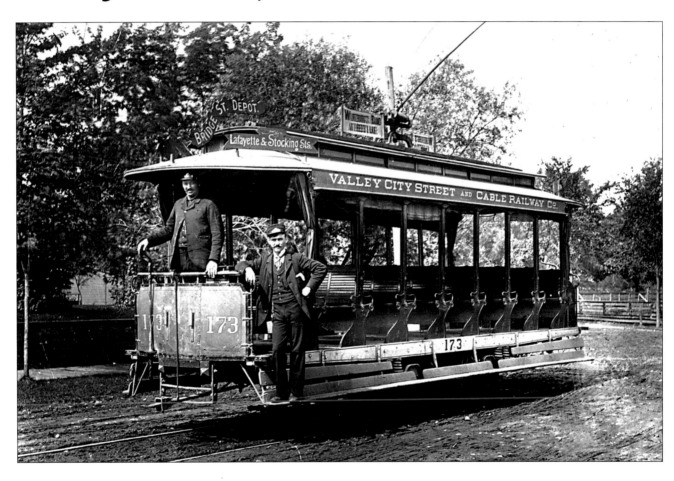

Bulletin 148 of the
Central Electric Railfans' Association

ISSN 0069-1623

The Street Railways of
Grand Rapids

Horsecars • Cable Cars
Steam Dummies • Electric Streetcars

by Carl Bajema and Tom Maas

Bulletin 148 of the
Central Electric Railfans' Association

ISSN 0069-1623

CERA DIRECTORS 2015

© 2017 by the Central Electric Railfans' Association
An Illinois Not-for-Profit Corporation
Post Office Box 503, Chicago, Illinois 60690. U.S.A.

The Street Railways of Grand Rapids was designed
by Jack and Ad Sowchin

Edited by Tom Maas and John D. Nicholson

Production was coordinated By John D. Nicholson

Library of Congress Cataloging-in-Publication Data

Names: Bajema, Carl Jay, 1937- author. | Maas, Tom, 1959- author.

Title: The street railways of Grand Rapids : horsecars, cable cars, steam
       dummies, electric streetcars / by Carl Bajema and Tom Maas.

Description: Chicago, Illinois : Central Electric Railfans' Association,[2017] |
       Series: Bulletin ... of the Central Electric Railfans' Association,
       ISSN 0069-1623 ; 148 | Includes bibliographical references and index.

Identifiers: LCCN 2017022447 | ISBN 9780915348480 (hardcover : alk. paper)

Subjects: LCSH: Street-railroads—Michigan—Grand Rapids—History.

Classification: LCC HE4491.G72 B35 2017 | DDC 388.4/60977456—dc23

Foreword

Step back in time and take a ride with us on the streetcars of Grand Rapids. Horsecars (1865-1892) first ran on Canal Street and Monroe Avenue; cable cars (1888-1891) ran up and down the hills of Lyon Street and East Bridge Street (now Michigan Avenue); steam dummy trains went to Ramona Park at Reed's Lake and to North Park resort on the banks of the Grand River; electric streetcars (1891-1935) and interurban cars (1901-1928) ushered Grand Rapids into the modern transit era. All carried passengers over the decades to and from Grand Rapids and within the city itself. They provide us with a window to view what it was like to live in Grand Rapids between 1865 and 1935 when these cars were in operation.

The first horsecar line ran south from the Detroit and Milwaukee Railroad depot down Canal street (now lower Monroe Avenue) and passed through the factory district along the east side power canal, the business and shopping district, Campau Square, up Monroe Avenue and ended at the Fulton Street and Jefferson Avenue intersection. A horsecar line was built south on Division Avenue to Hall Street in 1873 ending at the fairgrounds. Jerry Boynton, a local promoter, built a horsecar line all the way to Reed's Lake, the area's most popular local resort, in 1875. Horses pulled short cars of 10 to14 feet in length whose speed seldom exceeded 6 mph. Extra horses were often necessary to help tow a car up a grade on a street. All the horsecar lines were consolidated in the years 1882 through1885.

Small steam dummy locomotives replaced horses on the line to Reed's Lake in 1882 enabling the line to transport more passengers in a shorter time to the Reed's Lake resorts. Another steam dummy line was built to Soldiers' Home and North Park Resort in 1890.

Cable cars began running up and down the steep Lyon Street hill in 1888 and the East Bridge Street hill in 1889 forming a loop. Cable cars could be pulled up the hills that were too steep for horses to pull cars. The cable cars also provided faster service, traveling at speeds of up to 12 mph. The cable railway era lasted only 3 ½ years and was a financial disaster because of the high cost of the initial investment and the fast rate at which the cables wore out.

The electric streetcar era began in 1891 after the financially ailing horse and cable railway companies merged. As many as 100 electric streetcars could be seen traveling through Campau Square in downtown Grand Rapids in an hour by 1894. Electric streetcars had several advantages over horsecars and cable cars. Electric power made it possible to not only run streetcars at speeds as high as 20-30 mph, but also to run heavier and thus longer cars, which meant more passengers could be carried per car.

The streetcar system served three major resorts: Ramona Park adjacent Reed's Lake, North Park Resort adjacent Grand River and John Ball Park in addition to providing transportation for workers, businesses, downtown shoppers and theater goers.

The turn of the century ushered in the era of interurban travel allowing city folks to move to the suburbs or escape the city's hustle and bustle by taking an electric car from downtown Grand Rapids to the shores of Lake Michigan at Holland, Grand Haven, and Muskegon. Connecting steamer lines carried passengers across the lake to Chicago or Milwaukee.

The Grand Rapids streetcar system became a national leader in innovation with respect to streetcar design, efficient operation, courteous service, and promotion during the 1920s. Motor buses, which could be operated more efficiently, began replacing Grand Rapids streetcar lines in 1932. Within three years there was only one streetcar line remaining.

Miles McDonald, an employee of the streetcar company for 40 years was the conductor on the last electric trolley car to run in Grand Rapids on August 26, 1935. With his four decades of faithful service to the public and the company, Miles McDonald was an example of the dedicated employees who were "the soul of the corporation." It is to these employees to whom we dedicate this book.

Carl Bajema
Tom Maas
Grand Rapids, Michigan
February 2017

Acknowledgments

The authors wish to thank the following whose knowledge and assistance made this book possible:

- James Anderson
- Richard Andrews
- Sam Ashendorf
- Claudia Bajema
- Ed Bawden
- Tom Beutner
- Brian Bluekamp
- William Branz
- David Britten
- Jim Budzynski
- Tim Bultman
- Chris Byron
- Sue Carpenter
- Coopersville Museum
- Thomas Dilley
- Rev. Stephen S. Dudek
- East Grand Rapids History Room
- Tim Gleisner
- Grand Rapids City Archives
- Grand Rapids Public Library
- Grand Rapids Public Museum
- Grand Valley State University Library
- Jenison Historical Association
- Gordon Hubenet
- Karl Heckman
- Mark Hildebrandt
- Historical Society of Pennsylvania
- Dave Kindem (deceased)
- Norm Krentel
- Ron Kuiper
- Miles McDonald's descendants
- Graydon Meintz
- Jim Miller
- Minnesota Railroad Museum
- Roger Monk
- Allen Morrison
- Art Peterson
- Joe Rogers
- John Rothwell
- Gail Snow
- Smithsonian Institution
- Ron Strauss
- Dave Tinder
- Dana Troub
- University of Michigan Libraries
- Marilyn Van Orden
- West Michigan Railroad Historical Society
- Tom Wilson
- David Winick
- Shawn Wigant
- Jim Winslow Sr.
- Mark Worrall
- Charles Wrege
- Wyoming Historical Commission
- Many more…

The authors especially want to thank Roy Benedict for his assistance with the manuscript and also for his essay on James Russell Chapman.

The Street Railways of Grand Rapids

Contents

Horse-drawn cars on Canal Street, View looking north from
Campau Place (Square), Note passing siding on Canal Street.
Grand Rapids Public Library

The Street Railways of Grand Rapids

Riding Horsecars on the Streets of Grand Rapids (1865-1891)

Grand Rapids Street Railway Company (1865-1869)

Grand Rapids, Michigan celebrated two major events during the spring of 1865. The Civil War ended in April with a victory for the Union. Grand Rapids citizens also celebrated May 10, 1865, "with music, fire-works, speeches and free rides on the one-horse cars." The city of 9,000 now had its own street railway.

The young city of Grand Rapids was built in a narrow valley along the east bank of the Grand River. Water in the river dropped approximately eighteen feet in about one-half mile while flowing down the rapids. Pioneers harnessed some of the water power of the river by building a power canal along the east side of the river and constructing a wing dam to divert some of the water. Industries used the water flowing down the canal to operate machinery.

The "iron horse" arrived in 1858, connecting Grand Rapids to a rapidly growing network of iron rails. However, the steam railroad track and the Detroit & Milwaukee Railroad (D & M) depot were located more than one and one-half miles north of the center of the city. Citizens were riding horses, horse-drawn wagons, carryalls, omnibuses, hacks, two-wheel drays, and private carriages or walking to move from one section to another in the city.

William A. Richmond, Henry Grinnell, John W. Pierce, William Withey and a few other prominent citizens obtained a franchise on May 19, 1864 to build a streetcar line. The franchise gave the company the right to build and operate the line south from the D & M depot through the factory and business districts on Canal and Monroe streets. The line went east where it ended on Fulton Street at Jefferson Street, the beginning of the residential district.

They were unable to raise enough money locally, in part because of the opposition of omnibus and hack owners who did not want new competition for their business. Opponents contended that streetcars would be a nuisance in a small city of 9,000.

The local promoters turned to "foreign investors"—George Jerome in Detroit, Thomas Sprague in Saginaw and Daniel Owen in New York City, to raise most of the money necessary to build the streetcar line. These outside investors formed the Grand Rapids Street Railway Company and on October 1, 1864, obtained a franchise from the Grand Rapids Common Council to begin construction. The new company began running

horse-drawn streetcars on May 10, 1865.

The two and one-fifth-mile long standard gauge track connected the Canal Street business district with the steam railroad depot at the northern end of the line and with a large residential district on the southern end. The streetcar track was standard gauge (4 feet 8 ½ inches wide) and consisted of thin strap iron rail nailed to long wooden stringers laid on railroad ties buried in the unpaved streets.

The track left the D & M depot going a short distance south down Plainfield Road then on Coldbrook Street to Ottawa Street, and west on Newberry Street to reach Canal Street. The track ran south on Canal Street (now lower Monroe Avenue) adjacent to the factory district along the east side power canal, and into the business and shopping district adjacent to Campau Square (known then as Campau Place). The track made a zig-zag turn into Campau Square via Pearl Street and headed southeast on Monroe Street (now Avenue) to

First street car newspaper ad about time schedules and passenger fares published in the May 15, 1865 Grand Rapids Eagle.

Grand Rapids Public Library

The Street Cars.

Grand Rapids, May 15, 1865.

Ed. Eagle—Our Street Railway having been so nearly completed as to warrant commencing operations, on and after this date, cars will be run every half hour from each terminus. The first car will leave Jefferson street at 4½ o'clock every morning, for the depot, and then a car every half hour through the day. The first car from the depot will leave at 7 o'clock, A M. Special pains will be taken to make close connections with trains on the Detroit and Milwaukee railway at all hours.

The fare will be five cents for each person, babes in arms only being carried free. For each carpet bag, valise and trunk, five cents additional will be charged. Arrangements will soon be made for taking up and delivering baggage in all parts of the city.

For *this afternoon only,* everybody, citizens and children are respectfully invited to ride free.   Thos. S. Sprague,

Secretary and Sup't.

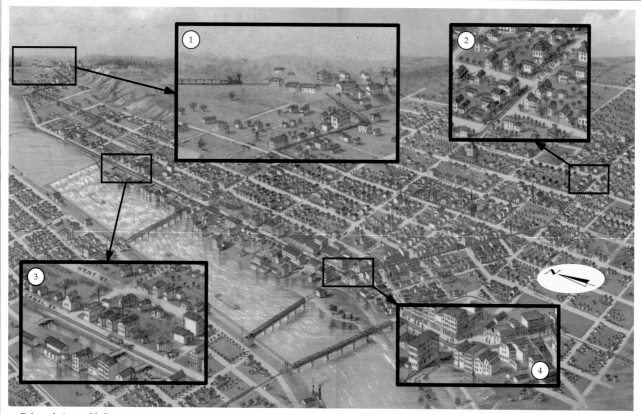

Enlarged views added:

1. Detroit & Milwaukee RR Depot at the north end of route (near Leonard St.)

2. South end of route on E. Fulton St. at Jefferson Ave.

3. Canal St. (now Monroe Ave.)

4. Campau Square before 1873 zigzag fix

First streetcar route superimposed as a red line on a bird's eye view map of Grand Rapids in 1868

Map courtesy of Grand Rapids Public Museum
© 2017 Tom Maas

Map showing the route of the first streetcar line in Grand Rapids superimposed on an excerpt from 1868 bird's-eye view of a Grand Rapids map showing route of the streetcar line from Detroit & Milwaukee RR station to Fulton and Jefferson intersection.

Fulton Street. The street railway line turned east traveling a short distance before ending at the corner of Fulton and Jefferson streets.

Service every thirty minutes in each direction could not be maintained on the single-track line without a passing siding. A switch was built on Canal Street near Bridge Street allowed southbound and northbound cars to pass each other. A bell attached to the horse's harness jingled when the horse moved so people knew that a streetcar was coming. The franchise passed by the Grand Rapids Common Council and accepted by the street railway set the speed limit at six miles per hour. At least one driver was arrested and paid a fine for exceeding this speed limit during the horsecar era.

The one-horse streetcars were small—twelve to fourteen feet in length. Passengers sat on wooden benches running the length of the car. The cars ran on four wheels with the axle bearings spring-supported in pedestals attached directly to the wooden floor beams.

The company employed a crew of two during the busy warm months—a horse driver and a conductor who collected fares. The conductor used a bell or whistle to communicate to the driver. One bell meant stop and two bells meant start. Both the driver and conductor were required to use watches to maintain their schedule. Often only one man was employed during the slower winter months to drive the car and also collect the fares.

The small streetcars frequently derailed at switches and curves. Passengers had to get out of the car and the men helped the driver and conductor lift and move the car back onto the track. When the end of the line was reached, the driver set the hand brakes. He then unhitched his horse, moved it to the other end of the streetcar where he hitched the horse, released the brakes, and began the return trip.

The new streetcar company had a roster of six horsecars by the end of 1865. Included was a freight car that could be quickly converted into an excursion car by installing four long benches that ran the length of the car.

The streetcar route included two hills to climb. A horse going northbound had to pull the streetcar up a short hill near the D & M depot while a horse going southbound had to pull a streetcar up a long hill on Canal Street from Campau Place to Fulton Street. Horses strained to pull the short passenger-laden cars up these

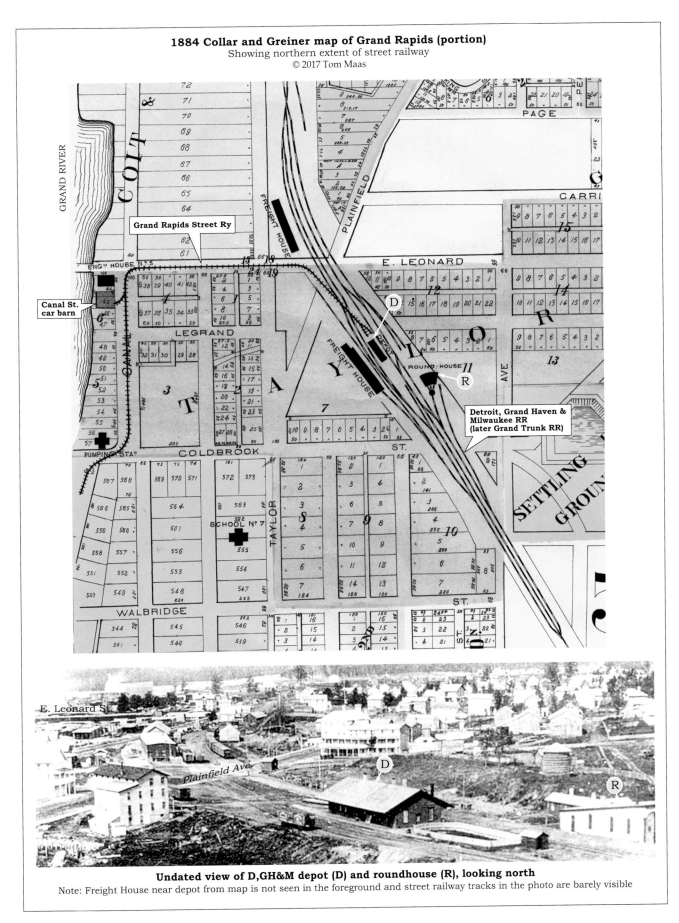

1884 Collar and Greiner map of Grand Rapids (portion)
Showing northern extent of street railway
© 2017 Tom Maas

Grand Rapids Street Ry

Canal St. car barn

Detroit, Grand Haven & Milwaukee RR (later Grand Trunk RR)

Undated view of D,GH&M depot (D) and roundhouse (R), looking north
Note: Freight House near depot from map is not seen in the foreground and street railway tracks in the photo are barely visible

Color map of streetcar tracks to the platform at the Detroit & Milwaukee Railroad station.

Chapter 1: Riding Horsecars on the Streets of Grand Rapids: 1865-1891

Zig-zag streetcar track in Campau Place circa 1868. View looking northwest.

Grand Rapids Public Library

two grades. Bad weather made the problem worse. The streetcar company was forced to add a team of one, two and even three horses to get the car up the grade.

Bad weather caused problems. A horse-drawn snow plow was often used to clear snow from the track for the horsecars. The accumulation of ice and frozen mud in the flangeways forced the street railway to discontinue service on a number of occasions. The company operated sleighs in an attempt to maintain schedules required by the franchise until the ice melted and the dirt could be removed.

Canal Street was in the Grand River flood plain. Rain storms frequently converted the unpaved street into a muddy swamp. One newspaper jokingly went so far as to ask the street railroad to provide passengers with stilts to walk over the knee-deep mud when they got off the car. City fathers tried to solve this problem by raising the grade of Canal Street several feet. Canal Street merchants used jack screws to raise their buildings to the new street grade levels.

The original route of the street railroad left Canal Street and ran on Trowbridge, Ottawa, Coldbrook streets and Plainfield Road to reach the D & M depot. The street railway tracks, being higher than the road surface, made it very difficult for other horse-drawn vehicles to travel north because they had to cross these higher tracks. Consequently, the Common Council ordered the street railway to change the route. The council ordered the company to relay its track going farther north on Canal Street to Leonard Street, then east on Leonard a short distance, and then southeast to the D & M depot. This change was completed in August 1868. The street railway also built a new horse and carbarn on Canal Street near Leonard Street later that year.

The streetcar track at the north end of the line was finally laid up to the platform of the D & M depot in early October 1869. Passengers now could "step directly from the cars to the platform and thus save wading in mud and water when it rains."

Horsecars in Campau Place and Monroe Avenue. View is looking northwest toward Campau Square (Place) circa 1887-1891 after zig-zag curve was removed.

Dave Tinder Collection, Wm Clements Library, University of Michigan

Financial Problems

Thomas Sprague, superintendent of the street railway, estimated it cost $50,000 to build the line. Passenger fares and baggage charges were the only source of income.

Fares were five cents in May 1865 and raised to ten cents later that year. Riders could save money by buying twenty commutation tickets for one dollar. (A five-cent fare in 1865, adjusted for inflation, would be around seventy-five cents in 2016 prices.) The street railway charged extra for baggage. The company reduced fares on August 15, 1866, but then raised them again on December 4, 1866.

Citizens complained about the high fares, the antiquated horsecars, and the use of worn-out horse flesh. The local newspaper reported in April 1867 that the street railway was not a paying proposition.

The street railway faced more than the basic operating expenses—paying the drivers, conductors, stable and carbarn workers, feeding and caring for the horses, and basic wear and tear on the tracks. The street railway also had to pay for raising and re-grading the right-of-way, relaying the track and repaving inside the two rails to conform to the new higher street grades on Canal Street that the Common Council ordered in 1868.

The Grand Rapids Street Railway Company, unable to pay its bills or any dividends, was sold at Chancery sale in December 1869 for $39,200 to George F. Frost of Detroit, trustee for himself and others. The company was reorganized as the Street Railway Company of Grand Rapids.

A horse-drawn streetcar turns on to East Fulton Street from Monroe Avenue. View is looking northeast at Fulton Park and the Park Congregational Church.

Thomas Dilley Collection, Grand Rapids Public Library

Street Railway Company of Grand Rapids (1870-1880)

George W. Thayer of Grand Rapids was hired to manage the streetcar line now operating in a city of 16,507 citizens, more than 6,000 more than in 1865. Thayer hired Ebenezer Anderson as his representative and active manager. The company now had cash to meet its need. Fares were set at ten cents for one ride or eight tickets for fifty cents between 6 A.M. and 9 P.M. Fares after 9 P.M. and before 6 A.M. were twenty cents a ride. The company had to pay the city a $15 license fee for each car.

The new company established a thirty-minute schedule with the first car starting from the northern end at 5:30 A.M., followed by a second car at 6 A.M. Each of the two cars made twelve round trips daily for a total distance of about fifty miles each. A third car was run when

ridership was heavy. Sixteen horses were used in pulling the cars, each team of horses working three hours and then replaced by other teams. After being stabled about four hours, the first team of horses resumed its work.

Business improved. The company began paying dividends to investors in the early 1870s. The Street Railway Company of Grand Rapids continued to operate its horsecar line, but was not interested in extending the original route, even though the franchise gave the company exclusive first right to build on a street and be the only company operating on that street. Grand Rapids citizens organized three street railway companies to build and operate separate lines—one running on south Division Street (1873-1883), another going all the way from the east side city limits to the west side city limits (1875-1879), and one running on Scribner Street on the west side. This line was extended

View of the rear of a horsecar at Campau Square, about to go under the 50' high patriotic Centennial Arch of 1876. View looks northwest.

Dave Tinder collection, Wm Clements Library, University of Michigan

to cross the river and go all the way to the Union Station on south Ionia Street (1878-1883).

In 1875 riders complained about long headways (thirty minutes or more) on the Canal-Monroe Street line of the "old company". They pointed out, as presently managed, "nobody ever thinks of waiting for a car even if he has a mile or more to walk." The Common Council finally ordered the company to operate a thirty-minute schedule between 6:30 A.M. and 6:30 P.M. stating cars must run every fifteen minutes within two months. In August the council ordered the company to build a double-track line on Monroe and Canal streets to Bridge Street while the two streets were being re-graded and paved. The company refused, contending the council did not have the legal authority to require a double-track line to be built. However, the company did agree to lay new and better track and to put improved rolling stock in service and run them on a fifteen-minute schedule once the streets were fully re-graded.

The Street Railway Company of Grand Rapids bought six "bobtail" horse-drawn street cars in 1876 to provide fifteen-minute service to lower operating costs. Bobtail cars had only one platform in the front, thus the name "bob-

tail" because their rear platform ("tail") was "lopped off." These cars were cheaper to operate as they only needed a driver. The conductor was replaced by a cash fare register. Being smaller and lighter a bobtail car was easier for a horse to pull. When a bobtail car reached the end of a streetcar line, it was reversed on a turntable or on a wye which required three switches.

The street railway company also purchased three large two-horse streetcars to carry passengers and their baggage to and from the hotels and the D & M depot. The company built a new stable and carbarn on Canal Street just south of Leonard Street in 1876. The barn contained 28 horse stalls and two 102 ft. long tracks for the cars.

Service on the streetcar lines in Grand Rapids had deteriorated badly by 1879. The local press cited, among other problems, poor track, dilapidated equipment, and insufficient number of cars in service.

The Street Railway Company of Grand Rapids purchased the bankrupt Grand Rapids and Reed's Lake Street Railway Company in November 1879, but operated the two street railways as separate companies at the beginning of the 1880s.

The Division Street Railway Company (1873-1883)

The State Fair scheduled for the Kent County Fair Ground in September 1873 led some prominent Grand Rapids citizens to organize the Division Street Railway Company to build a second street railway in Grand Rapids. A standard-gauge line was constructed that ran south for more than a mile on Division Avenue from Fulton Street to Hall Street. The line turned east and traveled a short distance on Hall Street until it reached Jefferson Avenue, at the entrance to the Kent County Fair Ground located on the south side of Hall Street.

The line began operating in September, just in time to carry passengers to and from the 1873 State Fair. The company purchased ten one-horse cars, each of which accommodated ten to twelve persons nicely.

The Division Street Railway provided citizens with an easier way to attend horse races, circuses, baseball games and fairs at the Kent County Fair Ground, in addition to traveling to and from the southern part of Grand Rapids. The streetcar company put in three switches by July 1874 so that southbound and northbound cars could pass one another while maintaining a schedule with horsecars starting from both the northern and southern ends of the line every fifteen minutes. While fast service was important, the Common Council's

franchise stated no car could exceed six miles an hour. Louis H. Winegar, the thirteen-year-old son of Superintendent Winegar of the Division Street Railway, was arrested and fined $5.45 on August 31, 1883, for driving a two-horse streetcar faster than the six miles an hour limit.

There was no physical connection between the two street railways at the northern terminus of the Division Street car line. Passengers not only had to walk a short distance between the old street railway on Monroe Avenue and the Division Street car line at the Division and Monroe Avenue intersection, they also had to pay a second fare when they climbed aboard the streetcar of another company to continue their journey.

The Division Street Railway extended its track on Hall Street farther east to Oak Hill and Valley City cemeteries in July 1881. The company also built a line that went east on Fifth Street (now Franklin Avenue) to Lafayette Street (now Avenue) and extended the branch south on Lafayette to Hall Street forming a circuit with the Hall Street branch.

The Street Railway of Grand Rapids purchased the Division Street Railway Company in December 1883, in addition to having just purchased the Grand Rapids & Reed's Lake Street Railway Company and the West Side Street Railway of Grand Rapids. The new owners installed a switch in January 1884 that connected the Division Street line with Monroe Avenue so that the Division line cars started from Campau Square at the south end of Canal Street.

Grand Rapids and Reed's Lake Street Railway Company (1875-1879)

The Grand Rapids & Reed's Lake Street Railway Company, the third and the longest horse-drawn street railway in Grand Rapids, was organized in March 1875 and built in 1875 and 1876. Jeremiah W. Boynton, better known to locals as "Jerry," was one of the most colorful promoters of street railroads in Grand Rapids, eventually building three separate divisions of the Grand Rapids and Reed's Lake Street Railway Company. See Jerry's biography in Chapter 12.

Boynton always seemed to be on the verge of financial ruin. Yet somehow he was able to raise just enough cash and loans from local citizens, strap iron rail from manufacturers, and rolling stock from horsecar builders to build a streetcar line. It extended east from the southeastern edge of downtown at LaGrave Avenue-Fulton Street intersection all the way to the city limit at East Street (now Eastern Avenue). Boynton's goal was to build a street railroad east from the city limit all the way to Reed's Lake where he also planned to build a resort. He succeeded in constructing a streetcar line that went beyond the city two and one-third miles into Grand Rapids Township to reach Reed's Lake at the end of July 1875.

Reed's Lake was a major resort destination for six months of the year—late April to October. Sundays were the busiest because laborers and store clerks had their one and only day off each week. The Reed's Lake division of the Grand Rapids & Reed's Lake street car line was only a seasonal operation. The company often ran cars only on Sundays during late April, early May, and late September to early October.

Nearly 4,000 persons visited Reed's Lake on Sunday, August 1, 1875. The new Reed's Lake horsecar line carried 2,800 riders to the lake. Reed's Lake was rapidly on its way to becoming the most popular resort in the Grand Rapids region. The street railway had to work hard to change the atmosphere around Reed's Lake from that of drunken men to daytime family resorts.

Jerry Boynton started building the west side division of the Grand Rapids & Reed's Lake Street Railway in July 1875 just after he had completed the Reed's Lake division street railway line that went east through Grand Rapids Township to Reed's Lake. The West Bridge Street division was completed and operating by January 1876. It went north on Kent Street from Lyon Street and then west on Bridge Street all the way to the city limits near the foot of west Bridge Street hill.

Each division of Boynton's Grand Rapids & Reed's Lake Railway had its own franchise which allowed each to be treated as a separate

legal entity—a five-cent fare for each division and no free transfers. The three were:

- **West Bridge Street division** from Lyon-Kent Street intersection in downtown Grand Rapids to the end of the line at bottom of the hill on west Bridge Street
- **Eastern division within city of Grand Rapids** from Lyon-Kent Street intersection to the city limit on East Street at Sherman Street
- **Eastern division in Suburban Grand Rapids Township** from the city limit at East Avenue east on Sherman Street to Reed's Lake

Jerry Boynton finally got the eastern and western divisions within Grand Rapids connected at the intersection of Lyon and Kent streets in November 1876. While the two divisions were now connected, passengers still had to leave the car they on which they arrived and board a car headed out the remaining third division, paying an additional five-cent fare.

Eastbound cars on the West Bridge Street division stopped at the Kent-Lyon Street intersection and were reversed on a turntable. The cars headed back north on Kent Street to East Bridge Street (later to become Michigan Avenue, then Michigan Street), turned west on East Bridge Street, went downhill to cross Canal Street and the Grand River until reaching the turntable forming the western terminus of the line at Lincoln Park at the foot of West Bridge Street hill.

Cars on the eastern division line of the Grand Rapids & Reed's Lake Railroad left the turntable heading east on Lyon street, turned south on Division Avenue to Monroe Avenue where the cars traversed the track of the "old" street railway a short distance to LaGrave Street (now Avenue) where the cars went south to Wealthy Street. The cars continued east on Wealthy Street to East Avenue at the city limit. Finally the cars went south a short distance on East Avenue to the end of the line at the station and carbarn, which were located on the south side of Sherman Street which intersected with East Avenue.

Passengers could pay another five cents and board a car on the line of the Grand Rapids & Reed's Lake Street Railway that was built in Grand Rapids Township and travel east two and one-third miles and get off at the end of the line to enjoy the resorts at Reed's Lake.

Jerry Boynton hoped to purchase a steam dummy to run in Grand Rapids Township to Reed's Lake as early as 1875. However, Jerry never was able to raise enough money to purchase the heavy rail required for even a small steam locomotive to run on. Almost always short of the cash and operating with the rolling stock and rails mortgaged to the hilt, Boynton finally lost control of the Grand Rapids & Reed's Lake Street Railway Company

Grand Rapids & Reed's Lake car on Bridge Street.

Thomas Dilley Collection, Grand Rapids Public Library

when it was sold at a sheriff's sale on November 24, 1879, for $1,500 plus a $15,000 mortgage against the rolling stock, horses, and track. The Street Railway Company of Grand Rapids took possession of the line but ran it as a separate subsidiary until August 17, 1885. The company did make a major change in 1881 when it purchased steam dummies to run on the Sherman Street line in Grand Rapids Township to Reed's Lake.

The West Side Street Railway Company of Grand Rapids (1878-1883)

Jerry Boynton obtained a franchise on May 27, 1878, to build a street railway on Scribner Street and other streets in the city. Jerry lacked capital but not enthusiasm nor the time and energy to get the "Scribner Street car line" built and equipped. Jerry asked "every man he met, strangers as well as friends, to invest in stock. When he could not induce them to invest he asked for a personal loan of ten or twenty dollars."

The Scribner Street Railway initially ran north on its namesake street from West Bridge Street to Webster Street, north of West Leonard Street. Scribner Street cars began running on the tracks of the Grand Rapids & Reed's Lake Railway at west Bridge Street and went across the Grand River as far as the corner of Division and Monroe streets.

Boynton managed somehow to maintain control of his west side Scribner Street railway line when he could not raise the necessary money to prevent others from buying his heavily mortgaged Grand Rapids & Reed's Lake Street Railway. He continued his street railway building efforts and succeeded in building an extension from West Bridge Street south through

Court, Allen, Front and then east on Pearl Street going across Pearl Street bridge. The line continued to Sweet's Hotel on the corner of Canal and Pearl streets at the foot of Monroe Avenue by June 1881. The company built new carbarns on Scribner that were completed in July.

The "old company" (running on Canal and Monroe streets) entered into a political and legal battle with the West Side Street Railway over whether a street railway can have "exclusive rights" allowing only that company to run on a particular public street. The legal battle went all the way to the Michigan Supreme Court which ruled against the old company. Boynton rapidly extended the west side streetcar line from Pearl Street south on Campau Avenue, Waterloo Street (now Market Avenue) and then south on Ionia Avenue to the Grand Rapids & Indiana Railroad (GR&I RR) Union Depot on south Ionia Avenue. The first horsecars ran over the new extension to the GR&IRR Union Depot on August 30, 1882.

Boynton succeeded in extending the Scribner Avenue streetcar line all the way north to the west side Detroit & Milwaukee Railroad depot at the Detroit, Grand Haven & Milwaukee Railroad junction by August 9, 1883.

Jerry Boynton wasn't through making it more convenient for the citizens to travel by streetcar in Grand Rapids. Less than a month later he played a leading role in bringing about the merger of three of the four streetcar lines operating in Grand Rapids.

On September 1, 1883, newspapers announced that Jerry Boynton was working with Cleveland investors to purchase the three streetcar lines and bring all three under a single management, that of the West Side Street Railway Company. The merger became official when the investors, who already controlled the Street Railway of Grand Rapids, exercised their option to buy the Grand Rapids & Reed's Lake

Street Railway Company and the West Side Street Railway Company of Grand Rapids on December 1, 1883. The Cleveland syndicate included John J. Shepherd, C. A. Otis, W. H. Hayes, Thomas Jopling and Samuel Mather. The company then purchased the fourth street railway, the Division Street Railway.

Street Railway Company of Grand Rapids Operations (1880-1890)

The four street railways operating in Grand Rapids now served a population of 32,000 people in 1880, twice the number living in Grand Rapids ten years earlier.

Mrs. Lucetta Medbury of Detroit, practically the sole owner of the Street Railway Company of Grand Rapids, along with Allen Rabineau of Detroit, James H. McKee of Minneapolis, and George Thayer of Grand Rapids, bought the bankrupt Grand Rapids and Reed's Lake Street Railway in July 1880. They made major changes in the easternmost division running east on East Street from the city limit into Grand Rapids Township ending at Reed's Lake. The very next year, 1881, steam dummies and passenger cars replaced the line's horsecars. The history of the Reed's Lake steam dummy locomotive line (1881-1891), the improvements in the line, and the company's resort adjacent Reed's Lake are chronicled in Chapter 2 in this book.

The new owners made numerous changes in 1884. The streetcars on all the lines except those of the Scribner Street car line were now to depart from Campau Square, the center of the city rather than from the intersection of Fulton and Division streets or from the intersection of Kent and Lyon streets as in the past. The company leased a store to serve as an office and waiting room at the corner of Pearl and Canal streets.

New Cars Purchased

The cars were also scheduled to leave every quarter and half hour. Fares were reduced if passengers bought a group of tickets in advance.

The street railway had forty-five cars and 130 horses in stock at the beginning of April 1884. The reorganized company ordered eighteen new twelve-foot-long bobtail cars from Brownell & Wight Company of St. Louis, Missouri in April.

Manager Atwood planned to run the new cars on the "old" Canal Street route to Campau Square every five minutes. Some of the Canal Street cars would continue running on the south Division line and LaGrave lines every ten minutes while the rest of the Canal Street cars would run on the Reed's Lake line every thirty minutes.

The company finally began building double track in 1884. The first streets to be double tracked were Canal Street north from Campau Square to Bridge Street and southeast on Monroe Street during May and June, 1884. Politicians had been campaigning for double track on these streets for almost ten years.

Track was abandoned in several streets where duplicate routes existed. Track was removed on Louis, Ionia, Kent and Lyon streets. Old worn out strap iron rails on the Scribner and LaGrave streets was also removed. The old rail made up of strap iron mounted on wooden rails (stringers) was discarded and replaced with solid iron rail.

Dustin Atwood, superintendent of the street railroad, reported at the end of May 1884 that eighty-eight cars (including open cars) were in use. He also reported that the company operated on more than sixteen miles of track and owned 170 horses.

Both Fulton Street and LaGrave Street were double tracked during the fall of 1884. Andries Bevier took over as general manager of the company's affairs in Grand Rapids by late October.

The company painted broad stripes around each car to minimize the confusion created by so many cars going through the same downtown location—Campau Place. The color of the wide panel stripe around a car indicated which line the car was going to travel on from downtown— where virtually all cars ran on the same track—to and from Campau Place. The company chose the following colors: red for LaGrave-Wealthy cars on the Reed's Lake line; a light cream color for Division, Monroe and Canal line cars; blue for West Bridge-Union depot cars; green for the Scribner line cars; and yellow for the Stocking line cars.

The city had been using pine planks for pavement on major streets since 1874 when it began to abandon stone. The street railway used cobblestones between the rails. Both the city and the street railway began using cedar blocks for pavement in 1884.

Labor Issues in 1884

Labor became a major issue in September 1884 when the street railway reduced wages by fifteen cents a day from $1.65 to $1.50 for conductors and from $1.50 to $1.35 a day for horsecar drivers. Hours were long with many of the crew working a sixteen-hour day, seven days a week.

The streetcar company also issued an order at the beginning of October that required drivers and conductors to wear gray uniforms similar to the uniforms mail carriers wore and they were required to pay $20 for the uniforms. ($20 in 1884, adjusted for inflation, is $535 in 2016 dollars.)

The Knights of Labor began a boycott of

the street railway in late October citing two reasons. A division foreman discharged twenty laborers because they belonged to the order and because the company reduced the wages paid to barn hands. Twenty-two horse-drawn carryall wagons began running on the same streets as the horsecars. The boycott lasted almost three months ending on January 12 when the Knights stopped operating carryalls which at the time were running on sleigh runners rather than wheels. The Knights of Labor most likely ran out of money supporting the boycott while the street railway company had enough funds to outlast the strikers.

The "Old" Company Makes a Big Mistake

Residents living on top of what is now known as the Heritage Hill district, east of the Grand River overlooking downtown Grand Rapids, wanted streetcar service. The Common Council finally ordered the Street Railway Company of Grand Rapids to build a cable line to serve the hill district on November 10, 1884. The "old" company declined and gave up their exclusive right to build the line. A. Bevier, manager of the street railway, stated that they had allowed their exclusive privilege to build a cable line up the hill to lapse because "They had all they could attend to in perfecting the roads now in use, both as to discipline of the men, improving the roadbed, replacing old iron with steel rails, and in fact, making them metropolitan in every respect."

This decision came back to haunt the Street Railway Company of Grand Rapids. The cable company began building horsecar lines as well as cable car lines in 1887 and became a major competitor operating numerous horsecar feeder lines in addition to the Lyon and East Bridge Street cable car lines. See chapter 3 for more information about the cable company.

Streetcar Operations

A short section of the northern end of the Scribner streetcar line from Long's Mill to the Detroit, Grand Haven & Milwaukee Railroad junction on the west side was abandoned in May. Street railway officials said that there was "but little traffic and hoodlums interfere with the drivers" as the reasons abandoning the end of the line. Track was taken up in Front Street south of West Bridge Street because the Scribner line cars had started crossing the Grand River on the Bridge Street bridge rather than the Pearl Street bridge.

Streetcar service was inaugurated between the Detroit, Grand Haven & Milwaukee Railroad depot and the Union Depot in connection with all trains in June. A branch line going

northwest on Stocking Street from West Leonard Street began operating in October.

The street railway company paved all of its lines with cobblestones. The company proudly announced at its annual meeting in July 1885 that every foot of track had been replaced with steel track and not a car or horse remained that was in service when the company began operating the street railway in 1883.

The city council finally passed a new ordinance on August 17, 1885, enabling the Street Car Company of Grand Rapids to operate all of its lines as one franchise. The company now operated 14 ½ miles on streets, of which 4 ½ miles were double track. The average number of cars in use was reported to be 21, with each car making 10 trips and running about 70 miles each. The company owned 50 cars and 172 horses, employing 71 men exclusive of track layers. The company also owned two steam dummies that ran on the Reed's Lake line in Grand Rapids Township to the lake, where the streetcar company owned and operated a resort.

The city served notice to the street railway in July 1885 that the company had to eliminate the suffocating odors coming out of the company's Canal Street barn. The company was accused of creating a cesspool by allowing horse manure and urine to fall through the floor of the barn.

Serious consideration was given to operating a steam dummy on city streets in Grand Rapids between the East Street station at the west end of the Reed's Lake line and the Grand Rapids & Indiana's Union Passenger Railroad Depot near downtown Grand Rapids. However, the city council refused to pass an ordinance allowing steam locomotives to operate on city streets. The city council and the company also fought over the type of rail to use. The company preferred T-rail while the council tried to force them to use Johnson rail. Road vehicles could cross Johnson girder rail more easily than T-rail.

The company had been putting straw on the floor of the cars to keep the passengers' feet from getting too cold. A physician pointed out that the straw on the floor provided a means for spreading disease. He reminded citizens that the filthy as well as the clean rode the streetcars. Individuals spit saliva and tobacco juice while dirt and manure on the bottom of passengers' shoes and boots brought more filth into the cars. The straw got ground into small pieces and got kicked up. This put passengers at risk of breathing in germs and getting "consumption."

Service frequency was increased through the purchase of additional horse and cars. Open cars were used in the summer months and closed cars were used the rest of the year.

Conductors had to do more than collect fares and help women and children get on and off the streetcars. They had to keep a keen eye

Grand Rapids horsecar No. 11 built by Brownell & Wight Company in 1884 on parade in the 1920s, long after its service days ended.

Pomarius Collection

on their cash boxes. Thieves stole several cash boxes while the conductors were busy and thus distracted. The company discharged several conductors for "knocking down" the fares, a polite way to describe the behavior of conductors who were suspected of or caught in the act of stealing money.

Improvements Continue

Service improvements were made on several lines by building double track. West Bridge Street was double tracked beyond Scribner Street to increase service frequency on three lines. The double track on south Division was extended almost to Wealthy Street. The company and the city council debated whether an extension of the steam dummy line into Grand Rapids all the way to the Union station should be built. The company decided to save money by using bobtail cars on the Wealthy Street line for the winter. The driver served both as driver and conductor driver, meaning he had to make sure that fares were being deposited in the cash box. A number of conductors became drivers during the slow winter months.

The company bought nine stoves in an attempt to make a few cars more comfortable during the cold winter months. They also installed new wire floor mats rather than use straw to cover the floor on these cars.

The first major snowstorm of the season saw fierce wind and flying snow cover the rails faster than the snow plows and shovelers could remove it. More than one car started bobbing and then skidding off the icy track when approaching a downhill curve.

The fight over whether to allow a steam dummy line to run on a Grand Rapids street heated up again in early January 1887. The city council finally passed a resolution in favor but the mayor quickly vetoed it.

The city council finally granted permission

that allowed the street railway to run steam dummy trains a short distance about 80 rods (1,320 feet) north on East street from the old Sherman Street station to a new station being built at Buckeye Street on East Street. The controversy, the injunctions, and the "East Street Riot" where track was torn up are discussed in Chapter 2.

New Lines built in 1887

The Street Railway Construction Company, a new subsidiary of the Street Railway of Grand Rapids, obtained an ordinance on April 5, 1887, to build a streetcar line to the west side. The line started at Campau Square. A double track was built going west on Pearl Street across the bridge to Front Street. A single-track line continued west on Shawmut Avenue to Gold Street, south to Butterworth Street, and west to Indiana Street. The company built a barn and car house on the northwest corner of Butterworth Street and Indiana Avenue.

The Common Council approved the street railway company's petition to extend its new Third Ward line from Cherry Street on East Street to Wealthy Street to reach the present terminus of the steam dummy line. The mayor vetoed the ordinance and wealthy citizens were able to file injunctions to prevent construction of the Cherry Street line. The controversy continued for several months.

The aldermen finally had enough votes to override the mayor's veto on October 10. The company had men working that very night on the line. Horsecars began running on the Cherry Street line in November 1887. The cars carried the inscription "State and Cherry streets, Shawmut and Butterworth avenues."

The company received a franchise to build the Plainfield line on October 17, accepted the franchise on November 21, and began building north on Plainfield to Coit Street and north on

Two horse-drawn cars on Monroe Avenue after double tracking. View looking northwest.

Thomas Dilley Collection at Grand Rapids

Coit to the city limit at Sweet Street. This line was later changed. Track on Coit street was taken up and the line was moved to go further north on Plainfield.

The Street Railway Company of Grand Rapids had a virtual monopoly in the city when 1887 began. That changed drastically when the Valley City Street and Cable Railway Company was organized and quickly obtained franchises to build three horsecar feeder lines in addition to its cable car line franchise. These were to be built on Lyon and East Bridge Street hills. Jerry Boynton organized the City Street Railway Company and tried to obtain a franchise to build a line starting from the Kent Street-Lyon Street intersection and going north on Kent Street and via several streets to finally continue north on Taylor Street to the northern city limits. While Boynton's efforts to build competing lines failed, it was obvious that the cable railway company was becoming a major competitor.

At the beginning of 1887 the Street Railway Company of Grand Rapids was operating on 12 ½ miles of streets within the city with only one mile of double track at the beginning of 1887. The company used 200 horses that pulled cars an average of 1,600 miles daily. By the end of that year the company was operating almost 15 miles of lines, and nearly four miles of double track. Over 300 horses were used and the daily average mileage was over 2,500 miles.

The Street Railway Company of Grand Rapids finally began working on plans for building and operating new streetcar lines to compete with the new horsecar lines the cable railway company had begun operating. The Street Railway Company of Grand Rapids declined to accept a franchise to build a new line in the third ward—in southeast Grand Rapids—if the Common Council persisted in changing the route the company proposed. They relinquished their right to build on Lafayette Street and pointed out that any new line in that sparsely settled section of the city would only lead to a financial loss for both companies. Several companies submitted petitions for new streetcar lines to the Common Council. Mayor Weston was glad because he wanted to see streetcar tracks within two blocks of every residence in Grand Rapids.

The street railway did improve service on at least one very busy line. The company began running a second car following the first car on the Wealthy line during the 5 to 7 P.M. rush hour at the beginning of March. Wealthy Street was double tracked all the way to East Street.

Additional Cars Purchased in 1888

Additional cars were needed if the company was to increase service frequency on its lines. The company placed an order for twenty-three new cars with the Pullman Company at the beginning of February 1888. Three of these cars were to be the size of steam railroad passenger cars, each with a seating capacity of one hundred passengers, and were to be used on the steam dummy line running from the city's east side limit at East Street to Reed's Lake in Grand Rapids Township. The remaining twenty passenger cars were to be the much smaller open streetcars for use on three lines—Division, Cherry and Wealthy Street lines. These open cars were to be equipped with drop-down curtains to provide protection against a storm or a glaring sun. The cars were equipped with wooden end frames for sash and glass so that they could be operated later in the fall. Riders still did not receive free transfers even if the same company owned both lines.

Conflicting Trackage Rights on Canal Street

The Common Council of Grand Rapids passed an ordinance on March 5, 1888, granting the Valley City Street & Cable Car Company the right to run on Canal Street. The "old" company, as the Street Car Company of Grand Rap-

ids was known, already had two tracks on Canal Street. The old company also was heir to the 1864 franchise that granted exclusive right to run on Canal Street to the very first street railway to operate in Grand Rapids. This started a legal controversy eventually leading to a decision by a U.S. District Court judge who had just been appointed associate justice of the United States Supreme Court.

The Valley City Street & Cable Car Company was building a long north-south cable line and had planned to run through downtown on Ottawa Street. The downtown Canal Street merchants wanted to capture as much business as possible from streetcar passengers. The merchants convinced the Common Council to pass an ordinance granting the cable company the right to build on Canal Street even though the old company had an exclusive right to be the only street railway on that street. The Street Car Company of Grand Rapids opposed the Common Council's decision and contended the action was illegal.

The old company asked for and obtained an injunction restraining the cable company from constructing and operating a cable line on Canal Street. Circuit Court Judge Grove modified the injunction on Saturday evening, October 27, 1888, giving the cable company the right to construct a track on the east side of Canal Street.

Just a few hours later after midnight on Sunday morning, the managers of the cable railway showed up with 200 men who began

Horsecar at Campau Square; view looking southeast up Monroe.
Grand Rapids
Public Library

digging trenches so that they could install the conduit necessary for operating a cable line on the east side of Canal street. They worked all day and evening on Sunday digging and installing the cable conduit.

The Canal Street merchants soon found out that they were getting more than they had bargained for. They thought that the two streetcar companies would come to an agreement enabling cable cars to operate on the old company's existing two tracks in Canal Street; that didn't happen. The cable company built two tracks, one on each side of the horsecar company's tracks for a distance of three blocks from Lyon Street north to Bridge Street. The four tracks in Canal Street created problems and became widely known as the "Four Track Nuisance." This track configuration remained a thorn in the side of Canal Street merchants and city aldermen for more than twelve years until the turn of the century.

Newly appointed United States Supreme Court Justice Brown finished his service as a U.S. District Court judge in Michigan by ruling on June 28, 1891, that no Common Council had the right to give any company exclusive rights to use a public street.

1889: Cable vs. Electric

The cable railway company began operating the newly-completed extension of its north cable line on March 7, 1889. The old street railway company now faced competition from a cable line paralleling its Canal Street horsecar line north to the Detroit, Grand Haven & Milwaukee depot. The cable railway also was running cable cars on Canal Street between Lyon and Bridge streets.

Grand Rapids Township granted a franchise to the Street Railway of Grand Rapids enabling it to extend its streetcar line on Coit Avenue north from the city limits to Fifth Street, and to extend its line on Wealthy and Barnard streets all the way to Ramona Park at Reed's Lake, but with one major condition. If

the street railway extended the line to Ramona Park via Wealthy Street it would have to provide year-round service and charge only a single five-cent fare rather than two five-cent fares to the center of Grand Rapids.

The Cleveland investors who owned a controlling interest in the Street Railway of Grand Rapids had been watching the successes of electric railways in the Cleveland region. They realized that the Street Railway Company of Grand Rapids would have to convert to electric power if it was going to successfully compete with the Valley City Street & Cable Railway Company. They submitted their request and on October 14, 1889, the Common Council granted the street railway a new franchise giving them the right to convert to electric power.

Review Operations at the End of 1889

Two Grand Rapids newspapers ran similar year-end stories on the state of the Street Railway of Grand Rapids. The *Grand Rapids Eagle* noted on December 25 that the Street Railway of Grand Rapids was operating 26 miles of track including its 2½-mile long steam dummy line to Reed's Lake resort at the end of 1889. It employed 488 horses and 180 men to operate 120 cars that traveled an average of 4,500 miles a day. It had seven barns for the horses and cars. It also had its own car shops. The company had $1,000,000 of capital invested and planned to spend $500,000 to convert its horse lines to electric power as rapidly as possible.

The *Grand Rapids Eagle* drew attention to the fact that all five of the company's horse-drawn streetcar lines ran through Campau Square, the center of the business district:

• Canal, Monroe and Division streetcar line, 5 miles long
• Wealthy and Scribner streetcar line, 5 miles long
• Stocking Street and Jefferson Avenue streetcar line, 4½ miles long

- Cherry Street and Eighth Ward streetcar line, 4½ miles long
- West Bridge streetcar line, 2½ miles long
- The steam dummy line ran 2½ miles long to Ramona Resort on Reed's Lake

Debate over the "Four Track Nuisance"

The Common Council spent so much time discussing the "Four Track Nuisance" in early 1890 that the May 2 *Grand Rapids Telegram-Herald* summed up the council's special meeting to solve the problem in its headline—"Three Hours Wind Wasted on the Four Track Nuisance."

The quickest and least costly solution would have required Canal Street merchants to shrink their eighteen-foot-wide wooden sidewalks on both sides of Canal Street by a total of four feet—two feet on each side. Meanwhile as many as sixty-seven cars were running on the four parallel tracks every hour during the day.

Companies on Verge of Bankruptcy

The Valley City Street & Cable Railway became a major competitor when it came under new management in 1888, backed by what seemed to be untold wealth. The old company, crowded by competition with rapidly growing parallel cable and horsecar feeder railway lines, realized that horse power was doomed. The old company decided to convert to electric power and obtained a franchise that gave it the option to do so.

Local investors and other wealthy citizens played a major role in merging two companies "on the ropes" financially and in bringing about the rapid and successful conversion of the horse and cable lines into an efficient electric street railway system.

The Cleveland investors who had controlled the old company for the past five years were made "an offer they could not refuse." The cable company syndicate made up of Grand Rapids and Chicago investors purchased at 50 cents on the dollar $400,000 of stock that the old company had purchased for 25 cents on the dollar, and assumed all the bonded debt of the old company and $50,000 in excess of the bonded debt. The debt above this was assumed by stockholders of the old company which reduced their actual consideration to about 40 per cent of the capital stock.

The formal transfer of the Street Railway of Grand Rapids Company to the Valley City Street & Cable Railway Company took place on October 22, 1890. These two companies continued to operate independently but had the same general managers.

At the time of consolidation, the Street Railway Company of Grand Rapids had 26 miles of track, 113 cars, two steam dummy locomotives, 483 horses, 9 barns and shops, 12 acres of land and the Ramona Park Pavilion at Reed's Lake. The company had 260 men in its employ. The company was beginning to grow and it would grow even larger in the years to come. Electric traction was in its infancy and for many optimistic investors, "the sky's the limit" would be their credo.

This view of Canal Street looking north from Lyon Street illustrates what locals called the "Four Track Nuisance". The outer two tracks laid for cable-driven cars in 1888 stayed intact well beyond the merger of the two competing companies and the advent of electrification as shown here.

Credit: Grand Rapids Public Library

The Steam Dummies (1881-1894)

Open 0-4-0 steam locomotive and passenger car pose at Reed's Lake in the late afternoon sun.

David V. Tinder Collection, Clements Library

Reed's Lake Steam Dummy Line (1881-1890/91)

Jerry Boynton's bankrupt Grand Rapids and Reed's Lake Street Railway Company was sold at a Sheriff's sale on November 24, 1879. The new owners included Mrs. Lucetta Medbury of Detroit, Allen A. Rabineau also of Detroit, James H. McKee of Minneapolis, and George Thayer and Ebenezer Anderson, both of Grand Rapids. The new owners treated the Reed's Lake division in Grand Rapids Township of the Grand Rapids & Reed's Lake Street Railway as a separate railroad company which enabled them to continue charging passengers a separate fare with no free transfers.

The new owners possessed to two things Jerry Boynton almost always lacked—cash and good credit. They purchased two one-horse light open excursion cars from J. M. Jones Manufactory in Schenectady, New York, that arrived and immediately were put to use on June 16, 1880. Michigan Iron Works, a local Grand Rapids company, built two more one-horse open streetcars. The line then had ten cars in all with enough horses to pull them during the rest of the 1880 resort season at Reed's Lake.

Management began improving the track

and motive power as Jerry Boynton had wanted to do but couldn't because of lack of capital. They rebuilt the Sherman Street horsecar track with T-rail weighing thirty-five to forty pounds to the yard. The heavier rail was necessary so the company could run steam dummies on the track during the 1881 resort season.

Baldwin Locomotive Works of Philadelphia was contracted to build a small 0-4-0 steam locomotive, similar to those in use on the elevated railways in New York City. This locomotive arrived in May and commenced operation on May 14, 1881. Later that month the last T-rail was laid on the line.

The street railway company also built a large two-story brick station on the southeast corner of the Sherman Street-East Street intersection in 1881. The station included a waiting room, blacksmith shop, engine room, and sleeping rooms for employees. Additional structures included a horse and carbarn, as well as turntables and track switches which connected the buildings to the main track.

The steam locomotive began pulling a passenger car all the way to the eastern terminus of the line at Reed's Lake in late May, 1881. The locomotive was reversed on a turntable at the Sherman Street station, the western terminus

The Street Railways of Grand Rapids

Baldwin 0-4-0 locomotive and passenger car at Reed's Lake. Sam "By" Alley is the member of the crew holding the oiling can. This car has twelve rows of seats—room for perhaps 48 passengers. A fully loaded car of this size would be too heavy for a team of horses to pull.

Grand Rapids
Public Library

of the line. A passing siding was built at Reed's Lake, the eastern end of the line, which enabled the locomotive to run around the passenger car and pull the train back to the station at the Sherman Street-East Street intersection.

The first small 0-4-0 Baldwin tank locomotive was named *Samuel Medbury* for the husband of Mrs. Medbury, the chief stockholder of the Street Railway Company of Grand Rapids. Thomas Van Wormer was the first engineer at the throttle of the new locomotive, while Sam "By" Alley served as conductor on the passenger car. The train began making regular round trips in late June 1881 on a thirty-minute headway, going two and one-third miles from East Street to Reed's Lake on Sherman Street and returning the same way on Sherman Street to East Street. The Reed's Lake steam engine made its last trip for the 1881 resort season on Sunday, October 9, 1881. The steam line to Reed's Lake operated only during the resort season each year.

The Company Builds a New Summer Resort

The Reed's Lake Street Railway began establishing a summer resort in March 1882 on a ten-acre tract just north of the street railroad terminus at its namesake. A spacious pavilion was built with a center and four wings. The center and three of the four wings were provided with tables and chairs to be used by the public who could carry their own lunches as well as those who wished to purchase lunches. The portion of Judd's Grove on the street railway property was cleared, more trees planted, and seats, swings, and other recreational items were set out for visitors to use. The company's resort was adjacent to Miller's Landing where visitors could take advantage of boats.

A *Grand Rapids Saturday Evening Post* columnist reported on June 17, 1882, that:

> The season at Reed's Lake had opened as usual with liquor flowing freely, brawls and drunkenness.

In contrast, the street railway company's new resort was designed to attract families by providing a quieter and more "moral" place to enjoy Reed's Lake. Beer, spirits, and undesirable people were excluded from the grounds.

Almost 4,000 people visited Reed's Lake on July 4, 1882. Of them, 1,400 rode on the steam dummy line passenger cars both to and from the Lake, while carryalls and private carriages transported the rest.

A year later the July 23, 1883, *Grand Rapids Eagle* reported that:

> Reed's Lake was crowded with visitors yesterday, and the condition of many of those returning was not that of sober people. Residents along the railway track and drivers report that a drunken man can make more noise than a steam calliope.

Jerry Boynton played a major role one more time in September 1883 when he helped bring about the consolidation under one management of the four street railway companies operating in Grand Rapids. Superintendent Boynton immediately began promoting one of his many pet projects: running a steam dummy all the way from the East Street-Sherman Street intersection at the city limit to downtown Grand Rapids. So many citizens opposed the idea that the Common Council rejected all proposals to run a steam locomotive on any street within the city of Grand Rapids.

Street Railway Routes between Grand Rapids and Reed's Lake 1875-1892

Based on several maps including 1894 and 1907 Ogle & Co. Kent Co. Atlas and news accounts
© 2017 Tom Maas

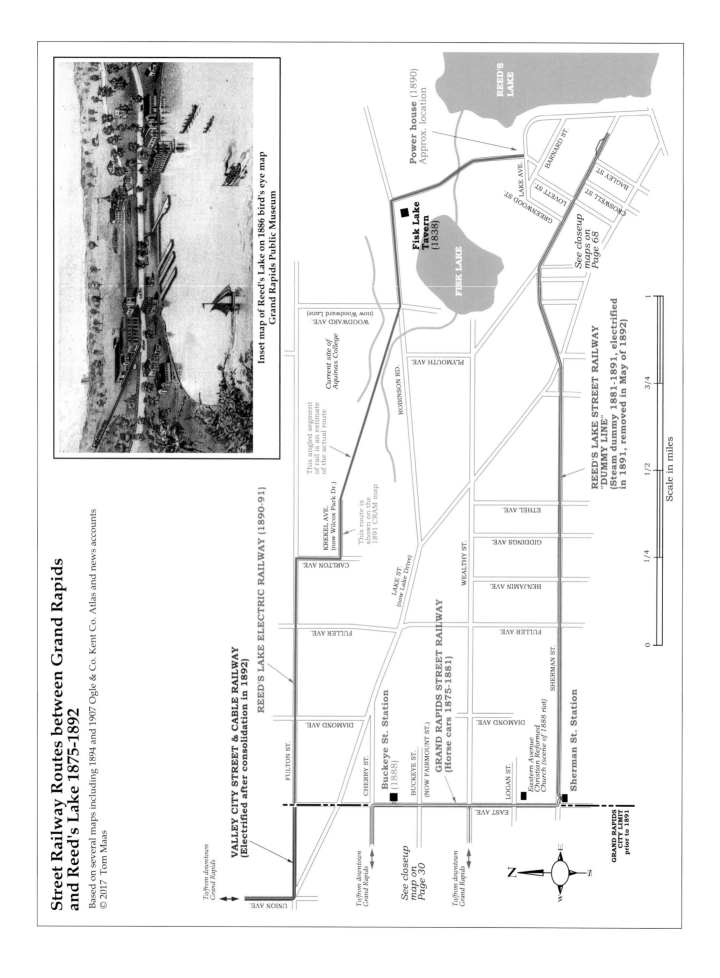

Inset map of Reed's Lake on 1886 bird's eye map
Grand Rapids Public Museum

VALLEY CITY STREET & CABLE RAILWAY
(Electrified after consolidation in 1892)

REED'S LAKE ELECTRIC RAILWAY (1890-91)

This angled segment
of rail is an estimate
of the actual route

This route is
shown on the
1891 CRAM map

Current site of
Aquinas College

KREKEL AVE.
(now Wilcox Park Dr.)

WOODWARD AVE.
(now Woodward Lane)

ROBINSON RD.

FISK LAKE

Fisk Lake
Tavern
(1838)

Power house (1890)
Approx. location

REED'S
LAKE

See closeup
maps on
Page 68

BARNARD ST.

LAKE AVE.

GREENWOOD ST.

LOVETT ST.

CROSWELL ST.

BAGLEY ST.

PLYMOUTH AVE.

LAKE ST.
(now Lake Drive)

FULTON ST.

CARLTON AVE.

FULLER AVE.

DIAMOND AVE.

CHERRY ST.

Buckeye St. Station
(1888)

BUCKEYE ST.
(NOW FAIRMOUNT ST.)

GRAND RAPIDS STREET RAILWAY
(Horse cars 1875-1881)

ETHEL AVE.

GIDDINGS AVE.

WEALTHY ST.

BENJAMIN AVE.

FULLER AVE.

SHERMAN ST.

**REED'S LAKE STREET RAILWAY
"DUMMY LINE"**
(Steam dummy 1881-1891, electrified
in 1891, removed in May of 1892)

DIAMOND AVE.

LOGAN ST.

EAST AVE.

Eastern Avenue
Christian Reformed
Church (scene of 1888 riot)

Sherman St. Station

UNION AVE.

To/from downtown
Grand Rapids

To/from downtown
Grand Rapids

See closeup
map on
Page 30

To/from downtown
Grand Rapids

**GRAND RAPIDS
CITY LIMIT**
prior to 1891

N
W E
S

0   1/4   1/2   3/4   1
Scale in miles

26   *The Street Railways of Grand Rapids*

Street Railway Routes between Grand Rapids and Reed's Lake 1892-1935

Based on several maps including 1907 Ogle & Co. Kent Co. Atlas map
© 2017 Tom Maas

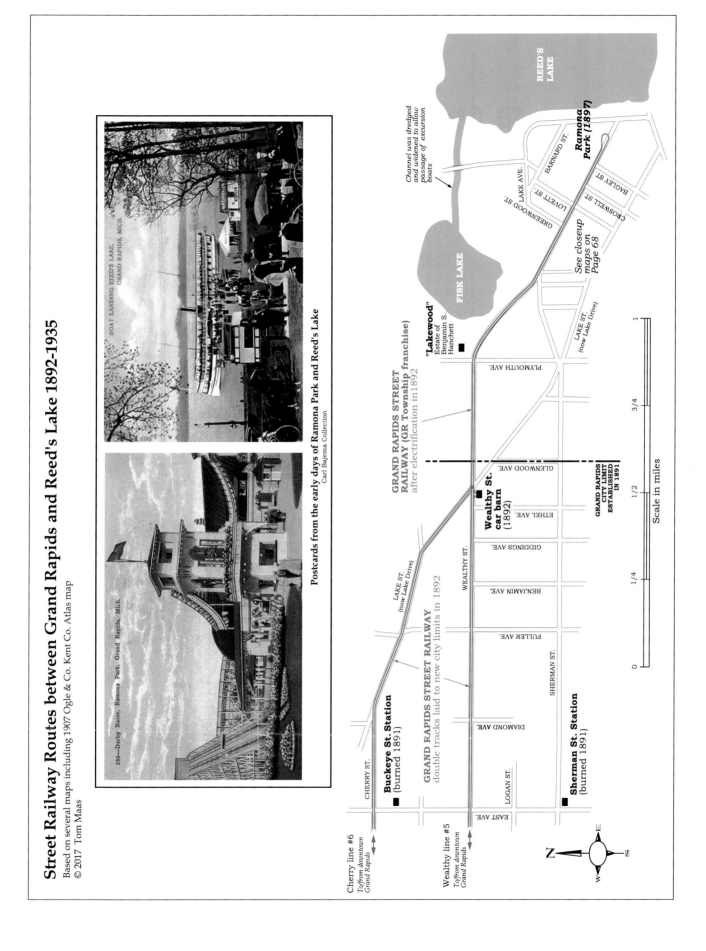

250—Derby Racer, Ramona Park, Grand Rapids, Mich.

BOAT LANDING REED'S LAKE, GRAND RAPIDS, MICH.

Postcards from the early days of Ramona Park and Reed's Lake
Carl Bajema Collection

REED'S LAKE

FISK LAKE

Channel was dredged and widened to allow passage of excursion boats

Ramona Park (1897)

BARNARD ST.
LAKE AVE.
LOVETT ST.
CROSWELL ST.
BAGLEY ST.
GREENWOOD ST.

See closeup maps on Page 68

"Lakewood"
Estate of Benjamin S. Hanchett

LAKE ST. (now Lake Drive)

PLYMOUTH AVE.

GRAND RAPIDS STREET RAILWAY (GR Township franchise) after electrification in 1892

GLENWOOD AVE.

Wealthy St. car barn (1892)

ETHEL AVE.
GIDDINGS AVE.
BENJAMIN AVE.
FULLER AVE.

WEALTHY ST.

SHERMAN ST.

GRAND RAPIDS CITY LIMIT ESTABLISHED IN 1891

0   1/4   1/2   3/4   1

Scale in miles

LAKE ST. (now Lake Drive)

GRAND RAPIDS STREET RAILWAY double tracks laid to new city limits in 1892

CHERRY ST.

Buckeye St. Station (burned 1891)

DIAMOND AVE.
LOGAN ST.
EAST AVE.

Sherman St. Station (burned 1891)

Cherry line #6
To/from downtown Grand Rapids

Wealthy line #5
To/from downtown Grand Rapids

N E S W

Newspaper ad promoting Reed's Lake, 04 June 1883.

Grand Rapids Eagle

Improvements Continue

The company made several improvements at the beginning of the 1884 resort season to better serve the visitors to the company's resort which was being advertised as the "Saratoga of Grand Rapids." Track was extended forty feet to shorten the walk to the pavilion at Reed's Lake. The company also purchased a second steam locomotive that arrived in June 1884. In contrast to the first locomotive, which was not enclosed, this engine was a true steam dummy that was "covered so that it would not frighten horses more than a car does, and is quite as noiseless."

The Street Railway Company of Grand Rapids stated in 1885 that it was ready to run the Reed's Lake steam dummy all the way from the lake to the Union Station adjacent to downtown "whenever public sentiment will cause the Common Council to give them right of way."

The ferry boat system for collecting fares was adopted by the line in 1885. Gates were erected at the Sherman Street station on the corner of East Street. Passengers going to Reed's Lake were required to place their tickets in a box before entering the cars. This eliminated the conductor's problem of trying to collect fares enroute when the cars were crowded. However, while some passengers liked the new system because they spent far less time waiting for and boarding a streetcar, others did not like "being driven like a herd of sheep into the enclosure and packed together in great masses

on the platform" while waiting for the next train.

The two locomotives operated on a schedule leaving every twenty minutes each way between East Street and Reed's Lake during the 1885 season. The horsecars, which could not carry as many passengers, operated on a ten-minute schedule between downtown and the East Street station at the western terminus of the steam line.

The Women's Christian Temperance Union (WCTU) started a campaign during April 1883 to get the street railway resort on Reed's Lake closed on Sundays. The WCTU pointed out conditions were so bad at Reed's Lake that the street railway had found it necessary to keep a police force at the lake to control the debasing influence of those who commune with beer and whisky rather than communing with nature, pure air and delightful lake breezes. The street railway did employ police whose major function was to keep the rowdies who visited the illegal saloons along the lake out of the company's resort where no alcoholic beverages were allowed.

The 1886 resort season was profitable for the street railway. Approximately 5,000 people visited Reed's Lake on Sunday, May 2, when the company opened its resort and began running the steam train for the season. The cars carried 30,500 passengers to and from Reed's Lake over the July 4 weekend. The trains continued to operate until October when autumn weather ended the busy season.

The street railway held a very successful ladies' contest in the summer of 1886 to choose an official name for the company's resort at Reed's Lake. "Ramona", the romantic name of an Indian maiden in a popular novel, was chosen and became the official name of the street railway resort on August 20, 1886. The unique name helped distinguish the company's resort from the numerous saloons that dotted the shores of the lake.

The street railway's continued attempts to secure an ordinance to allow steam dummy operation on city streets from the East Street station to Union Depot failed. Citizens and politicians did not want to open Pandora's Box by permitting a steam locomotive to run on any street inside the Grand Rapids city limits.

Major Improvements in 1887

The street railway made two major improvements at Ramona Park to make the 1887 resort season more pleasant for visitors. The pavilion was enlarged and made into a two-story building equipped with a cupola. A new 16-foot wide dock that stretched 239 feet out from the shore, had a cross dock built at 149 feet out in the water and provided additional dockage of 32 by 49 feet. This part of the dock was covered with heavy canvas enabling more

visitors to sit in the shade and enjoy the cool lake breezes.

The street railway company advertised Reed's Lake as the place to go "whether you want boating, rowing, sailing, a siesta, pleasant company, bathing, forest beauties, coolness, rest, a delightful prospect—anything of that nature—no better place for them can be found than at Reed's Lake." Bands, rides on steamboats, a regatta, and other events made Ramona Park the place to visit

Track Extensions

The street railway company began extending its existing double track on both Wealthy and Cherry streets the rest of the way to East Street in the early spring of 1888.

The one half-mile of track that the company already had in East Street was on the west side of the street just inside the east city limit of Grand Rapids. In April, the street railway company began constructing a single half mile-long track on the east side of East Street just inside Grand Rapids township, from Sherman Street station, then the western terminus of the steam dummy line from Reed's Lake in April. The company planned to have the new large passenger station and carbarn they were building on East Street at the Buckeye Street (now Fairmont Street) intersection just one block south of Cherry Street completed in time for the beginning of the Reed's Lake resort season. Resort goers would be able to ride either the Cherry Street horsecars or the Wealthy Street horsecars to and from the Buckeye station which would be the new western terminus of the steam dummy line.

The company was trying to solve two problems by enabling the steam dummy locomotives to haul full-size passenger cars north on East Street to the Buckeye Street station rather than carry inbound passengers only as far as the Sherman Street Station on East Street. First, horses had a very difficult time when pulling a downtown-bound streetcar loaded with passengers north up the steep grade on East Street hill at Wealthy Street. Second, the company also wanted to more efficiently handle the huge crowds on Sundays and holidays that too often had to wait for long periods before they could board an outbound car headed for the lake. Steam dummies could move more inbound passengers more quickly because a locomotive could pull a train of three or four full-size passenger cars north up the grade on East Street hill.

One citizen opposed to the operation of steam locomotives on East Street succeeded in obtaining a temporary injunction on April 21 restraining the company from building a track for steam operation on the east side of East Street, which was in Grand Rapids township, rather than in the city of Grand Rapids. The company responded stating that it had been granted the right to build such a track on the east side of East Street by the township. The street railway already had a track on the west side of East Street which was within the city of Grand Rapids and was presently used by horsecars.

The injunction was dissolved by the judge on Wednesday, May 9, but the judge required the streetcar company to use only steam locomotives that were enclosed and noiseless. By 9 P.M. that very day the street railway company had a crew of nearly fifty men laying track on the east side of East Street.

Enclosed "noiseless" 0-4-0 dummy steam locomotive No. 2 and passenger car at Reed's Lake. An enclosed locomotive like this fits the classic definition of "dummy" as it was meant to mimic the typical horsecars of the era so as not to scare the horses it encountered on the streets.

David V. Tinder Collection, Clements Library

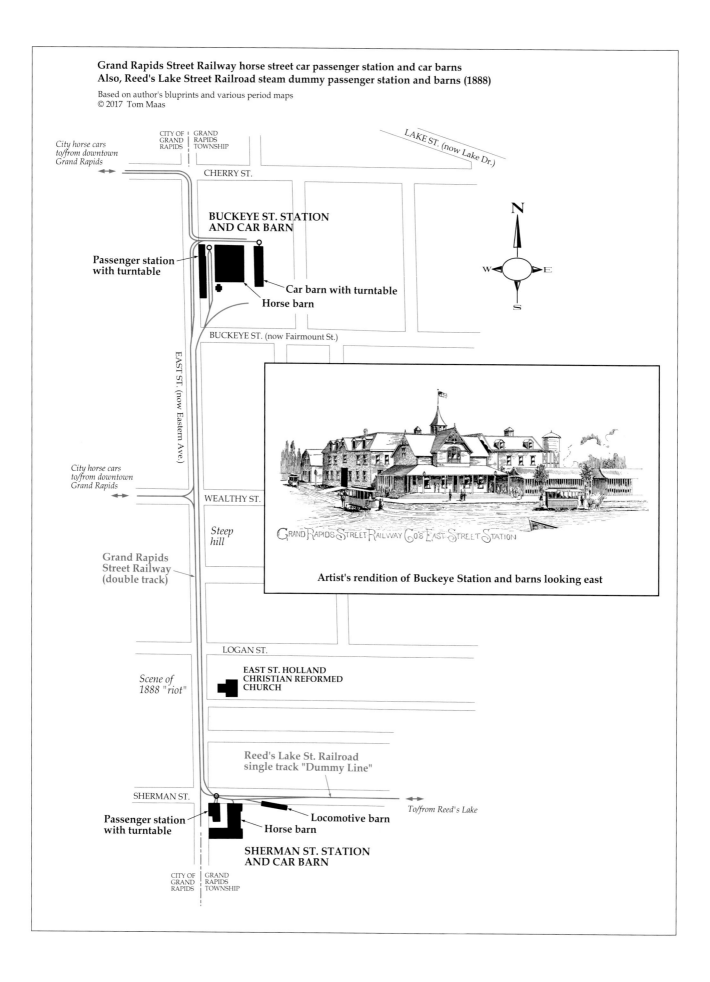

Grand Rapids Street Railway horse street car passenger station and car barns
Also, Reed's Lake Street Railroad steam dummy passenger station and barns (1888)

Based on author's bluprints and various period maps
© 2017 Tom Maas

City horse cars
to/from downtown
Grand Rapids

CITY OF GRAND RAPIDS | GRAND RAPIDS TOWNSHIP

LAKE ST. (now Lake Dr.)

CHERRY ST.

BUCKEYE ST. STATION AND CAR BARN

Passenger station with turntable

Car barn with turntable

Horse barn

BUCKEYE ST. (now Fairmount St.)

EAST ST. (now Eastern Ave.)

City horse cars
to/from downtown
Grand Rapids

WEALTHY ST.

Steep hill

Grand Rapids Street Railway (double track)

Artist's rendition of Buckeye Station and barns looking east

LOGAN ST.

Scene of 1888 "riot"

EAST ST. HOLLAND CHRISTIAN REFORMED CHURCH

Reed's Lake St. Railroad single track "Dummy Line"

SHERMAN ST.

Passenger station with turntable

Locomotive barn

Horse barn

To/from Reed's Lake

SHERMAN ST. STATION AND CAR BARN

CITY OF GRAND RAPIDS | GRAND RAPIDS TOWNSHIP

The Dummy Line Riot Begins

Someone began ringing the church bell causing a large crowd of men and boys to gather and begin to threaten the workers. The crowd decided the company would not be allowed to lay track in front of the East Street Holland Christian Reformed Church. As fast as the workers tried to spike the rails to the ties the crowd tried to pick up the rails and carry them away. When that failed the crowd began showering track workers with cobblestones.

Two deputy sheriffs were called to the scene but decided that nothing could be done with such an unruly crowd in the dark. The protesters dispersed around midnight and the work crew finished laying track. Once the work was completed a steam dummy pulled a train of cars over the new line.

The East Street Holland Christian Reformed Church filed a lawsuit against the street railway company on May 10 and the judge issued an order to show cause by the defendant.

Hollanders resumed rioting during the nights of May 10 and May 11. About twenty-five policemen went to the site of the rioting on the night of May 11. The *Grand Rapids Telegram-Herald* newspaper had a reporter on the scene of the "East Street War" for at least two nights. The reporter contended that certain property owners on East Street and beyond were responsible for the trouble accusing them of "urging on the deluded ignorant Dutchmen to do what they have been doing night after night." One of the rioters threw a stone that smashed one of the headlights of a steam dummy running on the track on the night of May 11. He was arrested and taken to jail, but later released. This action by the police ended the three-night war against the street railway.

The *Grand Rapids Eagle* newspaper editor wrote on May 12 that

> All good citizens will rejoice in the termination of this affair. It is a bad thing to take the law into one's own hands. For this very thing men were hanged in Chicago on the eleventh day of November last and this lesson should remain fresh in the memory of every American citizen, whether this country be his home by birth or by adoption.

1888 Resort Season

The official 1888 resort season began when the steam dummy trains commenced operation on May 24.

New open passenger cars, which were wider and longer than the ordinary cars, arrived in June. Each car was equipped with fourteen seats and each seat could hold seven to

---

HO FOR REEDS LAKE.

The Dummy Line Time Card—Sunday Trains.

Hereafter, and until further notice, the dummy train for the Lake will leave the dummy Station—terminus of both the Cherry street and the Wealthy avenue lines—at 8:40 a. m. and every thirty-five minutes thereafter until 9:20 in the evening.

The last train will leave the Lake at 9:40 p. m. for the present. Later in the season it will leave later. On Sundays, and on busy days only for the present, there will be two dummy trains for the Lake, and trips will be made every eighteen minutes; until the new noiseless motor arrives the trains will exchange locomotives at the switch.

The band gives concerts every afternoon and evening at the Lake, and the Street Railway Company will spare no pains or expense to make that popular resort more pleasant than ever before, this season.

Reed's Lake dummy line newspaper timetable, 25 May 1888.

Grand Rapids Eagle

---

eight people. The two locomotives each pulled three passenger cars while making twenty-minute round trips on June 3.

The enclosed "noiseless" steam dummy transported passengers on East Street between Buckeye Street and Sherman Street stations while the old tank locomotive pulled the train of passenger cars from the Sherman Street station to Reed's Lake and back. Another "noiseless" steam dummy arrived in late June and ended the problem of having to switch every train at Sherman Street station to avoid running the conventional tank locomotive on East Street.

The East Street Holland Christian Reformed Church succeeded in filing a temporary injunction on June 13 that prohibited the street railway from running steam locomotives on East Street. The street railway was unable to persuade the judge to dissolve the injunction. The company was forced to use carryall wagons and horsecars to transport passengers between the Sherman street station and the Buckeye Street station.

Judge Montgomery ruled on August 13 that the court had no reason for dissolving the injunction against the operation of steam locomotives on East Street. That very evening the Grand Rapids Common Council amended the East Street motor ordinance in an attempt to get the injunction overturned. Judge Montgomery then ruled on August 20 that the amendments to the city's ordinance made on August 14 allowed enclosed noiseless steam dummies to run on East Street and dissolved the injunction. The company immediately began starting and terminating their steam passenger trains to Reed's Lake at the new big Buckeye Street station on East Street north of Wealthy Street.

The political war over running trains of

FOR SALE. 1 Baldwin Saddle Tank Engine. weight, 9 tons, cylinders 9 x 12 in., built in 1881. Price $1,000. 1 Baldwin Steam Motor, weight, 20 tons; cylinders 9 x 12 in.; built in 1884. Price, $1,500. 1 Baldwin Steam Motor, weight, 11 tons; cylinders, 10 x 14 in., built in 1887. Price, $2,000. All the above standard gauge, have Eames brake, and are in excellent condition. Also 400 Tons 48 lb. Slot Rail, 2 Walker U Frames with 12 ft. Staggered Arm Sheaves, 1 Set Double Cable Driving machinery, with four Ring Walker Differential Drums. 1 Hazelton Tripod Boiler, 150 H. P. 1 Hazelton Tripod Boiler, 300 H. P. All the above but little used and in excellent condition. CONSOLIDATED STREET RAILWAY CO., Grand Rapids, Mich.

When electrification came in 1892, the steam dummy engines and cable driving equipment were advertised for sale.

Street Railway Review

passenger cars pulled by steam dummy locomotives did not end in August 1888. The Common Council placed a time limit on the ordinance allowing such locomotives to run on the one half mile track on East Street, a border shared by both the city and Grand Rapids Township.

The Final Years

The Sherman Street station became the western terminus of the steam dummy line rather than the Buckeye Street station for most of 1889. Political and legal conflicts prevented the company from using the Buckeye Street Station as the western terminus that year. The company bought a new Baldwin steam dummy that was delivered in the spring of 1889.

The steam dummy passenger trains began running from the Sherman street station on East Street on May 24, 1890, officially opening the resort season at Ramona Park and other Reed's Lake resorts. The Common Council finally passed an amendment to the street railway ordinance on May 26 that allowed steam dummy locomotives to operate on East Street until December 1. Two days later the street railway commenced running its steam dummy trains the full length of the line to the Buckeye Street station. The Street Railway Company of Grand Rapids published a summer timetable effective June 30, 1890. The service continued until Sunday, September 28, 1890, when the lake's resort season ended.

The Valley City Street & Cable Railway Company purchased the Street Railway Company of Grand Rapids which included the Reed's Lake division in October 1890. The cable railway company planned to electrify the lines under their ownership as soon as possible.

The End of Steam

Steam dummy-hauled passenger trains operated to Reed's Lake at least once in early 1891 when the new Masonic Home near Reed's Lake was dedicated on January 27.

The old carbarn adjacent the Sherman Street station burned down on May 5, 1891. The fire destroyed thirty-six cars which were being stored inside. All of these cars were open streetcars with a value of $950 each, which the company's insurance company paid. The closed cars that had been running on the streets during the cold months had to continue in operation until open car bodies could be obtained.

The street railway company began erecting poles and stringing wire during the spring of 1891 so the Sherman Street line could be electrified. An electric car made a trial run on Sherman Street to Reed's Lake on June 9. Electric cars hauling trailers started carrying passengers to and from Reed's Lake on the old dummy line on June 15.

The rails, poles, and ties were taken up on Sherman Street when the resort season at Reed's Lake ended in the early fall of 1891. Looking back, horsecars ran on Sherman Street to Reed's Lake in 1875, steam dummy passenger trains operated over the same line in 1881, and finally with electric streetcars in 1891.

The Consolidated Street Railway Company began providing year-round electric streetcar service to the new village of East Grand Rapids as well as Reed's Lake via an extension of the Wealthy Street line in 1892.

The oldest steam dummy locomotive, affectionately called the "Goat" by employees was sold in the spring of 1892. The Goat's shrill whistle and clanging bell would no longer be heard running to Reed's Lake; it was on its way to be heard in the lumber camps of Arkansas. One of the remaining two Baldwin steam dummies was sold to the Jamestown & Newport Railroad in North Dakota. The remaining locomotive was shipped to Milwaukee in August 1892 where it provided service to a resort on the Milwaukee & Wauwatosa suburban railroad.

North Park Steam Dummy Line (1890-1894)

The North Park Street Railway Company was incorporated in 1889 by Charles Carter Comstock and others to build a railway connecting Grand Rapids to the new Michigan Soldiers' Home and North Park where Comstock planned to build a resort on the east bank of the Grand River. Comstock was a former mayor of Grand Rapids (1863-65) and ran for a number of political offices, including state governor in 1870. He made his fortune as a lumberman and wooden ware manufacturer. Comstock had invested in lands just above the northern city limit of Grand Rapids and wanted a railway built through his properties.

In 1889-1890 the company built a two and one-third mile standard-gauge steam railroad north from its junction with the Valley City Street & Cable Railway at the intersection of Taylor and Sweet streets, the northern city limit of Grand Rapids. The line was built on private right-of-way except for passing through Michigan Soldiers' Home on state-owned land. It ended just north of the Soldiers' Home at the new North Park Resort which C. C. Comstock was developing adjacent to what was then known as the Canal Street gravel road toll bridge which spanned the Grand River.

The North Park Street Railway signed a contract with the cable railway company to meet at the northern city limit where Taylor Street ends at Sweet Street. The railway also had an interchange track with the Detroit, Grand Haven & Milwaukee Railroad at Sweet Street to allow railroad cars carrying coal and other freight to the Soldiers' Home.

Passenger service began on the North Park Street Railway on June 15, 1890, when one of the two brand new Baldwin steam dummy locomotives was put in running order. The locomotive took a new open passenger car on the two-mile trip to the Soldiers' Home. It cost a nickel each way to take the trip.

The company was busy building stations to accommodate passengers in 1890: one at Sweet Street at the southern end of the line, one at Soldiers' Home, and one near the newly built two-story pavilion in the North Park Street Railway company's new North Park Resort. There were switches for sidings at both ends of the line. A carbarn was built just northeast of the North Park Pavilion.

Large crowds began traveling via the new Taylor street extension of the cable company's north Ottawa Street cable line to reach the temporary Sweet Street junction station where they could transfer to the steam dummy line and spend a day at the new North Park resort. The two railway companies agreed to collect a joint fare of only seven cents (instead of the regular ten cents) to travel all the way to North Park

North Park Railway 0-4-2 locomotive equipped with front and rear headlights.
Ron Kuiper Collection

North Park Railway open passenger car No. 1.
Ron Kuiper Collection

North Park Railway closed passenger car No. 10.
Ron Kuiper Collection

Resort from any cable line or horsecar feeder line in Grand Rapids.

A nineteen by fifty-foot two-story station house was built later in the summer to serve both the cable railway and North Park Street Railway at Sweet Street. A fifty by one hundred-foot train shed was also built at the north end of Sweet Street station. The roof of the train shed extended over both the cable and steam dummy line tracks which were located on opposite sides of the station.

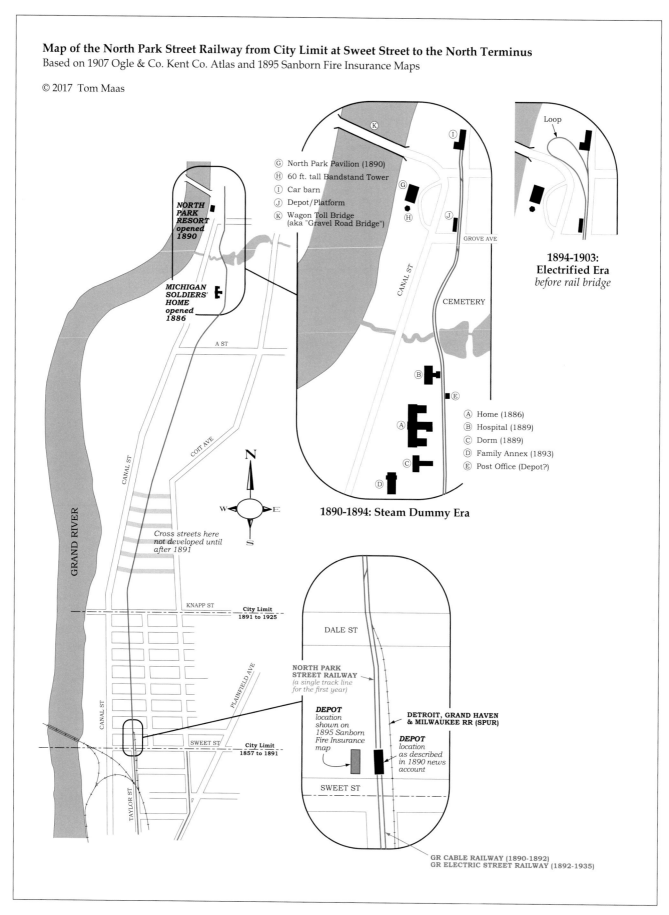

Map of the North Park Street Railway from City Limit at Sweet Street to the North Terminus
Based on 1907 Ogle & Co. Kent Co. Atlas and 1895 Sanborn Fire Insurance Maps

© 2017 Tom Maas

G North Park Pavilion (1890)
H 60 ft. tall Bandstand Tower
I Car barn
J Depot/Platform
K Wagon Toll Bridge
  (aka "Gravel Road Bridge")

NORTH PARK RESORT *opened 1890*

MICHIGAN SOLDIERS' HOME *opened 1886*

A ST

GROVE AVE

CANAL ST

CEMETERY

Cross streets here *not developed until after 1891*

KNAPP ST

City Limit 1891 to 1925

N
W E
S

A Home (1886)
B Hospital (1889)
C Dorm (1889)
D Family Annex (1893)
E Post Office (Depot?)

1890-1894: Steam Dummy Era

1894-1903: Electrified Era *before rail bridge*

Loop

GRAND RIVER

CANAL ST

COIT AVE

PLAINFIELD AVE

CANAL ST

TAYLOR ST

DALE ST

NORTH PARK STREET RAILWAY *(a single track line for the first year)*

DEPOT location shown on 1895 Sanborn Fire Insurance map

DETROIT, GRAND HAVEN & MILWAUKEE RR (SPUR)

DEPOT location as described in 1890 news account

SWEET ST

City Limit 1857 to 1891

SWEET ST

GR CABLE RAILWAY (1890-1892)
GR ELECTRIC STREET RAILWAY (1892-1935)

Map of the North Park Street Railway including Soldiers' Home, 1890-94.

Dummy Station of the North Park Railway Co., taken in 1890, when they pulled the cars with steam engines. Photo submitted by Helen Morrill, 576 Prospect Ave. S.E.

The North Park Resort

The North Park Street Railway Company also built a sixty-foot tall four-story bandstand just south of the pavilion in July 1890. The band music could be heard throughout the two shady picnic groves in the fourteen-acre resort. An Edison generator provided electricity for lights in the pavilion, in the bandstand, and throughout the picnic groves. In early September 1890 special attractions at the company's North Park resort included tight wire and trapeze performances and diving from a seventy-five-foot platform into the Grand River. Balloon ascensions and parachute jumping entertained resort visitors in October.

The company planned to operate the North Park Street Railway during the winter months to serve both the Michigan Soldiers' Home and the company's resort. Two handsome new enclosed passenger cars were added to the rolling stock for use during the cold weather. Each coach was built to comfortably carry seventy-five passengers. The company built an ice skating rink adjacent the pavilion at the North Park to attract winter riders.

Amusements and the End of an Era

The North Park Street Railway double tracked the entire length of its line from Sweet Street station to the North Park Resort in the early spring of 1891 to better handle weekend crowds. The railway now had eight passenger cars and two closed passenger cars so that each of the two Baldwin steam dummies could pull a train of as many as five cars.

C. C. Comstock had an eighty-five-foot long side-wheel steamboat built over the winter of 1890-1891. The boat, named *North Park*, had one main deck and could carry 300 passengers. The gravel road toll bridge at North Park was raised two feet in June to enable the boat to pass under the bridge and steam north on the Grand River to Grand Island and other river resort destinations.

Above and below: *Depot at Soldiers' Home about 1890.*
Grand Rapids Herald

219. North Park Pavilion from Bridge, Grand Rapids, Mich.

The dock side of the North Park Pavilion as seen from above the Grand River looking east.
Carl Bajema collection

NORTH PARK

*North Park Resort,
view looking west
at railway station,
resort bandstand and
pavilion, and railway
car barn in 1890.*

Grand Rapids As It Is,
1890-1891 edition.

NORTH PARK

*North Park Resort:
view looking east from
Grand River showing
toll bridge, pavilion,
bandstand in 1890.*

Grand Rapids As It Is,
1890-1891 edition

Thousands of people visited North Park Resort on the glorious Fourth of July 1891. They celebrated by enjoying cool breezes under the limbs of majestic oaks and elms in the picnic grounds, taking a ride in one of forty rowboats or on the steamboat. They could listen to the music of the Wurzburg & Bronson band, watch double aerial trapeze acts and a diver jumping off a high platform into the river, go bathing, look for deer in the new five-acre deer park across the river, and finally watch fireworks after dark.

Thousands of citizens rode the steam dummy line to North Park on September 15 and then crossed the river to visit the first West Michigan Fair to be held in Mill Creek (now Comstock Park). Citizens had another transportation choice. They could board a Chicago & West Michigan Railroad train or a Grand Rapids & Indiana Railroad train

at Union Station in Grand Rapids and alight at Mill Creek station adjacent to the new fair grounds. Most citizens preferred to ride the streetcars for two reasons: frequency of service and cheaper fares.

When the cable car era ended in Grand Rapids on November 12, 1891, the roof of the Sweet Street station platform had to be raised to allow space for the overhead trolley wire.

The North Park Street Railway had an excellent safety record. The steam dummy trains traveled more than 150,000 miles and carried 1,200,000 passengers during the four years they operated, never injuring an employee or passenger. Unfortunately, the locomotives did run over a number of individuals who were walking, staggering, or sleeping while drunk on the tracks. Many of these men were veterans living in the Michigan Soldiers' Home.

The steam dummy line trains ran on the North Park line for the last time in the spring of 1894. John P. O'Dell and C. R. Cummings, the millionaire bankers of Chicago who owned a controlling interest in the Consolidated Street Railway Company of Grand Rapids, visited the city on March 21, 1894. They joined James R. Chapman, the general manager of the Consolidated Street Railway Company's electric street railway system. All went on an inspection tour of the North Park line and ended their visit by signing papers for the purchase of the North Park Street Railway. The steam dummy line and resort were acquired for $50,000 in twenty-year five-percent bonds, exclusive of the railway stock that Mr. Comstock retained.

The Electric Streetcar Era Begins on the North Park Line

In early spring 1894 the Consolidated Street Railway Company of Grand Rapids began making the necessary changes to convert the line from steam to electric power so electric streetcar operation could begin by early spring of 1894. The company erected poles and trolley wire; it also built a loop at the north end

of the line that enabled streetcars to reverse direction. Passengers now could get on and off the cars at the north end of the pavilion. Passengers rode electric streetcars to the Michigan Soldiers' Home and to North Park and North Park Resort for the first time on May 15, 1894. The cars operated on a ten-minute headway. The Consolidated Street Railway lowered the fare from seven cents to five cents from anywhere on the Grand Rapids streetcar lines.

This suburban streetcar extension was treated as a part of the electric railway system in Grand Rapids, as was the line to suburban Ramona Park and Reed's Lake in East Grand Rapids. The two resorts were now linked by a continuous line of streetcars. A person could travel between the two resorts in a Wealthy-Taylor line streetcar, a distance of eight miles, for only five cents.

North Park Streetcar Line (1894-1935)

The North Park Street Car Railway had begun as a steam dummy line in 1890. The Consolidated Street Railway Company purchased the North Park line in 1894 and immediately converted it to electric operation. This line became widely known as the Taylor Street line. The cars ran south to Campau Square in downtown Grand Rapids. From there the cars continued south and east on the Wealthy Street line all the way to Ramona Park adjacent to Reed's Lake in East Grand Rapids. At eight miles long, the Taylor-Wealthy line was the longest streetcar line in Grand Rapids. The last streetcar to run in Grand Rapids left Comstock Park on Sunday night, August 25, 1935, entered Grand Rapids at Northwood Street (the 1935 northern city limit), continued through Campau Square and ended at Ramona Park adjacent Reed's Lake.

Numerous events occurred during the forty-one years that electric streetcars ran on the North Park line. These are related in greater detail in this book in the electric street railway era chapters for the period between 1893 and 1935.

Panoramic view looking east at Car Barn, Baldwin 0-4-0 dummy locomotive pulling 3 open passenger cars and the North Park Railway Station at North Park. Circa 1890,

West Michigan Railroad Historical Society

Valley City Street and Cable Railway Company – Grand Rapids, MI

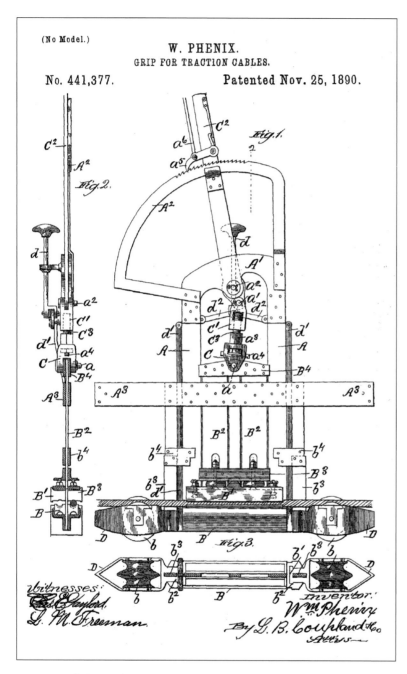

(No Model.)

W. PHENIX.
GRIP FOR TRACTION CABLES.

No. 441,377.   Patented Nov. 25, 1890.

Diagram of Phenix double cable grip which was adopted for use in Grand Rapids since it allowed two cables to travel in opposing directions inside the same conduit. This provided traction for cars traveling in both directions using a single track.

U.S. Patent Office

The high hill that rose abruptly a mere three blocks east of the business district in Grand Rapids made horse-drawn street railway operation virtually impossible in the hill district. Horses could not pull streetcars up the long steep eight per cent grades on Lyon Street or the even steeper nine and ten per cent grades on East Bridge Street (became Michigan Avenue, now Michigan Street) hill. Consequently, the residents living on top of what is now known as the Heritage Hill district were without horse-drawn streetcar service.

A solution emerged by the mid-1880s when it became widely known that streetcars drawn by a continuous moving steel cable below the street surface had conquered not only the steep hills of San Francisco but also the nasty winters in Chicago. The Street Railway Company of Grand Rapids ignored requests by citizens living on the hill and by the Common Council to build a cable railway to serve the hill district. On November 10, 1884, the Common Council finally ordered the company to build a cable line to serve this area. The company declined and gave up its exclusive right to build the line claiming that it was too busy upgrading its existing street railway lines.

The horsecar company's decision not to build a cable line probably was motivated partly by the cost and partly by the time required to build a new system embracing new technology. Nonetheless, this decision came back to haunt the Street Railway Company of Grand Rapids. The cable company would soon build numerous horse-drawn streetcar lines that served as feeders to the cable lines. These horsecar lines would enable the cable railway company to become a major competitor of the "old" Street Railway Company of Grand Rapids.

Cable cars had two big advantages over horse-drawn streetcars. The first was power. The cars could easily be pulled up steep hills by the cable. Power plants were built that provided more than enough power to pull the cable in the conduit so a single grip car could pull two or more trailers thereby increasing its carrying capacity. Unfortunately, a grip car was unable to act like a locomotive in an emergency because it could not alter its speed or reverse its direction.

Speed was the second advantage cable cars had over horsecars. Cable cars could be pulled faster, seven to twelve miles an hour, depending on how fast the cable was being pulled by the machinery in the powerhouse. Cars pulled by horses on a level grade, in contrast, were limited to an average of four to six

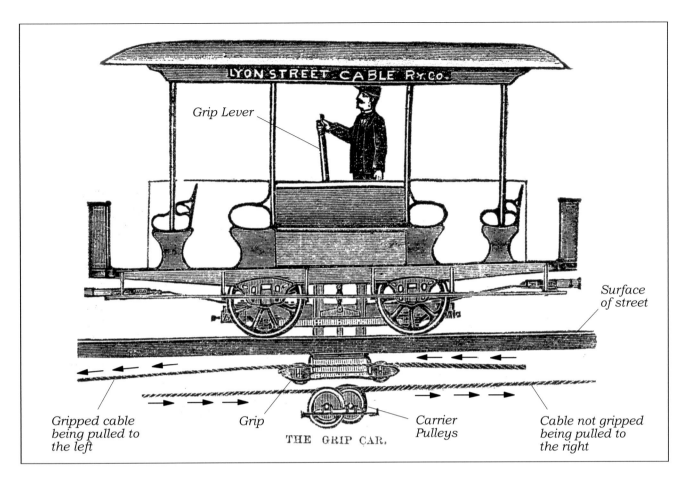

Grip Lever

Surface
of street

Gripped cable
being pulled to
the left

Grip

THE GRIP CAR.

Carrier
Pulleys

Cable not gripped
being pulled to
the right

miles an hour depending on the combined weight of the car and the passengers.

Unfortunately, there were two big cost disadvantages of using cables to move passengers: construction and maintenance. It was expensive to construct and install the underground conduits in which the cable ran. Also, it was expensive to keep the cables in good repair and replace cables that had worn out. Cables wore out faster in northern cities because ice could clog the conduits and damage the cable. When a cable broke, all the cars being pulled by that cable came to a halt and were stranded.

The Valley City Cable Street Railway Company was organized in 1885 to build the cable line but failed to raise the necessary capital. Two years later The *Grand Rapids Eagle* announced, "With the return of spring the cable road is being warmed back into existence, and when the frost is out of the ground the old chestnut promises to put on new life."

A second company, the Valley City Street and Cable Railway, was incorporated on June 8, 1887, by H. P. Breed of Minneapolis, A. J. Bowne of Grand Rapids and associates. The officers of the new company were William P. Innes, president and Robert W. Innes, secretary and treasurer. William Phenix, who helped build the cable system in Chicago, became the engineer. The Common Council granted them a franchise on July 11, 1887.

Phenix Single-Track System Adopted

The Valley City Street and Cable Railway Company adopted William Phenix's single track system to build the Lyon Street line. This system had two cables running in opposite directions on different pulleys inside the same underground conduit. As previously noted, one of the disadvantages of a cable railway system was its very high initial cost associated with building the underground yokes to hold the cable and the concrete conduits around the yokes to stabilize their position. Phenix's two cables in the same yoke system dramatically lowered the cost of building the Lyon Street cable line because the company had to construct just one set of yokes and one conduit rather than two.

Phenix's double-jaw side grip system enabled the gripman to choose one of the two running cables to grasp when starting his cable car, which in turn determined which direction the cable car would be pulled. The gripman could tighten the grip or let go of one of the two cables. The diagram is of a cable car going forward by gripping the forward-moving cable of the two.

Diagram of a gripman working a grip in the Phenix single conduit system used in Grand Rapids where two cables being pulled in opposite directions were in the same conduit. The diagram is of a cable car going in the same direction as the cable the grip man is gripping (labels added for clarity).

The Cable Car in America by George W. Hilton

Rails

Cable conduit

View Looking west down Lyon St. hill showing slot opening to the conduit where the cables run between the two rails that a cable car rides on. Note the large home on the hill was known as the David Leavitt house, built in 1858 at Ransom Avenue and Lyon Street.

Grand Rapids Public Library

Building the Lyon Street Cable Railway Line

The Valley City Street and Cable Railway Company hired Samuel Tibbetts to build the cable railway line in Grand Rapids. The new company ran into trouble with politicians when Tibbetts announced in August that the one-track line on Lyon Street hill was going to run on one side of Lyon Street rather than in the middle of the street.

The Grand Rapids Common Council had practically become an open forum for complaints about the old horsecar company, proposals to run steam dummy locomotives on certain city streets, and what rights and responsibilities the various street railway companies should have in the new franchises under consideration. The proposals and counter proposals got so out of control that the *Lansing Journal* reported in early September, "When it comes to discussing street railways, dummy lines and cable roads, they have high old times at the meetings of the Grand Rapids Common Council. They say that it is better than half a dozen clowns at a circus."

Sam Tibbetts who was supervising the construction of the Lyon Street line contended that "There are more G-d d—d fools here than in any town I ever saw" in response to all the complaints and counterproposals to his decision to place the cable railway track on one side of Lyon street. He pointed out that the company planned to double track the street next

year and that the center of the street was not an option as sewer line and manhole covers were already occupying that portion of the street.

The company was unable to complete the construction of the cable line on Lyon Street before winter due to delays in receiving raw materials and parts. Winter brought snow and ice that clogged the conduit.

The Cable

The cable rope for the Lyon Street line consisted of six steel strands, each of which were made of seventeen smaller wires twisted together. The six strands were twisted about a hemp rope, making a cable one and one-eighth inch in diameter, weighing two pounds to the foot. The cable was delivered in two sections which were spliced together to make one continuous cable. The cable was about 12,000 feet in length going down and up the Lyon Street hill, a distance of 5,471 feet each way plus going around the wheels and drums at the powerhouse, and at the lower end of Lyon Street where the continuous cable was turned around.

When the first cable was installed, Superintendent Phenix estimated that it would provide reliable service for two years. Phenix's estimate proved to be overly optimistic. But before its unreality was discovered, it led the company to build a long north-south cable line in addition to building the loop hill lines that went up and down both East Bridge and Lyon streets.

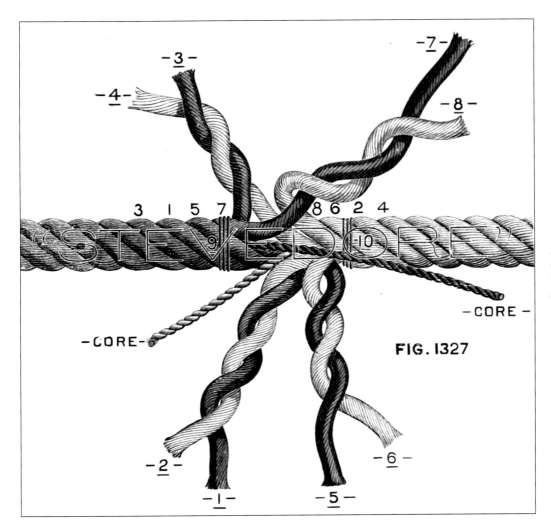

Drawing of a typical cable splice as shown in this 1892 ad.

Street Railway Review

Threading the Cable and Opening the Lyon Street Cable Railway Line

The opening of the Lyon Street line was delayed until the spring of 1888 because ice had clogged the conduit. The company finally was able to thread its cable on April 13. A cable grip car towed by four horses pulled the cable into the conduit going west from the power house and arrived at Campau and Lyon streets—the western terminus of the line—nineteen minutes later. It took forty minutes to pass the cable through the drum at the foot of Lyon Street and then twenty-eight minutes for eight horses to tow the grip car and the cable back up Lyon Street hill to the powerhouse. The *Grand Rapids Eagle* reporter was so impressed with the ease at which the cable ran in the conduit that he wrote "That eight horses, could drag a cable over two miles long, weighing almost thirty thousand pounds on end, up a steep hill even over the pulleys, shows how friction has been reduced to a minimum in the machinery."

The first grip car using cable power to operate on the Lyon Street hill tested the line on April 16, 1888.

Cable Road Regulations

The Grand Rapids Cable company has been adopting metropolitan(?) ideas in regard to the running of the cable cars. The orders that have recently been issued are that the conductors on all cable trains are implicitly prohibited from going on the grip car for any reason, except the collection of fares, and it shall further be the duty of conductors to stand upon the rear end of the train and as the train approaches a switch it shall come to a full stop and it shall be the duty of the conductor to alight from the end of the train and proceed forward and examine the switch and if said switch is all right it shall be his duty to give the gripman the proper signal and thence forward it will be plain sailing until another switch is reached. The gripmen as well as the conductors are very much worked up over the way affairs are conducted and the probalities are that a strike will be one of the interesting things the company will have to contend with in the near future. A conductor said last night to a reporter that he never heard so much "kicking" from passengers as there is at present, further remarked that a cable train would be a "dandy" place for a man to sleep off a drunk as a very drunken man could easily get "sobered" in the time it takes to go from Sweet street to Hall street.

The April 17, 1888, *Grand Rapids Daily Democrat* published the account of the triumphant trial run of the previous day, as shown on the next two pages.

HEAR IT HUM!

The Cable in the Conduit Begins Its Song

Even the croakers can no longer doubt. The long expected has at length come to pass. At six minutes before 2 o'clock yesterday afternoon the endless steel cable that will hereafter propel cars up and down Lyon Street hill, was set in motion by the machinery at the power house. The cable was run for two hours for the purpose of effectively coating it with tar and adjusting its tension, and everything running it a perfectly satisfactory manner, at 4 o'clock the car was fastened by the grip to the endless chain and moved swiftly, smoothly and steadily down the line.

Portrait Sketch of Wm. Phenix, April 17, 1888.

Grand Rapids Democrat

Sketch of Sam B. Tibbetts, April 17, 1888.

Grand Rapids Democrat

Aldermen Creque, De Graaf, Saunders, Shanahan, Launiere, Eisenhardt and Brenner, City Marshal Wilson, Mayor Dikeman, and Messrs. Eggleston, Tibbetts and Phenix of the cable railway company, and the representatives of the press occupied seats in the car.

Nearly everybody on the hill had been called out by the unusual sound of the cable as it hummed away out of sight under the surface of the street, and many were the attempts to see the mysterious hummer. No one, however, succeeded except the ubiquitous small boy who was willing to sacrifice his dignity and put his eye down to the crack. When the car hove in sight, all eyes riveted upon it and its crowd of passengers increased as it progressed downwards. In front of the high school, almost the whole school turned out to watch the car which is to save so much icy hill climbing to students especially, watched it with favorable comments as it passed down the hill and remained waiting for its return.

The Excitement Down Town

Streets Crowded Black with People Watching for the First Cable Car.

At just before 2 o'clock yesterday afternoon the attention of pedestrians on Canal, Ottawa and other streets, at their intersections with Lyon was attracted by a peculiar low, singing, humming noise, which, at first, seemed to come from nowhere. It was soon discovered that the noise was caused by the cable spinning over the pulleys in the Lyon Street conduit, and onlookers said one to another, "The Cable company is going to run its first car over the track this afternoon." ''No, they're just stretching the cable, there'll be no car till tomorrow or the next day." The crowd, however gradually thickened; men, women and children stopped at the Ionia, Ottawa and Lyon street crossings, peered anxiously down through the narrow slot into the dark conduit in the endeavor to get a glimpse at the cable which was to drag cars up the Lyon Street hill (eight feet rise to the hundred): they could see nothing, however, and had to content themselves with the music

of the hum. "Is the grip car really running down this afternoon?" was the question asked over and over again; but no one seemed to know, though the impression grew that it certainly would. Between three and four o'clock people began to thicken perceptibly all along Lyon Street from the post office building to the river, and by 4 o'clock the sidewalks and the street were quite [packed] black with crowds, all looking earnestly up Lyon street hill. Still no cable car; but the streets grew blacker with people; an unusual number of policemen put in an appearance along the cable track; supt. I. C. Smith was seen spurring his horse about the various crossings; and then the crowd knew for sure they'd see the first grip car if they only waited.

Sketch of Mr. Tibbetts orating from cable car, April 17, 1888.

Grand Rapids Democrat

At 4:27 precisely by the tower clock the long-looked for grip car hove in sight on Lyon Street hill at about Lafayette Street. "There she comes," shouted a voice, a chorus of voices echoed the words; all faces were turned hillwards, the noise of the crowds settled to a low murmur, and everybody watched the car as it

HEAR IT HUM!

steadily moved down the hill with no visible way. When the grip car bell rang for the Canal street crossing the Tower marked 4:33, and when the grip stopped at the river terminus it was 4:34, car having been just seven minutes taking the run from Lafayette Street to the river bank. Not until the car stopped at the foot of Lyon Street did most of the people remove their steady gaze from it. Then they all seemed to take a long breath, propelling power, stopping at various street crossings along the way.

HE WILL TAKE A REST.

Sketch of a worn out horse with "HE WILL TAKE A REST" caption, April 17, 1888.
Grand Rapids Democrat

THE CAR PASSING OTTAWA STR[...]

Sketch of the Cable Car on Lyon Street Passing Ottawa Avenue, April 17, 1888.
Grand Rapids Democrat

their toes in or walk backwards in order to ascend the icy inclines in the winter or toil upwards in the wilting heats of summer; for the cable road is an accomplished fact…

At 4:36 the car started back up the hill, and a still larger crowd watched its return course, and as it steadily climbed the hill . . . At just 4:43 the returning car disappeared behind the hill having made the return from the river to Lafayette Street at the top of the hill in seven minutes, exactly the same time in which it made the downward trip between the same two points.

The car was out of sight, but still the cable hummed and sung in the conduit, and the people waited, discussing the question as to whether or not another trip would be made. But after some 15 minutes waiting the information seemed mysteriously to distribute itself along the lines that there would be no further cars for a day or two-and the crowds gradually but slowly dispersed.

The cable road is now virtually open. Cars will be run today to further test the machinery and stretch the cable, but the company will be ready for business by tomorrow or Thursday at the furthest. A slight error in the gauge of the curves of the 800 foot siding above Lafayette Street and the further adjustment and trial of the machinery so as to avoid all danger of accidents makes this delay necessary. But citizens on the hill who do not keep a carriage may rejoice. No longer will it be necessary for them to stick

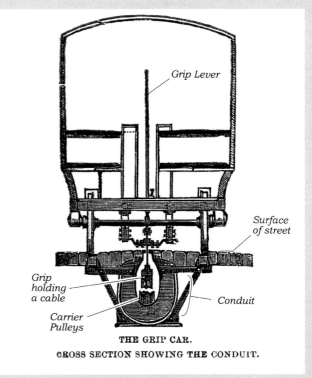

Grip Lever

Surface of street

Grip holding a cable

Conduit

Carrier Pulleys

THE GRIP CAR.
CROSS SECTION SHOWING THE CONDUIT.

Sketch of cable gripcar cross section showing the conduit (labels added for clarity).
The Cable Car in America by George W. Hilton

*Interior of Upper Lyon Street
powerhouse showing cables in 1892.*

Street Railway Review

Cable company engineers and politicians rode the grip car on April 17, the day after the trial run, and citizens began paying five cents to ride the cable car on April 18. The cable company was operating trains consisting of one grip car and two trailers every ten minutes up and down Lyon Street hill by early May. The company built an open grip car in its shop in June that could carry twenty passengers. This car was popular in part because smoking was allowed as it was an open car.

The Lyon Street cable line cars started from the Canal Street intersection at the foot of Lyon Street and went east going up a lengthy grade of more than eight per cent on Lyon Street hill between Division and Lafayette Street (now Avenue). The Lyon Street cable line continued east going beyond Union Avenue and ended at the cable powerhouse between Union and Grand avenues. The Lyon Street line was unusual in that it started as a single-track operation with a siding allowing ascending and descending cars to pass each other. The Lyon Street hill cable line was converted to a double-track system on November 7, 1890, after the East Bridge Street hill double-track cable line was built.

Grand Rapids Investors Purchase One-Half Interest in the Cable Railway

Grand Rapids investors, impressed by the early success of the Lyon Street cable line and horsecar feeder lines, bought more stock and became the major owners of the cable railway in June 1888. Messrs. A. J. Bowne and Delos A. Blodgett each purchased a one-fourth interest in the Valley City Street and Cable Railway Company. Several other Grand Rapids investors including Col. Geo. G. Briggs, E. B. Dikeman, P.C. Fuller, Thomas Peck, A. D. Rathbone, I. Stewart White, J. H. Wonderly, James Blair and Willard Kingsley joined them by investing $200 to $3,000.

Chicago investors such as John M. Hagar and John J. O'Dell also were major owners of the cable railway company. Chicago investors owned slightly more than one-third of the stock in the company.

Horsecar Feeder Lines Built by the Cable Company

The Valley City Street and Cable Railway Company built approximately seven miles of horsecar lines that acted as feeders to the 6.9 miles of cable car lines the company built between 1888 and 1891. On July 11, 1887, the Common Council granted the ordinances to build the Grandville and the Butterworth

horsecar feeder lines, the same time the council granted an ordinance for the cable lines on Lyon and East Bridge Street hills. The cable company began building horsecar lines as feeders to the Lyon Street cable line in August 1887.

The Grandville Avenue horsecar line, the first of four horsecar cable feeder lines, began running its horsecars on November 14, 1887. The Grandville Avenue line started from the intersection of Lyon and North Division streets, headed west on Lyon and then turned south on Campau Street to Louis Street; Louis Street to Waterloo Street (now known as Market Avenue); thence along Waterloo Street to Ellsworth Avenue; and south on Ellsworth (now northern end of Grandville Avenue) and south on Grandville Avenue to the city limits at Fifth (now Franklin) Street. A horse barn with room for twenty-six horses was built on Ellsworth Avenue between Island and Cherry streets in November 1887. The company built an extension enabling cars to run as far south as Hall Street by the end of 1888.

The Butterworth Avenue horsecar line, also known as the West Side line, the West Fulton line and the Eighth Ward line, began operating in November 1887, a few days after horsecars began running on the Grandville Avenue line. The cars started from the intersection of Lyon and North Division streets, headed west on Lyon to Campau Street and then traveled south on Campau, Louis, and

Waterloo streets to Fulton Street. Then the cars turned west going over the Grand River on the Fulton Street Bridge. The horsecars continued going west on West Fulton Street until reaching the Straight Street-West Fulton Street junction where the horsecars turned south to Butterworth and then west on Butterworth to south Jefferson (now Lexington) Avenue, the western terminus of the Butterworth branch line.

The West Side horsecar line branch of the Butterworth line, started at the Straight Street-West Fulton Street junction and went north on Straight Street to Jackson Street, turned west on Jackson until the line reached Pine Street where the line finally turned north to reach the terminus at the intersection of Pine and West Bridge streets. This horsecar line competed with the "old" company's horsecar line then running on West Bridge Street.

The Barclay-Coit Street horsecar line was the third horsecar feeder line that the cable company built. The Common Council passed the ordinance granting the cable company the right to build the line on October 10, 1887. The Barclay line horsecars started going north on Barclay Street from the Lyon Street-Barclay Street intersection and then turned to go north on Coit Street where the line crossed East Bridge Street. The horsecars then traveled north on Coit Street to Trowbridge, and Clancy streets and finally reached the Detroit, Grand Haven and Milwaukee Railway Company pas-

Cable grip car No. 13 with two trailers and crew at the the north terminus on Ottawa Avenue about 1890.

Grand Rapids
Public Library

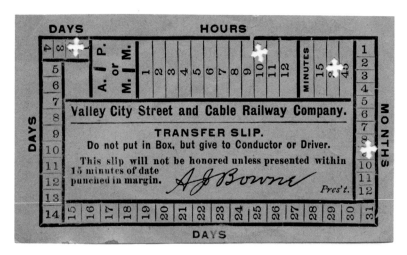

Punched transfer ticket of the Valley City Street and Cable Railway Company.

Ed Bawden Collection

senger station. The first part of this line began operating after January 1, 1888. The company completed building a horse barn on Clancy Street just north of the DGH&M railroad tracks by December 21, 1888. The southern part of the Barclay line which ran between Lyon and East Bridge streets was abandoned when the North Ottawa Street cable railway line began operating in March 1889.

The South Ionia Street horsecar line, built in the fall of 1889, was the fourth and last horsecar feeder to be built. The South Ionia line fed the south cable line connecting at the Spring Street-Wealthy Street intersection. The horsecars ran on Johnson brand girder rails and went west one block on Wealthy and then south on South Ionia Avenue to the city limits at Hall Street. Horsecars began operating on the South Ionia line on January 1, 1890, in accordance with the city ordinance and were running every five minutes by February 18, 1890.

The first horsecars that the cable company purchased were very short—ten to twelve feet in length. Cars purchased later were longer—fourteen to sixteen feet in length. The cars were painted a canary yellow and lettered with the names of the streets the cars ran on by early January 1888. Some of the horsecars were designed so that a car also could be used as a trailer hitched to a grip car and run on cable lines. Many of the cars were double-ended cars on which the driver simply unhitched the horse and walked it to the other end of the car.

The cable railway company provided free transfer tickets to passengers who wanted to transfer to another cable railway line or horsecar feeder line. These transfer tickets had to be used within fifteen minutes of the time punched on the transfer slip ticket.

Building the Cable Railway Lines

The Valley City Street and Cable Railway built more than just a cable loop line up and down East Bridge Street and Lyon Street hills. The company also built a long north-south cable line that was unique in that it had the longest continuous cable—32,000 feet—of any cable railway in the United States. The company built a total of 6.9 miles of cable railway between 1887 and 1890 and ran cable cars on one or more cable line routes between April 18, 1888, and November 12, 1891.

The Lyon Street cable line, one and one-fifth miles long, ran from April 18, 1888, to April 1, 1890, and then became part of the larger loop line that included East Bridge Street. In the latter form it operated from April 6, 1890, to November 12, 1891. The Lyon Street cable line started going east on Lyon Street from the Campau Street intersection at the foot of Lyon Street. The cable line crossed Canal Street and began going up a lengthy grade of more than eight per cent on Lyon Street hill between Division and Lafayette Street (now Avenue). The Lyon Street cable line then continued east on Lyon Street beyond Union Avenue to a cable power house between Union and Grand avenues. The cable was about 12,000 feet in length traveling up and down the Lyon Street hill a distance of 5,471 feet each way plus going through the wheels and drums at both ends of the line.

The Lyon Street cable line was unusual in that it initially used the Phenix double grip system. The lower western part of the Lyon Street single track cable line was converted to a double-track line in the fall of 1888. The rest of the hilltop section of the Lyon Street line was double tracked and connected to the East Bridge Street line forming a double-track loop that operated between April 6, 1890, and October 8, 1891. The part of this loop line ran on Canal Street between Lyon and East Bridge streets and became known as part of the "Four Track Nuisance."

See maps on pages 48 A-48B.

The "Four-Track Nuisance" on Canal Street

On March 5, 1888, the Common Council granted the cable company the right to build a line on Canal Street as part of an ordinance to build the north and south cable lines. The cable company had originally planned to build the north-south cable line on Ottawa Street through downtown Grand Rapids. However, Canal Street merchants wanted to capture the business of these potential riders. The merchants persuaded the Common Council aldermen, who then informed the cable railway company that its proposal to run through downtown on Ottawa Street would not be approved, but that a proposal to run on Canal Street between Lyon and East Bridge Street would be approved. Therefore the cable company asked for an amendment to its proposed ordinance to allow it to build a street railway on Canal Street; this was granted.

The Street Railway Company of Grand Rapids opposed the Common Council's decision to grant the cable company the right to build a track on Canal Street. The horsecar company obtained an injunction in state court on October 14 preventing the cable company from constructing tracks on that street. On Saturday evening of October 27, a judge partially dissolved the injunction which allowed the cable company to build one track on Canal Street's east side.

Ten minutes after midnight on Sunday, October 28, the cable company fielded a force of more than a hundred men with picks and shovels who went to work digging the trench for the yokes and conduits. They labored day and night to complete one track on Canal Street. The second cable line track on this section of Canal Street was completed later converting the street between Lyon Street and East Bridge Street into what became known as the "Four-Track Nuisance." The old company continued to fight in court against what it considered to be an illegal action. The lawsuit was on its way to the Michigan Supreme Court but ended when the defendant, the Valley City Street and Cable Railway Company, purchased the plaintiff, the Street Railway Company of Grand Rapids, on October 17, 1890.

In a curious reversal of roles, the Valley City and Cable Railway, originally the defendant in the "Four Track Nuisance" lawsuit, was now the plaintiff in federal court a few months later in an attempt to block the Lake Electric Railway from building 200 feet of track on East Fulton Street by contending that it had the exclusive right to use East Fulton street.

The North Canal-North Ottawa Street cable line, two and one-half miles long, operated from March 7, 1889, to November 12, 1891. This line initially ran two miles from Lyon Street north on Canal Street, east on East Bridge Street, north on Ottawa Street, east on Walbridge, north on North Ionia to Leonard Street near the Detroit, Grand Haven and Milwaukee Railway depot.

Next, the cable company built the Taylor Street extension of the North Ottawa cable line in 1889-1890. This extension, about one-half mile long, went north on Taylor Street from Leonard Street near the Detroit, Grand Haven and Milwaukee Railway depot to the city limit at Sweet Street. It was intended to be steam powered, but the Common Council rejected the petition for a franchise to run a steam dummy on Taylor Street inside the city. Therefore horses were temporarily used to haul

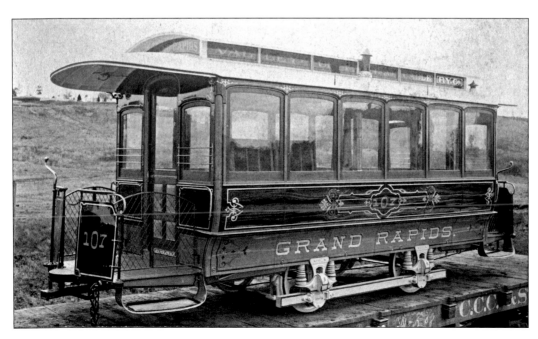

Valley City Street & Cable Railway Car No. 107 built by Ellis Car Company, Amesbury, Mass.

Carl Bajema Collection

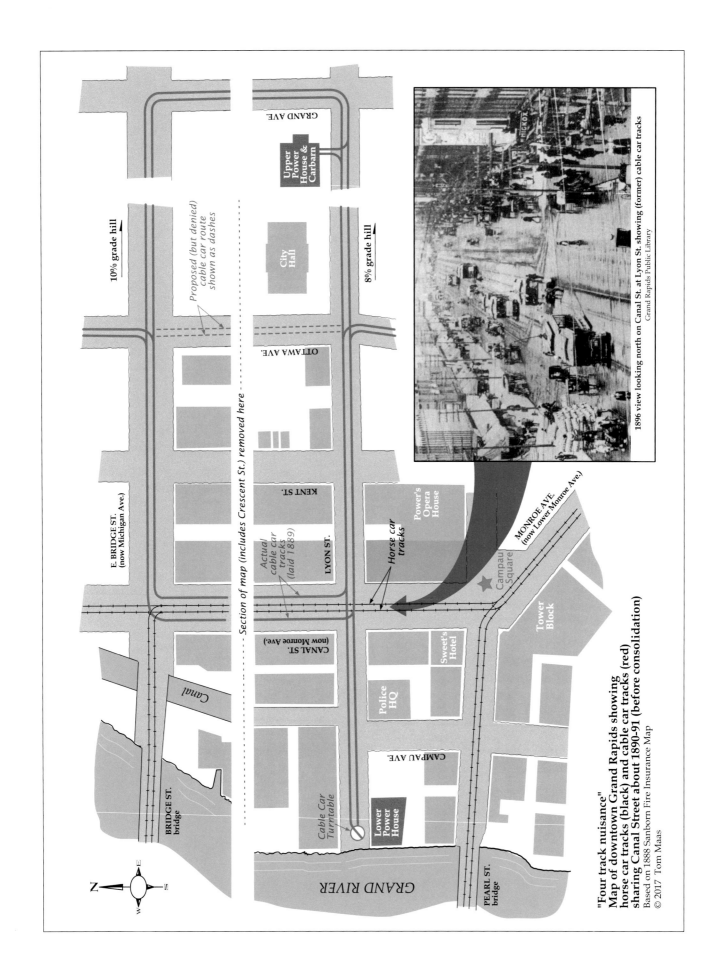

1896 view looking north on Canal St. at Lyon St. showing (former) cable car tracks
Grand Rapids Public Library

10% grade hill

Proposed (but denied)
cable car route
shown as dashes

8% grade hill

GRAND AVE.

Upper Power
House &
Carbarn

City Hall

OTTAWA AVE.

Section of map (includes Crescent St.) removed here

KENT ST.

Actual
cable car
tracks
(laid 1889)

LYON ST.

E. BRIDGE ST.
(now Michigan Ave.)

Power's Opera
House

Horse car
tracks

MONROE AVE.
(now Lower Monroe Ave.)

Canal

CANAL ST.
(now Monroe Ave.)

Campau
Square

Sweet's
Hotel

Tower
Block

Police
HQ

BRIDGE ST.
bridge

CAMPAU AVE.

Cable Car
Turntable

Lower Power
House

GRAND RIVER

PEARL ST.
bridge

N

"Four track nuisance"
Map of downtown Grand Rapids showing
horse car tracks (black) and cable car tracks (red)
sharing Canal Street about 1890-91 (before consolidation)
Based on 1888 Sanborn Fire Insurance Map
© 2017 Tom Maas

Valley City Street and Cable Railway of Grand Rapids - Five maps spanning from 1888 to 1891

as documented by George W. Hilton in 1967 for the American Railroad Journal, Vol. 2.
Illustrations represent development phases and are numbered ① through ⑤ to show changes.
© 2017 Tom Maas

Note: Grand River, Campau Square, Union Station, power house illustration and City Limits were added to maps for clarity.

p.h. = power house

Upper power house was on the north side of Lyon Street near present day Grand Avenue.

Lower power house was on the south side of Lyon Street nearly on the bank of the Grand River.

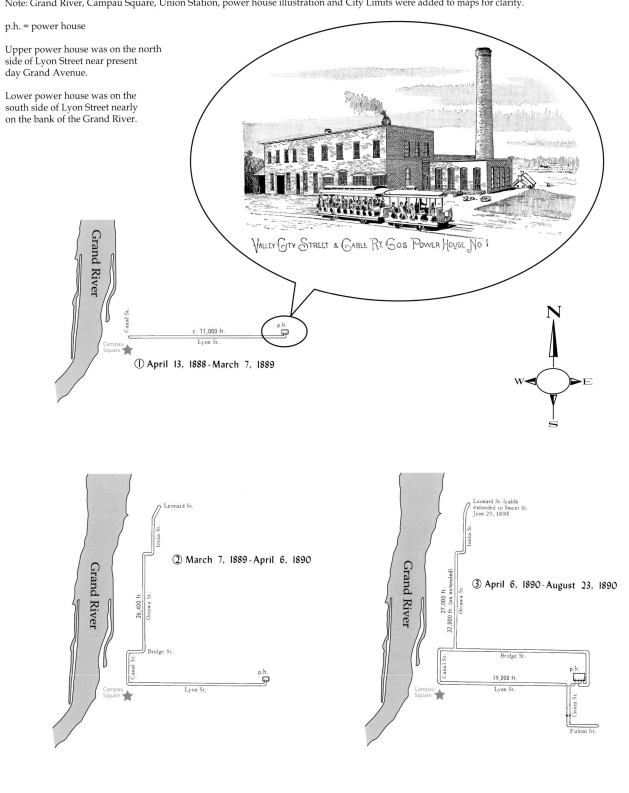

Valley City Street & Cable Ry Go.s Power House No 1

① April 13, 1888 - March 7, 1889

② March 7, 1889 - April 6, 1890

③ April 6, 1890 - August 23, 1890

Leonard St. (cable extended to Sweet St. June 29, 1890)

trification overlaid on bird's eye map of Grand Rapids
e)

391

Map Legend

Black dashed lines - Grand Rapids city limits
Green lines - Grand Rapids Street Railway
Orange lines - Valley City Street and Cable Railway cable lines
Brown lines - Valley City Street and Cable Railway horse feeder lines
Blue line - North Park Railway
Violet line - Reed's Lake Railway
Black rail lines - Primary steam passenger lines

1 - Union Station (GR&I RR, MC RR, DL&N RR and C&WM RR) on S. Ionia Ave.
2 - DGH&M RR Station on Plainfield Ave.
3 - LS&MS RR Station on Bridge St.
4 - Campau Square
5 - Upper Lyon Power House (drove East/West Loop cables)
6 - Lower Lyon Power House (drove North/South cables)
7 - Sweet St. Station - North Park line south terminus
8 - Buckeye St. Station
9 - Sherman St. Station of the Ramona Lake Dummy Line
10 - Horse car barn built prior to Ramona Lake Dummy Line

DGH&MRR

Grand Ave.

⑤

CITY LIMIT

Union Ave.

E. Fulton St.

End: East St.
(now Eastern Ave.)

Cherry St.

⑩

Jefferson Ave.

⑧

Sherman St.

To Reed's Lake
(via "Dummy Line")

Wealthy St.

⑨

Logan Ave.

Sheldon Ave.

Buckley St.

Lafayette Ave.

S. Division Ave.

Jefferson Ave.

S. Ionia Ave.

Hall St.

End: 5th Ave.
(now Franklin St.)

DL&N RR

GR&I RR

MC RR

© 2017   Tom Maas

Map of streetcar and cable railway lines in 1890 before consolidation and ele

(City limits and primary steam passenger railroad routes are shown for referen

Track map sources: Common Council of the City of Grand Rapids Ordinance of 1887, Map by George F. Cram

Note: Track routes overlaid on original 1892 bird's eye view (color converted to greyscale) from the Gr

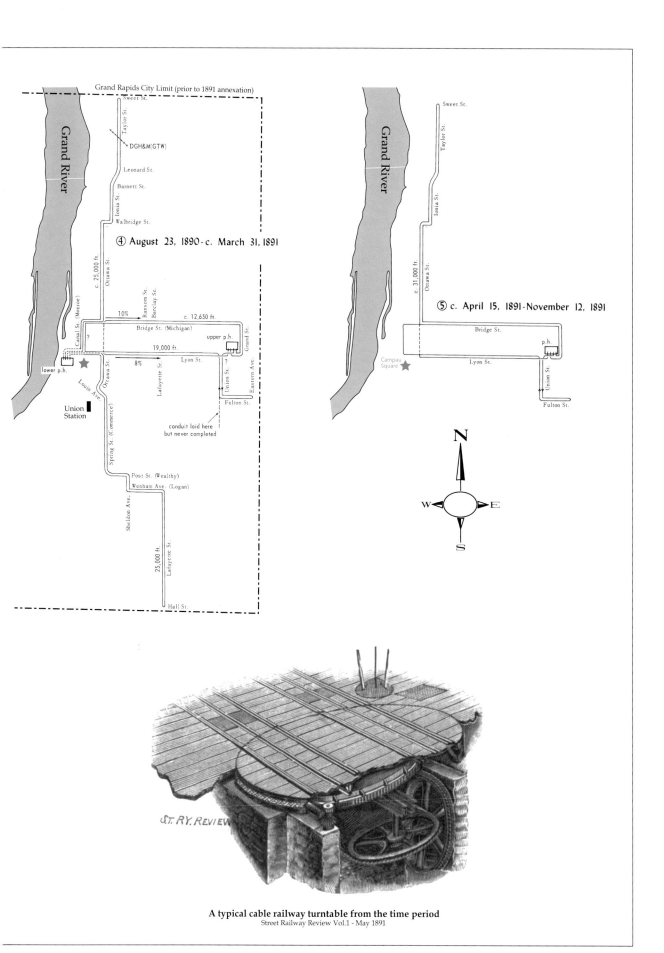

Grand Rapids City Limit (prior to 1891 annexation)

Grand River

Sweet St.

Taylor St.

DGH&M(GTW)

Leonard St.

Barnett St.

Ionia St.

Walbridge St.

④ August 23, 1890 - c. March 31, 1891

c. 25,000 ft

Ottawa St.

Ransom St.

Barclay St.

Canal St. (Monroe)

10%   c. 12,650 ft.

Bridge St. (Michigan)   upper p.h.

?   19,000 ft.   Grand St.

?   8%   Lyon St.

lower p.h.   ★   Ottawa St.   Lafayette St.   Union St.   Eastern Ave.

Louis Ave.   Fulton St.

Union
Station   conduit laid here
but never completed

Spring St. (Commerce)

Post St. (Wealthy)

Wenham Ave. (Logan)

Sheldon Ave.

25,000 ft.

Lafayette St.

Hall St.

Grand River

Sweet St.

Taylor St.

Ionia St.

⑤ c. April 15, 1891 - November 12, 1891

c. 31,000 ft.

Ottawa St.

Bridge St.   p.h.

Campau
Square   ★   Lyon St.

Union St.

Fulton St.

N
W   E
S

A typical cable railway turntable from the time period
Street Railway Review Vol.1 - May 1891

ST. RY. REVIEW

48A

Map of electrified railway lines at the end of 1892 after consolidation and electrificati

(Newly expanded city limits and primary steam passenger railroad routes are shown fo

Track map source: Common Council of the City of Grand Rapids Franchise agreement

Note: Track routes overlaid on original 1892 bird's eye view (color converted to greyscale) from the Grand Rapids

overlaid on bird's eye map of Grand Rapids
(eference)

Map Legend

Black dashed lines - Grand Rapids city limits
Red lines with white dots - Grand Rapids Consolidated Street Railway (electric)
Blue line - North Park Railway
Black rail lines - Primary steam passenger lines

1 - Union Station (GR&I RR, MC RR, DL&N RR and C&WM RR) on S. Ionia Ave.
2 - DGH&M RR Station on Plainfield Ave.
3 - LS&MS RR Station on W. Fulton St.
4 - Campau Square

CITY LIMIT

DGH&MRR

REEDS LAKE

End:
Grand Ave.

Union Ave.

E. Fulton St.

End:
Fuller Ave.

Lake Dr.

Cherry St.

Ave.

To Reed's Lake

Ave.

Wealthy St.

East St.
(now Eastern Ave.)

End:
East St.

Fifth Ave. *(now Franklin St.)*

Blakeley St.

Lafayette Ave.

S. Division Ave.

Hall St.

DL&N RR

© 2017 Tom Maas

R&I RR

MC RR

End: Burton St.
(City Limit)

ublic Museum Collection

48C

streetcars on the Taylor line until it was rebuilt as a cable railway. Grip cars began operating on it on June 29, 1890.

This 1890 northern extension of the Ottawa Street line ended at the city limits at Sweet Street. Passengers could transfer there to the North Park Street Railway and continue north on the steam dummy passenger train in Grand Rapids township to reach Soldiers' Home and North Park on the banks of the Grand River. A station was built at Sweet Street that served both the cable cars and the new North Park Street Railway.

The last cable car train ran on the North Ottawa-Taylor cable line on November 12, 1891. Electric streetcars began operation on Taylor Street north to Sweet Street the next day.

The history of the North Park Street Railway, which was electrified in 1894, can be found in Chapter 2 in this book.

The East Bridge Street cable line, more than a mile long, ran from April 6, 1890, to November 12, 1891. The East Bridge Street cable line was built east from Canal Street going up the steep East Bridge Street hill which included a ten per cent grade between Ottawa and Ransom streets. The steep part of the cable line was double tracked. The cable cars ran on a single track on top of the hill with switches and passing sidings that enabled cars going in opposite directions to pass one another. The line on East Bridge Street hill continued east going down to Grand Street where the cable line turned south to Lyon Street where it connected with the double-track Lyon Street cable line. The East Bridge Street and Lyon Street cable lines formed a loop that operated between April 6, 1890, and November 12, 1891.

The Union-East Fulton Street cable Line, ran south on Union Street from Lyon Street, and then east on Fulton Street and ended at the city limits at East Street. This line operated between April 6, 1890, and October 8, 1891. Passengers could pay another five-cent fare and board a Reed's Lake Electric Railway car and ride all the way to Reed's Lake.

The cable running on this line was an extension of the cable that pulled the cars on the Lyon Street line. Broken cables were frequent on this route. Whenever a section of the Lyon Street cable broke where it couldn't be repaired, the damaged section was cut out. The good part of the cable was rerouted, leaving the Union-East Fulton Street line without cable power for weeks at a time. Meanwhile the Reed's Lake Electric Railway was left isolated until the cable company was able to obtain a replacement cable.

The South End-Lafayette Street (now Avenue) cable line began operating on August 23, 1890, and was abandoned on March 31, 1891. The line began at a junction with the loop line at the Lyon Street-Ottawa Street intersection, ran south on Ottawa Street, southeast on Louis Street, on Spring Street (now Commerce Avenue), east on Post (now Wealthy) Street, south on Sheldon, east on Wenham (now Logan) Street and finally south on Lafayette Street to end at Hall Street.

In retrospect, there were two problems with the south end cable line. First, the line had seven sharp right-angle curves. Flexing and straightening the cable as it navigated street corners drastically shortened the life of a cable. Second, this new cable car line roughly paralleled an old horsecar line a few streets away on Division Avenue. Consequently the income from passenger fares did not even pay for the maintenance costs associated with the cable on the south end line.

Change in Ownership

Samuel B. Tibbetts resigned as manager of the Valley City Street and Cable Railway Company on June 20, 1889, after selling his interest in the company to a syndicate composed of John M. Hagar of Chicago and other "foreign" investors. The *Grand Rapids Daily Leader* cheerfully reported that it was "General Manager Sam B. Tibbetts is no more. The hifalutin' windy official could no longer stand the pressure of adverse public opinion . . ."

Buying, Building, and Modifying Cable Cars in 1888 and 1889

Five elegant cars, numbered 0, 2, 10, 11 and 13, all built in the Pullman car shops for the exclusive use on the cable portion of the lines, arrived in Grand Rapids in early 1888. Two of them were outfitted with grips in Grand Rapids. One of the three trailer cars was finished in mahogany and fitted with stained glass windows and elaborate upholstery. This car could be chartered for special events.

The cable company also built a large open grip car in its shop at its upper Lyon Street powerhouse. This car could easily carry twenty passengers. The car was very popular both with gripmen, who had an unobstructed view on both sides of the car, and with passengers who wanted to smoke as the car was a designated smoking car. Two more grip cars equipped with long side seats were built at the powerhouse shop during the first months of 1889.

The Common Council ordered the cable company to put connecting chains between grip cars and trailers. The aldermen contended that if the lightweight link and coupling pin that held the cars together broke, then the rear trailer or trailers could go thundering down the steep Lyon Street hill, endangering the lives of all passengers aboard.

The Pullman Palace Car Company built at

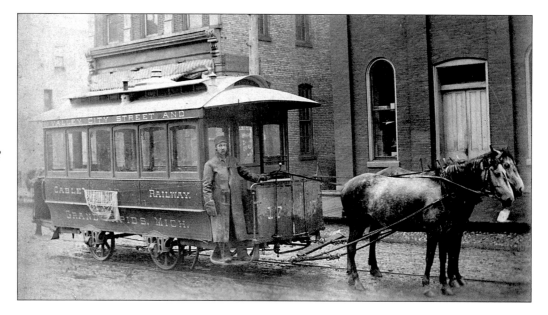

Horse feeder car No. 12 for the cable railway.

Gordon Hubernet Collection

least four new open cars for the Valley City Street and Cable Railway Company during the summer of 1889. The company also purchased a huge snow sweeper to keep its tracks clear during the winter. The *Grand Rapids Telegram-Herald* described the new steam snow sweeper as a formidable looking engine and when coming down the street "resembles a cross between a steam sawmill and a Nebraska cyclone."

By the end of 1889 the cable company had invested more than $425,000 (over $11 million in 2016 dollars) to build and operate the lines. The company was operating between two and three miles of cable line in addition to its horsecar lines. It employed 150 men. The company had ten horsecars and forty-four cable and grip cars in use (counting some that would be in use within a few weeks). It reported that its cable cars were being pulled at an average speed of from six to eight miles an hour.

Operations in 1890

Horsecars began running on the south Ionia Street line by the beginning of January 1890. The cable company petitioned in early March to operate cable cars on Canal Street between Pearl and Lyon streets to connect the north Ottawa and the south end cable lines. It even proposed to put a conduit within the tracks of the old company. The Street Railway Company of Grand Rapids opposed the idea and drew attention to the fact that four horsecars of their "old company" passed over Canal Street between Pearl and Lyon streets every three minutes during rush hour.

Cable cars started running up and down the new East Bridge Street cable line on Sunday, April 6, 1890. The horsecar feeder line running on Barclay Street from East Fulton Street to East Bridge Street was torn up because the cable line now served the East Bridge Street hill

region. The Lyon Street hill was double tracked in September, 1890.

The company built a double-track extension from Leonard Street north to Sweet Street in the spring of 1890. Passengers could transfer to the new North Park Street Railway steam dummy trains at Sweet Street and ride to Soldiers' Home as well as to North Park where a new resort was being built.

As noted in the previous chapter, the change of cars was eased by a joint two-story station house at Sweet Street junction. A big train shed was located at the north end of the station that extended over both the North Park Street Railway and the cable railway tracks. Cable cars began operating on the South End cable car line on Sunday, August 31, 1890.

Battle over the "Four Track Nuisance" Continues

The political and legal fight over the "Four Track Nuisance" in Canal Street began early in 1888 and showed no signs of ending soon. Canal Street merchants and aldermen spent as much time arguing about who was to blame as they did trying to devise a solution during the month of March 1890.

Samuel Mather of Cleveland, the major stockholder in the Street Railway of Grand Rapids Company, made the case for the importance of a streetcar company's exclusive right to operate on a particular street when he spoke before the Common Council on May 2, 1890. He reminded the alderman this right was reaffirmed at the August 17, 1885, Common Council meeting. The cable company claimed it was no fault of theirs because they had wanted to build their connecting cable line on Ottawa, not Canal Street.

The controversy continued throughout May. Some citizens even advocated extending the cable railway tracks on Canal Street south from Lyon Street to Pearl Street. This led the editor of the *Grand Rapids Evening Leader* to contend that it "would be sheer lunacy to permit the repetition in Canal Street south of Lyon of the four-track folly perpetuated north of it."

Can a Streetcar Company Own a Street?

A new legal battle arose over the same issue but on a broader scale that would apply to any company and any street. The Valley City Street and Cable Railway Company, which was the defendant in the Canal Street lawsuit, contended that only it had the right to operate streetcars on East Fulton Street and filed a lawsuit in federal court in an attempt to prevent the Reed's Lake Electric Railway from building street railway track on East Fulton Street inside the city.

Newly appointed U.S. Supreme Court Associate Justice Henry B. Brown heard the case of the Street Railway Company of Grand Rapids et al. vs. Reed's Lake Electric Railway Company. Judge Brown handed down his decision in U. S. Circuit Court, Western Division of Michigan, on June 27, 1891. He denied the petition of the Valley City Street and Cable Railway Company, the owner of the old Street Railway Company of Grand Rapids, for an injunction that would prevent the Reed's Lake Electric Railway Company from laying a track in a 200-foot section of East Fulton Street where the plaintiff already had a track. Judge Brown decided that although one council had granted the old company permission to use a street, the same council or succeeding council could grant similar rights to others.

This decision ended the legal struggle, but the "Four Track Nuisance" in Canal Street survived to create problems for merchants and vehicular traffic until the beginning of the twentieth century.

Additional Power and New Cars

During the winter and early spring of 1890 the cable railway installed new, more powerful Wheelock engines in the upper Lyon Street powerhouse. The additional power produced at this facility was not enough to run the new East Bridge Street and the new south end-Lafayette Street cable lines in addition to the power demands that the company was meeting at the beginning of 1890. Therefore, the cable company also built a lower Lyon Street powerhouse on the southwest corner of the Lyon Street-Campau Street intersection. The new powerhouse machines pulled the cables for the cars using the Lyon Street cable line and the Union-East Bridge Street cable line.

Four of the seven new streetcars arriving

in late February began running on the new South Ionia horsecar line. The remaining three cars commenced service from the Grand Avenue terminus on the new East Bridge Street cable car line on Sunday, April 6, 1890. The cable street railway received five new open cars on May 5, 1890. These five were the first cars of a twenty-three-car order to be received. Open cable grip car No. 31 built by Pullman Company was involved in an accident at the Canal Street-East Bridge Street intersection on July 26, 1890.

Twelve new, but long-delayed grip cars built by the Ellis Car Company of Amesbury, Massachusetts, arrived in September, 1890.

Cable Railway on Verge of Bankruptcy

The cable car era in Grand Rapids lasted less than four years. The company was facing bankruptcy in the fall of 1890. Why were cable cars in Grand Rapids such a financial disaster?

Many of the lines the cable company built paralleled the older horsecar company lines. This proved to be unprofitable for both companies because they were competing for virtually the same small population of riders. With the huge expenses for both installation and maintenance the cable company was unable to gain enough income from passenger fares to pay more than half its bills.

Also, the cable company experienced major problems with respect to its cables. A cable had to be oiled for flexibility and tarred on a daily basis to make the strands smooth. This was done to minimize the damage to the cable that could occur whenever gripmen grasped the cable with the vise-like grip. Excessive lubrication could spread tar and oil on the winding machinery and pulleys carrying the cables, decreasing the speed at which the cables could be moved.

When the company began to run its first cable in 1888, Superintendent Phenix had believed that a cable would provide good service for two years before it needed to be replaced. His estimate fell short of reality and led to disastrous financial problems. The Valley City Street and Cable Railway Company was forced to deal with a parade of problems involving cables.

Pulling cables at speeds approaching twelve miles an hour and continually flexing the cable on the many ninety-degree curves in Grand Rapids shortened the service life of the cables. Expensive replacement cables had to be ordered more frequently than the cable railway company had expected.

Breaks in cable running on the southern route had become so frequent that on December 5, 1890, an editorial writer for the *Grand Rapids Eagle* drew attention to a local rumor that the cable rope was very old when he wrote, tongue-in-cheek: "There is a tradition that it

Pullman Company Builder's photo of car No. 31.

Smithsonian Institution

was used for towing the ark to Mount Ararat but this is not well authenticated."

Bad weather also shortened the life of a cable. Wet weather accelerated the rate at which the wires in a cable corroded. Freezing temperatures caused water in conduits to freeze and cables to break when a section of cable was frozen in position. The accumulation of dirt and fecal material from horses in a conduit could clog the conduit and cause a cable to break. Water and dirt caused cables to be stripped of their protective lubricants against damage by grips.

The north-south cable was submerged in two and one-half feet of water when Grand River flood waters flowed into the lower Lyon Street powerhouse on March 2, 1891. The flood waters scoured the cable bright and wore off all the oil and tar used to protect it.

Gripmen could damage a cable in a number of ways as they attached their grips to the cable while it was moving. When the grip squeezed the cable it could cause thinning of the cable or strands of the cable to break. The friction from attaching a grip to a cable and keeping the grip attached increases exponentially with the speed the cable is moving. The company wanted to run its cables at twelve miles an hour so its cars could be pulled at those speeds between passenger stops. Faced with the increasing frequency of cable maintenance, repair and replacement costs, the company began running its cables at speeds so slow that travel by cable car no longer represented a saving in time over horse-drawn streetcars. The company reported its grip cars were being pulled at an average speed of six to eight miles an hour.

The cable used on the North Ottawa line was breaking down so frequently during January and early February 1891 that the cable company decided not to make the costly repairs or order another expensive replacement cable. The company stopped running a cable between East Bridge Street and Sweet Street.

The company began running a free horsecar for the half-mile ride on Taylor Street between Leonard Street and the end of the line at Sweet Street and provided free transfers to the old Canal Street horsecar line the cable company now owned. Providing free transportation for passengers boarding the free horsecar line not only was much cheaper than replacing the cable. It helped placate aldermen on the Common Council who threatened to require either the cable be replaced or they would vote to declare the franchise null and void because a cable railway was part of the franchise agreement.

James R. Chapman, the new superintendent of the newly combined companies, described the problem that the company faced by pointing out that the North Ottawa cable cost $6,000 new and that when he arrived in Grand Rapids almost two months ago. "That cable had been running for ninety days and it had broken and been spliced at that time. We have been patching it up every night since until there is no use trying to keep it up longer. I saw that it was useless and we asked the council to allow us to suspend pending the passage of the electric ordinance."

Chapman went on to estimate ". . . how well that line was paying. I will tell you that the actual cost of the last cable was $49 per day" during its lifetime." Chapman then estimated that the receipts from fares averaged less than $15 per day and that "When one gets such figures, the situation is absurd; such business is ruinous. Just consider the income from that line has not more than one-half paid for the cable. The other expenses are not figured in at all."

Cable Railway Company Buys the "Old" Horse Railway Company

Both the Valley City Street and Cable Railway Company and the Street Railway Company of Grand Rapids were on the verge of bankruptcy when the cable railway company devised a plan that to salvage its investment by buying the Street Railway Company of Grand Rapids. The cable railway company could accomplish two goals by this purchase. First, the cable company would eliminate its competitor for fare-paying passengers. Second, the cable railway company would own the Street Railway Company of Grand Rapids' 1889 franchise which included the right to electrify its streetcar system. The cable railway company called a special meeting of stockholders on October 9, 1890. The stockholders voted unanimously to borrow up to $2,500,000 so they could purchase the Street Railway Company of Grand Rapids and begin electrifying the city's streetcar system. The Valley City Street and Cable Railway Company purchased the other company on October 17 and announced the two companies would remain distinct but under one general management.

The Cleveland investor Sam Mather stated the reason the Cleveland investors paid a high figure for the Grand Rapids street railways was the ultimate value of the franchises they purchased giving them exclusive rights on the streets the cars ran on and first choice for exclusive right on any street that any company proposed to build a streetcar line. They did not purchase the line for the worn out streetcars nor the old rusty strap iron rails. They were not willing to invest more money if their exclusive franchise rights were not being protected. The cable company also made an offer to buy their stock at a price they found impossible to refuse—fifty cents per dollar for stock that they had only paid twenty-five cents per dollar for eight years earlier.

Cable Railway Operations at the End of 1890

The Lyon Street cable hill line began operating as a double-track line on November 7, 1890. The cable company started taking up the new cable line on Union Street south of Fulton Street in accordance with the wishes of the residents of that street in mid-November. At the same time the Grand Rapids Township granted a franchise enabling the cable company to build a cable line on the east side of East Street in mid-November.

Labor Problems Lead to Strikes in 1890 and 1891

Many cable car gripmen, horsecar drivers, and conductors had joined the Street Railway Employees' Union by November 26, 1890. Their goal was to make the company agree to higher wages and shorter working hours. The strike that began on May 10, 1891 was fairly peaceful until the night of June 9 when an organized group of striking employees attempted to use dynamite to destroy the terminal wheel and wheel pit of the North Ottawa cable line at Sweet Street station. The police had been alerted and a group of policemen were sent to protect the station. A riot ensued and several of the rioters were arrested. The violence turned the public, who had been on the side of the striking employees, against them. The strike ended in failure on June 23 after forty-four days.

The Valley City Street and Cable Railway Gets a New Name

Notwithstanding the previous year's plan to keep the two companies "distinct," the Street Railway Company of Grand Rapids and the Valley City Street and Cable Railway Company ceased to legally exist on June 30, 1891. Both companies were combined into a new legal corporation on July 1, 1891, accurately named the Consolidated Street Railway Company of Grand Rapids.

The new company continued to operate cable cars for several months while electrifying horsecar lines and some of the cable car lines. Newspapers reported that north end cable line grip cars drew two trailers each on July 12, 1891, and were crowded with passengers going to and from the North Park resort. The newspapers also reported the cable railway tracks in Ottawa Street south of Monroe Street were being removed at the end of August. A cable pulled a cable car on the rails in Grand Rapids for the last time on November 12, 1891.

The *Grand Rapids Evening Leader* published a farewell to cable car operations in Grand Rapids on Nov 13, 1891:

GOOD BYE, CABLE

Last night the hill cables were pulled out of their conduits and coiled away, and the hill service is today furnished by the new electric motors, which have now superseded the grips throughout the city. The days of the cable road in Grand Rapids are undoubtedly done, and of citizens, and especially the hill people, when the grips began running some three-and-a-half years ago, it is the almost universal opinion that great as was the improvement then of the cable over horse-power, the substitution now of electric power for both makes a still greater advance toward perfection in rapid street-car transit . . .

Looking back over the marvelous improvements in street-car travel which the three-and-a-half years of cable transit have been directly or indirectly the means of bringing about, it is hard to repress a mild feeling of regret that the hum of the cable is to be no more heard in this bailiwick. But it has done its good work, and the citizens of Grand Rapids are greatly indebted to it for the existing superior system of rapid transit—a system now unequaled by that of any city of its size in the country.

Electric Traction Begins in Grand Rapids

View showing the interior of the Hall Streetcar barn with its repair pits. These pits became necessary after electrification to provide access to repair the electric motors which were exposed to all kinds of foul weather conditions.

Thomas Dilley Collection at Grand Rapids Public Library

If It Works in Cleveland . .

The industrialists Samuel Mather and W. J. Hayes, owners of the controlling interest in the Street Railway Company of Grand Rapids, observed the successful introduction of electric streetcars in their home town of Cleveland in 1888. They realized that if their Grand Rapids street railway company was going to successfully compete with the cable railway company it would have to replace horse-drawn streetcars with electric-powered ones. The Grand Rapids Common Council granted the street railway's request for a new thirty-year franchise that included the right to convert to electric power on October 14, 1889.

In January 1890 the Cleveland investors sent their Grand Rapids superintendent Andries Bevier to Cleveland to study how the electric cars were operating in that city. Upon returning, Bevier announced that the company was going to accept a modified version of the Common Council's proposed franchise at the latter's next meeting on February 3, 1890. He stated, "We will go to work as fast as the sea-son will permit, changing our entire plant to be operated by the overhead electric system."

The Street Railway Company of Grand Rapids estimated that it would cost approximately $500,000 to convert their horsecar routes to an electric system. Streetcars would have to be equipped with electric motors which added to the weight of the cars. New heavier rails would have to replace almost all of the existing rails which were too light to support the heavier electric cars. An overhead electric wire power system supported by poles would have to be built.

Mather and Hayes were very hesitant with respect to investing the necessary capital to convert their horse-drawn streetcar system to electric power. Mather stated that the plans of the company had received a serious setback by the Common Council's support for one or more companies to operate competing lines on Canal, Monroe, and East Fulton streets. Mather told a newspaper reporter that "We will await the action of the Common Council before we expend any large amount of money in this city."

The First Strike: 150 Conductors and Drivers Go on Strike

The newly organized Street Railway Employee's Union made three demands they called "requests:"

- The number of hours an employee works be reduced from about seventeen hours to about twelve hours per day
- The pay per day be increased from $1.65 to $1.75
- The employees when laid off or discharged by the company be given a reason for such action, or a fair hearing

The strike began on Sunday morning, July 27, 1890. On Monday the company superintendent Bevier said that employees were averaging thirteen to fourteen hours per day and that he thought that, "We can settle the hours question as soon as we hear from Cleveland." Bevier received a telegram from Mr. Hayes that read: "Mather and I both absent yesterday. You may concede twelve hours." The company conceded to the first two requests but not the third on July 28. The union accepted the company's offer and the striking employees went back to work on July 29 after a two-day strike.

Less than a year later, in early May 1891, employees would go on strike again for what they called "living wages."

The Old Company to Electrify Its Horsecar Lines

The "old" Street Railway Company of Grand Rapids finally decided to officially begin to convert its horsecar lines to electric power at its annual board of directors meeting on July 8, 1890. The company planned to pay for the conversion to electric streetcars by adding $900,000 to their present capital of $600,000, which was to be preferred stock. The old company ordered 500 tons of steel girder rails, 70 pounds to the linear yard, which were shipped to Grand Rapids in September 1890.

The Grand Rapids Common Council aldermen refused to make a decision as to whether the street railway would have to install steel or wooden trolley poles to support the electric power wires unless the new company agreed to provide free transfers from one line to another. The company filed a lawsuit against the city contending that the franchise that the city gave the street railway did not give the city the right to refuse making a decision that was required by the franchise. The Michigan Supreme Court ruled in late December 1890 that the city had to specify the type of poles to be used to support the company's elec-

tric wires. It also ruled that the Common Council had no right to force the company to furnish free transfers by making the granting of the privilege to erect wooden poles outside the fire limits contingent upon such a concession by the company.

Cable Company Buys the Old Street Railway Company of Grand Rapids

In 1888 the Valley City Street and Cable Railway came under new management and with it new sources of investment capital. Local investors worked to bring about a consolidation of the two companies which helped clear the way for the successful conversion of the horse and cable lines into a modern electric street railway system.

The consolidation occurred on October 22, 1890, and enabled investors in the cable street railway system to salvage much of their worthless investments by transferring the value to a new company. The conversion of the hodgepodge system of Grand Rapids horse and cable railways into one citywide electric railway system would have been delayed by more than a year if the two companies had been allowed to go bankrupt.

1891: Chapman Enters the Scene

The new owners brought James R. Chapman, the general manager of the Kansas City and Independence Rapid Transit Railroad to Grand Rapids and offered to make him superintendent of both the cable and horsecar systems. Chapman had taken over the Kansas City cable line when it was practically bankrupt and made it into a profitable enterprise.

Chapman initially refused the offer to become superintendent of both lines in Grand Rapids because, "There were too many lines in the center of the city where people could walk and not enough in the suburbs where they need car service." Chapman concluded that the Grand Rapids system of street railways could not become profitable unless it eliminated duplicate lines and furnished rapid transit to the outskirts of the city. The new owners agreed to take Chapman's criticism of the merged systems seriously. Chapman then accepted the offer to become general superintendent of the consolidated system of companies' lines.

Newly-appointed superintendent Chapman immediately went to work identifying changes that needed to be made in operations and designing a new franchise that would enable the company to survive financially while improving service. At the February 11, 1891, meeting of the Common Council

*James R. Chapman.
See his biography in
chapter 12.*

Chapman outlined many of the changes the company needed to make while it was converting the whole Grand Rapids streetcar system to electric power. Chapman announced that the new company intended to abandon lines on South Ionia Avenue; Jefferson Avenue; Canal Street north from Hastings Street to Coldbrook; Ottawa Avenue south of Monroe streets, Louis and Spring streets; Wealthy Street; Sheldon Street, Wenham Street and Lafayette Avenue north of Blakeley Avenue.

Chapman noted the proximity of several lines to each other and how this duplication of service led to added costs of operation. He also discussed the company's plans to reroute and extend lines including a summer line out West Fulton Street to John Ball Park, a new city park named in honor of John Ball, a Grand Rapids pioneer. The new management promised to arrange a transfer system where a patron could ride to any portion of the city from any starting point for one five-cent fare. Many of these changes were incorporated into requirements by the time the new company finally accepted a new thirty-year franchise.

Chapman estimated that it would cost approximately $500,000 (approximately $12 million in 2016 dollars) to convert the street railway system to electric power, of which $175,000 was for labor and the remainder for track, material, and equipment. All the rails except those of the old company on Monroe and Canal streets needed to be replaced with heavier rail.

The Valley City Street and Cable Railway Company submitted a petition for a new franchise embodying these changes at the February 18, 1891, meeting of the Common Council. The proposed new franchise would authorize the company to convert its own cable lines and horsecar lines as well as the lines of the Street Railway Company of Grand Rapids into an electric system.

The Second Strike: No Concessions This Time

The cable street railway company purchased the old horse street railway company in October 1890, but tried to manage the two companies as separate entities. The men working for the Valley City Street and Cable Ry Company worked longer hours than the Street Railway Employees Union workers who were working for the Street Railway of Grand Rapids. Several conferences were held to bring about greater equality with respect to pay and hours per day. The state of Michigan's Bureau of Labor and Industrial Statistics Annual Report for 1891 concluded that, "The chief causes of the failure to agree being the number of hours of labor required of the men for a day's work and an obnoxious contract which the men were compelled to sign or leave the employment of the company."

This "obnoxious contract" [see appendix] was reprinted in the *Grand Rapids Morning Press* for its readers to examine. In it, the street railway company was forcing its employees to sign an individual contract forbidding them from joining a union or simply attending a union meeting. Either act could result in immediate dismissal.

About one hundred streetcar company employees went on strike on May 1, 1891. They contended they needed $1.50 per day rather than the $1.25 per day they were currently paid. The strikers and management also failed to agree on the number of hours required for a day's work.

Street railway union men met with the Central Labor Union (CLU) of Grand Rapids on Friday, May 8 and overwhelmingly voted to go on strike. The strike, one of the worst in the history of Grand Rapids, began on Sunday, May 10, 1891, when more than 400 employees walked out. The public was on the side of the street railway employees at the beginning of the strike. The city made the situation worse by swearing in 500 policemen and having the streets patrolled by men in civilian clothes.

Public support for the strikers changed dramatically when a group of street railway union men attempted to use dynamite to blow up the terminal wheel of the cable railway at Sweet Street Station. The police, informed of the attack ahead of time, were waiting at the station when the attempt was made at 2 AM on Sunday morning, June 10. Thirteen men were arrested in the ensuing mayhem and fifteen more were arrested for alleged conspiracy to destroy street railway property. The strikers, having lost public support and without funds to continue their walkout, officially ended it on June 23 after forty-four days.

The New Company and Aldermen Battle over Proposed Franchise.

One of the most radical changes in street railway service involved its proposal to temporarily suspend operation on the North Ottawa-Taylor Street line and on the Spring Street-Lafayette Avenue cable line as soon as the cable wore out. The company then proposed to use horses on the Taylor Street line. While the company explained the exorbitant expense of cable operation and the need to end it, the council aldermen were indignant over the prospect of losing any streetcar lines. One alderman even proposed that the Common Council revoke the charter of the merged railway for abandoning the North Ottawa cable line.

Aldermen suggested numerous changes in the proposed franchise, but the company would not accept these due to the cost of operating so many planned short lines. As the *Grand Rapids Democrat* reported, "A large lobby of prominent citizens headed by the Hon. T. D. Gilbert, C. C. Comstock and Harvey Hollister filled the council chamber" on the evening of March 6 to champion the franchise submitted by the street railway.

The new streetcar company presented a long petition to the Common Council on March 9, 1891, strongly protesting against several features in the new proposed franchise. The company claimed the changes were too costly since all could not be completed within a year as required by the new franchise. The council met several times during the next month to discuss and on occasion pass various amendments to the electric streetcar franchise under discussion.

Finally ten aldermen met in secret with representatives of the cable company in a private office on Friday, April 11. The ten aldermen wanted a franchise that at least fifteen of the twenty aldermen could support which would make the franchise "veto proof." They succeeded and the Common Council by a vote of fifteen to five approved the final version of the franchise on April 24.

The Valley City Street and Cable Railway Company accepted the franchise as submitted at the May 18, 1891, meeting of the Common Council. The Consolidated Street Railway Company finally had a thirty-year franchise to work with.

The editor of the *Grand Rapids Eagle* announced that, "The time for haggling is happily past" and that, "The time for practical work has arrived."

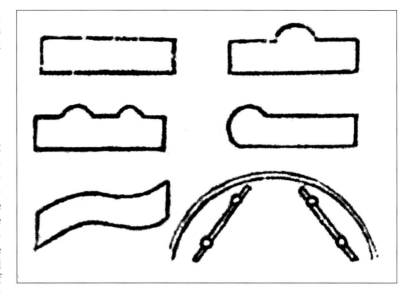

Diagram of possible shapes of streetcar signs and angle of diagonal roof view.

Grand Rapids Democrat, 19 Feb 1891

Who Owns the City— the Street Railway?

The new franchise gave the street railway rights with respect to what could not be used as pavement between the rails of its track, and what the company could do in using salt to clear ice from the track. These rights placed limits on what the city could and could not do. The city attorney, the city marshal, the city clerk, and the city engineer all publicly complained that the new franchise gave the street railway too much control over the city streets where the railway had tracks. This led the *Detroit Journal* to sarcastically raise the question as to whether the people of Grand Rapids would soon have to get the street railway company's permission to breathe.

The citizens of Grand Rapids were frustrated over the ongoing construction in so many streets and how long it took to complete some of the projects. The city had contracted many of the projects—digging and installing sewers, grading and re-grading streets, and paving streets. The street railway company added to all the construction confusion by tearing up the old track, installing heavier rails, setting poles to support electric trolley wire, and even re-grading streets to match new grades established by the city.

Routing Streetcar Lines through Campau Square

Superintendent Chapman designed the streetcar lines so that virtually all the cars would pass through Campau Square in downtown Grand Rapids. This created a problem. How would citizens identify which car they needed to board in order to ride to where they wanted to go?

Chapman proposed that all the streetcars have changeable signs to indicate what route

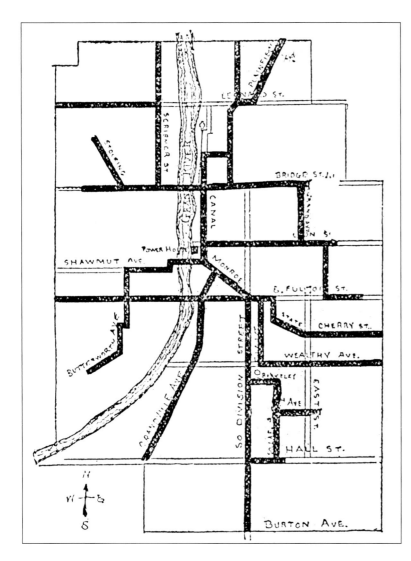

Map of proposed new streetcar system showing the streets over which the ten lines are to be built and the electric street cars are to run.

Grand Rapids Democrat, 26 Apr 1891

the car was traveling. He stated that none of the new streetcars were to have permanent signs indicating the route or street the car ran on. Each streetcar would carry a changeable set of route signs indicating the car's destination when it left downtown. These signs were designed to help riders identify the proper car to board in order to reach their destination. The route signs on a car could be quickly changed. This enabled the company to provide better service while also saving money. Any car could be quickly reassigned to a different route to maintain service on a line or to increase service to handle more passengers on their way to and from sporting events, theaters and other activities. Fewer streetcars would be needed to provide better service thus lowering operating costs.

Changeable signs were to be placed diagonally across the four corners of the car roof so the car's destination could be identified by reading the sign or identifying its shape during the day. At night the route a car operated on after leaving downtown was designated by lighted colored glass in the front and rear transoms of the car. This could also be replaced by glass of a different color to indicate the car's new route. Colors and shapes of signs allowed illiterate individuals as well as immigrants who hadn't yet learned English, to successfully navigate the streetcar system.

Converting Horse, Cable and Steam Dummy Lines to Electric Operation

At the end of 1890, the Valley City Street and Cable Railway Company had started making the necessary arrangements to convert to an all-electric streetcar system. Agents representing the Thomson-Houston, the Short, the Edison and the Daft electric systems had come to Grand Rapids to evaluate the two power-houses of the cable company, to map every line that was likely to be electrified, and to carefully estimate the grades on each line.

Superintendent Chapman immediately began compiling two lists: one list identified streetcar lines to be abandoned because they duplicated service on adjacent lines or where ridership was too low to cover operating expenses.

See map on page 64A.

Chapman identified the following streets where service would be abandoned:

- The Clancy Avenue line (where there were not even enough riders to even pay the driver)
- The South Ionia Street/Avenue line
- The South Jefferson Avenue line
- The Hall Street line from South Division to Lafayette
- The Canal Street line north of Hastings Street to Coldbrook Street
- The North Ottawa cable line (until electrified)

The second list Chapman compiled was a list of lines to be extended or rerouted:

- South Division Avenue line extension to Burton Street once the toll road problem was resolved
- Grandville Avenue line to Fifth (now Franklin) Street south to Hall Street
- Lafayette Avenue line to be rerouted west from Madison Avenue on Hall, then north on Lafayette, west on Blakely, north on South Division, and north on Monroe
- Wealthy Street line to be extended to Reed's Lake
- Cherry Street east from East Street (now Eastern Avenue) to Fuller Street, then south on Fuller to Wealthy Street
- Taylor Street line to turn west on East Leonard, then south on Canal to Ottawa and south on Ottawa Avenue.

After more than two months of almost continuous controversial proposals made by aldermen before the Common Council, a franchise acceptable to the street railway was finally approved at the Common Council meetings on April 17 and April 24, 1891. Nineteen lines were combined to form ten streetcar routes under the franchise. Nine of the routes ran through downtown Grand Rapids, eight of the routes went through Campau Square, while one ran on Canal Street, a block west of the square.

Electrifying the First Line

The company decided the first line to electrify would be the one connecting Canal Street and Campau Square in the center of the city with Ramona Park, the company's popular resort adjacent to Reed's Lake. The horsecar line running on Canal from Lyon street, southeast up Monroe, then east on Fulton, south on LaGrave and finally east on Wealthy Street, would be converted to electric power, and the line on Wealthy Street would be extended from East Street 2.2 miles east to Reed's Lake. This would enable the company to provide excellent service, even when faced with thousands of riders trying to go to one of the many Reed's Lake resorts on Sundays and holidays.

Unfortunately, the city was unable to grade Wealthy Street east of East Street which would have allowed the company to build its extension on Wealthy to Reed's Lake. Consequently, the street railway company temporarily electrified the old steam dummy line running south from Wealthy Street on East Street and then east on Sherman Street in Grand Rapids Township (now East Grand Rapids) to Reed's Lake.

Sherman Street was graded so the company could convert the old single-track line to double track, lay heavier rail, erect poles and string wire. An electric car made a trial run from downtown to Reed's Lake via Sherman Street on June 9, 1891. Electric cars hauling trailers started carrying passengers all the way from downtown Grand Rapids to Reed's Lake via the old dummy line route by June 15. The company no longer charged an extra five-cent fare to ride the line from East Street to Reed's Lake. Most of the estimated 30,000 visitors to Reed's Lake on July 4 arrived and departed via the open streetcars which were loaded down to the running boards.

Daniel Campbell, superintendent of transportation and construction for the Grand Rapids streetcar system, reminisced about the changes that had occurred during his twenty-three years of service to a *Grand Rapids Herald* reporter in early January 1902. Campbell described how many of the first electric streetcars to run in Grand Rapids were horse and cable car bodies mounted on the trucks and motors the company had purchased. He pointed out that, "The little cars now used oc-casionally as trailers were the first in the city to be graced with motors and it was several years before regularly built motor cars were put into operation." Campbell remembered that some of the cars were so flimsy that, "Several times on the lake run such crowds were packed into these little cars that they were literally broken in two in the middle, and left disabled, with both ends resting on the ground."

When the resort season ended in the early fall of 1891, the poles, rails and ties were taken up on Sherman Street ending seventeen resort seasons during which time horses pulled streetcars (six years), steam dummies pulled full-sized passenger cars (ten years) and electric streetcars ran with trailers (one year) on Sherman street.

Electric power was extended north on Canal Street to East Bridge Street on July 9, 1891. Work continued on this line north until electric cars could travel to Leonard Street where it connected to the Taylor Street line.

Rebuilding the Taylor Street Line North to Sweet Street Station

The Taylor Street line was built in 1890 to connect the cable railway with the new North Park Street Railway that ran to Soldiers' Home and North Park Resort in Grand Rapids Township. Cable cars ceased operation on this line in late February 1891 as the cable had worn out and deemed too costly to replace. Horsecars temporarily filled the gap by operating north from Leonard Street on the old company's horsecar line to Taylor Street and north to Sweet Street station at the city limits.

The south end cable line was abandoned in early April 1891 and a portion of that cable was transferred to the North Ottawa Street line so cable cars could again run to Sweet Street station. There passengers had to pay an extra three cents to climb aboard one of the North Park Railway passenger cars. North end cable trains consisting of a grip car and two trailer cars, all three of which were crowded with passengers, went north and south via Sweet Street station on July 12.

The Consolidated Street Railway Company began taking up the cable on North Ottawa Street in early September. The roof over the two tracks at Sweet Street station was raised in late October to allow streetcars to reach the station platform. Passengers could now get on and off the electric cars directly from the covered platform. The last cable train was pulled by the North Ottawa line cable to Sweet Street station on November 11, 1891. Electric streetcars began operating on the Taylor line the very next day.

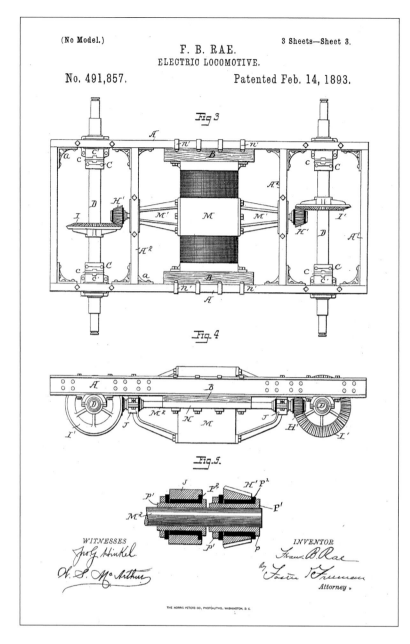

Patent drawing submitted in 1891 by Frank B. Rae for his popular streetcar motor.

U.S. Patent Office

Cherry Street Line

The new company concluded an agreement on March 27, 1891, with the Reed's Lake Gravel Road company to purchase the right to build and operate a street railway east on Cherry Street from East Street to its intersection with Lake Street (now Lake Drive). This extension was completed by June. Electric cars stopped running on the Cherry Street line in August because State Street and part of Cherry Street were torn up for relaying heavier rail and for paving State Street. The streetcar company planned to extend the Cherry line east on Lake Street to Wealthy Street as soon as the city gained control of the thoroughfare from the Reed's Lake Gravel Road Company's toll road.

Equipping Horsecars, Cable Cars and New Cars to Use Electric Power

Many of the open cars running on the horsecar and cable lines were in good enough condition that the company needed only to install an electrical transmission system, an electric motor, gears and heavier trucks to adapt them for electric railway operation. Unfortunately many of these cars were among the fifty-eight cars destroyed on the night of May 5, 1891, when the Sherman Street carbarn burned down. The company purchased fifteen large cars that arrived on June 12 to take the place of the smaller cars destroyed in the fire.

Shopmen installed thirty-horsepower Rae motors in ten cars in late June. Rae motors, manufactured by the newly expanded Detroit Electric Works Company, were unusual in having a single motor in a four-wheel streetcar truck with gears that drove both the front and rear wheels of the truck. These thirty-horsepower electric cars were powerful enough for a car to pull one heavily loaded trailer up the Wealthy Street hill and pull two or three trailers on level streets. Superintendent Chapman reported while Rae motors were giving excellent service, the company proposed to try every good motor in the market until it secured the best obtainable.

Chapman also drew attention to the fact that "It takes seven times the electric power to start a car moving than it does to keep the car in motion" to justify the practice of cars making a passenger stop only after they had crossed an intersection.

Seventeen other cars were equipped with motors from the Edison Company that had bought the Sprague patent. The Consolidated Street Railway Company often was unable to begin running electric streetcars as soon as each car line was electrified because the company could not obtain sufficient electric motors in time to convert many of the old horse and cable cars.

The company equipped a new motor car with two twenty-five-horsepower Edison-built motors with six-inch gearing underneath the car hoping to provide enough power on the steep East Bridge and Lyon Street hills.

The street railway had nearly twenty cars equipped with electric motors and running at the beginning of September. Electricity was being used exclusively on the Reed's Lake line and interchangeably with horse power on two or three other lines.

Many of the early electric motors proved so unreliable that the Consolidated Street Railway even had to run horsecars again until better motors could be installed on the electric cars. Superintendent Chapman described the problem to a reporter who wrote the following in the October 14, 1891, issue of the *Grand Rapids Evening Leader*:

THE MOTORS GAVE OUT.
And the Street Railway Company Falls Back on the Faithful Horse.

It looks like old times to see horsecars running again on Cherry Street and South Division streetcar lines. Manager Chapman explained the reason for the change in this way.

"In regard to the motors now in use, I will say that they proved to be a failure within the first thirty-six hours we used them. These single resistance motors now in use were put on the market last spring by all the electric companies. We were the first fellows on the books of the Edison Company and we got twelve of their motors. The trouble is an electrical one. The old double resistance motors were troublesome mechanically, but electrically they were all right.

"These single motors heat, and when anything electrical heats, the resistance is increased, causing it to heat more. We have had three of these motors play out right on Monroe Street, and it keeps a gang of men putting in new fields all the time. We have 14 of the double resistance motors on the road and will have them here in a week or two. These motors that we are now running must all go back to the factory and be rebuilt and remodeled before they will be satisfactory."

J. J. P. O'Dell, president of Union National Bank of Chicago (and recent survivor of injuries from a freak tornado touch down in downtown Chicago) and now president of the Consolidated Street Railway Company, pointed out to a reporter on November 2 that, "The single reason why our lines in this city have not had a more adequate equipment is that the electric companies of the country have been unable to fill our orders." O'Dell went on to point out that, "The great advantage of electricity is that it solves the problem of rapid transit, thus satisfying the public and increasing the efficiency of each car."

The street railway finally had enough electric cars in service by December 1891. Only the Grandville Avenue line still used horses to pull the cars.

J. M. Hagar, a Chicago businessman who had a major investment in the Consolidated Street Railway Company, visited Grand Rapids in mid-December and described the problems that the company was experiencing with respect to electric motors:

"The Edison motors are here on trial only and will be superseded by Rae motors. We could not get enough to operate the lines and were forced to take some of the Edison motors to fill out. Those old howlers, the Sprague [double-reduction] motors, will also be fired out of service. Electrically they are very good but mechanically they are poor."

Hagar also stated that the company planned to double the number of electric motor cars by next spring so that the streetcars could run on a five-minute schedule rather than the current ten-minute schedule.

Slot Brakes: Grand Rapids' Braking Solution for Steep Hills

The Edison Company had a force of men in Grand Rapids during November 1891 remodeling the electric streetcars originally intended for use on the Lyon and East Bridge street hills. A remodeled experimental car running on the hill proved to be very satisfactory and carried more passengers every day than the cable cars. The experimental car was equipped with a wheel brake and a slot brake, the latter being a unique invention designed locally by the Consolidated Street Railway Company. It was a device in the shape of a wedge, running horizontally under the car. When the car was descending the steep hill, the motorman, by turning a small wheel, could cause this brake to descend and wedge into the slot in the old cable conduit.

Electric Street Railway Car Houses Replace Horsecar Barns

The street railway needed new brick carbarns equipped with pits for repairing motors and trucks. They also had to be strategically located so the electric cars could be stored overnight at the most convenient sites close to where the cars would begin service in the morning.

The new brick carbarn at the corner of Scribner and First streets was the first new barn to be completed and filled with cars in November. The streetcar company had eight horsecar barns for sale in early February 1892. It planned to keep both the Hall Street and Canal Street carbarns to store equipment. The carbarns at East Street and Buckeye Avenue were to be disposed of as soon as a new barn on the corner of Lake and Wealthy streets was completed. The old upper Lyon Street cable powerhouse was converted into a car repair and paint shop.

The End of the Beginning

The progress made with respect to converting an eclectic jumble of horsecar, cable car, and steam dummy lines during 1891 was truly remarkable, particularly when the system was on the verge of bankruptcy only a year earlier. Additional challenges included delays due to city street construction projects, legal issues over control of streets, and employee strikes.

The *Grand Rapids Daily Democrat* published an article on January 1, 1892, summarizing all the improvements that had been made in the previous year:

RAPID TRANSIT NOW.
Wonders a Year Has Wrought
The Magnificent System of Electric Street Railways Provided by the Consolidated Company— How Change Was Wrought

The year just closed has witnessed a great improvement in the intramural transportation system of this city. At the opening of 1891 there were in Grand Rapids thirty-six miles of street railway track, operated by 470 horses and two cable power houses. The close of the year finds forty-five miles of track, operated by sixty horses and one electric power house, generating current for the entire system and equipped by forty-one electric motors. Of the track itself, thirty-one miles is entirely new. The rail laid has, for the most part, weighed sixty-seven pounds to the yard. On Scribner Street three and one-half miles of rail, weighing eighty pounds to the yard, with groove rail on curves weighing 100 pounds to the yard, have been placed in position. The weight of this rail is as great as any used for steam railways. Over all of this track, a No. 1 hard drawn copper wire is carried attached to supports by the best system known to electric railway construction.

The Powerhouse

At the power station four engines, of 400 horsepower each, furnish the power. Eight boilers furnish the steam. Five Edison Railway generators of 235 horse power each are in service, and two more are being placed into position.

"The electric current is carried from the powerhouse by eight feed wires, each of which supplies its own district and is independent of any other; thus the opening of a switch at a station shuts off the current from that section of the city supplied by that feed wire. On each of these eight feed wires is placed a "limit switch," which opens automatically in case of any ground on the line.

With their valuable plant in position and ready for operation, an increase in the number of vehicles is all the system will require for the service of the city for many years.

While no system of city transportation is perfect, the electric system for surface roads is more flexible than any other, and that it is popular the enormous growth of the business throughout the country proves. That it is more satisfactory to the public than either the cable or the horse cars, is proved by the passengers carried on the various lines of this city now, as compared with one year ago.

The Transfer System

Of course quite a large percentage of growth in business is due to the inauguration of a liberal transfer system. That it is appreciated by the public is proved by the daily issue of transfers. The first issue of the "clock dial" transfer slip, 1,000,000 in number was placed in use Nov. 15, and so great has been the demand

Lower Lyon Street Power House and Offices. This power house was originally built to supply power for the north/south cable lines.

Street Railway Review, 15 Apr 1892

for them, that a second order was placed fifteen days ago for another million.

Few people appreciate the cost of such a system of street railways as this city now possesses. Over $600,000 has already been spent in changing the system. There are already forty-one motor cars in operation and orders are placed whereby the number will be increased to eighty as soon as they can be obtained. These cars are not only very expensive in the first place, but it costs a great deal of money to keep them in repair. The first cars bought were of the Rae type, built by the Detroit Electrical Works. By this system one large motor is attached to each axle of the car truck. The cars which conveyed the immense crowds to Reed's Lake last summer were of this pattern.

The Edison Motors.

While these cars were in use, contracts were made with the Edison Company for a large number of single reduction motors, two to a car. This was a new departure in the street car motor which all prominent companies offered to their customers for the first time in 1891. The type, while theoretically correct, did not meet the expectations nor fulfill the builders and the Edison Company has been working out the problems of perfecting them on the streets of this city.

As a Time Saver.

The saving of time to the public by the new system of transportation, as compared with the old, amounts to thirty-five per cent. The time from Hall street to Sweet street is now thirty-three minutes, while it was formerly fifty minutes. The distance is four miles. This is about the average rate of all the lines in the city.

This speed, though much greater than ever given the public in this city before, is not as great as that of many other cities. The Duquesne Company, of Pittsburg, makes a six-mile's run in thirty-

nine and one-half minutes, and one mile of the distance is in the heart of that city. The cars in use by that company are the double truck pattern, with bodies nearly twice the size of those in use here, requiring more time for starting and stopping. When the public demands fast time in this city the company will be ready to meet the demand.

Plans for the Future.

As soon as the season opens in 1892, the line to John Ball Park will be completed; also, the line on Grandville avenue and other streets contemplated by the original ordinance. The additional cars ordered will be place in service, the use of horses entirely abandoned, and the system brought up to even a higher standard than it sustains at present.

The Consolidation.

This splendid system is the outgrowth of a consolidation of the Street Railway Company of Grand Rapids and the Valley City Street & Cable Railway Company in operation Jan. 1, 1891. The new company had its inception in a charter granted to the Valley City Company April 18, last, which was accepted by that corporation May 18, following. The charter granted permission to the corporation to absorb the property and franchises of the Street Railway Company. Immediately after the acceptance of this charter the Valley City company became proprietors of the property of the Street Railway Company, and on July 1 changed its name to the Consolidated Street Railway of Grand Rapids. In additions to the improvements made by the consolidated company within the year, the North Park Railway Company has, during the same period, greatly improved its property by the addition of several first-class coaches and additional buildings.

The Reed's Lake Electric Road did a thrifty business during the summer, suspending operations with the close of the season.

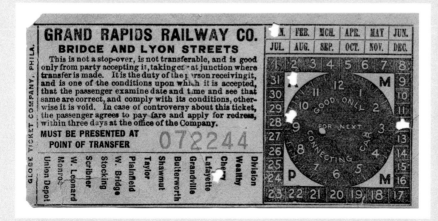

Punched transfer ticket for Bridge and Lyon Streets featuring the "Clock Dial."
Ed Bawden Collection

The intended route of the South Grand Rapids Street Railway - 1888 to 1894
Based on 1891 George Cram map provided by Bill Branz
© 2017 Tom Maas

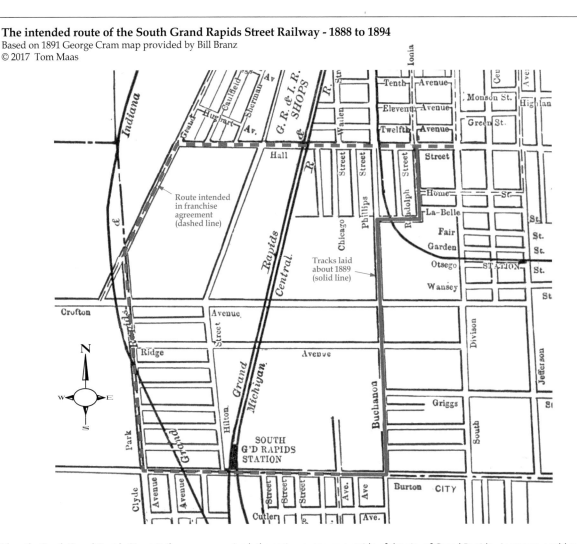

When the South Grand Rapids Street Railway was conceived, the entire route was outside of the city of Grand Rapids. Investors could see that the city was growing, and were ready to invest in the southern suburbs soon to be developing in that direction. The company sought and gained a franchise to lay rails in this area's streets from the board of Wyoming Township in November of 1888. The intent of the railway was to provide the people of the South Grand Rapids area with a way to gain access to the Grand Rapids Street Railway lines at Hall Street and the Valley City Cable horse feeder lines running on Grandville Avenue. The City of Grand Rapids book published in 1889 by B.F. Conrad describes the newly formed railway. The company president at this time is listed as Joseph C. McKee. The Wyoming Township franchise was for three and a half miles of street railway and Conrad claims that "one and a half miles of track are now under construction and will be in operation in thirty days". Grand Rapids expanded its southern city limit in 1891 to Burton Street and the Wyoming Township franchise was honored by the city.

The Grand Rapids Street Railway was electrified in 1892 and the new city limits allowed expansion of service southward down Division Avenue, effectively servicing many of the people of the South Grand Rapids area (later known as Burton Heights).

By 1894 however, the city decided to establish several new streets which crossed Buchanan Street and during the process the city cut and removed rails and ties, making the line impassable. The Grand Rapids Press mentions in July of 1894 that this railway line was in a state of abandonment and that Jerry Boynton was interested in purchasing the franchise. Developers of the area accused Boynton of trying to raise the value of the land with promises of bringing the railway back to life with no intention of actually putting a railway back into operation.

A newspaper article in March of 1897 described the tracks being torn up by an angry crowd of farmers with crowbars during the night. The article says this about the railway: "For a time a single car went over the route and held the right of way, but for long months nothing whatever has been done on the line. The rails have rusted and warped and many complaints have been made of the condition of the road. Farmers living south of the city have complained repeatedly, but the township board took no action toward revoking the franchise." (GR Press, 23Mar1897) The same article reveals that the well-known local businessman and lumber baron, Colonel E. Crofton Fox was president of the company.

The South Grand Rapids Street Railway Company commenced a lawsuit in 1900 against the city to prevent any further damage to the tracks. The city had still not replaced the track that it cut back in 1894, even though it was ordered to by the court. The newspaper writer concludes with this: "The South Grand Rapids railway is a relic of the boom days of Grand Rapids. It was built at a time when suburban property was changing hands rather freely, and it was thought that a good sized city would be built up in the neighborhood of Burton avenue and Plaster creek. The road was built and cars drawn by a steam dummy were run over it, connecting with cars operated by the old cable company. When the cable road and the horse car line were consolidated and the motive power was changed to electricity the electric line was extended out South Division street and it soon placed the old steam line in the shade."

The last mention of this shortlived railway in the local press was in October 1900, when Judge Newnham dissolved the injunction restraining the city from disturbing the tracks in Buchanan Street because the street railway company "since the spring of 1894 has not claimed to even attempt operation".

Map of southeast Grand Rapids showing the intended route of the South Park & Crystal Springs Street Railway
Based on 1894 Polk Atlas map of Paris Township
© 2017 Tom Maas

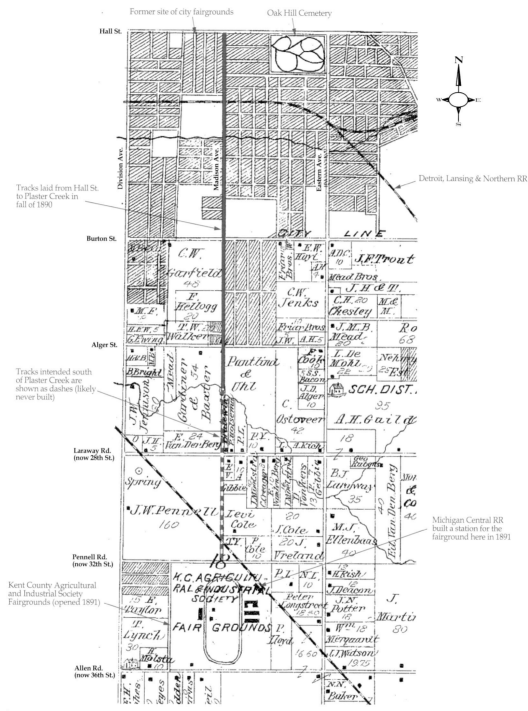

The fall of 1890 saw a flurry of activity as the new Kent County Agricultural and Industrial Society Fairgrounds was being constructed on acreage south of the city limits near the new suburban development known as Oakdale Park. A large racetrack was being prepared and at the same time, ties and rails were being laid in Madison Avenue to take streetcar passengers there. The new railway company became known as the Crystal Springs Street Railway since half of its funding came from the Crystal Springs company, known for its bottled spring water captured from springs along the banks of Plaster Creek. This railway was intended to run on electric power from its inception and was to link up to the Grand Rapids Street Railway at Hall Street. In June of 1892, the line was referred to in the newspapers as the South Park & Crystal Springs Street Railway and in July of that year local banker and former mayor Edwin Uhl became involved in the company. News of the little railway becomes hard to find after this, so we can assume that the line was likely never completed beyond Plaster Creek. Visitors to the new fairgrounds were encouraged to use the existing Michigan Central (steam) line which had a new station built specifically to service the fairground traffic.

THE REED'S LAKE ELECTRIC RAILWAY, GRAND RAPIDS, MICH. (See page 285).

Reed's Lake Electric Railway (1890-1891)

Open motor passenger car and open double-truck passenger trailer car on Reed's Lake Electric Railway that carried a total of 249 passengers.

Electrical Engineer, Vol. 10, 10 Sep 1890

The Reed's Lake Electric Railway Company began operating the first electric street railway in the Grand Rapids region on August 6, 1890. The company built a 3 ½ mile long streetcar line in Grand Rapids Township that enabled Grand Rapids citizens to ride electric streetcars from the city limits at East Street to the northwest shore of Reed's Lake.

The first electric railway to Reed's Lake started as the Grand Rapids & Soldiers' Home Suburban Railway Company, incorporated on May 16, 1889. The incorporators were David E. Donnovan of Chicago, and Charles M. Ayer, Edmund B. Dikeman, George Dunton and Samuel B. Tibbets of Grand Rapids. The company became the Kent County Street Railway Company a week later and obtained a franchise from the Grand Rapids Township. The *Grand Rapids Evening Leader* newspaper quickly reminded readers that Tibbets had called the people of Grand Rapids "God damned fools" when he supervised the construction of the cable car line on Lyon Street hill, described him as having a "coarse, brutal nature" and even warned citizens to be prepared for a "chapter of horrors." Samuel Tibbets was forced to resign when the Kent County Street Railway Company was sold in April 1890.

The new owners filed papers to incorporate as the Reed's Lake Electric Railway Company on April 15 and Sybrant Wesselius, well-known local attorney and politician became president of the new company.

The newly organized Reed's Lake Electric Railway Company was able to build the electric railway and get the necessary equipment to run it in less than four months. The first regular train started carrying passengers at 2 PM on August 6, 1890. One twenty-six-foot-long car equipped with a thirty-horsepower electric motor pulled a thirty-five-foot double-truck trailer car that had seating capacity for fifty passengers. It took approximately twelve minutes to travel the three and one-half miles from the cable line terminus at the city limit at East Street to Reed's Lake. The electric railway track went east on Fulton Street, south two blocks on Carleton Street, then turned east and went on private right-of-way to a point just north of Fisk Lake, then southeast over the marsh and across the channel between Fisk Lake and Reed's Lake and finally east to a site adjacent to Huber's Pavilion resort near Reed's Lake and just north of Ramona Park.

The Reed's Lake Electric Railway planned to build a loop to turn their streetcars around which would enable them to run more cars on the line. The United Electric Traction Company of New York provided an electric motor for each motor car and built an electrical system powerhouse near the northwest end of Reed's Lake. A Minneapolis Company built the car bodies.

The Reed's Lake Electric Railway continued to run until mid-September 1890 when it was shut down for electrical and mechanical repairs. The electric railway resumed operation and had two cars running to and from the lake on Sunday, October 12, when it ceased operation again; Grand Rapids residents complained that the Reed's Lake Electric Railway was on "vacation." The electric railway resumed operating by Thursday, October 28 making regular fifteen-minute trips. Yet by November 16 the company was reported to be making one trip a day—sometimes only one trip every two days.

The Valley City Street & Cable Railway Company purchased the Street Railway Company of Grand Rapids which had its own line to Reed's Lake in October 1890. The two companies were reorganized as the Consolidated Street Railway Company of Grand Rapids. The Reed's Lake Electric Railway then became dependent on its consolidated rival for its connections to downtown Grand Rapids. The cable in the line that ran east on Fulton Street to East Street soon wore out and broke. The broken cable was removed for repairs and "either naturally or unnaturally" not replaced. That ended cable car service to the western terminus of the electric streetcar line. A horse-drawn bus line began running from downtown to the western terminus of the Reed's Lake Electric Railway. Unfortunately people preferred taking the Consolidated Street Car Company's line that involved riding on horse-drawn street cars and then transferring to passenger cars pulled by steam dummy locomotives to go to and from Reed's Lake resorts.

Sybrant Wesselius was a local attorney, politician and also president of the Reed's Lake Electric Railway Co.

Michigan Day Schools for the Teaching of Speech for the Deaf, 1905

Reed's Lake Electric Railway Asks for a Franchise to Build an Electric Street Railway to Downtown

The Reed's Lake Electric Railway petitioned the Grand Rapids Common Council in December 1890 for a franchise that would allow the company to build a line from East Street, its western terminus at the city limit, into the city going west on Fulton Street.

The Common Council discussed and rejected the franchise several times during the winter and early spring. Finally on May 25 the aldermen voted 15-4 in favor of granting the railway a franchise to enter the city. The franchise allowed the Reed's Lake Electric Railway to build a line going west into the city on Fulton Street, north on Ransom, west on Park, north on Division, and west on Pearl Street to Campau Square, the business center of the city. The motor cars on the electric railway flew flags to celebrate the passage of the franchise.

Property-owners along the route immediately filed suits for injunctions to prevent the Reed's Lake Electric Railway from constructing the track into Grand Rapids. Twenty lawsuits were filed for an injunction and served against the company in just one day. These lawsuits filed in local state courts were quickly dismissed. However, there was one suit filed in United States District Court on May 27, 1891.

About 250 feet of track on Fulton Street between Jefferson and Ransom avenues where horse-drawn cars had run for about twenty-five years became a legal battle ground. The Valley City Street & Cable Railway Company filed suit against the Reed's Lake Electric Railway in United States District Court. The cable company contended that the franchise it inherited when it purchased the Street Railway Company of Grand Rapids was a contract that gave it exclusive rights to run on the 250 feet section of Fulton Street

The court subsequently ruled that the common council did not have the right to grant exclusive rights in city streets and that although one council granted the old company permission to use the streets, the same council or any succeeding council could grant similar rights to others.

This ruling did not end the battles between the two streetcar companies. The cable line that ran east on Fulton street was the only street railroad connection that the Reed's Lake Electric Railway had with the street railway system in Grand Rapids. The Reed's Lake Electric Railway company had won the court battle to be able to build a line to downtown Grand Rapids but it was unable to raise the necessary money to build it.

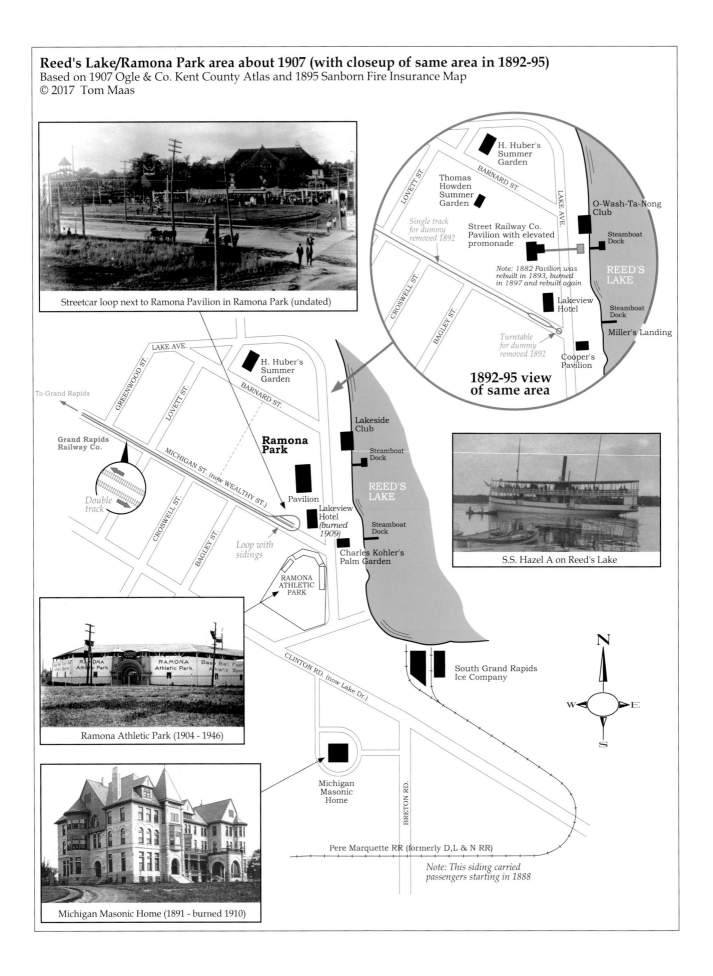

Reed's Lake/Ramona Park area about 1907 (with closeup of same area in 1892-95)

Based on 1907 Ogle & Co. Kent County Atlas and 1895 Sanborn Fire Insurance Map
© 2017 Tom Maas

Streetcar loop next to Ramona Pavilion in Ramona Park (undated)

H. Huber's Summer Garden

Thomas Howden Summer Garden

LOVETT ST.

BARNARD ST.

LAKE AVE.

Single track for dummy removed 1892

CROSWELL ST.

BAGLEY ST.

Street Railway Co. Pavilion with elevated promonade

Note: 1882 Pavilion was rebuilt in 1893, burned in 1897 and rebuilt again

O-Wash-Ta-Nong Club

Steamboat Dock

REED'S LAKE

Steamboat Dock

Miller's Landing

Lakeview Hotel

Turntable for dummy removed 1892

Cooper's Pavilion

1892-95 view of same area

LAKE AVE.

GREENWOOD ST.

LOVETT ST.

BARNARD ST.

H. Huber's Summer Garden

To Grand Rapids

Grand Rapids Railway Co.

MICHIGAN ST. (now WEALTHY ST.)

CROSWELL ST.

BAGLEY ST.

Double track

Ramona Park

Pavilion

Lakeview Hotel *(burned 1909)*

Loop with sidings

Lakeside Club

Steamboat Dock

REED'S LAKE

Steamboat Dock

Charles Kohler's Palm Garden

RAMONA ATHLETIC PARK

S.S. Hazel A on Reed's Lake

Ramona Athletic Park (1904 - 1946)

CLINTON RD. (now Lake Dr.)

South Grand Rapids Ice Company

N

W E

S

Michigan Masonic Home

BRETON RD.

Michigan Masonic Home (1891 - burned 1910)

Pere Marquette RR (formerly D,L & N RR)

Note: This siding carried passengers starting in 1888

The Brief Life of Reed's Lake Electric Railway Ends

The Reed's Lake Electric Railway began the 1891 resort season by running cars on Sunday, April 26, 1891, to and from its western terminus on Fulton Street at the city limit where passengers could transfer to and from the cable railway line. They could ride 3 ½ miles on the electric railway all the way to Reed's Lake. One electric motor car pulling a trailer car made numerous trips on April 26 and carried more than 2,000 passengers that day. The electric railway was able to run its cars to and from a site adjacent Reed's Lake that was located north of Huber's saloon until October 12, 1891.

During the streetcar strike of 1891, the Reed's Lake Electric Railway kept operating.

Income from fares dropped dramatically at the end of the 1891 resort season. The first electric street railway to operate in the Grand Rapids area no longer could afford to provide regular service and was well on its way to bankruptcy. Ironically, the cable company was able to replace the cable soon after the electric railway ceased operating and the cable line began running to East Street again.

The Reed's Lake Electric Railway was abandoned and bankruptcy proceedings started in 1892.

Bicycle riders who rode east on Robinson Road past Fisk Lake and the old Lake House in June 1894 had a fine view of Reed's Lake and the relics of the ill- fated Reed's Lake Electric Railway. A couple of old streetcars could be seen lying out in the field north of the Ramona resort grounds, badly bleached by the weather. One person reported that "everything about the cars, except the wheels, that could be sold for old junk has been stolen and the wheels would have been toted away if the roads had been in good condition." The wreckage of what once was the old powerhouse stood but all the machinery had long since vanished.

Electrification of the Consolidated Railway Progresses

The Consolidated Street Railway Company made substantial progress on electrification during 1891:

- The two cable lines running on Lyon and East Bridge Street hills and the Taylor Street cable line on the north end were converted to electric power in 1891.
- The long north-south cable line was removed.
- The company also converted the Reed's Lake steam dummy line on Sherman Street to an electric streetcar line in 1891.
- The company also almost succeeded in converting all the horse-drawn car lines to electric power by December 31, 1891.

THERE IS

NO STRIKE

ON THE

Reed's Lake

ELECTRIC ROAD.

———

You can take a CARRY-ALL from any part of the City to their Road for

5 CENTS.

This recurring newspaper ad ran during the street railway strike of 1891 to make readers aware that the Reed's Lake Electric Railway was still in operation.

Grand Rapids Morning Press, 14 June 1891

The city franchise of April 24, 1891, required all the streetcar lines be converted to electric power by December 1, 1892. Several miles of new heavy rail still had to be laid by the year-end deadline.

Fighting Winter Weather Prior to Construction

Cold, rainy, and snowy weather dominated the streets of Grand Rapids in early 1892 just as Michigan's annual "disaster" has almost always done. The street railway had to wait until early spring before it could resume construction to electrify the few remaining horsecar line sections.

The cold wet weather associated with periodic thaws during the winter created problems for passengers as well as streetcars. The *Grand Rapids Democrat* sarcastically suggested on January 2, 1892, that the streetcar company "might be asked to carry stilts, good high ones, on their cars, so that passengers could alight at the cross walks without getting over the tops of their shoes in mud." The same newspaper reported on March 26 of a streetcar striking an old man and knocking him into the gutter. "Fortunately the mud was quite deep where he struck, and he was not seriously injured."

Grand Rapids electric streetcars seen on the 8 per cent grade of East Bridge Street, circa 1891-early 1892. View looking east. Car no. 118 has just crossed Ottawa Avenue.

Street Railway Review, Vol. 2, 15 April 1891

Twenty New Open Streetcars Purchased

Early in January 1892 the Consolidated Street Railway Company placed an order for twenty new open cars with the Brownell Car Company of St. Louis, Missouri. Ten of these cars had arrived by March. On March 4 The *Grand Rapids Evening Leader* described these open cars as being "like railroad passenger coaches with an aisle running down the center and the seats are on either side and face the front. Each seat will hold two passengers, although three can be crowded in if the people are not built on a too liberal plan." The platforms at either end of the car were a foot lower than the car floor and side step. The new cars were nearly twenty-eight feet in length-longer than the current summer cars and with seats for about the same number of persons. Each new car came equipped with "a side foot board as in the older cars where people can hang on to if they are in a hurry to ride." The new cars were also equipped with wooden blinds rather than curtains which could slide up and down. Superintendent Chapman expected that most of these new cars would be running on the Reed's Lake line. He went on to say that these cars would be equipped with motors powerful enough to enable the cars to run at fifteen miles an hour.

The Michigan Supreme Court ruled in early March 1892 that all streetcars must carry headlights and ring their bells to alert other vehicles.

Grand Rapids Street Car System Featured in Street Railway Review

The Grand Rapids street railway system was the topic of a feature article in the April 15, 1892, issue of the *Street Railway Review.* The *Review* reported the Consolidated Street Railway Company of Grand Rapids had laid 39.7 miles of track and strung overhead trolley wire for electric streetcar operation during the last nine months of 1891. Most of the heavier rail the company installed during 1891 was 66 ½-pound or 70-pound rail produced by the Johnson Steel Street Rail Company of Johnstown, Pennsylvania. The steepest grades were on the two hill lines—one was 8 per cent for 800 feet and the other was 9 per cent for 400 feet.

The company reported it was using four different types of electric motors to power the forty-two electric cars: ten cars with one thirty-horse power Detroit (Rae) motor, seven cars with two twenty-five-horsepower Edison single reduction motors, and twenty-four cars with two fifteen-horsepower Edison motors. One car had been scheduled to be equipped with a twenty-horsepower Short gearless motor but the motor had not yet arrived by early April so the order was cancelled. The company still had seven horsecars and sixty horses to assist as feeders to the main lines.

Weather Not the Only Problem Delaying Construction

The street railway originally had planned to build twelve more miles of track in 1892. However, the company decided to wait until the city graded the streets on which the lines were to be built. The reason was obvious. The street railway could not afford to pay for an electric line twice: lay the new track to match the current grade and then relay the same track again to a newly established street grade. The company had laid track on Monroe Avenue eight inches higher to match the new city grade in 1890 only to have to raise the tracks another seven inches to match the newest city grade for the street. The company faced the same problem on Scribner Avenue only four months after it built the new track. Superintendent Chapman discussed the problems the railway faced with respect to the Cherry Street line, the John Ball Park line on west Fulton Street and the Grandville Avenue line. Chapman wanted to extend the Grandville Avenue line in the early spring but didn't know what the city was planning to do with the street, especially since there was talk about lowering the grade by as much as four feet at Fourth Street (now known as Graham Street).

The railway asked the Common Council in March to allow it to build a line on Ottawa Street from Monroe to Lyon streets and from East Bridge to Trowbridge streets. The company wanted to avoid a streetcar "blockade" as many more cars would be passing through Campau Square with new lines coming into operation. Also contributing to possible congestion would be the increased service frequency.

Electric Power Replaces the Last Horse Power

Friday, May 6, 1892, marked a milestone for the company: it succeeded in achieving its goal of all-electric operation over its streetcar lines. The next day—Saturday, May 7, 1892- marked the beginning of a new era in electric streetcar operation in Grand Rapids. The last horse-drawn streetcar ran on the West Fulton Street line the previous day. The Consolidated Street Railway Company of Grand Rapids had succeeded in transforming a mismatched collection of horsecar lines, cable car lines and a steam dummy line into a complete electric streetcar system in one year!

The company still had to make decisions about single-track lines to be double tracked, lines be extended, and what equipment to buy or rebuild to ensure profitability while still keeping the peace with the aldermen.

Four Grand Rapids electric streetcars are posed in the business district of Monroe Avenue, circa 1891- early 1892. Note that the four cars are on separate parallel tracks.

Street Railway Review, Vol. 2, 15 April 1892

The *Grand Rapids Herald* drew attention to the historic importance of this event by publishing the following news account two days later on May 8:

Building and Operating the "Bee Line"

In 1891 the company was unable to complete a one-mile "bee line" extension of the Wealthy Street car line from East Street (now Eastern Avenue) to the junction with Lake Drive and another 1.2 miles beyond to Ramona Park adjacent to Reed's Lake. The regrading of Wealthy Street by the city contractor had not been completed. The Sherman Street line to Reed's Lake that had been converted from a steam dummy line to an electric line in 1891 was kept in operation until the two extensions of the Wealthy Street line were completed in 1892.

The new village of East Grand Rapids (incorporated in 1891) granted a franchise to the Consolidated Street Railway Company at the end of March 1892. This franchise specified the line going out on Wealthy Street would veer off to the southeast over private right- of-way to the country club instead of running east along the south shore of Fisk Lake. It would join the present line in operation on Michigan Avenue at a point a short distance east of the intersection of Lake Drive. The extension of the Wealthy Street line running via the new route ended in a loop on the south side of Ramona Park. The new double-track line was almost one-half mile shorter than the old Sherman Street line and the loop at Ramona Park enabled streetcars to turn around rapidly. The company was doing its best to provide rapid transit to and from Ramona Park.

Electric streetcars began making hourly trips to Reed's Lake in early April 1892 via the Sherman Street line while the new extension of the Wealthy Street line was under construction. A gang of men began laying iron on Wealthy Street east of Eastern Avenue on April 13. The trolley wire was added a few days later.

The company inaugurated service on the new route to Reed's Lake on May 21. Cars ran every ten minutes during the week and every five minutes on Sundays. The *Grand Rapids Evening Leader* drew attention to one shortcoming with the new line reporting on May 23 that, "The new line to the lake is a dandy or will be when the track is thoroughly ballasted."

Fully 12,000 people were reported to have visited Reed's Lake on May 30. The street railway handled the large crowds by using a motor car to pull a trailer. The two cars were able to carry 130 to 18 passengers on a five-minute headway to the Ramona pavilion grounds.

The fate of the old buildings on East Street (the Buckeye and Sherman Stations) was determined by separate fires in 1891. The streetcar company lost 30 open cars in the Buckeye Station fire. There was no longer a need for passengers to change cars and so the damaged buildings were razed and the property was sold. The unused tracks on East Street between Wealthy and Sherman streets were removed in June of 1892.

Resort Season Operations

The company had 103 open streetcars ready for business in the summer of 1892. Patronage was heavy that season. Indicative of the level of summer ridership was on July 4 when electric cars pulled trailers heavily loaded with passengers every two minutes to Ramona Park on Reed's Lake.

Fifty-six cars, motors and trailers, created what seemed like an almost endless procession of electric trains carrying huge crowds from downtown Grand Rapids to Reed's Lake as soon as the Labor Day parade concluded on Monday, September 5. The resort season ended in early October. The pavilion at Ramona Park was then torn down to make way for a new and much larger one.

Service on the line to Reed's Lake no longer ended at the conclusion of the resort season. In December cars were scheduled to run from Campau Square all the way to the loop at Reed's Lake every ten minutes from 6 A.M. until 10 P.M.

REEDS LAKE

NORTH PARK

New Structures and Ongoing Equipment Maintenance

The company built a sixty-five-car capacity brick carbarn and passenger waiting room on the south side of Wealthy Street where it intersected with both Norwood Avenue and Lake Drive during the fall of 1892. The old carbarns on East Street were torn down in November and streetcars at the end of that day were run over the Wealthy line to the new brick barns.

Workmen were busy removing motors from open cars and installing the motors in newly repainted closed cars that were to operate in cold weather. The open cars were stored in the carbarns until spring when the newly repaired and painted open cars would have motors installed for operation in the late spring, summer, and early fall months.

Remnants of Old Cable System Junked While "Four-Track Nuisance" Remains

Street railway workers began removing old timbers that underlaid the rails of the cable line on Canal Street but they did not remove the two outer cable line tracks. The Canal Street merchants continued to contend that four tracks in their street were two tracks too many.

The street railway company refused to remove the old cable car tracks contending that these two "extra" tracks were needed for the Lyon-East Bridge Street hill line to operate efficiently. (More likely, these two "extra" tracks were kept as a bargaining chip in negotiations with the Common Council aldermen. The "extra" tracks lasted until the beginning of the next century.)

Street railway workers were busy in July removing the conduit slot from the south track on East Bridge Street once by cable cars going up the hill. The conduit slot on the north side of the street remained in place because it was part of the street railway's unique emergency wedge braking system used when streetcars were going downhill.

Improvements and Extensions Continue

The street railway stopped running horsecars on Grandville Avenue on April 12 because the street was torn up for grading and paving. The company decided to wait and resume service as an electric line once the contractor completed the work. The Grandville Avenue line was extended from Fifth Street (now Franklin) to the newly established 1891 city limit at Hall Street. Electric cars began running on the Grandville Avenue line on August 6 going through downtown Grand Rapids and

Views of local attractions featured in Street Railway Review.

Street Railway Review 1894

No. 106 Michigan Avenue, Grand Rapids, Mich.

continuing over the West Bridge Street line.

The railway planned to double track the projected extension of the South Division Avenue line after the city graded Division from Hall Street south to the new city limit at Burton Street. The city finally established the grade and the street railway was able to build its line at new grade and start running electric cars on south Division Avenue all the way to Burton Street on August 17, 1892.

The Consolidated Street Railway Company prepared to begin building the extension of the Lyon Street line from Eastern Avenue on East Fulton Street one-half mile east to Fuller Avenue in June. However, a lawsuit involving the Reed's Lake Electric Railway stood in the way of extending the East Fulton line.

West side residents were delighted in April 1892 to observe a street railway construction gang begin rerouting the Shawmut Avenue line to reach John Ball Park "... instead of wandering pretty much all over the west side." The old Shawmut Avenue line went west across Pearl Street bridge and continued west on Shawmut (now Lake Michigan Drive) until the line reached Straight Street where the line headed south on Straight to West Fulton and then west on West Fulton Street toward John Ball Park. It could not go any farther than the large depression (referred to by the locals as the "Big Ditch")

at Garfield Avenue because the grade had not yet been established by the city.

The street railway originally planned to extend the west Fulton Street car line from Garfield Avenue all the way to the entrance to John Ball Park in 1892. The *Grand Rapids Democrat* complained that passengers who rode west on the West Fulton Street car line were compelled to alight at Garfield and "to walk nearly half a mile over the dustiest and most uneven road within miles of the city." Three days later the newspaper complained "People who have enjoyed a cool ride as far as the big ditch are swearing at the barbarous condition of the path which winds among bushes, stones and stumps for a half a mile between the terminus of the car line and the park." But the street railway did not want to put down a tie or rail west of Garfield until the city had clear title to West Fulton Street. Service on the John Ball line was shortened in September 1892. The streetcars could only go as far as Sheppard (now Lane) Street according to the provisions of a city ordinance.

Fall and Winter 1892-1893 Timetables

Two Grand Rapids newspapers published an abbreviated form of the fall 1892 and winter 1892-1893 timetables. It included the times in the morning when the first cars were scheduled to begin running on each of the eight lines, the times when the last cars were scheduled to make their late evening departures, and the times at night when the last car passed through Tower block adjacent to Campau Square. The East Bridge and Lyon Street cars turned at the corner of Lyon and Canal streets, one block north of Campau Square. During the day and evening, cars were scheduled to run every ten minutes on each line.

FALL and WINTER SCHEDULE.

The street railroad company has arranged the following running schedule for the fall and winter.

Scribner and Wealthy Avenue.

First car leaves the west end going east at 6 a.m., last car leaves at 11:10 p.m.
First car leaves the lake going west at 6 a.m., last car leaves the city limits going west at 11:05 p.m.
Last car going west passes the Tower block at 11:22 p.m.
Last car going east passes the Tower block at 11:25 p.m.

Wealthy Avenue and Taylor Street.

First car going south leaves Sweet Street at 6:05 a.m., last car leaves Sweet Street at 11 p.m.
First car going north leaves East Street at 6:05 a.m., last car leaves East street 10:55 p.m.
Last car going south passes the Tower block at 11:10 p.m.
Last car going north passes the Tower block at 11:10 p.m.

Bridge and Lyon Streets.

First car leaves East street going north at 6 a.m.; last car leaves East street going north at 10:57 p.m.
First car leaves Grand avenue going south at 6:05 a.m.; last car leaves Grand avenue going south at 11 p.m.
Last car going south passes the corner of Lyon and Canal at 11:13 p.m.
Last car going north passes the corner of Lyon and Canal at 11:06 pm.

Division and Plainfield Avenue.

First car going south leaves the north end at 6 a.m.; last car going south leaves the north end at 11:20 p.m.
First car going north leaves the south end at 5:55 a.m.; last car going north the south end at 11:15 p.m.
Last car going north passes the Tower block at 11:36 p.m.
Last car going south passes the Tower block at 11:36 p.m.

Division and West Leonard Street.

First car leaves north end going south at 5:55 a.m.; last car leaves north end going south at 10:45 p.m.
First car leaves south end going north at 5:55 a.m.; last car leaves south end going north at 10:45 p.m.
Last car going north passes the Tower block at 10:58 p.m. Last car going south passes the Tower block at 11 p.m.

Lafayette and Stocking Street.

First car going south leaves the north end at 6 a.m.; last car going south leaves the north end at 10:50 p.m.
First car going north leaves south end at 6 a.m.; last car going north leaves south end at 10:50 p.m.
Last car going north passes the Tower block at 11:07 p.m.
Last car going north passes the Tower block at 11:02 p.m.

Grandville Avenue and West Bridge.

First car going east leaves the west end at 6:06 a.m.; last car going east leaves the west end at 10:42 p.m.
First car going north leaves Hall Street at 6 a.m.; last car going north leaves Hall street at 11:12 a.m.
Last car going east passes the Tower block at 10:55 p.m.
Last car going west passes the Tower block at 11:29 p.m.

Cherry Street and Shawmut Avenue.

First car going west leaves the east end at 5:50 a.m.; last car going west leaves the east end at 10:50 p.m.
First car going east leaves the west end at 6:15 a.m.; last car going east leaves the west end at 11:15 p.m.
Last car going east passes the Tower block at 11:05 p.m.
Last car going west passes the Tower block at 11:25 p.m.
On Sundays all cars start one hour later in the morning.

The Butterworth line was not included in this timetable because the Butterworth line was being rebuilt at the time this timetable was published.
The Tower Block was located on Monroe Avenue on the southwest side of Campau Square and became known later to many citizens as the dime store block during the first 60 years in the twentieth century.

Grand Rapids, Mich.,
John Ball Park.

If you look closely at this postcard view of the John Ball Park entry area from around 1908, streetcars can be seen in the far background as they deliver passengers for a relaxing stroll and a scenic picnic lunch.

Carl Bajema Collection

Rebuilding the Butterworth Line

The Butterworth Street car line, also known as Line No. 9, was rerouted. The line now went west over Fulton Street bridge, south on Gold Avenue, and turned west going on Butterworth to South Sheppard (now Lane Ave,) reaching the carbarn at that intersection.

The street railway experimented with two different paving methods on west side streets matching what the city had done earlier. Cedar blocks laid on planks were used to pave between the rails on West Fulton Street. The railway also used bricks for the first time, laying them on a concrete foundation for paving West Bridge Street.

Delays beyond the control of the company postponed the opening of the Butterworth line until Tuesday, November 29, 1892. Superintendent Chapman proudly announced the commencement of service on the Butterworth line. This completed all work the 1891 franchise ordinance required the Consolidated Street Railway Company to accomplish by December 1, 1892. Chapman went on to say that the company had achieved even more than the minimum required by the ordinance.

Police Watch for Speeding Motormen

The Grand Rapids superintendent of police was ordered to ensure that electric cars were not traveling faster than the ordinance allowed. On September 30 Superintendent Chapman was quoted in the *Grand Rapids Evening Leader* that:

We have not yet found a single violation of the laws. In the slow transit district, the cars don't run on the average over five miles an hour and we have not yet found one car which has run at seven miles an hour. In the open district they seldom run over ten miles and the highest we have found yet is 12 miles an hour. It is said that these Edison motors cannot go more than 12 miles an hour anyway. The old Rae motors will go faster but they are being rapidly superseded by the Edison pattern. The Rae cars have the wheels set under the center of the car and when it goes fast, the ends of the car bob up and down like a boat in a storm but the new Edison pattern has the wheels farther apart and they are easier to ride upon. Yes, we are keeping a close watch on them.

Twenty New Closed Streetcars

Workers were busy at the car shops repairing and painting the closed cars and installing motors so the cars would be ready for operating on Grand Rapids streets when cold weather arrived. Superintendent Chapman drew attention to the fact that the wheels on electric cars wore out three times as fast as they did on horsecars and cable cars. He pointed out that wheels on the latter vehicles carried only the weight of the car while the wheels on electric cars also supported the added weight of the motors.

During the summer of 1892, the street railway company ordered twenty closed streetcars for cold weather operation. The first of the St. Louis Car Company-built car bodies began arriving in early November on specially-designed railroad flatcars which carried two streetcars each. When the last of the twenty cars arrived in late November Superintendent Chapman was happy to announce the company now had 200 cars and that the rolling stock was in excellent shape for the winter campaign.

The latest streetcars were longer than any of the streetcars then running in Grand Rapids. These cars were twenty-five feet long with an eighteen-foot body and two three and one-half foot-long platforms. They were painted a yellow-orange, the color that Chapman said would be the standard color of all cars purchased thereafter.

Chapman assigned several of the new cars to west side lines so he could proudly announce that, "The starting of the Butterworth line [scheduled for Tuesday, November 29] completes our system. By the terms of our ordinance we were supposed to have certain lines running and certain work done by December 1, 1892. When this line starts we will have done everything we promised to do, and more." Superintendent Chapman went on to say that "We would have had the East Fulton and Lake Avenue lines built if there were not an injunction in the way."

Chicago Investors Pleased

J. J. P. O'Dell of Chicago, a prominent banker in the Windy City and a major investor in the Consolidated Street Railway of Grand Rapids (also a member of its board of directors) visited Grand Rapids in November. He was pleased with the progress the street railway company had made and stated that a good business was being done.

J. M. Hagar of Chicago, a major stockholder who also was a member of the board of directors and secretary of the Consolidated Street Railway in Grand Rapids, summarized how two companies that had been competing for many of the same riders and both on the verge of bankruptcy in 1890 had merged and now were in the final phase of giving Grand Rapids a first-rate transit system. This new arrangement made both investors and streetcar riders happy with improved efficiency (which translated into profits) and better service. Hagar was proud of the fact that, "Grand Rapids is known throughout the country for its efficient railway service."

The *Grand Rapids Democrat* reviewed what the street railway system accomplished over the previous year in its January 1, 1893, issue:

> In no one thing has Grand Rapids shown more marked improvement in the past two years than in the street railway system. Residents here during the period mentioned have seen the lines changed from horse and cable power to an electric system, second to none in the country. While the old horse car system was the best of its kind, it was a horse car system still, and the same may be said of the cable system. The year 1892 opened with thirty-four electric cars and seven horse cars in daily service on the streets of the city. There are now fifty-three daily moving cars.

The newspaper also made note of improvements to come:

> As the city is backward in providing pleasure grounds for its people the street railway company will endeavor to make the Reed's Lake resort even more popular than it has ever been in the past. The ground will be laid out as a park with plenty of shade and seats. The pavilion will furnish shelter and seating capacity for five times the people that have ever been able to find accommodations there before. The very best of music will be provided, and the building is designed so that the acoustic properties will be satisfactory and all who sit there upon the plazas or in the main building will be able to appreciate the music.

It was an auspicious beginning for the new company and an air of optimism prevailed among both management and the public.

Street Cars Run Right by the Door Of the elegant new passenger station of the Lake Shore & Michigan Southern railway on West Fulton street, affording passengers rapid transit from above station to hotels and all parts of the city.

Newspaper advertisement advising readers to take the streetcar to the Lake Shore & Michigan Southern RR depot which had recently opened on west Fulton Street.

Grand Rapids Morning Press, 01 Dec 1892

Overhead view looking southeast down "Our Broadway" (Monroe Ave.) in 1894. In the foreground you can see a wire repair crew high above the street on a lift.
It appears that the streetcars are all stopped, maybe due to an issue with the wires.

Karl Heckman Collection

1893 Looked like It Was Going to Be a Great Year

The collection of separate horse, cable and steam dummy lines serving Grand Rapids and vicinity at the beginning of the 1890s had been converted into a single electric streetcar system by the end of 1892. With free transfers, rides that once had cost as much as fifteen cents now cost only five cents.

Riders not only saved money, but also saved time riding on the new electric transit system because electrically-powered streetcars were able to operate at speeds three to four times faster than horse-drawn cars or cable cars. In addition the electric cars ran more frequently. Grand Rapids citizens riding the electric cars were pleased.

Investors were also happy because the new system was a model of efficiency with lower operating costs. This combination of happy investors and happy riders began to crumble in February 1893 when a nationwide financial panic burst the economic growth bubble.

The Great Depression of 1893 cost many investors not only profits but part or all they had invested. Grand Rapids citizens were hit

hard by the financial depression, which especially affected the furniture industry. High unemployment and lower wages meant fewer riders on the streetcars for both commuting and recreation. Fewer fares collected meant less money available to pay the bills for operating costs, new cars, new track extensions, interest on bonds, and dividends to shareholders. The great depression made it difficult for the Consolidated Street Railway Company of Grand Rapids to do much more than operate the streetcars and carry out basic maintenance.

Fight over a Proposed Ordinance in 1893

The Consolidated Street Railway requested an ordinance to allow construction of a line on Ottawa Avenue. The aldermen wanted costly concessions from the street railway in exchange for allowing it to build and operate the proposed line. Manager Chapman responded to the demands on January 14 stating that "There are twenty-four aldermen and there may be twenty-four conditions. No, gentlemen, perhaps the best thing I can offer is to say we propose to spend $96,000

Open car no. 173 on the Lafayette & Stocking streetcar line sporting a West Bridge Street station sign, this Valley City Street & Cable Railway car was converted to electric.

Orrie Sietsma, Coopersville Area Historical Society Museum Collection

Closed car no. 77 is still painted for the Division & North Canal streetcar line. This Street Railway Company of Grand Rapids horse-drawn car was converted to electric power, circa 1895.

Grand Rapids Public Library

and you can place it to suit yourselves."

The Common Council of the city finally passed their version of the street railway ordinance on June 12. The Company refused the ordinance and offered reasons why they rejected it, but the primary one was that the company could not afford to extend service where patronage did not warrant it.

Apparently, patronage warranted at least one extensionin 1893. The street railway built one-half mile of track on East Fulton Street, extending this part of the Lyon-East Bridge streetcar line from East Street further east to Fuller Avenue.

Closed car no. 49 on the Butterworth line at Gold Street, circa 1894. Conductor Henry Du Bois is left on the platform and motorman Matt Conley is on right holding the controller lever.

The Token, August 1926

Problems Building Streetcars and Operating the Streetcar System

Chapman planned to acquire additional cars in 1893 so the street railway could improve its service. He pointed out that during 1892 the company increased the number of cars in service from thirty-six to fifty-three and the company planned to add seven more cars in 1893.

The Consolidated Street Railway also planned to build streetcars in its own shops during the winter months of 1893. The company began building five cars at the old upper Lyon Street cable powerhouse. Piles of wooden car frames, floors and roofs were all that the company had to show at the beginning of spring. Unfortunately, while the frames and other wood parts had been built, the bolts and other metal parts that were ordered in late 1892 had not arrived. The design of these cars, the first to be built by the street railway company, was similar to those purchased in 1892 with seats facing forward and an aisle down the middle of the car.

The railway began stationing switchmen at the four busiest corners on the system in

April: Bridge and Canal streets, Monroe and Pearl streets, Monroe and Division streets, and Monroe and Waterloo (now Market) streets. This was done so that motormen would not lose the time required to stop and align switches at those intersections.

The street railway company employed approximately 350 workers in the fall of 1893. The motormen and conductors numbered 180. Others worked as trackmen or shopmen who did more than just clean, repair, and paint the cars. Car maintenance included overhauling and refitting the motor cars twice a year when the motors were moved from closed cars to open cars in the spring with the process reversed in the fall.

A track sprinkler was added to the roster in June 1893. Built like an oil tank car, it held forty barrels of water and could spray a stream of water on each of the two rails, washing the sand and dust away to improve the efficiency of the return electrical circuit and to lessen the dust caused by movement of the cars over the streets.

The Consolidated Street Railway shops even built a snow sweeper for another street railway in Michigan: the Manistee, Filer City & East Lake Railway.

Failures at the Powerhouse

A serious problem arose in late 1893 with the failure of five armatures in the electric generators in the powerhouse. All five were installed at the same time in 1891 and all five failed during a two-week span. Each of these armatures cost the street railway $1,500 to replace. The company had to reduce the number of streetcars running to avoid a complete breakdown of the electrical generating system in order to prevent a complete shutdown of the streetcar system. Two new armatures arrived by December 20 and service was soon again back on schedule with ten-minute headways.

The Financial Depression Continues

At the beginning of 1894, the Consolidated Street Railway Company announced that continued low ridership had forced a reduction of all wages by ten per cent. General Manager Chapman noted the payroll constituted two-thirds of the company's expenses, and that the cost of coal, which was primarily used in the powerhouse to generate electricity, was the next highest expense item.

As summer approached, the street railway announced on May 1 that it was restoring the pay scale for employees whose wages had been reduced by ten per cent at the beginning of the year. Spring was accompanied by an increase in riders going to the three daytime resorts that the street railway served.

The company began building an armature to be used in the powerhouse. It hoped to build armatures much cheaper than the $1,500 price

an outside purchase incurred. Chapman ruefully reported that while it took six weeks of experimentation to build an armature in the company's shops, it only took ten minutes to find out that it didn't work.

Consolidated Street Railway Company Buys the Suburban North Park Railway

John J. P. O'Dell and C. R. Cummings, the Chicago bankers who owned a controlling interest in the Consolidated Street Railway Company of Grand Rapids, visited the city on March 21, 1894. After inspecting the North Park Street Railway line in suburban Grand Rapids Township, its steam dummies, rolling stock, and resort at North Park with Manager Chapman, they agreed to sign the papers for the purchase of the four-year-old line.

The Consolidated Street Railway Company began making the necessary changes to convert the North Park line from steam to electric power so streetcars could operate by early spring 1894. The company erected poles and overhead trolley wire. It also built a loop at the north end of the line to enable streetcars to reverse direction and deliver passengers to the north end of the pavilion. Passengers rode electric streetcars to the Michigan Soldiers' Home and to North Park for the first time on May 15, 1894. The cars operated on a ten-minute headway. The Consolidated Street Railway lowered the fare on the system from seven cents to five cents.

This suburban streetcar extension was treated as a part of the electric railway system

A Grandville Avenue & West Bridge Street line open car no. 172, circa early 1890s.

Orrie Sietsma, CAHS Collection

in Grand Rapids, just as the line to suburban Ramona Park and Reed's Lake in East Grand Rapids was. The two resorts were now linked by streetcar service. A person could now travel between the two resorts on the Wealthy-Taylor line, a distance of seven miles, for only five cents.

The street railway carried 80,000 passengers on July 4. The North Park resort on the Grand River and Ramona Park on Reed's Lake were the most popular destinations. The last car from Reed's Lake arrived downtown at 1 A.M. and it was reported to be "loaded."

Chapman Resigns as General Manager

James R. Chapman, general manager of the Consolidated Street Railway for the past three years, who also had been serving as general manager of the South Chicago City Railway for the past two years, resigned in early May 1894. Now Chapman could take charge of Chicago street railway tycoon Charles T. Yerkes' massive project to build a large system of electric car lines and transform existing horsecar lines into electric ones on the North and West sides of Chicago. Chapman had succeeded in transforming the hodge-podge assortment of Grand Rapids horsecars, steam dummy lines,

and cable car lines into an efficient electric street railway system in less than three years.

James Chapman's successes in Grand Rapids made him an obvious choice to help Yerkes do the same in Chicago. G. Stewart Johnson, chief engineer for the Grand Rapids & Indiana steam railroad was appointed to fill Chapman's position as manager of the Consolidated Street Railway system. The reader is referred to Chapman's biography in Chapter 12.

New Motors Replace Old Worn-Out Motors

Twelve new motors arrived in early May 1894. The street railway company used ten of these motors to replace worn-out ones. The remaining two motors were to be used to power two freight motors which were to be used to haul coal and other freight to the Soldiers' Home on the North Park line.

1895 Starts on a Slippery Slope

A slot wedge brake broke as a streetcar started down the east Bridge Street hill on January 5. The car quickly picked up speed as it slid down the hill making "the passengers' hair stand erect." While the motorman was able to

CONSOLIDATED STREET RAILWAY COMPANY.

Time Card in Effect January 1, 1895.

The time card below gives the time of the departure of the first car in the morning and the last car at night on each of the various lines. The daily service between several points on the system is as follows:

Bridge and Canal Sts. to East Sts., every.......... 5 min
Bridge and Canal Sts. to First Ave. via Div. St....2½ min
Bridge and Canal Sts. to Hall St.................. 5 min
Campau Place to Stocking St...................... 5 min
Division and Monroe Sts. and W. Leonard St...... 5 min
Division and Monroe Sts. to D. & M. Depot........ 5 min
All other lines run under a 10 minute headway.

WEALTHY AVE. & TAYLOR ST.—NORTH PARK TO REED'S LAKE.

	First car Lvs. A.M.	Last car Lvs. P.M.
North Park....................	6 15	9 05	9 45*
Campau Place.................	6 40	9 30	10 10*
Reed's Lake	6 05	8 50	9 55†
Campau Place........	6 30	9 20	10 20†

*To East City Limits. †To Sweet St.

SWEET ST. TO EAST CITY LIMITS.

	First car Lv. A.M.	Last car Lv. P.M.		First car Lv. A.M.	Last Lv. P.M.
Sweet St......6 25	11 15	East City Lim 6 10	11 00
Campau Pl....6 40	11 20	Campau Pl....6 30	11 20

THEATER CAR—DAILY.

Lv. Campau Place for North Park and Reed's Lake..11 30
Returning, Lv. North Park and Reed's Lake........11 25

WEALTHY AVE. AND SCRIBNER ST.

| D. & M. June .6 10 | 11 20 | East St........6 00 | 11 00 |
| Campau Pl....6 25 | 11 35 | Campau Pl....6 15 | 11 35 |

DIVISION ST. AND PLAINFIELD AVE.

| Burton Ave....5 55 | 11 15 | Plainfield Ave 6 00 | 11 10 |
| Campau Pl....6 14 | 11 34 | Campau Pl....6 16 | 11 26 |

DIVISION & WEST LEONARD STS.

| Hall St........5 55 | 10 45 | W. Leonard....6 05 | 10 55 |
| Campau Pl....6 09 | 10 59 | Campau Pl....6 21 | 11 11 |

LAFAYETTE & STOCKING STS.

| Hall St........9 00 | 10 50 | North End.....6 10 | 11 00 |
| Campau Pl....9 17 | 11 07 | Campau Pl....6 22 | 11 13 |

FIFTH AVENUE.

| Lafayette St...5 55 | 11 25 | East St.........6 00 | 11 30 |

GRANDVILLE AVE. & WEST BRIDGE ST.

| Hall St........6 00 | 11.12 | West End.....6 00 | 10 42 |
| Campau Pl....6 16 | 11 28 | Campau Pl....6 20 | 10 56 |

BUTTERWORTH AVE.

| Butterwrth Av 6 13 | 11 27 | Bridge St......5 55 | 11 07 |
| Campau Pl....6 28 | 11 42 | Campau Pl....5 53 | 11 10 |

CHERRY ST. & SHAWMUT AVE.

| East End......5 50 | 11 00 | West End.....6 15 | 11 25 |
| Campau Pl....6 05 | 11 15 | Campau Pl....6 25 | 11 35 |

BRIDGE & LYON STS.

| Grand Ave....6.05 | 11 25 | Fuller St......6 00 | 11 20 |
| Canal & Lyon..6 15 | 11 35 | Canal & Lyon.6 15 | 11 35 |

UNION DEPOT CAR.

Car runs from Monroe St. to depot every 5 minutes from 6 a. m. to 11 p. m. daily except Sunday.

CONSOLIDATED STREET RAILWAY COMPANY

Time Card in Effect June 2, 1895.

The time card below gives the time of the departure of the first car in the morning and the last car at night on each of the various lines. The daily service between several points on the system is as follows:

Bridge and Canal Sts. to East St., every.......... 5 min
Bridge and Canal Sts. to First Ave. via Div. St....2½ min
Bridge and Canal Sts. to Hall St.................. 5 min
Campau Place to Stocking St...................... 5 min
Division and Monroe Sts. and W. Leonard St...... 5 min
Division and Monroe Sts. to D. & M. Depot........ 5 min
All other lines run under a 10 minute headway.

WEALTHY AVE. & TAYLOR ST.—NORTH PARK TO REED'S LAKE.

	First car Lvs. A.M.	Last car Lvs. P.M.
North Park....................	5 55	11 15*
Campau Place................	6 20	11 40*
Reed's Lake	5 55	11 15†
Campau Place......	6 20	11 40†

*To East City Limits. †To Sweet St.

WEALTHY AVE. AND SCRIBNER ST.

| D. & M. June .6 10 | 11 20 | East St........6 00 | 11 00 |
| Campau Pl....6 25 | 11 35 | Campau Pl....6 15 | 11 35 |

DIVISION ST. AND PLAINFIELD AVE.

| Burton Ave....5 55 | 11 15 | Plainfield Ave 6 00 | 11 10 |
| Campau Pl....6 14 | 11 34 | Campau Pl....6 16 | 11 26 |

DIVISION & WEST LEONARD STS.

| Hall St........5 55 | 10 45 | W. Leonard....6 05 | 10 55 |
| Campau Pl....6 09 | 10 59 | Campau Pl....6 21 | 11 11 |

LAFAYETTE & STOCKING STS.

| Hall St........6 00 | 10 50 | North End.....6 10 | 11 00 |
| Campau Pl....6 17 | 11 07 | Campau Pl....6 22 | 11 13 |

FIFTH AVENUE.

| Lafayette St...5 55 | 11 25 | East St.........6 00 | 11 30 |

GRANDVILLE AVE. & WEST BRIDGE ST.

| Hall St........6 00 | 11.12 | West End.....6 00 | 10 42 |
| Campau Pl....6 16 | 11 28 | Campau Pl....6 20 | 10 56 |

BUTTERWORTH AVE.

| Butterwrth Av 6 13 | 11 27 | Bridge St......5 55 | 11 07 |
| Campau Pl....6 28 | 11 42 | Campau Pl....5 53 | 11 10 |

CHERRY ST. & SHAWMUT AVE.

| East End......5 50 | 11 00 | West End.....6 15 | 11 25 |
| Campau Pl....6 05 | 11 15 | Campau Pl....6 25 | 11 35 |

BRIDGE & LYON STS.

| Grand Ave....6.05 | 11 25 | Fuller St......6 00 | 11 20 |
| Canal & Lyon..6 15 | 11 35 | Canal & Lyon.6 15 | 11 35 |

LINE TO THE LAKE VIA CHERRY ST. & EAST ST

Commencing Wednesday afternoon, June 5, a 10 minute service will be given every afternoon between John Ball Park and Reed's Lake via Shawmut-ave., Cherry and East-sts., and Wealthy-ave. At East and Cherry-sts. transfers will be given to east end of Cherry-st. line. This arrangement will continue until further notice.

G. S. JOHNSON, G. M.

Far left: *winter time card in effect January 1, 1895.*

Trolley Topics

Left: *summer time card in effect June 2, 1895.*

Trolley Topics

use the hand brake, the locked wheels continued to slide down the icy track as if it had been oiled. Several passengers were badly shaken up when the runaway car collided with another streetcar at the bottom of the hill.

Where Should Electric Street Cars Stop?

Horsecars had been required to stop at the far side of a street crossing and the electric cars were still doing the same in 1895. There were several good reasons for horsecars to stop at the far-side corner. Passengers boarded the rear of the car directly from the cross walks paved with broad smooth "crossing flag stones" which could be kept relatively clean of street dirt—an advantage women with their long skirts appreciated. They also did not have to walk close to the horse(s). Finally, riders entered the car at the rear where a uniformed conductor was stationed, away from the dusty or mud-spattered dash on the front platform where a relatively uncouth driver worked.

The *Grand Rapids Evening Press* published an editorial on May 30 contending that:

> The time has now come for a change. The only objection to stopping the cars at the near crossing disappeared with the poor old car horse, and it is high time for the custom to be reversed. At present there is perpetual danger to life and property because the cars are sent plunging over the cross streets before coming to a stop. The motorman is given little opportunity to observe vehicles approaching from the right and left. It is due to this fact that a large percentage of street railway accidents are due.

This would lead to continued controversy as the aldermen passed an ordinance requiring cars to stop at the near crossing only to change their minds and at the next council meeting and pass an ordinance reversing the ordinance they had just passed.

Resort Season Begins

Both of the company's suburban resorts at North Park and Reed's Lake officially opened the 1895 season on Sunday, May 12. The crowds going to the resorts were so large that the company had to double the number of cars serving the two resorts. Wurzburg's twenty-piece brass band was scheduled to perform daily free open air concerts at Ramona Park throughout the resort season. Music also was heard at the fourteen-acre North Park resort during most of the resort season. Bands played on the fourth floor of the bandstand while families enjoyed the picnic grounds or just plain relaxing along the shady tree-lined banks of the Grand River.

Improvements Continue into the Year

A very important technological improvement occurred when the company replaced the old controllers with the most modern type the available. Manager Johnson described the change on August 30, 1895:

When our cars were originally fitted out the best type of controller then known was used, the Edison seven-point switch. Later we tried the "K," five of which are now on the North Park line. Since then the "K-2" has been created and it represents the finest of the devices of that kind. We have just made a contract for these to be furnished on all our cars…a controller switch bears the same relation to a street car as the throttle does to a locomotive. The advantages of the new equipment will be a better control of the current and consequently of the car; a close contact for receiving the current and no burning in the box; a more economical use of electricity, and better yet, a steady and uniform acceleration of speed.

Open streetcar No. 159 with Motorman Miles McDonald on his first day on the job in 1895. A street railway inspector is standing at the rear.
Grand Rapids Public Library

In July, The Consolidated Street Railway ordered fifteen new Pullman Company streetcars equipped with vestibules. These cars began arriving in early September and were designed for cold weather operation. The *Grand Rapids Democrat* published the following description of these cars on October 9, 1895:

The new vestibuled street cars now being placed in commission are exceedingly popular during the present cold snap….There are twenty of the old cars now vestibuled and in service. The new Pullman vestibuled cars are the largest and most expensive ever purchased in the city. Fifteen have been purchased for use here and three are now running. They are elegantly finished in oak with seats running along the sides, upholstered in bamboo. The length of the cars is thirty feet including the spacious vestibules and their seating capacity is much larger than the old cars. The doors in each end of the cars are on the side nearest the entrance so that passengers passing in and out do not disturb those riding in the vestibule. The cars will be warmed by electricity, the heaters being concealed under the seats.

A Fight Over Franchise Changes

On September 23, 1895, the Consolidated Street Railway Company made a radical proposal to amend the 1891 street railway franchise that required ten-minute headways on all lines in the city. The company sought to change any specific street railway line schedule "when in the company's judgment the exigencies of traffic require it." Street railway General Manager Johnson drew attention to the fact that several of the city's streetcar lines did not pay seventy-five per cent of the operating expenses on a ten-minute time schedule and contended that "If the money wasted on these lines was saved it would enable the company to improve the road and service on lines which would be of more benefit to the public."

The *Grand Rapids Evening Press* published an editorial on October 14, 1895, criticizing the aldermen. "The council is not justified in regarding the street railway as a public enemy to be sandbagged on every occasion."

J. J. P. O'Dell, Chicago investor and chairman of the executive committee of the Consolidated Street Railway Company, made the case for the concessions the company wanted. He asserted that the Common Council aldermen had loaded the proposed ordinance with riders that made it harsh and unjust to the company, when he stated on October 26 that:

Four years' operation has demonstrated a number of things, and one is that the time restrictions put upon some of the lines are burdensome to the company, while they are not particularly valuable to the public. It seems to me that the council should consider that the interests of the city and of the company are to a large extent mutual . . . It is of no advantage to the public that we should run an empty car over the line, and it costs just as much to haul an empty car as it does one that is loaded. As I before said, we are anxious to run cars

Exterior of car body No. 109 supported on a temporary non-powered truck. Photo taken by the builder, the Pullman Company. This is one of the first cars with enclosed vestibules meant to keep the motorman protected from the elements.

Smithsonian Institution

Interior of car No. 109 showing longitudinal bench seats. Photo taken by the builder, the Pullman Company.

Smithsonian Institution

Single-truck car no. 104 on Cherry Street line, Motorman Frank Dumas in front, Conductor Arthur B. Cross in rear.

Jim Anderson Collection

and will run just as many as the traffic demands on all the lines, but I do not think we should be burdened with restrictions which bring the operating cost to a point so high that we can get no returns upon our investment . . .

As to extensions, the policy of the company is the same as that relative to service. It is anxious to get into new territory where there is traffic to justify it. We are asked to extend a line out East Leonard Street. Now we can demonstrate that a line there would not bring in enough to pay for axle grease for the cars. It costs us over $1,000 a year to run a single car. That means a good many nickels-and it doesn't include interest on investment simply operating expenses.

The aldermen continued amending the proposed ordinance. At the November 18, 1895, Common Council meeting the street railway submitted a long detailed statement as to why the pending ordinance could not be accepted. The points the street railway company most vigorously opposed were:

1. Laying rails on a concrete foundation.
2. Using ninety-pound rails exclusively.
3. Paying a due proportion of the expense of paving and "all other improvements" in streets where it has tracks.
4. Constructing a new line in East Leonard Street and College Avenue.

5. The fifteen-minute schedule proposed for three routes, in place of the twenty-minute headway at the company's discretion on all lines as asked.
6. Prohibition of the use of construction cars by the company.

The company was able to reduce the service on the parts of the Reed's Lake and North Park lines outside the city limits from a ten-minute to a twenty-minute headway for the winter months effective November 21, 1895. The ends of these two lines were in Grand Rapids Township whose street railway franchise did not require a minimum ten-minute headway.

1896

In January 1896 the company reported that 1895 street railway receipts from fares increased, but only slightly over 1894. In March the company noted that the bicycle riding fad was cutting deeply into the company's revenues.

The company also stated it was now operating streetcars on nearly fifty miles of track. It owned approximately 200 open and closed cars. All the cars operating during the winter months were fitted with vestibules before the winter of 1895-96 ensued. Fifteen of the latest Pullman company thirty-foot-long cars purchased in 1895 were electrically heated.

Motormen were able to keep warm during the cold winter months as they now were inside an enclosed vestibule while operating their streetcars. But these motormen now faced

new problems. Sleet and snow often accumulated on the front windows of the cars, obstructing the motorman's vision and forcing him to stop the car and clear the outside of the windows. In addition, the warm, moist breath of passengers condensed on the inside of the vestibule windows on chilly days. As there were no window defrosters in those days, all the motorman could do was to constantly wipe the inside of the windows.

Operating Costs

The company was operating at a financial loss; there had never been enough money to pay a dividend. When the franchise was granted in April 1891, the Consolidated Street Railway contended the time schedules demanded by the city were not justified as the expected population growth did not occur in the districts served by several lines. The Common Council passed a new street railway ordinance on October 19 that embodied practically every concession the street railway company asked for. The street railway finally had control over the frequency of service on individual streetcar lines, but only for one year.

There were two reasons why the Common Council was so liberal in granting concessions to Consolidated Street Railway. The first was the widespread belief that the financial condition of the company was so poor that rumors circulated that a receiver was going to be appointed. Also, the new ordinance had a time limit of one year after which the company would be required to operate under the terms of the old 1891 franchise if another one could not be agreed upon.

General Manager Johnson realized that while rails were wearing out the company could not afford to buy new rails necessary to replace them. To address the problem of rail wear, Warren Annable, the company's master mechanic, built an electrically-powered saw on a flat car. It was used to saw off the battered ends of rails in the streets so that they could be re-laid, saving the company the cost of all-new rail.

The heavy electric streetcars continued to cause the inner side of a rail that the wheel flanges rubbed against to wear out much faster than the outer side of the same rail. The street railway tried to solve the problem by taking up a rail and turning it around so the less worn outer side of the rail became the inner side. This

An electrically-powered rail saw car was designed and built locally.

Street Railway Review, Vol. 6, 15 Aug, 1896

enabled the company to extend the life of the rail and save money by not having to replace them as frequently.

The Consolidated Street Railway did not build any extensions during 1896. The company did pull up the rails on LaGrave Avenue, after building a track on Wealthy Street so the streetcars could travel down South Division Avenue to Wealthy Street. The street railway also re-laid track on the new Bridge Street bridge.

Accidents and Mishaps in 1897

The Consolidated Street Railway of Grand Rapids had a contract to deliver coal and other freight from an interchange track with the Detroit, Grand Haven and Milwaukee Railway at Sweet Street to the Michigan Soldiers' Home on the North Park line, a double-track line. The two tracks were connected by a crossover switch at the southeast end of the Soldiers' Home. A dead-end spur branched off going north along the back of the main building where the main boiler was located. How did a northbound streetcar car collide head-on with a gondola car loaded with coal?

The streetcar company used an electric freight motor to move railroad cars loaded with coal north to the Michigan Soldiers' Home, a distance of about two miles. The freight motor headed north pushing a loaded gondola car in front of it during a snowstorm on the evening of January 23, 1897. The loaded car was pushed beyond the switch that faced the opposite direction to the spur leading to the boiler house. Conductor S. S. Sliter and switchman Ed Clark climbed aboard the gondola that was uncoupled on the northbound main track which was slightly upgrade at that point. Their job was to set the brakes and keep the gondola north of the spur while the switch motor headed north on the spur to pick up empty coal cars. The switcher would then pull the empty coal cars to the southbound track and retreive the full car they left on the northbound track. This switching maneuver had worked successfully numerous times before, but it failed this time.

Unfortunately, the loaded car began to move south down the grade. The crewmen tried to tighten the brakes on the heavily loaded car but they failed. The car continued rolling southbound on the northbound track going right past the switch leading to the spur. The two men quickly realized not only could they not stop the car but that a scheduled streetcar on the same northbound main track was due anytime. Switchman Clark jumped off the gondola car and ran ahead to warn the motorman of the northbound streetcar. The light of day had faded and the trees on either side obscured the tracks.

Northbound streetcar No. 73 was traveling at about ten miles an hour as it rounded the curve at the north end of the grove of trees at the very south end of the Soldiers' Home. John Hake, the motorman, saw the runaway coal car coming at him just long enough to set the brakes and reverse the motor before the head-on collision killed him and destroyed both cars. Frank McKelvey, the conductor and the three passengers on board the trolley car were all thrown to the floor.

The inquest concluded that while no one was to blame, they recommended that the streetcar company perform their freight business after passenger traffic had ended for the day.

The streetcar company honored motorman John Hake with a tombstone on his grave in Hall Street cemetery that was engraved with the outline of a trolley car and inscribed with the words: "Killed at his post of duty."

A big earthen dam, rather than a bridge, was built across Lamberton Creek in 1890 to support the North Park Street Railway track so that the line could reach the North Park Resort. A small lake grew above the dam until it was more than thirty feet deep in some places. The sluiceway became clogged and the rising waters created enough pressure to cause the dam to collapse on April 26, 1897. Nearly the entire embankment which held up the street railway tracks was swept away. Another earthen dam was built at the same location but with a better system to keep water flowing. The street railway track was re-laid on top of the new earthen dam.

The pavilion at Ramona Park burned down on February 22, 1897. The Consolidated Street Railway spent $25,000 to build a new pagoda-style pavilion that was designed to attract even more visitors to the street railway's most popular resort.

Extra Cars Needed to Handle the Crowds

The streetcar company was well known for its efforts to provide extra cars to carry visitors as well as local citizens to and from special events such as theater performances, baseball games, horse races, circuses and even dedications of buildings. The dedication of the new Lakeside Club building at Reed's Lake on May 29, 1897, was a major event. The street railway ran forty special streetcars, motors and trailers, to take members of the Lakeside Club and their friends to Reed's Lake from

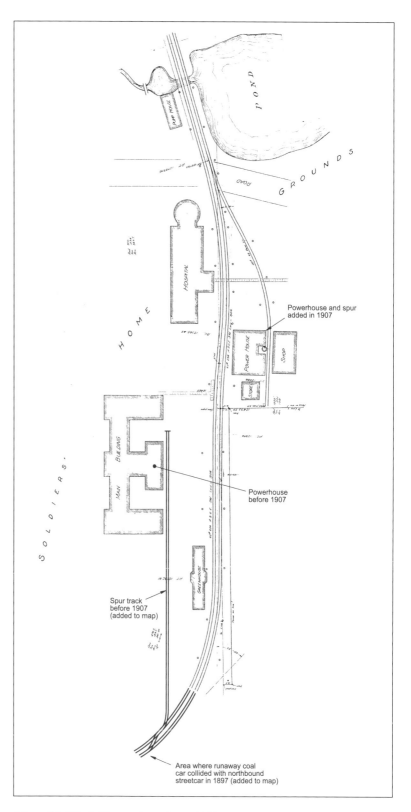

Map of Soldier's Home, circa about 1909.
The green tracks and text were added for clarity.
Grand Rapids Public Museum

Fight over the Franchise Resumes

The October 19, 1896, ordinance that both the Common Council and the street railway officials agreed upon had a time limit of twelve months. Once this expired the company would once again have to operate under the 1891 franchise regulations with respect to schedules unless a new franchise could be agreed upon.

A special Industrial edition of the *Grand Rapids Democrat* published on September 26, 1897, contained the following evaluation of the street railway's financial situation in an article entitled "Street Cars and Their Worth to Grand Rapids."

> During the past three years the company has had a very hard struggle; a very severe and tremendous battle to keep their property intact, and pay their just debts. They were forced to ask the council to give them some relief by changing a city ordinance. This matter the council gave their consideration, and it was granted; had it not have been they could not have pulled through. But they appreciated that it was in the best interests of the city to do so and they have shown a very fair and honorable disposition in this particular.

The Consolidated Street Railway Company petitioned the Common Council on November 22 for a new franchise to enable the company to control the routes and frequency of streetcar service on each line. The company proposed changes it would be willing to make in exchange for the passage of its proposed franchise. Also included was a list of specific streets where tracks would be extended. The company even offered to give up the outside two tracks on Canal Street, finally ending the "Four-Track Nuisance" provided it could build a line running on Ottawa Avenue between Lyon Street on the south and Trowbridge Street on the north. The Common Council discussed the proposed ordinance changes at several meetings and finally rejected them unanimously on December 31, 1897.

The Chicago investors who owned as much as three-fourths of the Consolidated Street Railway Company of Grand Rapids were getting some interest income on bonds but many investors did not receive any dividends at all on their common stock. Consequently, the company decreased its expenditures to upgrade the streetcar system. The company did make two large purchases designed to save money as well as upgrade the system in 1899 when it purchased ten new cars and installed a new electric generator in its powerhouse.

Motorman John Hake's marble tombstone at Oak Hill Cemetery on Hall Street with the faint image of a street car and "Killed at his post of duty". His last name is misspelled as Hath.

Photo by Tom Maas

downtown Grand Rapids. The lead streetcar was occupied by Wurzburg's band which furnished music enroute.

Trailers were often coupled to motor cars during the busiest times of the day to accommodate the crowds who wanted to get to and from downtown Grand Rapids.

229. Michigan Soldiers Home Grounds, Grand Rapids, Mich.

A postcard view of tracks through Soldier's Home before electrification (or this photo was retouched to remove wires). View is looking north towards the Lamberton Creek dam.

Carl Bajema Collection

1898 Brings Major Snow Storms

G. Stuart Johnson, president and general manager of Consolidated Street Railway Company, described the methods that the Grand Rapids Street Railway used to fight snow in a letter published in the March 15, 1898 issue of the *Street Railway Review*.

Fighting Snow

During the past winter we have had extraordinary snow storms and unusual difficulty in keeping our tracks open. A good many storms have prevailed, the one which visited us on February 19, and continued for three or four days, was, by far, the worst in the experience of this company, and taxed our resources to the utmost. The fall of snow was probably 2 ½ ft. on the level and, in many places, the accumulation caused by drifts, was over 5 ft. deep. In spite of the tremendous task which presented itself, we were determined that our lines should not be blockaded and that our service should not be stopped. To accomplish this every device in our possession and all the forces at our disposal were kept busy night and day. Our sweepers and snow plows left their shelters early in the evening and did not return to them for two nights and a day. When relieved, they were as much exhausted as the men.

We had two very large snow sweepers, a large switching motor and several horse snow plows in operation and probably a hundred men (extras) during this period. With this help and the determination to keep our lines open, we succeeded in preventing the interruption of traffic, while in a good many cities travel was entirely abandoned . . .

The switching motor is a 60-h.p. apparatus, and the motors are two Rae, or Detroit, motors of 30 h. p. each. The motors which operate the sweeper are two Edison No. 2s, which are 25 h. p. each. The sweepers are similar to those built elsewhere; the brushes being composed of rattan, placed in rollers and cut about 33 in. long. The brushes are so arranged at an angle with the track as to take the snow from the center of the way and throw it outside, clear from the rails. They are very effective.

We use a good deal of salt to keep our rails in suitable condition. Salt is a most disagreeable adjunct and leaves the streets in very bad condition, but it is an aid to electric railway operation which cannot be supplemented or duplicated. We regret its use, but have been unable to find a substitute. We would have great difficulty, at times, to operate without a liberal use of it.

Newspaper drawing of a new streetcar fender.

Grand Rapids Press,
16 April 1889

The fender adopted by the street railway company.

Attempting to Fend Off Accident Victims

The street railway had been experimenting with different styles of front fenders to help prevent accidents during 1897. The company gave up experimenting when it learned that there were about 2,000 patents for streetcar fenders. The street railway ordered 140 car fenders from a Providence, Rhode Island, company in April.

Interurbans Coming to Grand Rapids

The city had to begin making decisions in 1898 about an emerging mode of suburban and intercity electric rail transportation: interurbans. Both the Holland and Muskegon interurban companies asked the Common Council in 1898 to give them franchises to allow them to run over streetcar tracks within Grand Rapids. These negotiations took two years before the two interurban companies, the streetcar company, and the Common Council finally agreed to a franchise that all four were willing to accept.

Company Acquires Convertible Cars

Most streetcars had been built for a particular season. Open cars were built for running during the warm months and closed cars were built for operating in colder weather. The electrical equipment and trucks had to be moved from a closed car to an open car in the spring and in fall and then the process was reversed in the fall.

The controller used by the motorman had to be removed from each platform and installed in the other car and the wiring had to be connected. The open car bodies used in the summer had to be put on shop trucks and taken to the storage barns. Street railway workers in Grand Rapids converted the cars at a rate of about four or five cars per day twice a year.

The Consolidated Street Railway Company placed an order with the Pullman Company for ten new streetcars at the beginning of 1899. These cars were designed as all-purpose cars that could be used year-round. The company was able to save money by purchasing one set of streetcars to operate in all seasons rather than acquiring two sets. The sides of the new

Pullman-built cars were arranged so the window sashes could be folded and shoved out of sight during warm weather and could be put back in place for cold weather operation. The vestibules also were of the convertible type.

The cars had cane seats running the length of the car on both sides of the aisle. Five of the new cars were scheduled to run on the hill line and the remaining five were to run on the lake line. The new Pullman cars were about the same size as the large yellow cars already in use in Grand Rapids. These Pullman-built cars were numbered consecutively from 115 to 124.

Exterior mounted mail box on streetcar.
Thomas Dilley Collection at Grand Rapids Public Library

Other Developments in 1899

The company purchased a 1,200-horsepower Allis-Corliss engine that began converting steam into electric power on July 2, 1899. The new engine weighed 387 tons, had a 20-foot diameter flywheel, and generated enough electricity to operate all the streetcars in Grand Rapids at one time. This huge engine was designed to be more efficient and was predicted to use fifty per cent less coal to generate the same amount of electrical energy as the two old generators in the powerhouse had produced.

The U.S. Post Office obtained an ordinance on June 12, 1899, to have special streetcars carry bags of mail between the main post office and branch offices as well as between the main post office and the steam railroad depots in Grand Rapids.

The street railway company ordered 250 mail boxes and began attaching them to the front exterior of each streetcar so citizens could deliver their letters to the U.S. post office via the mail boxes attached on the front. The letters in the mail boxes were removed when a streetcar stopped briefly in downtown Campau Square. This service began on December 18, 1899.

A Look Back at the Decade

The electric streetcar era began in Grand Rapids in 1890 when the Reed's Lake Electric Railway began carrying passengers to the Reed's Lake resorts. James R. Chapman, an electrical engineer, became general manager of both the Valley City Street and Cable Car Company and the Street Railway Company of Grand Rapids at the beginning of 1891. He succeeded in converting the collection of horse, cable, and steam dummy lines into one of the best electric street railway systems in the nation in less than two years. Chicago businessmen led by J. J. P. O'Dell, John M. Hagar, and Columbus R. Cummings owned a controlling interest in the Consolidated Street Railway during the 1890s and supported efforts to main-

tain first class service in the depression years.

The electric streetcars provided faster and more frequent service which enabled Grand Rapids citizens to begin moving to the suburbs—East Grand Rapids, North Park and Burton Heights. Lower fares and free transfers made travel fast, convenient, and economical.

Using electric power to operate streetcars was accompanied by numerous benefits for the riding public to enjoy. A reporter compared the horse-drawn car era and the electric car era in Grand Rapids at the beginning of the twentieth century in the April 28, 1900, *Grand Rapids Evening Press*:

Old Horse Car Days in the Valley City

It has been only eight years since the last horse disappeared from the streets, and yet, as far as any traces of their use remain, the exodus might have taken place a century ago. The changes have been gradual, perhaps, but none the less radical.

There is little similarity between the present type of rolling stock and the old horse cars. In replacing the narrow platforms with capacious entries, in substituting electric and hard coal heaters for the damp hay which formerly covered the floor, in lighting the modern car with electricity instead of the little, foul, ill-smelling oil lamps, which hid in a box at one end of the car, leaked oil on the passenger below-in all of these things there has been progress. The old time tracks, which were used until they were little more than streaks of rust, have been replaced by rails which are heavy and strong, and which cost from two to three times as much to build as those of the horse car days. Even the old style uncovered wooden seats would hardly meet the fastidious demand of a public which has of late years been cushioned on springs.

Electric Railway Operations in the New Century (1900-1909)

U.S. Postal Car No. 22, one of three old GR streetcars rebuilt in local shops for mail distribution, circa 1900.

Grand Rapids Public Library

The Electric Interurban Railway Era Begins in Grand Rapids

Development in electric railway technology soon made travel between cities possible. The electric interurbans were the "dot coms" of their time. Very few industries rose so quickly and suffered as rapid a decline. Many of Michigan'a major cities were connected by interurban, but by 1932 the entire network had vanished. Certainly Michigan's early infatua-

tion with the automobile played a part and auto competition affected Michigan's interubans whether they were hill-and-dale operations or cut-and-fill high-speed roads.

Grand Rapids ultimately was served by three interurbans which are briefly described here. The histories of these lines are presented in greater detail in the chapters at the end of this book.

The "Holland interurban" as the Grand Rapids, Holland and Lake Michigan Rapid Railway (GRH&LMRRy) became known as regionally, began running into Grand Rapids in 1901 making it the first interurban to operate in that city.

The Grand Rapids, Grand Haven and Muskegon Railway (GRGH&MRy) was the second interurban electric railway to run in Grand Rapids. The "Muskegon interurban," as it was locally known, entered Grand Rapids on West Leonard Street at the Walker-Bristol street intersection in 1902.

The Michigan Railway that came into Grand Rapids in 1915 was the third interurban company to operate an electric line into Grand Rapids. The Michigan Railway company built its own private right-of-way that enabled the "Kalamazoo_interurban" cars to enter Grand Rapids after the city refused to allow them access to the city over a streetcar line.

This chapter covers the history of the Grand Rapids Street Railway Company system and all the street railway cars and interurban cars that operated within the city of Grand Rapids during the period of 1900-1909. More detailed histories of these interurbans will be found in Chapter 10.

Grand Rapids Railway Operations in the First Decade of the Twentieth Century

The Grand Rapids Railway Co. Buys the Consolidated Street Railway Co.

Early in 1900 a group of Grand Rapids citizens led by Lewis H. Withey and Anton G. Hodenpyl succeeded in getting E. W. Clark, a Philadelphia banker, to invest in the Grand Rapids street railway system. E. W. Clark, and J. W. Seligman of New York City, with the help of Grand Rapids investors, purchased the controlling interest in the Consolidated Street Railway Company in March 1900 from Chicago businessmen who were the major stockholders during the 1890s. The new owners chose Grand Rapids Railway Company as the new name of the streetcar company.

The Grand Rapids Railway Company operated a total of 51.3 miles of track in 1900. Streetcars ran on single-track streets for 7 miles and on double-track streets for 21.2 miles. Sidings added another 2 miles.

New Streetcars

The new owners immediately placed an order with Jewett Car Company of Newark, Ohio, for twenty new streetcars. The sample double-truck Jewett streetcar that arrived in Grand Rapids in April was thirty-eight feet in length and equipped with vestibules and twin doors. The interior of the car had longitudinal seats and was carpeted. The local car shops placed motors in the Jewett streetcar which aggregated between sixty- and seventy-horsepower.

General Manager G. Stewart Johnson also placed an order with the St. Louis Car Company for fifteen new closed city cars to be delivered in the fall when the company's closed cars were to be outfitted with controllers and double trucks. Each car was to be thirty-six feet in length overall and twenty-eight feet long inside. The Brill Company trucks for these new cars were equipped with four wheels of the same size instead of two large wheels and two small wheels found on trucks purchased earlier in the year.

These cars were equipped with longitudinal upholstered cane seats. The longitudinal seats not only made it easier for conductors to make their way through a car, but it also increased the car's carrying capacity by providing ample standing room. These new cars were to be painted orange and yellow in accordance with the company's color scheme for all cars as they went through the shops for repairs.

The St. Louis Car Company car bodies arrived in late September and were wired for lights, electrical heating, and motors. Some of the cars were equipped with a single fifty-seven-horsepower motor while other cars were fitted with two twenty-seven-horsepower motors. The two sizes were tried as an experiment. Hard coal stoves quickly replaced the electric heaters in the bigger streetcars in December because the electric heating apparatus used to heat the cars consumed as much electricity during a day as it took to run the car itself.

Street Route Signs on Streetcars

New street route signs were placed on the Bridge and Lyon Street trolleys that told riders the route on which those particular streetcars were headed. The signs, painted on the glass at the ends of the vestibules, were transparent. Tin shields were mounted behind them in which electric lights were placed so that at night the destination of the car could easily be read. Signs were also placed on top of the car on each side of the trolley and rendered transparent at night. The Bridge and Lyon street cars testing the new sign design were reported to have had an odd appearance at night, but the signs seemed to be serving their purpose—making it easier for passengers to board the right streetcar.

Mail boxes were mounted inside Grand Rapids street cars with slots provided for interior and exterior use .

Street Railway Review, 10 Jan 1900

Streetcars Serve as Mail Boxes

In December 1899 the streetcar company began equipping each car with two mail boxes, one inside each end of the car with a slot to the outside. Riders and passersby slipped letters into the slot while the car was stopped for passengers. The experiment was successful enough for the company to begin equipping its open summer cars with mail boxes.

Three old Grand Rapids streetcars were rebuilt in the Lyon Street shops in early 1900 to transport U.S. Mail. These special electric mail cars replaced wagons for transporting mail between the Union Depot which served the Grand Rapids and Indiana, Pere Marquette, and Michigan Central railroads, the Lake Shore and Michigan Southern depot and the Detroit, Grand Haven and Milwaukee Railroad depot as well as the main post office. Mail also was to be transported by these special postal cars to the main post office and three substations on the streetcar lines. The company completed spur tracks in early May into the downtown post office grounds on Lyon Street, and from Plainfield Avenue to the edge of the Detroit, Grand Haven and Milwaukee Railroad property so the mail streetcars could easily deliver and pick up mail bags.

These cars were painted in the company's yellow and orange livery and lettered "United States Postal Car." The windows on the sides and ends of the postal cars were covered on the inside with heavy wire screens and the end doors were permanently closed. The entrances to the postal cars were on the sides where double doors and wrought iron steps were provided.

Company Seeks Amendments to Franchise

The new Grand Rapids Railway Company proposed a new ordinance to allow the company to determine the streetcar routes and service frequency on its lines. It also wanted an ordinance to give the company the right to extend the Grandville Avenue line one half mile beyond Hall Street to the southwest city limits where the interurban line from Holland was expected to reach Grand Rapids. In addition, the company wanted to build a spur from the intersection of Oakes and Market streets to Island No. 3 and then run into the City Market on the island. The company also proposed to increase the twenty-one years remaining on the existing franchise to thirty years.

Grand Rapids Common Council aldermen debated the proposed ordinance and loaded it down with other amendments that would require the street railway to build and operate lines into remote and unprofitable territories. The company withdrew its proposal at the June 5 meeting of the council.

Grand Rapids Railway was successful on June 25 in obtaining passage of a specific ordi-

Artist's rendition of bird's eye view of GR&I Union Station, circa 1913. View looking northeast with Ionia Avenue in the foreground. The illustration is signed by Grand Rapids artist T. (Theo) W. Etzold.

Grand Rapids
Public Library

nance to allow the Holland interurban entry into Grand Rapids over the Grandville Avenue tracks of the street railway. The new ordinance allowed the company to build tracks on Grandville Avenue southwest from Hall Street one-half mile to the city limit and to build an entrance to the City Market on Market Street.

Per the provisions of the new ordinance the Grandville Avenue streetcar line was duly extended from Hall Street to the city limit at Clyde Park Avenue to enable Holland interurban cars entry into Grand Rapids to reach downtown via the Grandville Avenue line.

The street railway also considered changing the routes of some of the Wealthy and Lafayette cars to provide additional service to the GR&I Railroad Union Station on Ionia Avenue. The company improved Canal Street by laying new brick between the rails during 1900.

Track Construction Improvements

A mobile foundry for making "cast weld" rail joints on new track for better electrical conduction was under construction at the upper Lyon Street shops in May 1900. A heavy steel frame car mounted on two shop-built trucks was designed to support an eight-foot-high blast cupola forty-eight inches in diameter. The cupola was equipped with a blower that had its own motor and car supporting the cupola had two powerful motors for propulsion. The

steel foundry car weighed about thirty tons when the cupola was loaded and ready to charge. Workers carried ladles containing molten metal from the cupola to the rail joints to be bonded together. This new car was first used at night in July and enabled workers to weld thirty-four rails together in less than forty minutes.

The street railway company began placing strips of iron along the rails were being relaid on Canal Street to fill the flangeway along the side of each rail. The addition of these iron strips made a practically level surface between the two car tracks except for the flangeways themselves. This improvement was appreciated by wheelmen and others who frequently crossed the tracks.

New Track Extensions and Route Changes

The Grandville Avenue streetcar line was extended from Hall Street to the city limit at Clyde Park Avenue to enable Holland interurban cars to enter Grand Rapids and reach downtown via the Grandville Avenue line.

The street railway also considered changing the routes of some of the Wealthy and Lafayette cars so that they would provide more service for the GR&I Union railroad station on Ionia Avenue. The street railway company improved Canal Street by laying new brick between the rails during 1900.

HOW TO SEE GRAND RAPIDS

TAKE a Cherry St. and Shawmut Ave. car going west; this will take you to John Ball Park. When you have seen the park, go back (same line) to Canal St.; get a transfer for Wealthy Avenue and Taylor Street car going north. This car will carry you through the Soldier's Home grounds to North Park. After staying there as long as you wish, take a car for Reed's Lake. Free shows are given there every afternoon and evening during the season, commencing at 3:00 and 8:15 p.m. In addition there are many other amusements. Any of the cars will return you to the city from Reed's Lake, any time you desire, or return via Cherry Street.

THE WHOLE COST OF THIS 21-MILE RIDE IS BUT TWENTY CENTS

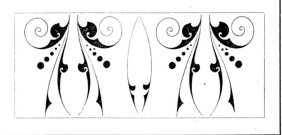

GRAND RAPIDS ENG. CO., PRINTERS.

Front and back cover of "Grand Rapids-Where and How to Go" tourist guide published by Grand Rapids Railway, 1900. The front cover features a line of open streetcars and the back features directions for visiting each of the big three resorts for 20 cents while traveling a total of 21 miles.
Grand Rapids Public Library

Three Local Resorts

The street railway company published a sixteen-page brochure to advertise the three daytime resorts in Grand Rapids that visitors as well as local citizens could reach by streetcar: Ramona Park adjacent to Reed's Lake, North Park adjacent to Grand River, and John Ball Park nestled in the west side hills at the end of West Fulton Street. The "Grand Rapids-Where and How to Go" tourist guide contained a two-page indexed map of the company's lines that identified points of interest and thirteen pages of photographs of scenes at the three parks.

The Grand Rapids Railway hired Craig Patee to become the company's first official excursion agent to publicize the "Big Three Resorts" not only to Grand Rapids citizens, but also to solicit groups in other cities to sponsor mid-weekday-long railroad excursions to Grand Rapids. Patee was successful in bringing more than a dozen group excursions to Grand Rapids during the 1901 season.

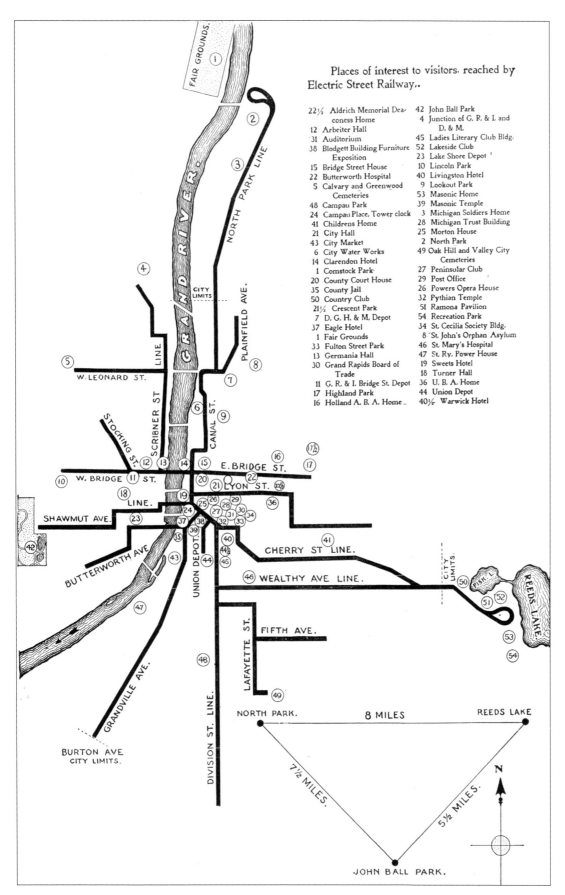

Places of interest to visitors, reached by Electric Street Railway.

22½	Aldrich Memorial Deaconess Home	42	John Ball Park
12	Arbeiter Hall	4	Junction of G. R. & I. and D. & M.
31	Auditorium	45	Ladies Literary Club Bldg.
38	Blodgett Building Furniture Exposition	52	Lakeside Club
15	Bridge Street House	23	Lake Shore Depot
22	Butterworth Hospital	10	Lincoln Park
5	Calvary and Greenwood Cemeteries	40	Livingston Hotel
		9	Lookout Park
48	Campau Park	53	Masonic Home
24	Campau Place, Tower clock	39	Masonic Temple
41	Childrens Home	3	Michigan Soldiers Home
21	City Hall	28	Michigan Trust Building
43	City Market	25	Morton House
6	City Water Works	2	North Park
14	Clarendon Hotel	49	Oak Hill and Valley City Cemeteries
1	Comstock Park	27	Peninsular Club
20	County Court House	29	Post Office
35	County Jail	26	Powers Opera House
50	Country Club	32	Pythian Temple
21½	Crescent Park	51	Ramona Pavilion
7	D. G. H. & M. Depot	54	Recreation Park
37	Eagle Hotel	34	St. Cecilia Society Bldg.
1	Fair Grounds	8	St. John's Orphan Asylum
33	Fulton Street Park	46	St. Mary's Hospital
13	Germania Hall	47	St. Ry. Power House
30	Grand Rapids Board of Trade	19	Sweets Hotel
		18	Turner Hall
11	G. R. & I. Bridge St. Depot	36	U. B. A. Home
17	Highland Park	44	Union Depot
16	Holland A. B. A. Home	40½	Warwick Hotel

Map of Grand Rapids Streetcar System and Grand Rapids
Three Summer Resorts-Where They Are and How to Find Them.

Grand Rapids Evening Press, 30 June 1900

Chapter 6: Electric Railway Operations in the New Century (1900-1909)

Hall Street carbarn showing doors to shops and car storage. Note that the arched window in the foreground can still be seen today, although it is bricked up.

Hilldebrandt Collection

New Hall Street Carbarn

The street railway began constructing a new carbarn with a thirty-foot ceiling during 1900 on the site of the old barn on Hall Street just east of Division Avenue. The right half of the new brick carbarn was about 150 feet wide and was used for storing as many as 80 streetcars. Each track in the car storage section of the building had its own direct outlet. The west side of the Hall Street carbarn housed a carpenter shop, machine shop and paint shop. There was a two-story employees' waiting room in the car storage section of the building.

1901 Streetcar Schedules

Clarence M. Clark, the son of E. W. Clark from Philadelphia, arrived in Grand Rapids in mid-January 1901 to evaluate the Grand Rapids Railway Company of which he was the vice-president, and to attend a board of directors' meeting. He was pleased with the progress the company had made since its reorganization the previous year.

Clark also drew attention to the fact the company was seeking an amendment to the franchise to enable it to lessen the service frequency on streetcar lines not operating on a paying basis while improving service on lines with higher ridership. The company needed to be able to plan and operate its own routes to better accommodate the riding public and at the same time remain afloat financially.

New Streetcars Ordered

The Jewett Car Company of Newark, Ohio, built ten new double-truck open streetcar bodies which started arriving in Grand Rapids during May 1901. The company shops outfitted the new cars with wires, motors, and trucks. These new streetcars were five feet longer than the big cars already running on several Grand Rapids lines. The cars were equipped with twenty-eight wooden seats that faced the front of the car and could seat fifty-six passengers. Each car had a wide center aisle which provided standing room for another forty-four riders. This made each new car the equivalent of two ordinary Grand Rapids streetcars then in use.

The new open Jewett streetcars differed from the open "bloomer" cars currently in use in Grand Rapids by dispensing with dangerous running boards. The only way one could enter or leave a car was via the front or rear platform. The sides of the car were built up to a point even with the seats. The motors mounted on the heavy trucks provided an aggregate of 120-horsepower. The electrically-lit signs were not mounted on the top of the car. Instead, the electric light signs were mounted on the front and rear of the car about four to five feet off the ground.

Old Horsecars Burned

The streetcar company ignited several bonfires to burn fifteen antiquated horsecars behind the old Canal Street car barn in late January 1901. These old horsecars were consigned to the flames not only to dispose of them but also to harvest what little iron they possessed. Four old cable cars were still in use as trailers or electric motor cars. The company also planned to scrap those four cars in the future.

The Street Railways of Grand Rapids

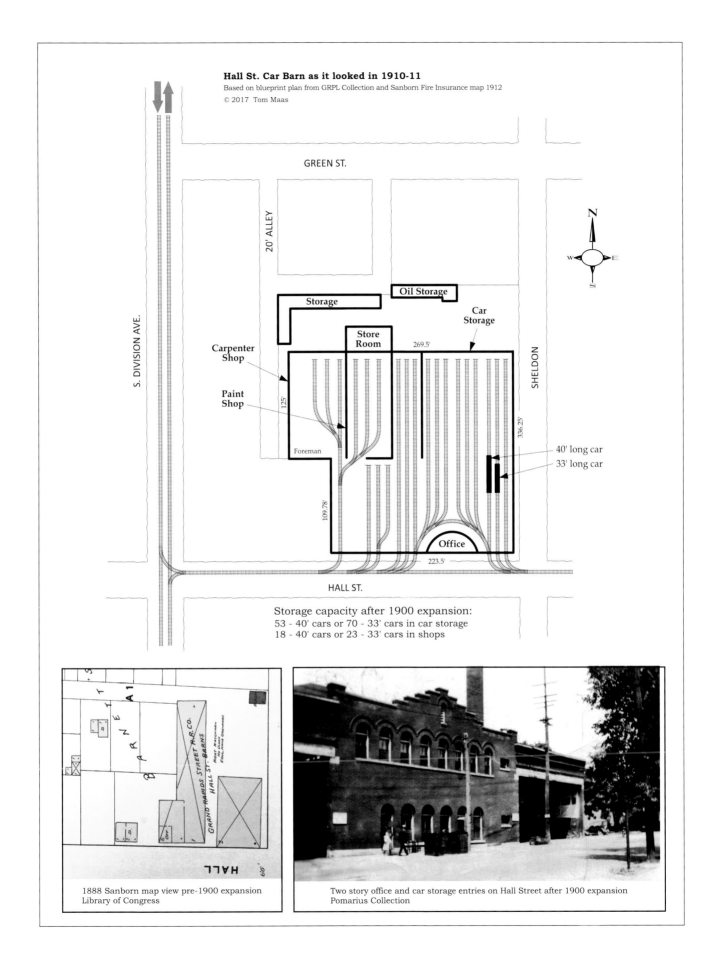

Hall St. Car Barn as it looked in 1910-11

Based on blueprint plan from GRPL Collection and Sanborn Fire Insurance map 1912

© 2017 Tom Maas

GREEN ST.

20' ALLEY

N
W E
S

Storage

Oil Storage

Car Storage

Carpenter Shop

Store Room

269.5'

SHELDON

Paint Shop

125'

Foreman

336.25'

40' long car

33' long car

109.78'

Office

223.5'

S. DIVISION AVE.

HALL ST.

Storage capacity after 1900 expansion:
53 - 40' cars or 70 - 33' cars in car storage
18 - 40' cars or 23 - 33' cars in shops

1888 Sanborn map view pre-1900 expansion
Library of Congress

Two story office and car storage entries on Hall Street after 1900 expansion
Pomarius Collection

Opening Up a Blocked Line.

Sketch of a snow sweeper car in a blizzard "Opening Up a Blocked Line."

Grand Rapids Herald, 03 Feb 1901

Magnetic Brakes for Hill Streetcars

General Manager Johnson wanted better brakes for Grand Rapids streetcars that traveled up and down the city's steep hills. Johnson visited Pittsburgh, a city with more and steeper hills than Grand Rapids, and was impressed with the Westinghouse magnetic brakes Pittsburgh streetcars had been using for over a year. To stop the car, the motorman made the electro-magnetic brake shoe go down to make contact with the rail where the magnetic brake shoe was held in place by the electric current. The Grandville line cars were the first to be equipped with the new magnetic brakes to enable the cars to stop on the steep Grandville Avenue hill between Wealthy and Franklin streets. The locally designed hand brakes the motormen had been using were kept on the cars so that if the magnetic brakes failed the motorman could still stop his car (with effort) with the hand-operated brake.

Streetcar Slides Backwards into a Steam Locomotive

A Grandville Avenue streetcar was going southwest up the steep hill south of Wealthy Street when it had to stop to let a passenger off the car. The motorman tried to resume his upward trip, but the car began sliding backwards on the slippery track. The car slid all the way down to the bottom of the hill where a Pere

Marquette locomotive was standing, waiting for a switch to be thrown.

Most of the passengers hurriedly abandoned the car as it slid downhill, but several were still on board when the streetcar slammed into the steam locomotive. The rear vestibule of the streetcar was demolished, but fortunately the passengers only received "injuries of a trifling kind." Six months later the incident was repeated but with a different streetcar and a different Pere Marquette locomotive.

Battling West Michigan's "Annual Disasters"

Located only twenty-five miles inland from Lake Michigan, Grand Rapids is on the eastern edge of what is known as the "lake shore effect" snow belt. Snow storms caused major problems for Grand Rapids streetcar operation so frequently that one can legitimately call the response "fighting west Michigan's annual disaster."

Snowstorms were just one of the weather problems encountered. Numerous electric motors were damaged when lightning struck the trolley wire. Melting snow caused water to accumulate in low spots on the streets causing the car motors to short out. Heavy rain storms in the summer also caused problems for traction motors.

New Powerhouse is Built

The Grand Rapids Railway Company built a new, larger powerhouse on Market Street just east of Godfrey Avenue in 1901. The new engine and its generator, rated at 800 kilowatts, were similar to their older counterparts in the lower Lyon Street powerhouse. Soon after the new equipment went into operation, the old engine and generator were moved to become a second unit in the new powerhouse. The new powerhouse had space for a third, even larger engine of 1,200 or 1,500 kilowatt capacity.

Two years later a huge new engine was installed in the Market Street power plant that greatly increased the power produced at this location. Additional power power was required to operate the newer and heavier cars with their more powerful motors.

The Interurbans Arrive

The Grand Rapids, Holland and Lake Michigan Rapid Railway became the first electric interurban to run into Grand Rapids. Construction of the "Holland Interurban," began at Jenison, six miles southwest of the Grand Rapids city limits in October 1900. The Grand Rapids-Jenison section of the Grand Rapids, Holland and Lake Michigan Railway was informally opened on July 9, 1901, when Benjamin

The Street Railways of Grand Rapids

The street railway company built this large coal burning powerhouse on Market Street just east of Godfrey Avenue. It opened in 1901.

Hilldebrandt Collection

Hanchett took a group of guests on a new double-ended Grand Rapids streetcar to Jenison and back.

The twenty-five year history of the Holland interurban cars running in Grand Rapids and suburbs such as Wyoming Park, Grandville, and Jenison (1901-1926) and the five-year history of the United Suburban Railway that ran only as far as Jenison (1927-1932) are covered in greater detail in Chapter 10.

The Grand Rapids, Grand Haven and Muskegon Railway (GRGH&MRy) was the second interurban to serve Grand Rapids. The "Muskegon Interurban" entered Grand Rapids on West Leonard Street at the Walker-Bristol street intersection in 1902.

The twenty-six year history of the Muskegon interurban operating in the suburbs is also covered in greater detail in Chapter 10.

Looping Interurban Cars in Downtown Grand Rapids

Both the Holland and the Muskegon interurban cars that operated in Grand Rapids were single ended and required a loop or wye to reverse direction. The streetcar company had built tracks on Ottawa and Lyon streets in downtown Grand Rapids during 1900 to form

a loop with Monroe and Canal streets so the interurban cars could easily reverse direction without having to wye, which would have delayed all streetcars going through Campau Square.

The streetcar company had to improve the 1900 downtown loop by building new switches with wider curves on Monroe Avenue so the big interurban cars could more easily navigate the curves without derailing. The Holland interurban cars were to leave the loop via Market and Grandville Avenues while the Muskegon interurban cars were to leave the loop via Canal Street (now lower Monroe Ave.), Bridge Street, Scribner Avenue, and finally West Leonard Street. This enabled the longer Holland and Muskegon interurban cars to reverse direction by circling two blocks, and leave downtown Grand Rapids on the same street on which they had entered downtown. Four years later, the radius of the curves was tightened four years later whe residents complained about the wider arrangement taking up too much space.

Grand Rapids streetcar No. 263, a new double-ended car, was chosen by Benjamin Hanchett to be the first electric car to run between Grand Rapids and Jenison. Only double-ended Grand Rapids streetcars were assigned to the Grand Rapids-Jenison interurban route

200. Michigan Avenue, Grand Rapids, Mich.

Bird's eye view colorized postcard. View looking west towards the Bridge Street bridge about 1908.

Thomas Dilley Collection

until the downtown loop was improved.

Until these improvements were made the Holland interurban company leased double-ended Grand Rapids streetcars to enable the company to begin operation between suburban Jenison and downtown Grand Rapids in early July 1901.

First Interurban Cars Travel into Grand Rapids

Passenger coach No. 14 of the Grand Rapids, Holland and Lake Michigan Rapid Railway was unloaded at the Detroit, Grand Haven and Milwaukee Railroad depot adjacent Plainfield Avenue in Grand Rapids on July 25, 1901. This was the first interurban car to ride over street railway's rails while being towed by a streetcar to the Hall Street carbarn. There it was to be outfitted so it could begin operation between Grand Rapids and Jenison the next day.

The new interurban car created much excitement while being towed through the streets. The car was much larger than the streetcars as it looked more like a Pullman sleeping car in comparison. The exterior color of the interurban car also drew attention to it as it was being towed. The car was painted a deep maroon with silver decoration and silver lettering making it stand out it in comparison to the orange-yellow color of the local streetcars.

Interurban cars finally were able to operate a regular schedule between Holland and

Grand Rapids on Monday, October 14, 1901. A person could ride from Holland to anywhere in Grand Rapids for forty-nine cents which included five cents for traveling into Grand Rapids. An interurban passenger could get a free transfer ticket to ride anywhere in the city on a Grand Rapids streetcar.

The street railway company extended its West Leonard Street line west going up the high hill between two cemeteries and down to the city limit at Bristol and Walker avenues in early fall 1901. The Grand Rapids, Grand Haven and Muskegon Railway was busy building the eastern end of its interurban line on West Leonard Street to the Grand Rapids city limit where the interurban would continue into Grand Rapids on street railway track.

A New Streetcar Line

The streetcar company also built a stub line to serve northeast Grand Rapids. Streetcars began running on the new Carrier Street line on August 3, 1901. This short one-mile-long line ran east up steep Carrier Street from the Plainfield Avenue streetcar line to College Avenue where the track turned north on College Avenue only to deadend at the country club adjacent to a golf course. While this line served a rapidly growing northeast Grand Rapids neighborhood, local legend had raised the issue that the Carrier Street line was built so Mrs. Hanchett could take her lady friends to

The Street Railways of Grand Rapids

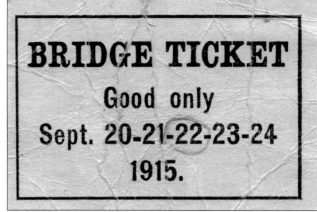

Front side and back side of 3 cent street railway toll bridge ticket from 1915.

Ed Bawden Collection

the country club. At least two motormen lost control of their streetcars going westbound down the steep Carrier Street hill, stopping only when they slammed into a grocery store on the west side of Plainfield Avenue during the first eighteen months of operation on Carrier street.

A total of eleven million passengers rode the streetcars in Grand Rapids during 1901. Some of these eleven million passengers were transferred from one line to another and were counted twice. Certain passengers such as firemen, policemen, and public officials were not required to pay a fare.

Modern carbarns, shops, and a powerhouse had been built in 1901 to provide more reliable service. Thousands of dollars were spent buying new streetcars and heavier rail was laid on several stretches of track. The street railway did not plan to make any large capital expenditures for 1902.

The street railway's old franchise required the streetcar company to pay a $5 annual license fee for each passenger streetcar in daily use. The company paid for 45 cars used daily in 1900 and for an average of 46.25 cars used daily in 1901. The statistics were calculated on the basis of daily trip sheets, not on the basis of the number of streetcars the company actually owned.

A New Year Begins

At the annual board of directors meeting on January 27, 1902, Anton Hodenpyl resigned as president of the Grand Rapids Railway but remained on the board. C. M. Clark of Philadelphia was chosen president to replace Hodenpyl, who had moved from Grand Rapids to New York City in 1901. Benjamin Hanchett was elected treasurer in addition to being re-elected secretary.

On Memorial Day in 1902, an estimated 90,000 people rode the streetcars. The company estimated each car carried more than 125 per cent of its normal carrying capacity. Approximately 20,000 of these passengers rode on the running boards or on platforms of crowded

cars without any accidents. The two engines and generators in the powerhouse ran at capacity and performed flawlessly. Over 15,000 excursionists came to Grand Rapids by train and rode the streetcars to visit one or more resorts.

Toll Bridge over the Grand River

The Grand Rapids Railway Company organized the North Park Bridge Company on April 7, 1902, to build a 600-foot-long double-track steel street railway toll bridge across the Grand River to enable streetcars to cross the river and reach the West Michigan Fairgrounds adjacent to the unincorporated village of Mill Creek (now known as Comstock Park). The North Park loop for reversing the streetcars had to be moved farther north to enable the two-track mainline to curve west before reaching the street railway toll bridge.

The construction of the toll bridge was delayed because the company received a shipment of poor-quality piles that could not safely support the temporary trestle. Streetcars began crossing the Grand River on a temporary trestle to reach the fairgrounds just before the annual fair in September 1902.

The raging waters of the Grand River carried away the temporary wooden street railway trestle and wrenched out two of the new hollow steel tubes of the street railway toll bridge under construction at North Park on March 7, 1903.

The new $40,000 double-track steel street railway toll bridge across the Grand River extended the Taylor Street-North Park line to the west Michigan fairgrounds and Mill Creek. The new bridge was completed two months later on May 15. Streetcars began running on a ten-minute schedule crossing the toll bridge over the Grand River to the village of Mill Creek a day later. Passengers had to pay an extra three cents to ride on a streetcar going across the toll bridge.

The street railway built two reversing loops: one loop just beyond the main entrance

Here we see an eastbound Grand Rapids streetcar on the double track street railway bridge over the Grand River between Mill Creek and North Park. View is looking east with the road bridge running parallel on the south side.

Gordon Hubenet Collection

Same bridge, but looking west towards Mill Creek, with the fairgrounds building on the right in the distance.

Hilldebrandt Collection

to the fairgrounds and the other loop at the far northwest end of the fairgrounds closer to Comstock Park. The Grand Rapids and Indiana Railroad built an interchange track with the street railway on the west side of the fairgrounds so that an electric freight motor could haul coal cars and other freight cars to and from the Soldiers' Home.

The street railway operated cars to and from the end of the line at the fairgrounds adjacent to the village of Mill Creek on a ten-minute schedule during the resort season, on a one- to two-minute schedule during the West Michigan Fair and on a twenty- minute schedule during the rest of the year.

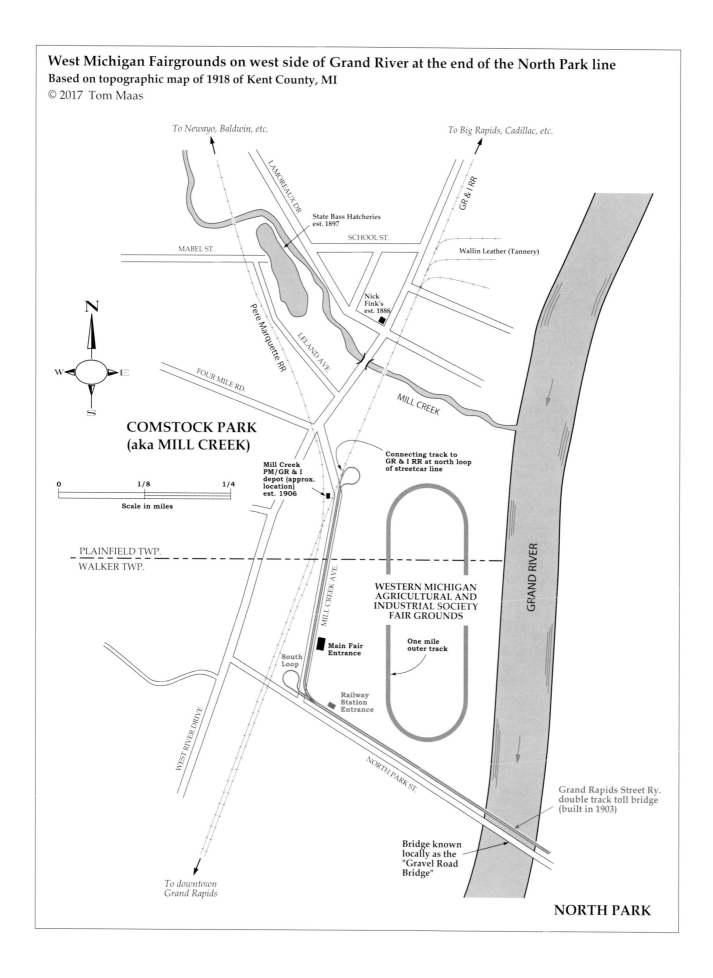

West Michigan Fairgrounds on west side of Grand River at the end of the North Park line

Based on topographic map of 1918 of Kent County, MI

© 2017 Tom Maas

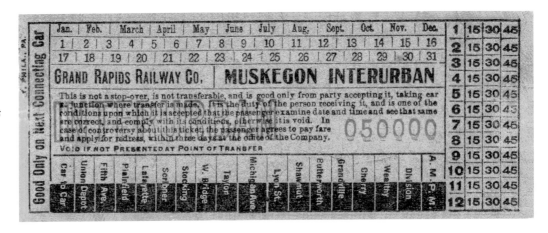

An undated and unused Muskegon (GRGH&M) Railway transfer ticket which interurban passengers could use to continue traveling in Grand Rapids on one of the street railway lines.

Richard Andrews Collection

Heavy Ridership Causes Problems

The street railway was not prepared to handle the crowds leaving the West Michigan Fair on October 2, 1902. The October 3, 1902, issue of the *Grand Rapids Press* reported the streetcar company was swamped and:

> Never in the history of Grand Rapids has the street railway been faced with such a problem as presented itself yesterday in the form of an attempt to move the great multitude who waited at the grounds for the last feature of the program, and then beat madly at the gates of the terminal house in an effort to pile on to a single car. The company was obliged to take cars off the regular traffic lines in the city and attach them to trailers, until there were upwards of 100 coaches running on the Taylor street line. The enormous drain on the trolley meant the concentration of every volt of electricity in the big feeders of that line, but even with the big wires smoking hot from the resistance, the cars could attain maximum speed only on the down grades. Today the company expects to handle nearly as many passengers as yesterday and there is not a little worry in store for the officials, who foresee great difficulty in caring for the thousands of youngsters who will board the cars, wild with delight at the prospect of a day at the fair and will ignore all thought of personal safety. The company dreads the rush that will come late in the afternoon, and every available policeman of the fair grounds and the deputies of Sheriff Chapman's force will be pressed into service at the station to see that the little ones are properly cared for. It is estimated to be little short of a miracle that out of the great crowd who fought for places on the cars of the street railway company late yesterday afternoon, none were seriously injured.

The temporary toll bridge trestle built over the Grand River in 1902 was destroyed by flood waters early in 1903.

New and Old Brakes

The first magnetic brakes that the company tested in 1901 proved to be unsatisfactory because this brake was controlled by the same lever that controlled the motors of the car. While the magnetic brake succeeded in stopping the car, the feat was accomplished so abruptly that passengers were practically hurled along the length of the car. The Westinghouse Company redesigned the magnetic brake providing the motorman with a separate controller. The street railway tested the new model which made braking more effective and smoother. The company placed an order for 100 magnetic brake systems in April. The old hand brakes were retained on the cars for emergency use.

When the cable lines were abandoned in 1891, company employees built wedge brakes that could be inserted ("wedged") into the slot of the old cable conduits. These wedge brakes helped the motorman slow or stop the car when it was coming down the steep Lyon or East Bridge Street hills. The company was very pleased to discontinue the wedge brakes when it had an alternative brake-the magnetic brake—because a wedge brake could get stuck in the conduit causing the streetcar to be jerked to an immediate stop.

Track Extensions Continue

The Muskegon interurban completed construction of its line to Grand Rapids and began operation to the city limits in February 1902. The Grand Rapids Railway added two extra streetcars to meet the Muskegon interurban cars on West Leonard Street at the city limits until arrangements for through interurban operation into downtown Grand Rapids were completed.

As soon as the Bridge Street bridge over the Grand River was modified to allow the big

interurban cars to cross it, the Muskegon interurban cars began going east into Grand Rapids on West Leonard Street, south on Scribner, east on West Bridge Street across the Grand River and finally south on Canal Street (now lower Monroe Avenue) to reach downtown.

The Muskegon cars, like the Holland interurban cars, were required to provide what was essentially a streetcar service within the city, picking up local passengers, charging them five cents, and stopping to let passengers off where requested.

Muskegon interurbans began operating on the downtown loop at the Lyon Street-Canal Street intersection to allow the single-ended cars to reverse direction for their return trips.

The Muskegon interurbans continued south on Canal street to Campau Square where the cars swung southeast on Monroe Avenue, then north on Ottawa Avenue, turned west on Lyon Street, finally reaching Canal Street. The cars then left the downtown loop and headed back toward Muskegon via Canal Street, West Bridge Street, Scribner Avenue and finally traveled west on West Leonard Street to the city limits. At this point the cars began running on Muskegon interurban track.

The street railway began building a branch from the Grandville Avenue streetcar line into the City Market in June 1902. The short branch line left Ellsworth Avenue and went west on Oakes Street, south on Market Street, west on Cherry Street and into the City Market. This branch enabled both the Holland and Muskegon interurban cars to enter the market to deliver and pick up fruit, vegetables, meat, fish, and other commodities. A wye track was built at the Ellsworth-Oakes Street intersection to permit the interurbans to turn around.

The company built a single-track line on Court Street on the west side of the river in July 1902. The track on Court Street (which became part of the north-south Scribner Ave in 1912) connected the lines running on West Bridge

Street with the line that ran on Shawmut Street. The Court Street cutoff track enabled streetcars to use either the Bridge Street bridge or the Pearl Street bridge if one of the bridges was blocked due to repairs. The Court Street cutoff track was almost immediately used when the Pearl Street bridge was shut down and rebuilt. When the Bridge Street bridge was shut down the Muskegon interurban cars used the wye at the Ottawa-Monroe Avenue intersection to turn around so that they could leave downtown and head back the same way they entered.

Both the Common Council and the street railway wanted an ordinance that would allow the company to build an extension to the Oak Hills Cemetery on the Hall Street hill. The company refused an ordinance in August that allowed it to build the cemetery extension because the council had included too many other costly projects. The Common Council finally passed an ordinance in December that gave the street railway permission to extend the Hall Street track east to the Oak Hills Cemetery without having to accept the other projects.

Company Builds Streetcar Bodies and Buys New Cars

The street railway began building new streetcar bodies during the spring of 1902. The company's shops had been repairing streetcars and rebuilding old equipment. The Hall Street car shops built a brand-new streetcar body that was the first single-truck aisle car that did not have the running boards that characterized the old "side-wheelers." The first new car was mounted on a single standard girder truck with a long wheel base and driven by motors that had been used on the hill lines. The car was assigned the number No. 200.

The company decided to build five more similar car bodies at the Hall Street shops in August with one major exception. These new open car bodies were to be built with paneled

Muskegon (GRGH&MRy) interurban car traveling east on Leonard Street hill just west of Walker Avenue and the Grand Rapids city limits. View is looking west.

Coopersville Area
Historical Society
Museum

sides that could easily be converted into closed cars ready for winter service. Five new motors were ordered for the new cars.

The Hall Street car shops began building what they expected to be seven-to-ten new streetcar bodies in January 1903. The new car bodies were to be twenty-two feet long with two six-foot-long platforms bringing the total length to thirty-four feet. The cars were to have cross seats and were slated to run on the steep grades of East Bridge and Lyon streets. Two 125-horsepower motors were to be mounted on a single girder-four wheel truck. One of the 125-horse power motors was to be mounted on the front axle of the front truck while the other 125-horsepower motor was to be mounted on the rear axle. These seven cars were to be equipped with electric brakes because electro-magnetic brakes would put too large a drain on the motors of the hill cars and shorten motor life.

Problems obtaining motors of proper size and power delayed the completion of these cars. The new cars were to be heavier, larger and seat twice as many passengers as the hill cars then in use. These cars would have to make the same time as much smaller cars then in operation on the hill line route. The street railway and the General Electric Company were attempting to solve the motor problem by using 125-horsepower General Electric No. 66 motors and testing their performance.

Only two of these hill cars were almost ready to go into commission in December 1903. These two cars were probably the heaviest powered single-truck streetcars in existence in 1903. The two 125-horsepower motors were expected to provide enough power to drive the cars up the two steep gradients on the hill route at speeds then achieved only when the hill cars ran on level ground. Both the electric brake

system and the trucks were designed by Master Mechanic Annable and were being built entirely of steel to withstand the terrific strain of accelerating and braking on the hills.

Ten new cars were needed to provide adequate service on the Wealthy Street, Division Avenue and Lafayette Avenue lines. The street railway company wanted to purchase ten double-truck convertible cars so they could be converted quickly for use in winter and again for summer operations. The cars were to be equipped with enough cross seats to accommodate sixty passengers and would be somewhat different from the cars currently in operation on the line in 1903. The company wanted to purchase the cars from one of the large car building companies, but none of the companies could promise delivery before January 1. Grand Rapids Railway decided to "do it yourself" and build these new cars in its local shops.

The street railway built two of these cars in the Hall Street shops. These experimental hill cars began running on the steep East Bridge and Lyon Street hill lines in late January 1904. These 250-horsepower cars were expected to take a heavy load of passengers up the steep hills at speeds previously attained only on level track. The new electric brakes had the power of approximately 200 horses that the motorman could use to slow down or stop by applying the brakes.

Postal Cars Become "Ghosts"

The first streetcar of what became known as the "Ghost" line or "White" line began carrying mail on July 14, 1903. The postal car had just been repainted a new color of white with gold trim stripes, which was practically a na-

Photo of one of three White Line postal streetcars.

GRPO Guide
January 1903

tional standard for U. S. Mail cars on street railways. The new colors not only improved the appearance of the postal service cars, but also made it much easier for citizens to realize that these were U. S. Mail cars and not passenger-carrying streetcars.

The street railway also began construction of two new U.S. Mail streetcars with a U. S. postal service contract for two mail cars that were to be eighteen feet in length, exclusive of platform. The street railway built two cars to be twenty feet long, six feet longer than the three fourteen-foot-long postal cars they replaced.

Streetcars Blockaded by Steam Locomotives

Streetcars running on the west side of Grand Rapids were so frequently blockaded by steam locomotives switching cars that a reporter for the *Grand Rapids Herald* employed humor in 1903 to describe the frustrations of those who left their houses on the west side in hope of getting to work on time:

> Have a large basket of lunch put up. You may also take your pajamas along if you desire to pass the night comfortably. Thus provided and having taken farewell of your friends, board a Cherry Street car. When you come to the tracks you will know that the tracks are there. Yard locomotives will be switching cars up and down across the street. Do not speak unkindly to the engineer or the motorman. The engineer thinks he is at a blind siding somewhere up north and the motorman is used to it. After you have eaten your luncheon and slept for a few hours the street car may be able to cross the tracks. If not, you can get out and walk to your destination . . .

The failure of the city to enforce its ordinance limiting the amount of time a train could block a street crossing to five minutes continued to be a problem for a street railway company that was required to run its cars on time. Almost twenty years later Benjamin Hanchett responded to complaints about streetcars not running on schedule by pointing out that one of the major reasons for this was the fault of the city because it did not enforce the five-minute time limit already on the books.

Track Extensions and Route Changes in 1903

The street railway company built a double-track extension of the Lafayette line on Hall Street 1,100 feet to the main entrance of the Oak Hill cemeteries (earlier known as Valley City Cemetery). The company also double tracked West Fulton Street from Straight Avenue, where the double track had ended, all the way west to John Ball Park by the middle of May even though the street was not yet paved.

The company also eliminated two "plug" lines by connecting the Fifth (now Franklin) Street and West Leonard Street "plug" lines to make one through line effective June 2, 1903.

Grand Rapids Railway Company reported it had spent $200,000 to pave between the rails during the past ten years or an average of $20,000 a year. The cost of paving between the rails had long been a point of contention between street railway companies and municipalities; Grand Rapids was no exception.

ANOTHER SUGGESTION

As how the switching blockade on Shawmut avenue may be avoided.

A humorous cartoon showing how the west side railroad switching blockade might be avoided by streetcar riders flying over the railroad tracks in airships.

Grand Rapids Press, 01 Oct 1901

More Streetcars and Interurbans on the Union Station Loop

It took four months of proposals and counterproposals before the Common Council and the street railway finally agreed on what streetcar lines should be rerouted to provide through line service to GR&I Union Station. The street railway company finally got the ordinance it wanted when the Common Council passed the Cherry Street car line rerouting ordinance on October 26, 1903. The Cherry Street line was rerouted to South Ionia Street, finally providing the GR&I station with a loop service in late October. The Grand Rapids, Grand Haven and Muskegon Railway obtained an agreement with the Grand Rapids Street Railway Company in October whereby all the Muskegon interurban cars would be allowed to run via Union Station which made a bigger downtown loop in Grand Rapids.

Both the Muskegon and Holland interurban railway cars carried logs to Grand Rapids for use by the furniture industry. Citizens complained that Holland interurban freight motors were towing flatcars loaded with logs on the Grandville Avenue streetcar line in early March 1903 which disrupted streetcar service.

New General Manager

Benjamin Hanchett, secretary-treasurer of the Grand Rapids Railway, was appointed general manager in February 1904 to fill the position made vacant by the death of General Manager G. Stewart Johnson.

New Cars and Rebuilds

The street railway placed an order in early January 1904 with the Cincinnati Car Company for six car bodies to be delivered by April. These bodies were similar in design to the two hill cars the company built in its shops. The company equipped the new hill cars with General Electric motors, Westinghouse magnetic brakes, and trucks built by Leitelt Iron Works, a local Grand Rapids company. The *Grand Rapids Evening Press* proudly announced that when these six cars were completed, the hill lines would then have "eight of the most modern, most powerful and safest urban electric cars in the world."

When the old hill cars stopped running on the hill lines, they were taken to the street railway's shops where they were repaired, repainted and thoroughly overhauled. The old hill cars' magnetic brakes and powerful motors made them an ideal choice for hard service on the Grandville Avenue line as it would provide that line with "a set of fast cars such as it has never seen in continuous service."

Master Mechanic Warren W. Annable completed a set of plans and specifications in April for three new combination double-truck cars for summer traffic on the Wealthy-Taylor line. They were to be two feet longer than the Division Avenue cars and built so as to be quickly convertible from summer-to-winter and winter-to-summer vehicles.

Master Mechanic Designs New Streetcar Fender

Two people died in spite of the fact that the cars that hit them were equipped with fenders that were supposed to prevent such deaths. In December the street railway company tried to cope with this continual problem by lowering fenders to give only a three-inch clearance above the rails.

The street railway tested a number of streetcar fenders during 1904. Master Mechanic W. W. Annable designed a streetcar fender that seemed to be the answer. He tested his fender against dummies the size of children and adults to determine how effective it would be in fending them off when hit by the front of a streetcar. The Common Council passed an ordinance to allow the streetcar company to use the new Annable-designed car fenders on July 18.

The city councilmen studied how the new fender performed on the city streetcars and came to an unexpected conclusion. The new Annable fender was considered a success on double-truck cars a poor choice for single-truck cars.

Aldermen considered outlawing the Annable fender in November 1906 citing too many accidents "in which the fender ground the victims hard and finally allowed them to slip under the wheels." Annable had tested his fender using dummies that "were filled with hay. Consequently they were light and offered no particular resistance when the fender hit them. The dummies appeared to be brushed off the track easily enough, but the human body, filled with something else than hay, offers too much resistance."

General Manager Hanchett defended the Annable car fender claiming it had saved many lives and said the fender was as effective as any other that might be installed. He mentioned the company had "another fender under consideration, with which it desires to experiment" and "asked the Common Council to suspend the present ordinance long enough to allow a test of the new device."

Extensions Continue in 1904

A new sidetrack extended along Court Street from West Bridge Street south to Shawmut Avenue in early April 1904. This track was needed to minimize delays when the old Bridge Street bridge across the Grand River was

6908. Stone Bridge, Grand Rapids, Mich.

The rebuilt bridge at Bridge Street is seen in this color postcard from the west bank of the Grand River looking east. The new Grand Trunk RR station with its five story tower has become a regular stop for streetcars. The large brick building seen on the right side is the Grand Rapids Brewing Company, known for their Silver Foam Beer.

Carl Bajema Collection

being replaced. The old bridge was shut down in early April and the streetcar lines using this bridge were rerouted via Court Street and across the Pearl Street bridge until early October.

The Wealthy-Scribner line streetcars were rerouted onto the GR&IRR Union Station loop providing ten-minute service to and from the Union Station. The Muskegon interurban also began to use this line.

Workmen double tracked the single-track section of West Fulton Street between Lane and Indiana avenues during the spring of 1905. The street railway also completed its extension to the Oakhill Cemetery adjacent to Hall Street. Track was relaid on Cherry Street between East Street and Carroll Avenue and on First Avenue between Division and Lafayette streets.

"Short Turning" of Streetcars Opposed

Aldermen opposed the practice of "cutting out" streetcars before reaching the end of the line. Passengers sometimes were told they had to leave an outbound streetcar before reaching their destination because the car was going to be turned back to pick up passengers waiting to ride toward downtown. Aldermen opposed "short turning" one or more cars before they reached the end of the line. The street railway company decided to do what the politicians thought they wanted. The company agreed to abandon the practice of short turning cars, but it pointed out that it was often

necessary to maintain schedules.

Two weeks later an alderman introduced a resolution to allow the street railway to "cut out" cars and turn them back on the West Bridge-Grandville line because cars on this particular route had to cross five railroad tracks. Delays from trains on the crossings caused the cars on this particular line to become more bunched together than on other routes. Such occurrences gave rise to a joke that found popularity among streetcar riders of Grand Rapids:

Question: "Can you tell me why the streetcars in this here town are like bananas?"
Answer: "Because they are yellow and they come in bunches."

New Streetcars Arrive in 1905

Three new double-truck car bodies ordered in 1904 arrived at the Hall Street shops in early January 1905 where they were prepared for service. The new car bodies were practically the same size and design as the double-truck cars already in service on the Division-Plainfield and Stocking-Lafayette Street car lines. No motors or trucks had been ordered for these cars because Grand Rapids Railway had initially planned to use the cars as extras. When one of the big cars needed refinishing, wiring, or repainting, the old car body was lifted from the trucks and one of the three new car bodies was substituted for continued operation.

The three new cars were reported to be the finest street cars ever brought to Grand Rapids. They had windows four feet in width similar to that of a railroad lounge or dining car. These new car bodies also were heavier because they were partially constructed of steel.

The Kuhlman Car Company built ten new semi-convertible streetcars for Grand Rapids Railway in the spring of 1905. These big double-truck cars had four motors and were equipped with rattan seats for forty-eight passengers. The cars, which cost $5,000 each, were running on Grand Rapids streets by June.

Another ten Kuhlman Car Company cars of the same class arrived in November. Most if not all of these cars were placed in service on the Division and Grandville Avenue streetcar lines. The *Grand Rapids Evening Press's* report of the Grand Rapids Railways annual meeting on January 23, 1906, drew attention to the fact that while these twenty cars were built in Cleveland, they were designed in the shops of the street railway company in Grand Rapids.

Equipping Cars with Meters

Two cars were equipped with meters to measure how much electricity a motorman used while operating his streetcar. The amount of electricity a motorman used during a day necessarily depended upon the miles he traveled, the number of passengers he carried and the number of stops he made. The amount of electricity a motorman used also depended on factors he could influence, such as coasting vs. braking when approaching a curve, or speeding up and slowing down to stop and pick up passengers. Motormen who used more than the estimated amount were promptly informed that wasting electric energy "decreases the dividends of the stockholders and is not permissible under any circumstances."

What Type of Rail Should be Used?

The Grand Rapids Common Council aldermen and the street railway company fought over many issues. An important and potentially the most expensive issue involved what type of rail the company could use on its routes in Grand Rapids. Street railway franchises usually had a clause that either prohibited certain types of rails or specified the type of rails that could be used in the initial construction and when new rail was used to replace old worn-out rail. One of the many debates over the type of rail to be used occurred in 1904 and early 1905.

Some Common Council aldermen wanted to require the street railway company to use Trilby grooved rail whenever worn-out rail was

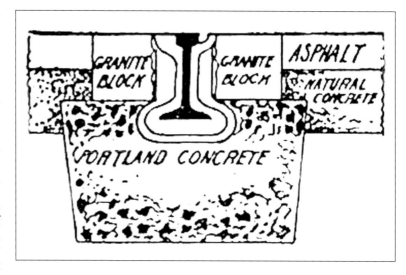

Diagram of t-rail with granite blocks design.

Grand Rapids Evening Press, 16 Dec 1904

replaced and whenever new rail was laid. Trilby rail was already being used on the Bridge Street bridge in Grand Rapids. General Manager Hanchett championed "Shanghai" rail which was T-rail with two rows of granite blocks fitted up to it, giving the grooved effect. This combination of T-rail and granite blocks was being used in the harsh Minneapolis climate to good effect and Hanchett believed this combination would work well in Grand Rapids with its similarly cold and snowy winters.

Alderman Rowson visited Saginaw, Michigan, to study how well grooved rail was working. Unfortunately, the groove became clogged with pebbles and dirt. Winter snow and ice compacted in the groove in the winter hampering electrical conductivity. The combination of T-rail with block ears proved to be the better option in Saginaw as it kept more of the dirt and ice out of the flangeways.

T-rail had several advantages over the Trilby grooved rail especially when used with block ears. The T-rails were much cheaper than the Trilby rails, an important consideration for the cost-conscious street railway company. It was also claimed that the wheels of a streetcar rode on top of the T-rail whereas with any of the other rail styles there was a side grind that soon wore out the rails. Grand Rapids Railway Master Mechanic Annable demonstrated how the wheels of an interurban car running on Trilby grooved rail gradually caused the Trilby rail to bend and knock pavement out of alignment.

The big advantage T-rail had over girder rail lay in the T-rail's "center-bearing" properties. The entire weight of the car rested on the center of the rail rendering impossible any tendency toward the tipping of the rail; on the old girder rails, the weight of the car was unevenly distributed causing excessive wear.

The Common Council spent nine months debating the type of rail to be placed in Grand Rapids streets before finally adopting an ordinance on April 17, 1905. The ordinance granted the Grand Rapids Railway's wish to lay Shanghai center-bearing T-rails with brick or granite "ears."

Girder rails weighing sixty-six pounds to the yard and nearly twenty-five years old, were pulled out from Monroe and Fulton streets in 1908 and replaced by new heavier T-rail weighing eighty pounds to the yard. The old lighter rail was strong enough to accommodate the lightweight cars used in the 1890s, but rails of more substance were needed in 1908 to accommodate the newer, heavier cars.

The joints between adjacent rails in the track began to be electrically welded in 1908 rather than being cast iron welded as was done during the previous eight years.

Controversy over Smoking Lights Up

Should smokers be allowed to smoke inside, on the platform, or no place at all on a streetcar? The Muskegon and the Holland interurban cars had smoking compartments for that purpose. The debate between those who wanted to smoke and those who did not want to inhale tobacco smoke-laden air while riding on a Grand Rapids streetcar heated up during the spring of 1905. One writer urged the street railway to have a motor streetcar for nonsmokers and a trailer car for smokers. The Common Council passed an ordinance that banned smoking on the rear platform of streetcars.

State Law Changed to Allow for Municipal Ownership

The State legislature passed a new charter for the city of Grand Rapids in June 1905 that allowed for the city of Grand Rapids to purchase its public utilities including the street railway company.

Common Stock Holders Finally Get a Dividend

The Grand Rapids Railway Company finally was able to pay the first dividend on common stock since the stock was issued five years earlier. Unfortunately, the payment of such dividends was to be exception rather than the rule during the course of the company's existence.

Improvements Planned for 1906

The Grand Rapids Railway Company announced that the company was not going to build any new extensions of streetcar lines during 1906. Instead it planned to spend $270,000 to improve existing track, for paving costs between tracks, to improve the powerhouse so

there was sufficient power for the heavy summer traffic, for new streetcar motors and car repairs, and for enlarging carbarns.

One of the most expensive track improvement projects involved Scribner Avenue where the city planned to lay new pavement. The street railway company's cost associated with installing new track and paving costs was estimated to total $62,000.

The Grand Rapids Railway decided in August 1906 it was not going to build any new streetcar line extensions or new lines during the remaining fifteen years of its franchise, due to expire in 1921, unless the city's new charter was amended. The street railway company did not want to come under the municipal ownership provision of the charter. The company interpreted this to mean that if Grand Rapids Railway accepted any new ordinance to build an extension or new line in the future, the city could automatically exercise its option under the provision to purchase the transit property.

Some citizens, including Common Council aldermen, wanted to organize a municipal street railway to build the lines the current company was refusing to build or extend. The *Grand Rapids Herald* published an editorial on September 15, 1906, that was very critical of any plan to organize a street railway to compete with the Grand Rapids Railway Company's streetcar system. The editorial writer pointed out that such a strategy had been tried before in Grand Rapids and the result had been disastrous. The cable railway became a major competitor with the old horsecar company and both were on the verge of bankruptcy when the two companies were merged in 1890 to form the Consolidated Street Railway. This 1890 merger added about $2,000,000 to the capitalization of the street railway system and increased the interest charges on the debt.

The Grand Rapids Common Council declared it was in favor of municipal ownership of street railway lines, and adopted a resolution requesting the state legislature to support an amendment to the state constitution to allow municipalities to own and operate street railways. The Common Council even went so far as to have estimates made to determine the cost of building the proposed street railway lines within the city.

The Grand Rapids Railway Company originally had planned to extend three streetcar lines out of ten proposed extensions during 1907: East Bridge Street from East Avenue to Diamond Avenue; Fifth Avenue from East Avenue to Carlton Avenue; remove track on Coit Avenue to Sweet Street, and relay rail on Plainfield Avenue as far as Sweet Street.

However, Grand Rapids Street Railway President C. M. Clark concluded the street railway company could not afford to build any of the proposed extensions. Clark went on to state

that, "If the Grand Rapids Railway was making money we would not hesitate for a minute to spend it. In the seven years in which I have been here, we have spent all the profits and twice again as much in improvements." The street railway was spending money in 1907 to buy new cars. Daniel Campbell, master of construction for the Grand Rapids Railway, reported the company spent approximately $250,000 in 1906 on rail replacement and anticipated expenditures for rail replacement in 1907 would be about the same.

Open Cars Phased Out

The streetcar company was slowly getting rid of its old open summer cars by selling them off to smaller and less modern properties or just stripping the cars and dumping the car bodies. The old open cars were being replaced almost entirely by convertible cars that could quickly be changed from open to closed cars.

Private Car "Honolulu"

General Manager Hanchett purchased a special private car in 1906 designed to accommodate private trolley parties. Although the car was to be used primarily by the general manager and his guests, the car also could be chartered by private parties for daylight or moonlight trolley rides.

The private car, christened the *Honolulu*, was built by the Cincinnati Car Company. The open car was twenty-three feet long (interior measurement not including platform), and was mounted on a long single truck. There was an observation platform on the end of the car and it was brilliantly lit by electricity. The *Honolulu* was equipped with two forty-horse-power motors and had a maximum speed of thirty miles an hour. The interior of the *Honolulu* was finished in mahogany and there were twelve leather-upholstered easy chairs. There was also a compartment where luncheons could be prepared.

The streetcar named "Honolulu" is posed with passengers and crew in front of the Hall Street carbarn.

Dave Winick Collection at Grand Rapids Public Museum

THE HONOLULU

The private car Honolulu, belonging to the Grand Rapids Railway company, has been purchased by General Manager Hanchett for the accommodation of private trolley parties. The car nicely accommodates twenty passengers, and furnishes means for a delightful and refreshing ride about Grand Rapids. It is placed at the disposal of the entire riding public and may be secured for daylight or moonlight trolley rides at a very reasonable price per hour, by telephoning J. C. Madigan, superintendent of transportation.

A newspaper ad featured the Honolulu as a car that can be chartered.

Grand Rapids Press, 01 Jan 1907

Water Sprinkler Cars Wet Down the Dust

A letter to the May 16, 1904, "Public Pulse" column in the *Grand Rapids Evening Press* asked, "Will the Grand Rapids Street Railway company put on sprinkling cars this summer so that a householder living near its lines may open a door or window to let in fresh air without filling the house with a shower of germ-laden filthy street dust?" The letter writer went on to complain about the unsanitary conditions of the air they breathed last summer. "Do you remember the odors of our streets and alleys on a hot day last summer? Will we miss them this summer? Let us hope so."

Sprinkler car No. 1, purchased in 1906, was a 2,480 gallon single-truck Brill centrifugal tank car. It was equipped with electromagnetic brakes similar to the brakes used on the hill line passenger street cars. The motors for sprinkler car No. 1 were chosen because they produced enough power to move the car with a full tank of water up either the steep East Bridge Street or Lyon Street grades.

Sprinkler car No. 2 purchased in 1907 was a 4,224-gallon double-truck Brill centrifugal tank car equipped with air brakes. This car was equipped with Brill No. 27-G2 trucks with a four-foot, six-inch wheelbase. Four forty-horsepower motors were installed on the trucks. Air for the brakes was compressed by a separate motor and compressor into tanks hung on the side frames. Both sprinkler cars could deliver water from storage tanks to the sprinkler nozzles under pressure capable of sprinkling a distance of up to fifty feet.

New Streetcars Arrive

Ten new cars were built at the Kuhlman Car Company in Cleveland in the spring of 1907 for use on the Division Avenue streetcar line. Six of these cars were thirty-foot-long double-truck cars.

The company ordered ten additional new double-truck cars on July 1, 1907. These cars were of the same type as the ones added to the Cherry Street line the previous year at the cost of the $5,000 each. The Division Avenue cars that these ten cars replaced were

The Grand Rapids Railway single truck sprinkler car No. 1, built by the J. G. Brill Co., had a capacity of 2,480 gallons.

Karl Heckman Collection

The Grand Rapids Railway two-truck sprinkler car No. 2, also built by the J. G. Brill Co., had a capacity of 4,224 gallons.

Historical Society of Pennsylvania

to be switched over to the Grandville Avenue line. The ten new semi-convertible cars were forty-three and one-half feet long, equipped with forty-horsepower motors, Brill trucks, and dash headlights. The cars were also equipped with Dietrich automatic apron trip fenders, the same as those on cars already in service.

New Dam Projects

Two ambitious hydroelectric power dam projects on the Muskegon River were completed in 1906 and 1907 by the Grand Rapids and Muskegon Power Company. The first to be completed was the Rogers Dam. This earthen-filled embankment dam, located fifty-one miles north of Grand Rapids on the Muskegon River, started generating 66,000 v AC of electricity in March of 1906. The power was intended to be shared between Grand Rapids, Muskegon, Holland and surrounding communities.

Only six miles away, the forty-foot high, reinforced concrete Croton Dam started operating in September of 1907. Soon, this newer dam would be producing 100,000 v AC using newly-invented transmission technology to attract visitors from around the world. As a result of this new surplus of electricity, the streetcar company decided to idle its big steam engines at the Market street power plant, keeping them maintained only for emergency power generation. Another result of these projects was the early adoption of electric tungsten lamp street lighting in Grand Rapids in 1908.

Carbarns Remodeled

The two-story brick Wealthy Street carbarn, located on the south side of Wealthy street just west of the Lake Street (now Lake Drive) intersection, was built in 1892. The carbarn covered an area 296 by 80 by feet. The facility was extensively remodeled during 1906-1907. An eighty-eight-foot clear span arched truss was put in place at the Wealthy Street facility at the beginning of 1907. The company built a club with several rooms for employees. This carbarn was a busy location for streetcar motormen and conductors at the beginning and end of their day's work. These employees enjoyed a restaurant, a reading room, a billiard room, and a dormitory. The addition to the building virtually doubled the streetcar storage capacity of the carbarn.

1908 Rail Replacement and Track Construction

The street railway built 1.17 miles of track extensions in 1908 including the West Bridge Street line west between Garfield and Valley avenues; the Plainfield Avenue line northeast from Caledonia Street to Palmer Avenue; and the Fifth Street line east from Eastern Avenue to Alto Avenue. The part of Fifth Street line between Madison Avenue and Eastern Avenue was double tracked. Almost 2 ½ miles of old worn-out rail also were replaced by heavier T-rail. The Grand Rapids Railway Company spent about $100,000 on improvements in 1908.

Streetcar Skids Down East Bridge Street Hill

Motorman Skiff stopped streetcar No. 302 at the top of East Bridge Street hill on January 21, 1908. Conductor Nichols made the required inspection of the brakes before signaling Skiff to start their westbound car down the ten per cent grade. They had hardly started their descent before the wheels of the car began to slide on the slippery rail rendering both the hand and electric brakes useless.

The streetcar began to pick up speed so rapidly that the four passengers and crew of two were unable to jump as the car skidded down the steep hill. Fortunately the car hit some sand on the track and skidded off the rails, tipping on its side into a trench previously dug for a sewer. While the four passengers were frightened and shaken up, none of them was seriously injured.

A similar incident happened on Lyon Street hill. This time it was Car 301 and it stayed upright.

City Opposes Use of Ottawa Street to Lay Over Interurban Cars

The city manager notified the Grand Rapids Railway Company that the storing of interurban cars on Ottawa street had been carried to the extreme and cars not in immediate use were to be stored elsewhere.

Annual Report for 1909

The 1909 annual report given at the Grand Rapids Railway Company's annual meeting held in January 1910 provided information about the company's activities in 1909:

A total of 20,780,000 passengers were carried and 5,735,167 transfers were issued in 1909. The street cars made a total run of 3,660,955 miles, a daily average per car of 160.96 miles of which 34.5 miles was on paved streets and 21.5 miles on unpaved streets. During the year the company paved between the tracks in Wealthy Avenue, Division, Monroe, West Leonard, East Leonard and Lafayette streets, to a total of 4.16 miles at a cost of $35,584. In reconstruction and other improvements including the paving tax, the expenditures were $197,687 for the year. The cost of equipment maintenance was $744 per car-mile, and of track maintenance $728 per track-mile. The electric welding of the rails, which was done last summer, cost $15,196. The amount expended on wages totaled $344,000, or nearly $1,000 a day, and the number of employes averaged 530.

What Was Accomplished in the Twentieth Century's First Decade?

In the spring of 1900 the Consolidated Street Car Company "was on the verge of bankruptcy, hardly earning interest charges and with a service that made people smile when they didn't have to ride and swear when they did." Anton Hodenpyl played a major role in buying out the Chicago interests in 1900. The old company was reorganized as the Grand Rapids Railway Company and adopted the policy of "trying to please the people" while making money at the same time. What did Anton Hodenpyl of Grand Rapids and C. M. Clark of Philadelphia accomplish during the ten years since they took control of the Grand Rapids Street Railway from Cummings and O'Dell of Chicago in 1900?

The 1909 annual report drew attention to the accomplishments of the past ten years,

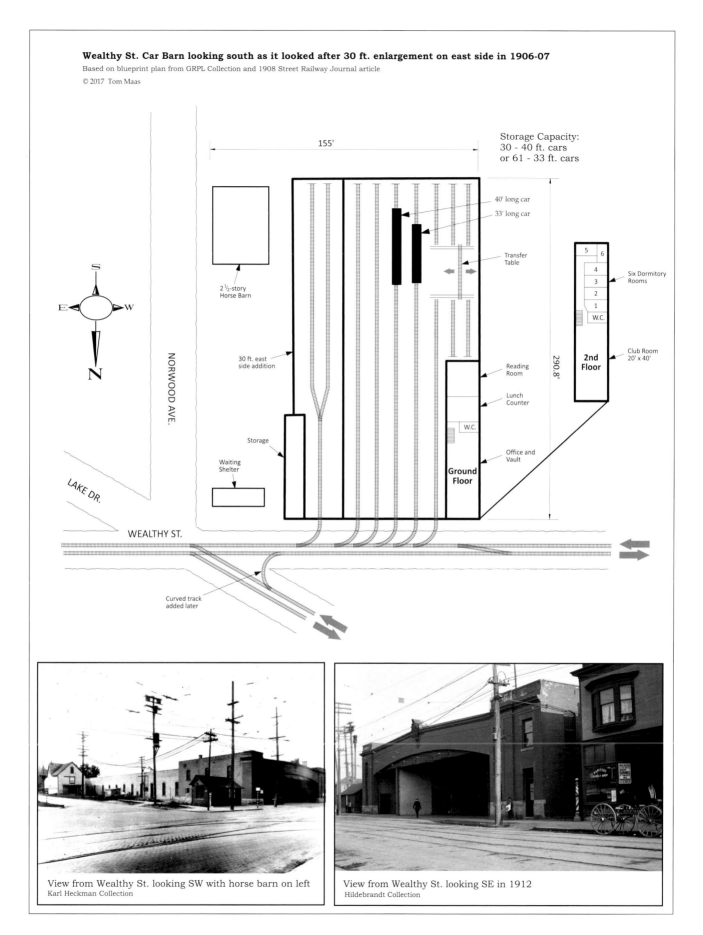

Wealthy St. Car Barn looking south as it looked after 30 ft. enlargement on east side in 1906-07
Based on blueprint plan from GRPL Collection and 1908 Street Railway Journal article
© 2017 Tom Maas

155'

Storage Capacity:
30 - 40 ft. cars
or 61 - 33 ft. cars

40' long car

33' long car

Transfer Table

2 ½-story Horse Barn

30 ft. east side addition

Storage

Waiting Shelter

NORWOOD AVE.

LAKE DR.

WEALTHY ST.

Curved track added later

Reading Room

Lunch Counter

W.C.

Office and Vault

Ground Floor

290.8'

5 6
4
3
2
1
W.C.

Six Dormitory Rooms

2nd Floor

Club Room 20' x 40'

View from Wealthy St. looking SW with horse barn on left
Karl Heckman Collection

View from Wealthy St. looking SE in 1912
Hildebrandt Collection

Map of Wealthy Street Carbarn showing tracks inside the car house and the location of the street car transfer table.

THE BILLIARD ROOM, SHOWING ARTISTIC SETTING

A ROOM OF THE DORMITORY

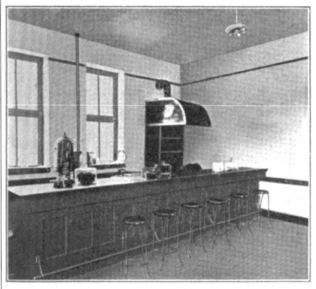

THE LUNCH COUNTER

THE READING ROOM

Interior views of the rebuilt Wealthy Street car house showing the accommodations available for use by employees of the streetcar company.

Street Railway Journal, 11 Jan 1908

Car No. 301 off the tracks on Lyon Street hill, winter of 1911.

Rebecca Smith-Hoffman Collection

Postcard showing Canal Street lit up at night.

Carl Bajema Collection

CANAL STREET AT NIGHT, GRAND RAPIDS, MICH. 6916.

1909 "Getting Crowded" cartoon captures some of the chaos experienced by one who dares to travel on foot in Campau Square.

Grand Rapids Press, 30 Jul 1909

stating that during this time 53.31 miles of the street railway had been rebuilt and only 9 miles of original track remained. Less than ten per cent of the cars in regular use in 1909 were in use in 1900. The total cost of reconstructing the track, building a larger powerhouse, buying new street-cars while rebuilding old electric cars, and other related expenses was estimated to be $2,167,397.00. The company also made enough money during the past ten years to not only pay interest on the debt it inherited in 1900 but to also pay some dividends to its stockholders.

Dealing with Economic Problems

The Grand Rapids Street Car Company, like many privately-owned public utilities, was having a difficult time trying to earn enough money from fares to cover the costs of operating a street railway system. There were three ways a street railway could increase income. It could raise the cost of fares, but too often this led to more individuals choosing to walk or seek other means of transportation.

The Grand Rapids street railway was able to increase the number of fare-paying passengers by operating three resorts: Ramona Park, North Park Resort, and John Ball Park, the latter owned by the city. Crowds of 20,000 were not unusual at both the Ramona and North Park resorts on a holiday while 10,000-15,000 passengers enjoyed John Ball Park.

The third and very obvious way a streetcar company could increase its income was by lowering its operating expenses. The Grand Rapids Railway Company was able to purchase new streetcars and rebuild some of its older cars which not only increased ridership but

GETTING RATHER CROWDED

The Campau square of the future, as we may expect to see it.

lowered operating costs at the same time. These new streetcars became known as Pay-As-You-Enter cars and they were to become the standard streetcar in Grand Rapids.

Grand Rapids Streetcar Operations (1910-1924)

New Owner of Grand Rapids Street Railway System

The annual meeting of the Grand Rapids Railway Company on January 25, 1910, marked ten years since Anton Hodenpyl and E. W. Clark took control of the street railway system. Benjamin Hanchett, a twenty-seven-year veteran employee, was elected president of the Grand Rapids Railway in addition to serving as general manager, a position he had held since 1904. Louis J. DeLamarter, assistant secretary, was advanced to secretary and assistant treasurer.

The Commonwealth Power, Railway & Light Company was incorporated on February 14, 1910, and took control of the Grand Rapids Railway as well as numerous other gas, electric, and traction companies. The organizers of this holding company included Hodenpyl, Hardy & Co. of New York, E. W. Clark & Co. of Philadelphia, and W. A. Foote of Jackson, Michigan.

Improvements and Extensions

The Grand Rapids Railway planned to spend about a quarter million dollars for construction and improvements during 1910. The company also planned to spend $60,000 to purchase twelve more streetcars, $80,000 associated with building a new car house on the west side, and $20,000 for improvements at Ramona Park. The company expected to spend $90,000 on construction work. The street rail-

way track construction projects included:

- Lafayette Street between Franklin (Fifth) and Hall streets to be filled in between the tracks
- Plainfield Avenue between the old Grand Trunk station and Caledonia Street to be re-tracked and paved
- West Leonard Street between Stocking Street and the Grand Rapids & Indiana Railroad tracks -to replace old sixty-six-pound girder rail with new eighty-pound T-rail
- West Leonard Street between Fremont and White streets to be paved and another track laid making this section of West Leonard Street double track
- West Bridge Street paved using eighty-pound T rail to replace sixty-six-pound girder rail
- Pearl Street from Canal Street west to and including the bridge over Grand River to be re-tracked.

A new car station was built in 1910 at the streetcar landing in Ramona Park. The station had a ticket window, waiting rooms and other conveniences. A covered walk was built connecting the station to the theater so that visitors could walk in comfort without worrying about the weather. The seating capacity of the Ramona Park Theater in the pavilion was increased to 2,000 by adding in a balcony, log seats in front, and garden seats on the side.

In the following year two crossover switches, one on Canal Street and one on

GRH&C Railway interurban car no. 28 being rebuilt in Hall Street car shops.

Carl Bajema Collection

Trowbridge Street, were installed near the Canal-Trowbridge intersection making it easier for streetcars to pass each other. A new switch was laid at the South Division Avenue and Cherry Street intersection. Nearly 100 feet of track was re-laid including heavy frogs and switches on busy track in less than two days without delaying traffic. Nearly seventy streetcars and interurban cars crossed through this intersection every hour.

A second track was added on Michigan Avenue between Grand and East streets converting the single-track line between those two streets into a double-track one. West Leonard Street was paved and double tracked as far as West Street.

Grand Rapids Leads in Streetcar Development

Something important happened during the summer of 1909. The first Pay-As-You-Enter streetcars (P.A.Y.E.) began running on the streets in Grand Rapids. The P.A.Y.E. cars (covered later in this chapter) quickly became a major standard streetcar for the rest of the Grand Rapids streetcar era. By operating P.A.Y.E. cars the street railway company was able to both lower the cost of operating streetcars and increase the income from fares by making it difficult for passengers to ride the streetcar without paying.

The new Pay-As-You-Enter cars operating in Grand Rapids were described in the August 18, 1910, *Grand Rapids Press* as:

> . . . the nearest approach to a Pullman on any city rapid transit line. The cars have air brakes, hot water heat, double exits, a safety door, a fare box, electric signaling buttons, wide aisles, comfortable seats, wide windows, an entrance separate from the exit, so that incoming passengers can board the car while outgoing passengers are being discharged, a safety exit door controlled by the motorman, the conductor always on the rear platform, and many other features that make them street car models.
>
> Grand Rapids . . . was the first city in Michigan to introduce the new models. There are now twenty-two of them in operation on the Division-Plainfield and Lafayette-Stocking lines while other lines are to be equipped in the near future. Every one of the twenty-two cars is new and all were built especially for P. A.Y.E service in Grand Rapids. They have features that distinguish them from similar cars found in other cities that have adopted the advanced system.

Downtown Loop Provides Extra Cars

The street railway was able to provide extra cars for almost any event or traffic problem. The downtown loop line that ran via Monroe, Canal, Lyon and North Ottawa streets enabled the street railway to concentrate the extra cars where the crowds were the largest during rush hour traffic or when crowds were leaving downtown theaters. Almost all the streetcar lines passed through Campau Square which was part of the downtown loop. If a crowd was on its way to Ramona Park and Reed's Lake, the street railway was able to assign extra cars to the Ramona Park line and when the extra cars returned to downtown the cars could go around the loop, pick up passengers and head back to Ramona Park without loss of time having to run over the entire line.

SOMETHING LIKE THIS—

Newspaper cartoon showing an indecisive Common Council alderman changing his vote on where streetcars should stop at an intersection so often that he was acting like he was on a turntable!

Grand Rapids Press, 18 June 1913

Would enable the aldermen to change the car stops as often as they liked without disturbing the city in general.

Car Stop Controversy Continues

Alderman Charles Brown proposed that all cars were to stop to allow passengers to board and alight at the nearest crossing instead of the farthest crossing as was required by the current ordinance of the city. This had been proposed and approved in the past only to have the Common Council reverse its vote later. Once again the Common Council debated the proposal but voted against changing the ordinance back to requiring near side stops in November 1912.

They somersaulted again and passed an ordinance effective May 1, 1913, reversing their previous vote. The aldermen then voted in June to repeal the near side ordinance they had approved less than two months earlier, but the

Mayor vetoed their repeal. It had gotten to where the Common Council was like Hamlet-it couldn't make up its mind. The *Grand Rapids Press* responded to the frequent reversals by publishing a cartoon showing an alderman changing his vote so often that he must be riding a streetcar on a turntable.

Many Streets Renamed in 1912

The Common Council approved a street renaming ordinance to standardize the names of streets in the city effective April 10, 1912. All streets running north-south were now Avenues and all streets running east-west were named Streets. All streets that had different names on opposite sides of an intersection now had the

Exterior view of the Scribner Avenue car barn. View looking northeast from Scribner Avenue.

Carl Bajema Collection

same names, with the exception of West Bridge Street and Michigan Street, which change names at Scribner Street.

Company Purchases Additional Power

The company's electric power distribution system was being stretched to its limit with the introduction of newer and heavier equipment. The Commonwealth Power Company, owner of the Grand Rapids Railway decided to provide additional power from the Grand Rapids-Muskegon Power Company, which it also owned. The latter company was busy building a new power plant on West Wealthy Street a half mile west of the Grand River that would have twice the power capacity of the old plant.

Lyon Street Hill Car Goes on a Wild Ride

Motorman Roy Van Keuren stopped streetcar No. 302 at the top of Lyon Street hill on January 28, 1911. He tested the magnetic brakes while conductor William McFall stepped out of the car to make sure the magnetic brakes took hold and to also check the sanding system. After completing these required tests, Van Keuren notched the controller to take the car west down the steep hill.

The streetcar started moving down the Lyon Street hill too rapidly and the magnetic brakes did not slow the car's momentum. It picked up speed as it dashed down the series of grades toward Canal Street. Motorman Van Keuren frantically sounded the warning gong and tried to set the hand brakes. Conductor McFall and one of the passengers tried to set the hand brake on the rear platform of the car, but the hand brakes did not slow the speed of the car.

Patrolman George Wells, who was directing traffic at the Lyon-Canal Street intersection, saw the streetcar coming toward him at breakneck speed. He immediately took a position between the two tracks and shouted a warning to pedestrians that a runaway streetcar was on its way. The front wheel of the streetcar started taking a switch going north onto Canal Street, but the momentum caused the car to leave the rails.

As the streetcar shot past Canal Street—now off the rails—it snapped a steel trolley pole as if it were a wooden match and skidded along for half a block before its wild ride down Lyon Street hill came to an end. All six passengers and the two streetcar employees survived the trip on the runway car.

The Grand Rapids Railway began installing air brakes and removing hand brakes on its streetcars in March.

Pay-As-You-Enter Cars Built for Hill Service

The Cincinnati Car Company built ten big double-truck P.A.Y.E. cars specially designed for the Michigan-Lyon Street hill line in 1912. The car body of these new streetcars was twenty-eight feet long and the total length was forty feet long when the front and rear platforms were included. Each car had a seating capacity of thirty-five passengers.

Derailers were installed on the uphill track on both the Michigan Avenue and Lyon Street hills as a safety measure to prevent runaway cars from sliding backwards down the steep hills all the way to the bottom. Derailing a car could not in itself stop the car but mud, dirt, gravel, or even street pavement offered more resistance than smooth steel rails, especially if damp or greasy. Railroads widely considered derailing an uncon-

Interior view of one bay of the Scribner Avenue carbarn.

Carl Bajema Collection

trollable car as the lesser of two evils.

The company's car roster numbered 134 cars at the end of 1912, including 24 P.A.Y.E. cars previously purchased by the company for the Division and Lafayette lines and the 10 new hill line P.A.Y.E. cars. None of the old streetcars had been converted to P.A.Y.E. cars by the end of 1912.

The big shops at the Hall Street carbarn were designed so that streetcars could be repaired quickly. The shops also equipped new car bodies with trucks, motors and control equipment as well as wiring. If necessary, the shops could turn out a car from the bottom wheels to the wheel on top of the trolley pole. The company rarely did so because it was more economical to purchase car bodies and other components from the companies that specialized in such equipment.

Eighty-five streetcars were cleaned every night at the carbarns to remove debris, dirt, and dust from the cars before they were sent out again the next day. Each carbarn was equipped with a fumigating machine that the crew used to spray disinfectants.

New Scribner Avenue Car House

The new Scribner Avenue carbarn that was completed in early December 1912 was a two-story brick building with 187 feet of frontage on the east side of Scribner Avenue just south of West Bridge Street. The car house occupied 200 feet along Bowery Street running through to Front Avenue. There were three bays, each bay having four tracks with pits for inspections and repairs. Each of the bays had a capacity of twelve P.A.Y.E. cars for a total capacity of thirty-six P.A.Y.E. cars.

The office was located on the southwest side of the Scribner Avenue-West Bridge Street intersection. The second floor contained a recreation room, a club house with parlors, a dining room, showers, and ten sleeping apartments, each with two beds. These facilities were a convenience for men whose start time was very early or unpredictable.

The old carbarns on Scribner Avenue north of West Bridge Street continued to be used by the company, but as the headquarters for the construction and maintenance departments.

P.A.Y.E. car named "Dwight Lydell" shown leaving the Scribner carbarn.

Roger Monk Collection

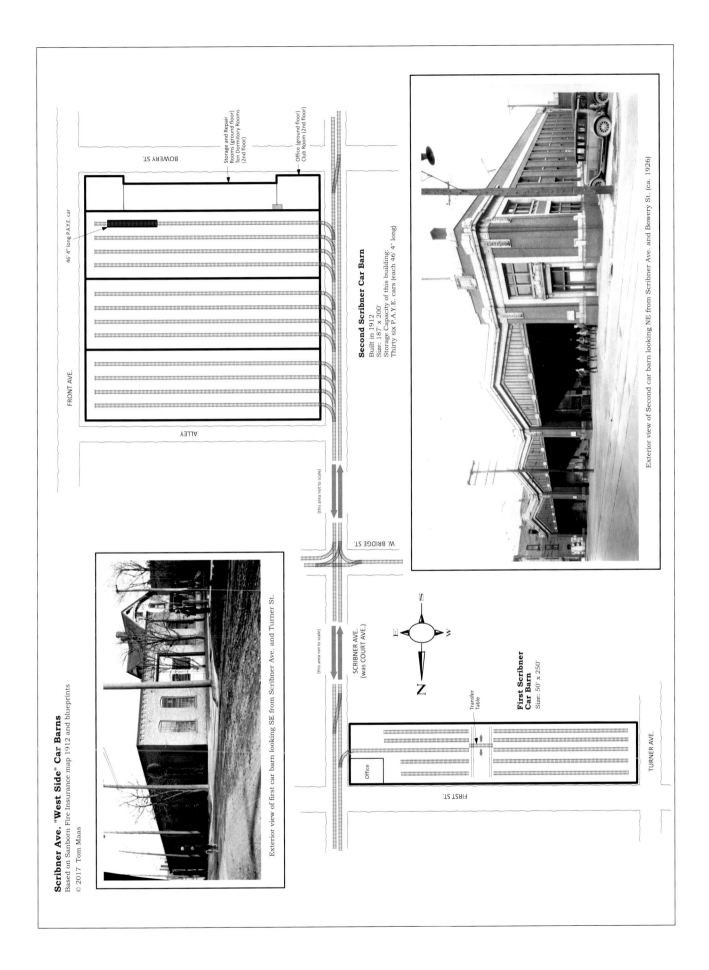

Scribner Ave. "West Side" Car Barns
Based on Sanborn Fire Insurance map 1912 and blueprints
© 2017 Tom Maas

Exterior view of first car barn looking SE from Scribner Ave. and Turner St.

BOWERY ST.

Storage and Repair
Rooms (ground floor)
Ten Dormitory Rooms
(2nd floor)

Office (ground floor)
Club Room (2nd floor)

46' 4" long P.A.Y.E. car

FRONT AVE.

ALLEY

(this area not to scale)

W. BRIDGE ST.

Second Scribner Car Barn
Built in 1912
Size: 187' x 200'
Storage Capacity of this building:
Thirty six P.A.Y.E. cars (each 46' 4" long)

Exterior view of Second car barn looking NE from Scribner Ave. and Bowery St. (ca. 1926)

(this area not to scale)

SCRIBNER AVE.
(was COURT AVE.)

Transfer
Table

Office

FIRST ST.

**First Scribner
Car Barn**
Size: 50' x 250'

TURNER AVE.

Street Railway Franchise Commission Established

Common Council aldermen argued with the Grand Rapids Railway over issues such as additional car line extensions and allowing smoking on streetcars. The aldermen, frustrated by their inability to make the street railway company spend money as they wanted, voted on September 30, 1912 to establish a street railway franchise commission to compile an overall study of street railway transportation. Among the matters considered were municipal ownership and operation of the street railway system, and the city owning the tracks and leasing them to an operating company. The Grand Rapids newspapers supported the aldermen's actions in large part because then the city would be better prepared when the street railway company's thirty-year franchise expired in 1921.

William McClelland, engineer for the public service commissioner of the state of New York, made a presentation to the street railway franchise committee in early March 1913. McClelland argued that, "The public service business no longer can be considered a private enterprise. It has grown far beyond that. Instead it is a partnership between capital, as represented in the investor, the operating company, and the public. To the investor . . . must be assured a fair return on his capital" which McClelland admitted "was easy to define but difficult to determine." McClelland asserted that, "The rights of the public are summed up in two words, 'good service.'"

Track Extensions and Rail Renewal Continue

The company finally installed an electric feeder on the West Leonard Street hill in April 1912 to solve a weighty problem. Streetcar traffic, both local and interurban, would now make better time going up the steep hill "where formerly the interurban cars were forced to creep laboriously up the long hill because of the lack of 'juice,' now sufficient power can be given the big interurban cars to rapidly ascend the hill and begin their journey to the lake terminal." The Leonard Street cars would no longer be delayed by Muskegon interurban cars that were not able to get enough electric power to rapidly climb the hill.

Track on new extensions and old track rebuilt during 1912 totaled 3.84 miles. The lines extended during 1912 included the East Fulton line from Union to Fuller streets and the Plainfield line from Quimby Street to Ann Street. Tracks that were re-laid included Buckley Street east from Division to Lafayette, Broadway Avenue from North Street to Indian Mill Creek, and Butterworth Avenue west from Gold to Lane avenues.

Grand Rapids streetcars traveled nearly 4 million miles and carried 18,209,083 passengers in 1912 which included 6,606,413 free transfers that conductors collected from passengers who continued their journeys by riding on another line owned by the Grand Rapids Railway.

Equipment not in use was stored in old carbarns such as the old Scribner barn located north of West Bridge Street. The rolling stock of the Grand Rapids Railway at the end of 1913 consisted of 137 passenger motor cars, 15 passenger trailers, 12 service cars and 3 postal cars.

The East Fulton Street car line was extended from Fuller Avenue to Carlton Avenue during the spring of 1913. A new waiting pavilion was built for North Park resort passengers during the summer of 1913.

The Grand Rapids, Grand Haven & Muskegon Railway built a combined freight and passenger station on the southeast corner of West Leonard Street and McReynolds Avenue in November 1913. This Muskegon interurban station became known as the "West Side Terminal" even though the station was not at the end of a streetcar line.

During 1914 the company spent $112,202 on building and rebuilding the lines in the city as follows: The loop adjacent to the West Michigan fairgrounds on the Taylor line; the Franklin Street line from Division to Lafayette Avenue; the Shawmut line from Front to Mt. Vernon; and same line from Seward to Straight. The Madison Avenue line was extended south from Hall Street to Beulah Street to serve the Garfield-Fletcher playground; the reconstruction of the Shawmut Street line west from Front to Mt. Vernon and west from Seward to Straight Avenue; and Michigan Avenue from Monroe Avenue west to the bridge over Grand River was rebuilt. Two miles of track were also paved.

The Madison Avenue line was extended from Madison Square south to the Burton Street region during 1915. The Plainfield Avenue line was also extended north from Ann Street to Knapp Street during 1915.

Kalamazoo-Grand Rapids Interurban Line

The Michigan Railway Company, a subsidiary of the Commonwealth Power, Railway and Light Company, built the last of the three interurban lines connecting Grand Rapids to other cities. The "Kalamazoo interurban," as dubbed by the locals, was built as a north-south line nearly fifty miles in length between downtown Kalamazoo and downtown Grand Rapids.

The Kalamazoo interurban cars did not

run into Grand Rapids until May 1915 because many Grand Rapids residents including the mayor and many aldermen were opposed to allowing heavy interurban cars to run over city streets to reach downtown. They were concerned that the longer and heavier interurban cars would block street intersections and damage the streetcar track. And for good reason as some of the new 800-class cars built by St. Louis in 1915 were 67 feet 6 inches in length and weighed a staggering 142,600 pounds while the heaviest streetcars weighed less than 50,000 pounds.

Consequently the Kalamazoo interurban company decided to build its line inside the city on private right-of-way which involved the building of two bridges across the Grand River.

The Michigan Railway company's interurban cars entered Grand Rapids for the first time on May 5, 1915, when the company ran a special car from Kalamazoo to Grand Rapids carrying two dozen newsmen to demonstrate what the new interurban line was capable of doing. The Michigan Railway interurban line became known in Grand Rapids as the "Kalamazoo interurban" to distinguish the line from the "Holland interurban" and the "Muskegon interurban," the other two interurban lines connecting Grand Rapids to other cities.

The official opening of the Michigan Railway's line connecting Grand Rapids with Kalamazoo, Battle Creek and other cities occurred on May 17, 1915. The Kalamazoo interurban used a third rail for power collection in the countryside, but went to overhead catenary trolley wire when operating inside the city. The history of the "Kalamazoo" interurban's operations in Grand Rapids and suburbs can be found in Chapter 10.

Street Railway Operates on Holland Interurban Track

When the Michigan Railway began running into Grand Rapids on its own private right-of-way in May 1915, the Holland interurban cars no longer entered Grand Rapids via Grandville Avenue but instead entered Grand Rapids by switching onto the Michigan Railway at their junction west of the city limit. This created a 1,000-foot gap between the end of the Grandville Avenue streetcar line at Clyde Park Avenue and where the Holland interurban cars turned north at the new Michigan Railway junction. The street railway obtained permission from Wyoming Township to extend its suburban service and started running on the newly abandoned Holland interurban track. This extension in service enabled individuals to ride rather than walk the 1,000 feet when transferring between the Grandville Avenue streetcars and the Holland interurban cars.

GRAND RAPIDS, MICHIGAN, THURSDAY, AUGUST 22, 1912.

SIDETRACKED

Newspaper cartoon of Grand Rapids Mayor Ellis sidetracking the Grand Rapids -Kalamazoo Interurban Railway onto a dead end siding while engaging in "Peanut Politics."

Grand Rapids News, 22 Aug 1912, pg 1

End of Line for the Postal Streetcars

The little electric motor cars used to transport the mails between the U.S. Post Office and the steam railroad stations, as well as the interurban stations for sixteen years, made their last trips in August 1914. The three stubby little cars had been built as cable line trailers about a quarter-century earlier to be pulled along the cable lines in Grand Rapids. These trailers were converted into motor cars when all Grand Rapids street railways were electrified in 1891. The three cars were rebuilt as postal cars in 1898.

The disappearance of these old "white ghost line" postal cars was not mourned by Grand Rapids citizens, many of whom had been annoyed more than once by being delayed by a postal car standing on the track while picking up or delivering mail pouches.

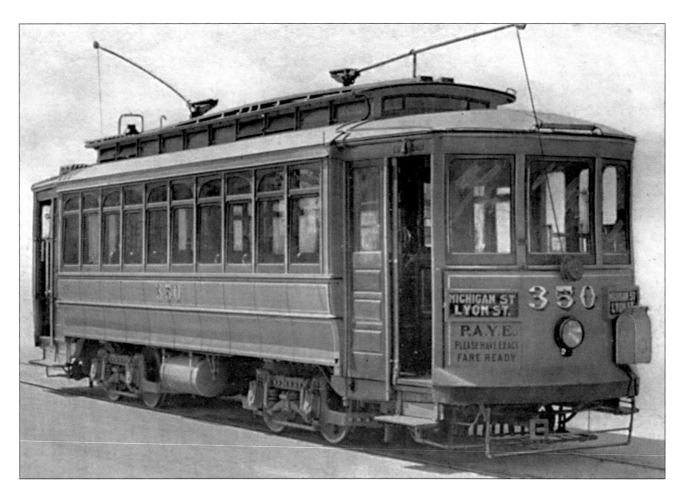

Grand Rapids Streetcar System Featured in *Brill Magazine*

The May 1914 issue of J. G. Brill Company's *Brill Magazine* featured Grand Rapids in its series on "Conditions Which Govern the Type of Car for City Service." Grand Rapids Railway Company had approximately sixty-five miles of track and most of the lines were double tracked, leaving only about nine miles of single track.

The company had 670 employees who kept 85 cars in normal operation. Practically all the streetcar lines passed through Campau Square in downtown Grand Rapids. During the rush hours between 6:20 and 8 A.M. and between 4:30 and 6:15 P.M., from 130 to 150 cars an hour passed through the square.

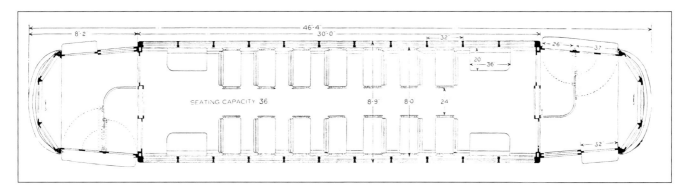

*Diagram of a double end P.A.Y.E. car with two vestibules.
Car Measurements: track to side sill, 2 ft. 9 in.; side sill to
trolley board, 9 ft. 2 in. ; floor to headlining, 8ft. 1 in.; track to
step, 18 in., step to platform, 13 in.; platform to floor, 10 in.;
weight of car. body, less electrical equipment, 22,880 lb.*

Brill Magazine, May 1914

P.A.Y.E. Car: The Standard Streetcar in Grand Rapids

In 1914 the standard streetcar in Grand Rapids was the "Pay-As-You-Enter" double-truck car equipped with a monitor-deck roof. The Grand Rapids Railway owned forty-seven P.A.Y.E. streetcars, some of which were built by American Car Company (a J. G. Brill Company affiliate), while others were the company's old double-truck Kuhlman company cars with their vestibules enlarged and doorways rearranged to conform to the P.A.Y.E. streetcar design. Many but not all of the P.A.Y.E. cars were double-end cars.

The American Car Company P.A.Y.E. cars operating on the streets in Grand Rapids had wooden underframes reinforced with steel; the side sills consisted of pine, plated with 15 ½-inch by 3/8-inch steel plates. These steel plates were reinforced at the top and bottom with angles of suitable size, which made the reinforced material have the structural characteristics of a Z-bar.

Color Light Codes, Destination Signs, and Route Numbers

Grand Rapids Railway devised color light codes for its lines so riders could identify streetcars at night. The color codes were as follows:

Green – Wealthy Street
Red – Cherry-Shawmut and Michigan-Lyon
Blue – Division-Plainfield
White – Franklin-West Leonard

Transfers were also color coded.

The street railway company decided to inaugurate a new system for car designation. The sign then in use on the front of a streetcar had two street names, but did not disclose which was the destination and which was the origin. The new sign was to have only one street name-the destination street. The Division-Plainfield line cars were to have the "Plainfield" sign if the car was headed north toward Plainfield Avenue

Interior of a Grand Rapids P.A.Y.E. street car. Seat-back grab handles are omitted but plenty of straps are provided.

Brill Magazine, May 1914

Four Grand Rapids streetcars at Campau Square, view looking northwest circa 1913-14.

Brill Magazine, May 1914

and to have the "Division Avenue" sign if the car was headed south toward Division Avenue.

The streetcars on all nine lines were assigned a number in addition to the single street destination name on January 1, 1916. The number was larger than the destination name plate so that it could be seen at a longer distance. The sign indicating the destination was to be displayed in the front right corner and the route number in the box at the left corner.

The streetcar lines were numbered as follows:

No. 1—Division and Plainfield;
No. 2—Franklin and West Leonard;
No. 3—Lafayette and Stocking;
No. 4—Wealthy and Taylor;
No. 5—Wealthy and Scribner;
No. 6—Cherry and Shawmut;
No. 7—Michigan and Lyon;
No. 8—Bridge and Grandville;
No. 9-Butterworth and Monroe.

Jitney Buses
Compete for Passengers

Five converted automobiles called "jitney" auto buses began competing against the street-car system for passengers on March 3, 1915. ("Jitney" was a slang word for five cents, the fares that many drivers were charging to ride their jitneys.) President Hanchett visited city hall the same day and talked briefly with Mayor Ellis about the company's new rival. Hanchett asked about what license fees the jitney owner was paying and what ordinance was being used to regulate the jitneys. Mayor Ellis responded by contending that it was up to the street railway or the aldermen on the Common Council to take action. President Hanchett drew attention to the fact that "the jitney bus does not pay taxes, any

street improvements; it does not pay for its right to the streets. It runs when it wants to."

Many politicians and local citizens initially contended that since the jitney buses required no poles, wire, or track, and were not a permanent fixture on the streets, there was no need for a local franchise. The jitney buses were called a number of names including "omnibuses" but often the jitneys were nothing more than private autos and jalopies. Some cities including Grand Rapids soon realized that street railways provided more comprehensive service, especially outside the morning and evening rush hours as part of their franchise requirement. Jitneys ran when it suited them. The Grand Rapids city council finally enacted strict jitney operating regulations as required by the street railway franchises.

Four Grand Rapids street cars were posed at the intersection of Monroe Avenue (was Canal Street) and Bridge Street, for this view looking northeast, circa 1913-14.

Brill Magazine, May 1914

Better Service to Union Station

Complaints about the frequency of streetcar service to downtown Union Station led the street railway to advertise that effective Thanksgiving Day, Franklin-West Leonard cars would be rerouted to Union Station via Ionia Avenue and Cherry Street.

A citizen complained about the quality of the new service and wrote a letter to the *Grand Rapids Press* asking, "Why must the Franklin-Leonard line with its ancient cars better known by patrons as 'dummies,' 'bowling alleys,' 'side wheelers,' etc. be the line to be routed by Union Station" rather than "the elegant P.A.Y.E. Lafayette-Stocking line cars?"

Franchise Commission Retains Lawyer

The street railway franchise commission retained attorney Shelby Schurtz early in 1916 to help it investigate the affairs of the Grand Rapids Railway Company and determine what the city needed to accomplish before negotiating a new franchise. Schurtz made a detailed 612-page report to the commission on October 6. Schurtz concluded that the franchise commission must do what he was unable to because he could not gain access to company or state records.

Schurtz stressed the importance of having a franchise that is explicit, clear, and carefully drawn—always with the idea in view that the new charter provided for a thirty-year franchise. Attorney Schurtz ended by concluding:

Never again should the City of Grand Rapids have to stoop to petty politics, to trading charter amendments for extensions of its streetcar service. These things should be provided for in the franchise, and some certain official of the city should have it his daily duty to see that franchise provisions are carried out to the letter.

Hodenpyl-Hardy Cars Arrive

The Grand Rapids Railway Company received fifteen new streetcars during the summer of 1917. Hodenpyl-Hardy & Company, the investment firm which owned numerous public utility companies including the Grand Rapids Railway Company, purchased twenty-five of these cars: fifteen for Grand Rapids and ten

New Hodenpyl-Hardy streetcar.
Electric Railway Journal, 15 Sep 1917

Diagram of the floor plan of the Hodenpyl-Hardy streetcar which has a seating capacity of forty-eight.
Electric Railway Journal, 15 Sep 1917

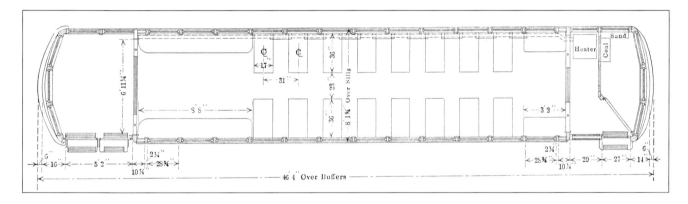

for Akron, Ohio. These cars were forty-six feet, four inches long over the vestibules—six feet longer than the biggest cars the company then used in the city.

These cars were single ended, were built to operate like P.A.Y.E. cars and were featured as "The New Standard Hodenpyl-Hardy Car" in the September 15, 1917, issue of *Electric Railway Journal*. Each car had sixteen cross-seats, two six-passenger longitudinal seats in the rear and two two-passenger longitudinal seats at the front of the car which gave a total seating capacity of forty eight.

The Hodenpyl-Hardy streetcars were designed for an enclosed "pay-within the rear platform" and for single-end operation. The motorman controlled the sliding exit door at the front of the car. The rear entrance and exit doors were of the folding type; the exit doors folded outward and the entrance doors folded

Rear end arrangement of Hodenpyl-Hardy street car showing door and enclosed platform.
Electric Railway Journal, 15 Sep 1917

inward. The conductor opened and closed the two rear doors manually using levers mounted on a center stand from his position on the rear platform. The conductor faced the rear of the car adjacent to the fare box just in front of the entrance to the rest of the car. The rear platform was large enough to allow for rapid loading and exiting with much of the fare collection accomplished once the car was underway.

The street railway began running these new cars on the Division-Plainfield Avenue line. Since the cars were single ended, the street railway built a loop for the cars to reverse direction at the north end of the Plainfield line and built a wye at Burton Street at the south end of the Division Avenue line.

No new track extensions were made during 1917 for two reasons. With a world war going on, it was almost impossible to procure rail and other materials. Also, the time to recoup an investment was short—four years— if the street railway franchise was not renewed in 1921.

New open-at-the-top mail boxes replaced the old mail boxes on Grand Rapids streetcars during 1917. The boxes kept the letters dry and it was easier to deposit mail in them.

Old Streetcars Rebuilt as P.A.Y.E. Cars

The street railway began rebuilding twenty of its thirty-foot double-truck streetcars to operate as P.A.Y.E. cars in the company's car shops in January 1919. The bulkheads were removed and platforms changed so the platforms at both ends of each car had a new design allowing each rebuilt car to operate in the same manner as the existing P.A.Y.E. cars on the system.

An April 15, 1919, editorial in the *Grand Rapids Press* asked the question, "Are the big, modern, double-ended streetcars dragging the street railway companies deeper into the financial mire?" and then reported that, "Traction managers are beginning to incline to that view, and experiments are now being made with a new type of light car." The new lightweight car would seat about thirty persons and be a one-man car. The motorman would also collect the fares from the passengers as they entered the streetcar because the only entrance and exit would be via the front end.

These cars of the future would be much cheaper to operate for two reasons. First, the

cars would consume much less power as the cars would be lighter. Second, the street railway company would need only one man rather than two men to operate the car. The editor then drew attention to experiments about to start in Kansas City and in Massachusetts that would provide a test of the theory. The editorial ended by stating it would be rather odd if the solution for street railways was a return to a "Bobtail" style car reminiscent of the 1880s and 1890s.

Accidents

A freight car being pushed by a Grand Trunk switch engine struck a Wealthy-Taylor streetcar carrying more than forty passengers at the Quimby Street and Taylor Avenue crossing north of Leonard Street on October 17, 1917. The big box car struck the platform of the streetcar, ripping it into pieces, reducing the front of the streetcar into kindling wood, breaking almost every window while tearing the trucks from the car. One passenger was killed and another died of injuries later. The coroner's jury found the crossing tower flagman and both the motorman and conductor responsible for the accident.

A Muskegon interurban motorman was unable to slow his freight motor enough to successfully negotiate the tight curve around the corner of Scribner Avenue and West Leonard Street on August 17, 1917. Muskegon freight motor No. 112 left the track, tipped over on its side along West Leonard Street where it wound up on the sidewalk in front of Wheeler's drug store at 325 West Leonard Street.

World War Restricts Street Railway Operations

The U.S. Fuel Administrator requested companies to conserve coal effective December 3, 1917. The street railway revised its operations in response to this request by discontinuing unnecessary service to conserve coal. Service was reduced by cutting the frequency of streetcars on a number of lines; eliminating "owl car" runs after midnight; and eliminating non-essential car stops effective January 28, 1918. "No Car Stop" signs were posted at the stops to be discontinued. Every start and stop a streetcar made used considerable power.

The impact of the war on street railway activities such as purchasing new streetcars and building new lines was summed up by Grand Rapids Railway president Benjamin Hanchett at a meeting of the City Commission's committee on street railway service in January: "Conditions make it absolutely impossible for us to get the rails if we had the money and we can't borrow the money even if we could get the rails."

Spanish Flu Epidemic, Jitneys, and Streetcar Fares

The 1918 influenza epidemic brought about a temporary decrease in the number of passengers the streetcars carried and thus reduced income from fares. The seven jitneys that been granted operating licenses by the Grand Rapids City Commission competed for passengers thus diverting more income from the street railway that year. The City Commission

Muskegon interurban freight ,motor No. 112 on its side on West Leonard Street in Grand Rapids on July 17, 1917. View looking south.

Coopersville Area Historical Society Museum collection

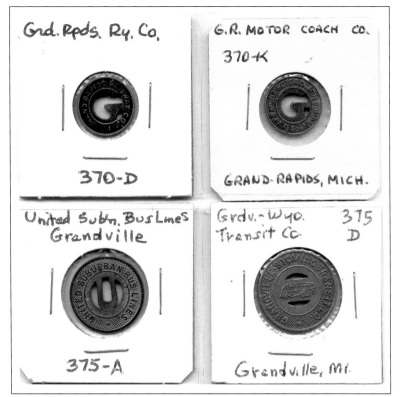

tally necessary privately-owned public utility such as the street railway system is a part and parcel of the community. Knowlton contended "It is not fair to assume that under existing conditions street railway companies can extend the lines without reasonable compensation" and that, "We can all talk over capitalization, justice and 6 cent fares, and so on, but . . . it is unreasonable to feel that we can ask the street railway companies for extensions without at least trying to see their side of the question."

The street railway company carried 24,884,739 fare paying passengers in 1918, a decrease of 963,887 paying passengers compared with the year before. The company also reported that 5,990,443 transfer passengers were carried in 1919, a decrease of 599,035.

Paper Tickets to "Liberty Discs" and Back

Benjamin Hanchett described the paper street car tickets as a nuisance and couldn't be used in the fare boxes. A new metal disc was devised to be used in place of the paper tickets which would be more readily accepted by the fare boxes. In keeping with the patriotic tenor of the era, the new tokens were tagged "Liberty Discs."

This fare collection system ended after the war. Notices were posted in streetcars and in carbarns forbidding motormen from accepting metal tokens beginning June 24, 1920. The *Grand Rapids Press* drew attention to one of the major reasons street railway officials gave for changing from metal back to paper was that "daily hundreds of discs from other cities and even beer checks found their way into the ticket boxes. These are of no financial value to the company and hundreds of dollars in revenue have been lost through their use."

President Hanchett contended he was not against street improvements as such but the street improvements that the city commission had scheduled for 1919 would cost the company $200,000 and he did not know where the money would come from.

The proposed paving of West Fulton Street from the Grand River to Lexington Avenue and from Straight Street to John Ball Park alone would cost the street railway company $89,000. This is because the company would not only have to pay for the paving of the two sections of West Fulton Street but would also have to buy new rails at $70 a ton as it would not pay to relay old rail when a street was being improved.

The strained financial condition of the street railway company led the Board of Directors to pay no preferred stock dividend, which in previous years was payable on February 1.

recognized these challenges and granted the streetcar company a fare increase from five cents to six cents.

The only improvements the streetcar company made in 1918 involved paving the Grandville Avenue line ($35,000) and replacing switches on Monroe Avenue ($7,000). The company planned to bide its time and await the end of the war before further improvements could be contemplated.

Labor Issues during the World War

General inflation during the war led to labor issues over wages. President Woodrow Wilson issued an order stating all railroad workers had the right to form a labor union. A group of street railway employees organized a local branch of the Amalgamated Association of Street and Electric Railway Employees in early August. The labor dispute was settled in September 1918 when the city commission acting as an arbitration board awarded the street railway employees much higher wages than the street railway company had offered.

Importance of Streetcar Service in a City

James R. Knowlton, a Grand Rapids realtor, drew attention to the important role streetcar service played with respect to real estate values in the April 19, 1919, *Grand Rapids Press.* He stressed it must be appreciated that a vi-

The Winter of 1919-1920 Causes a Street Railway Crisis

Grand Rapids citizens were tired of the horrendously poor service the street railway was providing during the beginning of the winter of 1919-1920. Benjamin S. Hanchett, the company's president and general manager, contended the impaired service was caused by continued cold weather and the company's inability to purchase the new cars necessary for improved service.

Hanchett even presented the commission with a report of each delay in service during the past few weeks along with a detailed report on car conditions. Hanchett drew attention to the fact there was an average of twenty-five streetcars a day in the shops undergoing repair. He agreed to furnish the commission with a daily report in the future.

Should the jitney buses return, Hanchett was certain no new streetcar equipment would be purchased.

Some of the city commissioners threated to amend the jitney ordinance and remove the restrictions that had restricted this bus service. The City Commission passed a resolution asking the streetcar company to continue service by instituting its own jitney service to solve the problem.

Hanchett left for New York City on January 19 to arrange for the purchase of nineteen more streetcars. However, he did take the time before leaving to point out the City Commission had the power to help the company improve service immediately if it passed a regulation giving streetcars the right of way over automobiles and other vehicles in the downtown district. He added the city needed to enforce the laws limiting the length of time a railroad could block a city street at a crossing.

Hanchett also drew attention to broken wire, broken axles, frozen air brakes, improvement of heating systems to heat vestibules as required by a new state law— all made it difficult for the street railway company to keep enough cars out on the lines to maintain respectable schedules.

Severe weather continued to plague western Michigan. A blizzard in early March and floods led to more than fifty per cent of the company's streetcars in the repair shops.

Fortunately the weather improved and the company's car shops were turning out repaired cars faster than they were breaking down.

Grand Rapids Railway Company posted this Daily Bulletin of "Tie-ups" and "Cars in Shops."

Grand Rapids Press, 16 Feb 1920

GRAND RAPIDS RAILWAY COMPANY

Daily bulletin of "tieups" and cars in shops as furnished the city manager for Feb. 13, 1920:

Service was interrupted on the following lines:

Division and Plainfield

16 minutes at 2:00 p. m., freight train.

16 minutes at 4:00 p. m.; motor case loose.

Franklin and W. Leonard

16 minutes at 6:30 a. m.; air froze.

20 minutes at 8:20 a. m.; hot journal.

16 minutes at 8:00 p. m.; traffic.

Lafayette and Stocking

16 minutes at 2:28 p. m.; stripped gear.

16 minutes at 3:25 p. m.; air froze.

16 minutes at 6:00 p. m.; air froze.

20 minutes at 9:00 p. m.; car off track.

Wealthy and Taylor

20 minutes at 1:05 p. m.; motor burned out.

20 minutes at 9:25 p. m.; traffic.

Cherry and Shawmut

16 minutes at 6:00 a. m.; trolley wheel off.

16 minutes at 12:50 p. m.; traffic.

24 minutes at 2:30 p. m.; wire down.

16 minutes at 4:28 p. m.; wire burned off.

20 minutes at 8:50 p. m.; air froze.

Bridge and Grandville

20 minutes at 7:50 a. m.; freight train.

20 minutes at 2:50 p. m.; truck on track.

16 minutes at 6:40 p. m.; traffic.

20 minutes at 8:25 p. m.; traffic.

20 minutes at 9:30 p. m.; car off track.

Disabled cars in car houses and shops in morning..30
Disabled during day.....22
———
Total disabled cars......52
Cars repaired in shop....17
———
Disabled cars remaining..35

Louis DeLamarter Becomes General Manager

Benjamin Hanchett decided to resign as general manager of the Grand Rapids Railway. Louis J. DeLamarter was appointed the new general manager at the end of January 1920. A biography of Louis DeLamarter appears in Chapter 12.

DeLamarter strove to improve the service by gathering information about what the public wanted and then made some inexpensive changes to initiate improvements.

New One-Man Birney Safety Streetcars

The streetcar company ordered nineteen new one-man Birney Safety Cars in January 1920 in an attempt to provide more frequent service at a lower cost. The new one-man Birney cars began operating in Grand Rapids by the end of June 1920. They were built by the J.G. Brill Company and numbered 367-385. The new one-man cars were assigned to run on the Cherry Street and on the new Shawmut-Butterworth street lines. (Refer to later in this chapter for more on these cars.)

Some Grand Rapids citizens were concerned that the one-man cars which met with disfavor in Saginaw were similar to the one-man cars being purchased by the street railway company. General Manager Louis J. DeLamarter responded:

> The one-man cars used in Saginaw were makeshifts, being simply old cars rebuilt. The cars we have ordered for Grand Rapids are new cars of a recently developed type design to give more frequent service and better service on lines where traffic is not as heavy to require the big cars. Where big cars are needed they will be used. The additions to the rolling stock will enable us to handle the rush hour crowds more satisfactorily.
>
> The one-man cars we have ordered are designed to give more efficient service-not less efficient service. They were developed to solve certain problems that the street railways of the country have been studying for years-particularly the problem of giving frequent and adequate service on lines where the traffic is steady but not heavy. I feel sure that after Grand Rapids has given the one-man cars a fair trial both the public and the railway employees will find much greater satisfaction in the general service rendered.

"A Frank Statement" by the railway company answering the question: "Why is service so poor?"
Grand Rapids Press, 10 Mar 1920

Rerouting of Several Lines Improves Service

Several lines were rerouted in 1920. The West Bridge-Grandville and the Cherry-Shawmut lines were split. Both the Grandville and Cherry lines now took the Ottawa Avenue loop staying on the east side of the Grand River rather than crossing over to the west side. The West Bridge Street line was combined with the Madison Avenue line on the east side of the river. The busiest lines in the city were to get five- to six-minute service in the morning and evening rush hours. General Manager DeLamarter announced that city officials would no longer be able to ride free on streetcars with the exception of policemen and firemen in uniform. Fares were increased to seven cents cash and sixteen tickets for one dollar on June 24.

The poor financial condition of the company in 1921 led it to adopt a very strict economic policy for the year. The only track expenditures were repairs and reconstruction with one small exception. A crossover switch near the Wealthy Street car house was removed and a new one placed further east to relieve the streetcar congestion problem in the proximity of the facility.

The Grand Rapids Railway made routing changes in October 1921. The Oakdale-West Bridge line was changed so the west end cars ran out on Stocking. The rerouted line was known as the Lafayette-Stocking Avenue-Seventh Street line.

The Madison-Stocking route was changed to become the Madison Avenue line and operate to Lyon Street from Madison and Burton during the busy hours and operate as a stub line the rest of the day with passengers transferring at Hall and Madison.

The Grandville line was designated as the Grandville-West Bridge line and was operated as a through line.

Street Railway Properties Appraised

The franchise the Grand Rapids Railway Company operated under in 1921 had been approved by both the Grand Rapids Common Council and the Consolidated Street Railway Company of Grand Rapids in 1891 with some changes made via ordinances and amendments. The franchise and amendments were scheduled to expire in 1921.

The city was operating under a new city charter adopted in 1916. The charter required rates that private utilities charged for their services such as streetcar fares be based on a physical valuation of the streetcar company properties including rails, car houses, and resorts as well as rolling stock. The City Commission hired Harry Barker and George W. Fuller of New York to appraise the value of all the Grand Rapids Railway Company's properties in June as required before a new franchise could be voted on by the City Commission and the voters.

Streetcar Service-at-Cost Plan

General Manager Louis DeLamarter and City Manager Fred Locks met on December 9, 1920, to discuss plans for badly-needed improvements the company was proposing to make in 1921. The city manager favored a service-at-cost plan to pay for operations and improvements until a new franchise could be submitted to the voters. City officials realized the eight-cent fare which was scheduled to become effective December 20 might not produce the necessary revenue.

The service-at-cost plan would enable the streetcar company to operate for a few months at a time by authority of city ordinances, and the fare would periodically be determined by operating costs.

The Grand Rapids streetcars ran on a total of 68.18 miles of track on 39.06 miles of city streets in 1921.

Street Railway Franchise Controversy

The street railway company's franchise expired on April 21, 1921, without any satisfactory agreement about the major issue separating the City Commission and the Grand Rapids Railway Company. The major controversy was over the valuation of the street railway properties which determined how much income could be paid to stockholders.

Four million dollars! That was the size of the difference between the city's estimate ($4,623,000) and the company's estimate ($8,500,000) that each wanted to be used as the value of the street railway properties. This dispute over the value of these properties lasted nine months from March 1921 until January 4, 1922, when both parties agreed upon a valuation of $5,500,000 plus 8 per cent annual yield on 5½ million dollars. These figures were used to calculate the cost plus interest when calculating the amount to pay for running expenses, interest on debt, replacements, and extensions. Grand Rapids citizens voted to accept the new street railway franchise on September 12, 1922.

Photo of Grand Rapids Railway Company auto bus in 1923.

Dave Winick Collection at Grand Rapids Public Museum

Jitney Service

Gerald Wagner, Director of Public Service for the city of Grand Rapids reported the American Society for Municipal Improvement's Committee on Traffic recommended at its 1921 convention: "In cities of large population the jitneys be placed under control of the street railways which are themselves controlled by municipal franchises." Wagner went on to conclude that, "It is universally recognized that continued toleration of irresponsible jitney competition is a real menace to the country. It strangles the street railway systems and then is utterly incapable adequately to replace them as public carriers."

Grand Rapids Press on 26 Mar 1915

Editor of The Press: Much has been said in the favor of the jitney bus in the last few weeks and if only a few of those who are afraid to ride on them would come forward and express themselves it might set the others to thinking more seriously. For the sake of getting to their destination two or three minutes quicker than the street car would take them they crowd from ten to as high as eighteen on a five or seven-passenger bus. What would happen if a tire or and axle should give away under such a load at the rate of speed they travel and during the rush hours when they crowd the buses to about three times their capacity?

Ladies and men, young and old, mingle in them and sit on one another's laps and stand thick on the running board with nothing but the frail top or the doors of the auto to hang on to in case of a jolt. I think it will be only a matter of time before the general public will be aroused over such dangerous transportation.

As for the time saved with the present style of bus, which runs haphazard without schedule and only make a very few stops compared to the many stops a street car has to make with the larger seating capacity, what would be the result with a heavy bus with seating capacity of about twenty or thirty with so many more stops and less comfort than can be had on a street car?

C.J.S.

The Company Rebuilds Streetcars

No new streetcars were purchased in 1921. The street railway company rebuilt fifteen of its cars into more modern types. Some were rebuilt as one-man cars while others were rebuilt as combination one-man/two-man streetcars. The improved service that was delivered at a lower cost led the company to plan the conversion of another fifteen double-truck cars into combination one-man/two-man cars in 1922.

While no new streetcars were purchased in 1922, the company rebuilt seventeen of its cars into a more modern P.A.Y.E. type of car. These cars were equipped with standard safety car devices so they could be operated as one-man cars. These double-truck cars were the same type as those on the Cherry and Madison lines where passengers entering and leaving the car did so at the front.

The first of these rebuilt cars began operation on the Grandville Avenue line on June 11, 1922. These streetcars were designated by a large red diamond displayed on the front so riders waiting for a car knew where to board. When the one-man double-truck safety cars began operating on the Lafayette-Stocking and Madison Avenue lines in November the company announced that all one-man cars with front entrances were to be marked by a red star.

Passenger platforms, "bull pen" and tourist info booth on Monroe Avenue in front of McKay Tower in Campau Square. View is looking southeast down Monroe Avenue. The spire of the Westminster Presbyterian Church on Jefferson Avenue can be seen in the distance.

Grand Rapids Press
(undated photo)

1923: New Cars, Rebuilt Cars, and Auto Buses

The street railway company had an active year during 1923. The Grand Rapids Railway spent $124,725 to:

1) Buy eight one-man Birney Safety Cars (estimated cost: $56,000)
2) Buy six motor buses (estimated cost: $44,000)
3) Rebuild twenty-eight double-truck streetcars with standard safety-car equipment so they could operate as one-man streetcars

The company also conducted an experiment in 1923 to accelerate service in congested areas. It equipped a one-man double-truck car with "rear door control." This device permitted opening the rear door from outside the car by an employee standing in the street collecting fares. He would be stationed at a major car stop during hours of heavy boarding. Thus waiting passengers entered at both ends of the car, practically doubling the rate at which they boarded. This experiment was so successful that the company began equipping other cars with this system.

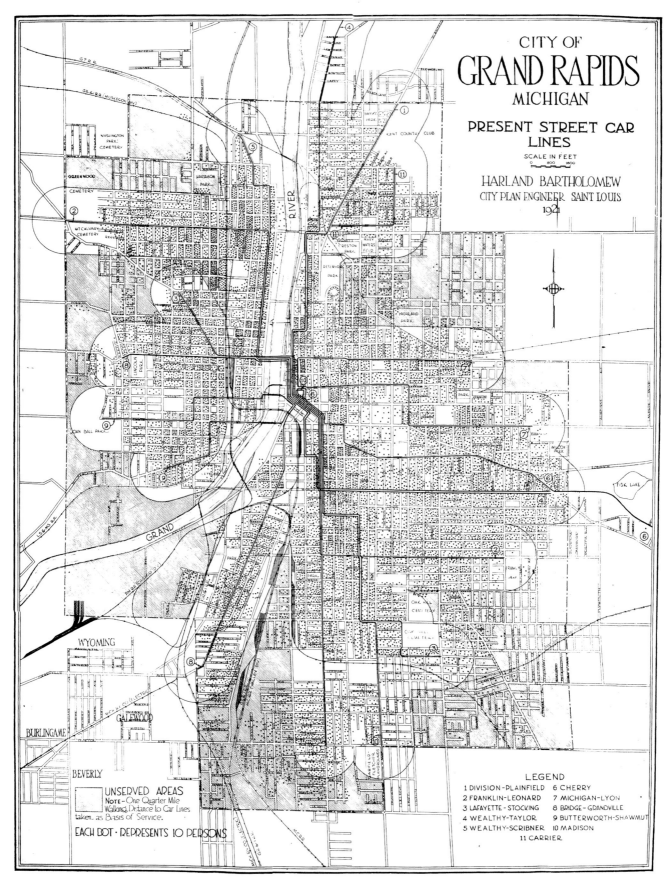

*1921 city map showing population and existing streetcar lines,
along with ¼ mile surrounding "walking distance" to these lines.*

Grand Rapids Public Library

FOR YOUR INFORMATION

THIS SPECIAL STREET RAILWAY WORK
WEIGHS 141,200 POUNDS
INCLUDING SWITCHES, FROGS & RAILS
IT WILL COST
12,680.00

9,500 FEET OF WHITE OAK TIES ARE REQUIRED TO SUPPORT IT
TIES WILL BE LAID ON
600 YDS. OF CONCRETE

The PAVING and FOUNDATION WILL REQUIRE
2 CARLOADS 32000 of BRICK
2 CARLOADS 1848(Sacks) OF CEMENT

TOTAL COST of THIS JOB # 20,000.00

This Cost Represents
240,000 STREET CAR FARES
ONE STREET CAR MUST TRAVEL 45,000 MILES
Or Nearly Twice Around The World
TO PAY FOR THIS WORK

GRAND RAPIDS RAILWAY COMPANY

Buses: a Harbinger?

The street railway company began operation under the new franchise in September 1922. The franchise allowed the company to supplement or replace streetcar lines with vehicles that ran under their own power. The company decided against building new streetcar lines or any major extension of existing lines. Starting a new route or extending a streetcar line with buses had one big advantage: the company did not have to make a large investment constructing track only to find out there were not enough riders to justify the investment. Six motor buses were purchased during 1923.

Streetcar company motor buses began running on a new route, the Monroe-Alpine line, on April 29, 1923. The buses started at the Rowe Hotel at the Monroe-Michigan Avenue intersection in downtown, went north on Monroe, west across Sixth Street Bridge to Turner, north on Turner to Seventh, and north on Alpine Avenue to Richmond and finally west on Richmond Street to Tamarack Avenue. The buses returned via on same route.

Improvements to the Property

The street railway company spent $221,404 on the following projects during 1923 to provide better service for streetcar riders:

• Building passenger loading platforms in congested districts
• Establishment of safety zones where streetcar riders could stand while waiting for a car on that line
• Establishing "skip-a-stop" operations on outbound cars during rush hours
• Establishing "Pay-As-You-Leave" cars on outbound traffic

The Ottawa Avenue cutoff track was laid between Monroe and Michigan avenues in 1924 to enable the company to reroute the Wealthy-Taylor-North Park line streetcars. This line was rerouted to help alleviate the growing congested downtown traffic conditions created by the increasing number of automobiles, es-

Sign posted at the construction site to display cost in dollars and number of fares. Construction is shown at the intersection of Ottawa Avenue and Lyon Street, looking north. City Hall would be off the right edge of the photo.

Dave Winick Collection at Grand Rapids Public Museum

Above: *A street railway construction crane with trolley pole at the intersection of Ottawa Avenue and Lyon Street.*
Dave Winick Collection at Grand Rapids Public Museum

Below: *Switch track construction at Ottawa Avenue and Lyon Street, view looking southeast at the Muskegon interurban terminal (vertical "I" sign) in the Houseman Building.*
Dave Winick Collection at Grand Rapids Public Museum

pecially on lower Monroe Avenue. Streetcars on The Wealthy-Taylor-North Park line began running on the Ottawa Avenue cutoff line on Monday, July 21, 1924.

The company also laid new track on Oakdale Street from Madison to Russell Avenue. The company was able to reroute the Oakdale cars and eliminate the expense associated with the duplication of service on the adjacent Oakdale and Madison Avenue lines. The Lafayette-Madison Avenue line began operating on the new route over Madison Avenue from Madison Square to Oakdale Street as far as Union Avenue on August 24.

Bus Service

The street railway company began bus operation on two new routes as feeders to two existing streetcar lines in 1924. Buses operated from the Valley Avenue terminus of the West Bridge Street car line going west up the very steep Bridge Street hill to the city limit at Bristol Avenue. The College Avenue-Leonard Street-Lafayette Avenue bus line delivered and picked up passengers at both the College and Lafayette Avenue intersections.

The company also began operating a Godfrey Avenue bus line. This service started at Campau Square and went southwest on Market Avenue to Godfrey Avenue and then south to Hall Street where the line ended.

A Disaster or an Opportunity?

A major fire (see Chapter 8) destroyed sixty streetcars at the Hall Street carbarn on July 19, 1924. Instead of bemoaning the loss of these old cars, General Manager Louis DeLamarter viewed this as an opportunity to modernize the streetcar fleet through new design and innovation. These efforts would bring Grand Rapids to national renown in the years to come.

Construction on Ottawa Avenue in 1924, view looking north from Fountain Street.

Dave Winick Collection at Grand Rapids Public Museum

Chicago City Railway Company car No. 5244 showing Loading and Unloading While the Pay-As-You-Enter car is at a Stop.

Electric Railway Review Vol.18, No. 12, Sept. 21 1907

The Pay-As-You-Enter Streetcar: The Standard Streetcar in Grand Rapids (1909-1924)

Streetcar Companies Need Better Streetcars

Streetcar companies faced a number of problems in finding ways to reduce operating expenses while maintaining or even increasing the quality of the service being provided to riders.

These companies were also looking at various means of increasing operating income. One source of additional revenue was the streetcar company-owned amusement park or resort. The Grand Rapids street railway company, like many other traction companies, worked with steam railroads to organize daylong excursions to the city where pleasure seekers paid to ride the streetcars to company-owned resorts such as Ramona Park. There they could enjoy the amusement park rides and theatrical performances.

Conductors Versus Fare Dodgers

The daily riders were the major source of income for street railways. Unfortunately some riders learned how to avoid paying fares, especially during the morning and evening rush hours.

People trying to beat the street railway out of a nickel fare were a major problem for streetcar conductors. A Grand Rapids streetcar conductor described the problems fare dodgers presented and how conductors tried to collect fares in the December 7, 1908, *Grand Rapids Herald*: "Under the system which prevails here, it is very difficult for a conductor to collect all the nickels during certain periods of the day. There are many who endeavor to avoid paying

fares at almost any old time, however. There is not a conductor with a few months' experience who had not a certain number of passengers 'spotted,' and from whom he always makes it a point to collect the fare early."

Conductors employed a number of strategies to ensure fare dodgers paid for their ride. Some conductors collected the fare immediately as the passenger boarded the streetcar. Other conductors kept track of who had not paid their fares "and simply stand in front of them until the coin is forthcoming."

At least one conductor was known to wait until his car had passed the shopping district before he tried to collect the fares. "He then goes through the entire car and gets his money because only a few fares have been previously collected."

A Solution to the Problem: the P.A.Y.E. Car

Street railway managers in Montreal, Canada, were frustrated with the way fare collections had become erratic, depending almost completely upon the accuracy of a constantly changing mental photograph that a conductor had to retain in his mind of the riders who had paid and who had not paid their fares. It was obvious that there were times it was an impossible task forcing the conductors to rely upon the honesty of the passengers; some of whose honesty was too often conspicuously wanting.

The Montreal Street Railway managers decided to model systems where tickets were sold at railway stations before the passengers entered the cars. They realized they could solve this problem if they designed a streetcar that enabled the conductor to act like a station agent, collecting fares before the rider entered the car. They designed a "pre-payment" streetcar where part of the rear platform became the equivalent of the ticket office and the entrance where boarding passengers had to pass by the conductor and pay before being allowed to enter the interior of the car. These "pre-payment" cars quickly became known as "Pay-As-You-Enter" (P.A.Y.E.) streetcars.

Passengers left the streetcar via the front platform or part of the rear platform, but they could only use a designated route when leaving via the rear platform. The division of the rear platform into a separate entrance and separate exit prevented the passengers getting off the streetcar from slowing down those individuals trying to board the car and pay their fares. The Montreal Street Railway solution provided a more efficient means of fare collection. Fewer missed fares translated into greater income for the company.

The Pay-As-You-Enter Car Company was organized by Montreal Street Railway officials and obtained a patent on the Pay-As-You-Enter system on September 26, 1905.

American streetcar companies began to adopt the P.A.Y.E. system car design when street railways in Chicago and New York City began purchasing large numbers of P.A.Y.E. cars in 1907.

P.A.Y.E Cars Begin Operation in Chicago

The Chicago City Railway Company began operating 130 newer version P.A.Y.E. cars on November 24, 1907. The Chicago P.A.Y.E. cars were different from the Montreal prototype in several important ways with respect to the arrangement of the doors and platforms. The Chicago cars were built for double-end operation and had seven-foot platforms in contrast to the Montreal cars which were built for single-end operation only.

Pay-As-You-Enter Cars Studied for Grand Rapids

Grand Rapids Railway General Manager Benjamin S. Hanchett and Superintendent J. C. Madigan had been following the experiments of other cities such as Chicago with P.A.Y.E. streetcar operation. Several features made these cars particularly attractive.

First, they had a good safety record by decreasing the number of accidents as the conductor was stationed where he could view the rear steps. Second, passengers could board and depart from a P.A.Y.E. car more easily because the two flows of passengers were separated. Third, a P.A.Y.E. streetcar did not lose as much time as other cars when stopped to pick up and drop off pas-

sengers. Fourth, fewer fares would be missed as all passengers had to pass directly in front of the conductor when boarding the car. Fifth, and finally, smokers would not be able to find a place on the rear platform where they could stand and blow smoke in the faces of other riders entering or leaving the streetcar.

Pay-As-You-Enter Streetcars Ordered

General Manager Benjamin Hanchett visited the American Car Company, a subsidiary of the J. G. Brill Company, in St. Louis, Missouri in March 1909 and placed an order for twelve P.A.Y.E. cars to be delivered by July 1.

The P.A.Y.E. cars purchased to operate in Grand Rapids, like the Chicago P.A.Y.E. cars, were equipped with extra-long platforms at each end of the car. Passengers entered the car only at the rear platform which was divided by a railing into two passageways, one labeled "Entrance" and

The P.A.Y.E. Car System advertisement.

Electric Traction Weekly January 9, 1908.

YOUR ROAD WILL
ULTIMATELY BE
A **P.A.Y.E.** SYSTEM

FROM 1907–1909
THE PAY AS YOU ENTER CAR
HAS BEEN ADOPTED BY
LEADING ROADS FROM
COAST TO COAST.

THE PAY AS YOU ENTER CAR CORP.
50 CHURCH ST. NEW YORK CITY

P.A.Y.E. Corporation advertisement map of the U.S.A. identifying Grand Rapids and 32 other cities where PAYE cars were already operating.

Electric Traction Weekly
Vol 5, No. 39,
September 25, 1909,
pp. 130-131

one labeled "Exit." Passengers left the P.A.Y.E. car by either the front or rear platform.

A passenger boarded the car by the rearmost steps, then continued around a dividing rail and had to deposit his fare in the fare box before he could enter through the rear bulkhead door of the car proper. The conductor stood by the fare box and rang up each fare as it was deposited.

The enclosed rear platform was extra-large to accommodate passengers who were waiting to pay their fares as well as passengers who were trying to find the coins to deposit in the fare box. The conductor made change for those who did not have exactly five cents. The conductor also provided transfers and watched incoming and exiting passengers. He was responsible for signaling the motorman to start or stop. If a crowd boarded the car, the signal to start the car could be given by the conductor while some of the passengers waiting to pay their fares were still on the rear platform. This choice usually was made if the car had fallen behind schedule.

Many P.A.Y.E. cars were designed for single-end operation only and required either a loop or wye at the end of the line. The Taylor-Wealthy line had north end loops at

North Park and West Michigan fair grounds at Comstock Park, and a southern end loop at Ramona Park. The Division-Plainfield line had a northern loop at Knapp and Plainfield intersection and a southern loop at Detroit Street-Division Avenue intersection. Several of the Grand Rapids street railway lines had wyes at both ends of the line.

Manager Hanchett stated that after the P.A.Y.E. cars had been thoroughly tested and shown to be efficient in service, then the thirty-three older double-truck cars would be gradually converted into P.A.Y.E. cars in the company's car shops. Hanchett noted the platforms of the thirty-three older cars would have to be extended, doors changed so they slid in the opposite direction from the way they formerly did, and be at the end of the exit and entrance passageways. Some stationary seats at each end of the car would have to be removed to allow for proper aisle width for separate entrance and exit doors, a fundamental part of the P.A.Y.E. patent.

The Grand Rapids Railway had to pay a royalty to the patent owner for every car built or converted into a P.A.Y.E. car. General Manager Hanchett was confident that the income the company received by collecting all the fares and the reduced cost associated with not requiring as many cars to maintain rush hour schedules would make the change to P.A.Y.E. cars a good investment. Passengers would also benefit as their trips would be faster.

Thomas W. Casey, Manager of the Pay-As-You-Enter Car Company of New York City visited Grand Rapids on March 16, 1909, to discuss plans to convert other cars to the P.A.Y.E. configuration. Casey stated twenty-one American cities already used the system including Chicago, Milwaukee, Cleveland, Columbus, and Buffalo. He remarked the streetcar companies were not the only ones pleased with the cars. Both employees and passengers approved of the cars as well.

The first P.A.Y.E. cars arriving in Grand Rapids were assigned car numbers 318-341. Car No. 320 was the first P.A.Y.E. car to make a trial run in Grand Rapids on August 17, 1909. Ten two-man crews and ten extra men received operating instructions in August. Special attention was given to operating the air brakes. The air for the brakes was supplied by an electric compressor at the front of the car. The motormen were also instructed how to operate the front exit door, over which they had sole control.

Several of the P.A.Y.E. cars derailed on curves while undergoing trial runs. Mechanics determined the bolts on the bottom of cars prevented the trucks from swinging freely on the king pins.

The Company published an advertisement on September 10 announcing that

> COMMENCING SUNDAY SEPTEMBER TWELFTH, PAY-AS-YOU-ENTER CARS WILL BE PLACED IN SERVICE ON THE DIVISION-PLAINFIELD AVE. LINE.

The advertisement included the following message:

> **By the adoption of this type of car the company expects to provide a better service, with greater safety and comfort to passengers . . .**

Both the *Grand Rapids Herald* and *Grand Rapids Evening Press* reported the P.A.Y.E. streetcars were an instantaneous success. The *Grand Rapids Evening Press* attributed the successful first day of operation to the street railway company's educational campaign to instruct passengers on how to board P.A.Y.E. cars, pay their fares, and how to exit the cars without interfering with boarding passengers.

When Paying Fares.

ENTRANCE   EXIT

By the adoption of this type of car the company expects to provide a better service, with greater safety and comfort to passengers, and this expectation can be realized only with the full co-operation of the public in obeying the following regulations:

1. All passengers are required to enter the car at the rear end only and by step marked "ENTRANCE."

2. Passengers will please have exact fare in hand before boarding car.

3. On boarding platform passengers will deposit cash fare in fare box and immediately pass into the car, moving as far as possible to the front.

4. Passengers riding on transfers will please have transfers unfolded, and ready to hand to the conductor.

5. Transfers will be issued only at the time fares are paid.

6. Passengers are urged to leave car by front door.

7. Passengers desiring information, presenting money to be changed, or with question as to transfer, will be requested to step aside until others on the platform have passed into the car.

GRAND RAPIDS RAILWAY COMPANY,
BENJ. S. HANCHETT,
General Manager and Treasurer.

The *Evening Press* concluded that:

> Experience showed, however, that had there not been a campaign of education it would have been almost impossible to operate the cars and the experience of Pittsburg might have been repeated. In the Steel City the company placed the cars in operation with comparatively little preliminary announcement. Passengers crowded upon the platforms as they had upon the other cars, few had the exact change ready, they became angry when held up, there were complaints and almost riots in a few instances and finally in despair the cars were taken off temporarily in order that schedules might be maintained.

The streetcar company published this notice of seven new regulations in the newspaper to help riders understand the new Pay-As-You-Enter cars.

Grand Rapids Herald
September 10, 1909

Upon boarding the new Pay-As-You-Enter cars, riders were given a fourteen- page pamphlet describing the new cars and extolling their advantages. The pamphlet contained pictures showing the front and rear doors of a P.A.Y.E. car, and the evolution of progress made beginning with a horsecar, a cable car, a single-truck electric car and finally a double-truck electric P.A.Y.E. car—an example of "the highest type of street cars ever built in America."

P.A.Y.E. streetcar No. 321, an example of the first standard double-end P.A.Y.E. cars that ran on Grand Rapids streets in 1909, on Monroe Ave.

Karl Heckman

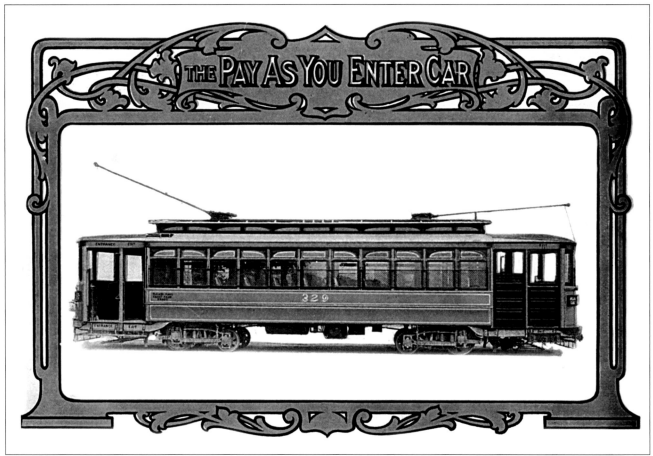

THE PAY AS YOU ENTER CAR

Pay-As-You-Enter streetcar on the front cover of P.A.Y.E. pamphlet published in September 1909 by the Grand Rapids Railway Company,

Grand Rapids Public Library

THE
PAY-AS-YOU-ENTER CAR

TO OUR PATRONS :

The Grand Rapids Railway Company, aiming at all times to provide for the people of Grand Rapids a modern, up-to-date street car system, has placed in operation on the Division and Plainfield Avenue line, twelve cars that are considered the highest type of the modern equipment, being the first of the style known as the "PAY-AS-YOU-ENTER" type to be introduced in Michigan. These cars are unsurpassed in comfort, finish, power and solidity of construction, and with the co-operation of our passengers will give a better service, with greater safety and comfort than has heretofore been possible with the old style of street car.

Very respectfully

BENJ. S. HANCHETT,

General Manager and Treasurer.

1

Pages 1-2 of P.A.Y.E. pamphlet.

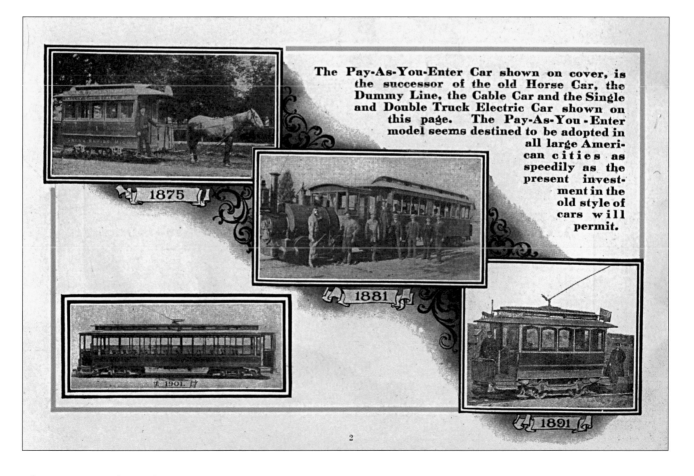

The Pay-As-You-Enter Car shown on cover, is the successor of the old Horse Car, the Dummy Line, the Cable Car and the Single and Double Truck Electric Car shown on this page. The Pay-As-You-Enter model seems destined to be adopted in all large American cities as speedily as the present investment in the old style of cars will permit.

1875

1881

1901.

1891

2

ADVANTAGES OF THE NEW CAR.

The New Pay-As-You-Enter Car Systematizes the Movement of Passengers.

A passenger entering the car meets no passengers struggling to get off. A passenger getting off meets nobody struggling to get on.

In the old style of cars the two steps, the two platforms and the two doors were used indiscriminately by incoming and outgoing passengers.

In the new car the entrance and the exits are separate and distinct.

The Pay-As-You-Enter Car introduces system in the place of absolute confusion, and necessarily adds greatly to the comfort and satisfaction as well as to the rapidity of service.

The New Pay-As-You-Enter Car Provides Much Better Ventilation.

It insures a regular and full supply of fresh air in the car, without the alteration of extreme drafts and stagnation experienced in the old style of cars.

3

Pages 3-4 of P.A.Y.E. pamphlet.

Correct position of conductor on rear platform and method of passenger paying fare.

Front exit door and correct
position of passenger alighting
from car.

5

Pages 5-6 of P.A.Y.E. pamphlet.

CO-OPERATION OF PASSENGERS.

Passengers are earnestly requested to co-operate in obtaining the great advantages which this car affords in Speed, Comfort and Safety, by systematically following these few rules:

1. Board the car at the rear platform at the part marked "Entrance."

2. Have exact fare, small change or unfolded transfer in hand; if cash fare, deposit same in fare box; or if transfer, hand to conductor. Ask for transfer, if one is needed, when paying fare; pass promptly into the car, and as far forward as possible,

3. One block, *or at least one-half block* before reaching cross-street where you wish to alight, use push button to notify conductor. Leave the car, through the *front* door if convenient, and face forward to avoid accidents.

4. *Do not remain on rear platform.*

Experience of years with the crowded platforms of the old style cars has shown to all that a clear platform is necessary for comfort and safety of passengers and rapidity of service.

6

Chapter 7: Grand Rapids Streetcar Operations (1910-1924)

The Pay-As-You-Enter Car Converted for Summer Use.

Pages 7-8 of P.A.Y.E. pamphlet.

DESCRIPTION

THE cut appearing on cover shows this car as it looks from the outside. The car is approximately forty-six feet long.

For the purpose of greater comfort to passengers and in order that less time may be consumed in making stops, entrance is restricted to the rear compartment, although persons may leave the car at either end, but the annoying situation created by the attempt of one set of persons to leave the car, by the same step as that by which other persons are seeking to board the car, at the same time, is eliminated. Persons who desire to enter the car may do so at the point marked "Entrance," stepping within a commodious compartment seven feet six inches long by approximately six feet wide. They then move in past the conductor who stands at the point shown, the cash fare is dropped in a fare box or the transfer handed conductor as the passenger enters the main part of the car. As soon as all of the passengers have stepped

8

within the vestibule (which will hold more than twenty persons) the conductor who always maintains his position in the rear compartment, gives the signal to the motorman to proceed, the passengers meanwhile entering the car as soon as the fare has been paid. Obviously it will promote the convenience of all passengers if each one has the exact fare in readiness to pay as he passes the conductor.

In order that there may be space in the vestibule for persons who may board the car at the next stopping place, passengers are not allowed to remain standing on the rear platform.

The view on page 4 shows the rear compartment of the car, which is enclosed on three sides so that ample protection from the weather is afforded. On page 5 is shown the forward compartment of the car with the exit-door open and a passenger alighting.

Between each window on either side of the car, there is placed a push-button by means of which a passenger desiring to leave the car may communicate his wishes to both the conductor and motorman as

9

Pages 9-10 of P.A.Y.E. pamphlet.

the car is approaching his destination, It is optional with the passenger as to whether he will leave the car through the sliding door at the rear, or through the door at the front of the car. This method of arranging the entrances and exits practically affords facilities three times as great as those provided on the present standard closed cars. The aisle within the car is about six inches wider than that on other cars and there will be an unobstructed view both forward and backward, through the plate-glass windows in the doors of the car.

Each car is driven by two powerful motors and is equipped with both air-brakes and hand-brakes. The electrical equipment has been carefully installed and in a manner in full accord with insurance regulations, especially heavy insulation being used. It is obvious that a car of this character is much heavier than our present closed cars and because of this fact the stopping and starting should never be attended with any discomfort, and the movement of the car is more agreeable.

10

Each car is also heated by the latest improved hot water heater assuring as uniform a temperature as it is possible to maintain.

Briefly then it will be seen that the use of such a car will systematize the entrance and exit of passengers, materially adding to their comfort and shortening the time now consumed in making stops; that there will be no necessity for the conductor to continually pass and repass through the car, a course of procedure always likely to be attended with more or less annoyance to passengers, especially to women; that by reason of the conductor's location he will always be able to definitely assure himself that all persons desirous of either entering or leaving the car have done so before the signal to proceed is given, and the likelihood that the starting signal will be given prematurely by some impatient passenger, as is now frequently the case, is almost entirely eliminated; the conditions of travel, particularly for women and children, will therefore be very greatly improved by the use of this car; but the success of these cars in service is dependent very largely

11

Pages 11-12 of P.A.Y.E. pamphlet.

upon the intelligent and cordial co-operation of the public. The use of the **PAY-AS-YOU-ENTER** Car will prove to be a step in advance toward the bettering of transportation conditions.

12

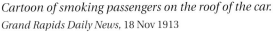
Cartoon of smoking passengers on the roof of the car.
Grand Rapids Daily News, 18 Nov 1913

Cartoon of woman leaving P.A.Y.E. car in a cloud of smoke.
Grand Rapids Press, 20 Dec 1913

The front vestibule of a P. A. Y. E. car.

The company purchased twelve more P.A.Y.E. streetcars. On August 18 the *Grand Rapids Press* praised the P.A.Y.E. streetcars operating in Grand Rapids as:

> . . . the nearest approach to a Pullman on any city rapid transit line. The cars have air brakes, hot water heat, double exits, a safety door, a fare box, electric signaling buttons, wide aisles, comfortable seats, wide windows, an entrance separate from the exit, so that incoming passengers can board the car while outgoing passengers are being discharged, a safety exit door controlled by the motorman, the conductor always on the rear platform, and many other features that make them street car models.

Smoking in Streetcars Continues To Be a Problem

Despite the hopes of the non-smoking riders, the new P.A.Y.E. cars proved to be just as smoky as the old cars. Offended riders were motivated to start circulating petitions calling for a smoking ban on the streetcars. One anti-smoker wrote a letter to *the Grand Rapids Evening Press* complaining that, "You let six or a dozen men get into the closed vestibule of

the front end of a P.A.Y.E. car with old pipes, most all qualities of cigars and vile cigarettes, you have a condition of things in regard to health and morals that you do not need to talk about, just stop it."

At least twenty news accounts and letters were published during the next month including a letter in which the author contended that there was no excuse for allowing the entrances to streetcars "to be filled with men belching forth fire, smoke and lava in the faces of people who wish to enter the car without being obliged to run the gauntlet to make it." One letter writer even suggested the street railway provide separate "Jim Crow" style cars for smokers.

Ten P.A.Y.E. Cars Built for Hill Service

The Cincinnati Car Company built ten big double-truck P.A.Y.E. cars specially designed for the Michigan-Lyon Street hill line in 1912. The first of these "hill cars" arrived in October and were sent to the shops to be outfitted with four fifty-horsepower motors and equipped with both air and hand brakes. Magnetic brakes were not installed in these hill cars because of a belief that magnetic brakes could not be used effectively on double-truck cars. The car bodies of the new streetcars were twenty-eight feet long and the total length was forty feet when the front and rear platforms were included. Each car had a seating capacity of thirty-five passengers.

Derailers were installed on the uphill track on both the Michigan Avenue and Lyon Street hills as a safety measure to prevent runaway cars from sliding backwards down the steep hills.

The company's car roster numbered 134 cars at the end of 1912, including the 24 P.A.Y.E. cars previously purchased by the company for the Division and Lafayette lines and the 10 new hill line P.A.Y.E. cars. None of the P.A.Y.E. cars were converted from older equipment.

New Streetcar Lamps Identify Routes of Each P.A.Y.E. Streetcar

Individuals who had been having difficulty reading street railway car line signs on the big P. A. Y. E. cars at night were surprised to see attractive colored electric lamps hanging over the front doors of the cars that indicating which car would get take home. The busy Division Avenue-Plainfield line cars had deep blue colored lamps; the Stocking-Lafayette cars had amber yellow lamps and the Michigan-Lyon line cars had red lamps which made nighttime identification of each line much easier for passengers.

Older Streetcars Converted to P.A.Y.E. Cars

The street railway began rebuilding twenty of its thirty-foot double-truck streetcars to P.A.Y.E. car configuration in the company's shops in January 1919. The bulkheads were removed and platforms changed so they conformed to P.A.Y.E. specifications. The streetcar company estimated that the cost of reconfiguring each old car to P.A.Y.E. standards at $500 per car. The first seven modified cars were assigned to service on the West Bridge-Grandville and the Wealthy-Taylor lines. Part of the next group of these was assigned to the Wealthy-Scribner line.

The P.A.Y.E. car became the standard streetcar of Grand Rapids until the Hall Street carbarn fire in July 1924 prompted management to seek new innovative designs for future streetcar orders.

Birney Safety Cars: the Second Standard Streetcar in Grand Rapids (1920-1935)

The nationwide success of the "wildcat" jitney buses during 1914-1915 severely hurt many streetcar companies through lost passengers and income. The Grand Rapids Railway Company was no exception. What made riding jitneys so attractive to enough streetcar riders to cause this decrease in patronage?

Jitneys were able travel faster and more frequently than streetcars. Also, streetcars had to meet franchise regulations that required numerous stops and operation for a much longer day rather than just the two daily rush hours.

It was obvious if street railway companies were to survive growing bus and private automobile competition they would need to provide faster and more frequent service at lower cost than the streetcars operating in 1914-1915. Unfortunately, the Pay-As-You-Enter streetcar that the Grand Rapids Railway had chosen as its standard car was economical to operate only when carrying more than thirty to forty passengers. The P.A.Y.E. cars were not economical to operate for base off-peak service on several lines or on lightly-traveled routes.

One of the Birney streetcar 367-385 series.

David Winick Collection at Grand Rapids Public Museum

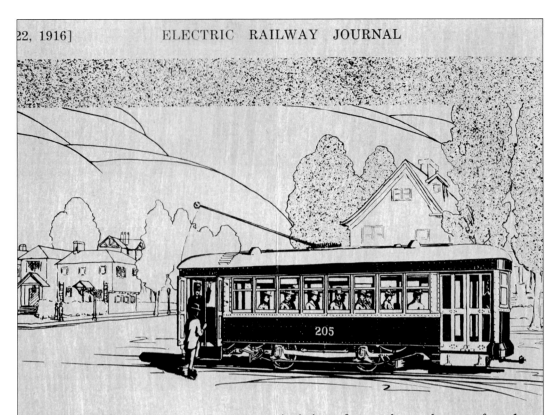

single-truck cars, judging from the volume of orders received, seem to have fitted themselves perfectly into the economic situation of the electric railway field. Many varying conditions well could be cited as having been responsible for the urgent necessity of the change by a large number of railways from heavy, double-truck equipment to the economical, light-weight, single-truck type of car. How the arising of these conditions has worked to the great advantage of the companies that were obliged to make the change may be seen very plainly from the fact that these companies are operating now at a profit. But the most convincing proof of the economic value of operating with single-truck cars and the fact that this economic value is well recognized by the field is that a very great number of the companies now using light-weight cars have done away with heavy, double-truck equipment because of their realization of the increase in net revenue accruing from such action rather than because they absolutely were forced into the step. The field seems to be finding in one instance after another that operations at one time regarded as unsuited for single-truck equipment are adapted perfectly well to it and as a consequence statistics are showing better returns on the investment of the stockholders of these roads.

THE J. G. BRILL COMPANY, PHILADELPHIA, PA.

AMERICAN CAR COMPANY, ST. LOUIS, MO.

G. C. KUHLMAN CAR COMPANY, CLEVELAND, OHIO

WASON MFG. COMPANY, SPRINGFIELD, MASS.

Pacific Coast Office: 907 Monadnock Building, San Francisco

Company advertisement for one man streetcars.

Electric Railway Journal, 22 Apr 1916

The First Birney Streetcar

Charles O. Birney, superintendent of construction for the Stone and Webster Corporation, an owner of numerous traction companies in the southwestern states, designed a unique streetcar in an attempt to solve the problem. The streetcar he designed was a small, lightweight single-truck car that could be operated very efficiently by a one-man crew. The substantial lower labor cost coupled with the lower energy required to operate the lightweight car, Birney argued, could allow a streetcar company to provide more frequent service—meaning more convenient service—which would attract more riders.

Birney built two demonstration streetcars in 1915 using components from the following companies: two car bodies by the American Car Company of St. Louis; the single truck for each car by J. G. Brill Company of Philadelphia; the electrical equipment by the General Electric Company of Schenectady; and the air brakes and other air-operated safety control equipment by the Westinghouse Traction Brake Company of Wilmerding, Pa.

Charles Birney called the streetcar he designed the "Safety Car" because of the safety devices included its design due to its being a one-man. These safety features included:

• The car could not be moved nor the brakes released until the door was closed.
• The car door could not be opened until the air brakes were applied and the controller moved to the off position. As no one could enter or leave the car once the car was in motion greatly reduced the number of accidents involving passengers trying to climb aboard or alight.
• The motorman of a Birney Safety Car had to keep his hand down on the controller or his foot on a special foot pedal. If he became incapacitated and released either before setting the brakes, the car was brought to a stop. Such a feature became known as a "dead man control."

The streetcar company ordered nineteen new one-man safety street cars in 1920 in an attempt to provide improved service at a lower cost. Rising operating costs were a significant problem in addition to jitney and private automobile competition that was eating into the streetcar company's income. By closely monitoring the operation of these new cars, the company would have a better idea as to how close the cars came to meeting the manufacturer's claims of safety, reliability, and economy. Management also wanted to see how well these new cars would be received by the riding public.

Grand Rapids Herald, 22 Feb 1920

Step Up, Ladies and Gentlemen, and Be Introduced to Your New Friend, The Only One-Door Street Car in Captivity That Can't Be Started while You Are Getting On Or Off. Nineteen of Them are Coming to Grand Rapids to Aid Better Transportation. They Have Proved Successful in Many Cities and Use Is Increasing.
By O. F. Beemer

Introducing the One-Man Safety Birney Street Car

Through investigations in almost all the cities of the country, it had been determined that the public desired a quicker transit from one point to another and wants a car available the instant desired . . .

Street railways wished to increase the sale of their product—Transportation—and thus produce a larger revenue to offset the increased cost of production due to increases in material and labor. At the same time they wanted to secure a return on the investment which will attract capital to the street railway industry.

The Grand Rapids Railway company was not an exception to this rule, although there have been some mighty acrid expressions by patrons who possess, or have possessed, the idea the local company did not have these objectives in mind . . .

Frequent and Rapid Transportation

Here is the history of the safety car. Approximately four years ago, the Stone and Webster Corporation discovered that rising costs and jitney bus competition were playing havoc with the net earnings of their properties in the south and west. A careful investigation was made as to ways and means of combating the jitney bus and the solution naturally resolved itself into more service and faster schedules.

The heavy weight of the old equipment and the cost of platform labor, however, made the cost of increased service more than the increased revenue could possibly bring them. This necessitated an attempt to cut down the cost of operations and thus the light weight safety car was developed through co-operation of the Stone and Webster engineers, the car builders and electrical and air brake manufacturers.

Benefits are Estimated

The success of the car, is claimed by H. G. Bradlee, of the Stone and Webster corporation, who says that in Houston, Texas, "The increase in car mileage has been 68.3 per cent, and the increased receipts 41.2 per cent; and in Seattle on two lines, the increase in car miles on one line has been 21.4 per cent and the increase in receipts 29.5 per cent; on the other line the increase in car mileage has been 29 per cent and the increase in receipts: 49 per cent."

In 1916, 8 per cent of all city surface cars purchased were safety cars; in 1917, 20 per cent, and in 1918, 40 per cent.

Madigan Predicted Conditions

So the Grand Rapids Railway company has turned to this type of car with a hope of meeting traffic conditions in Grand Rapids. John C. Madigan, one of the best known of the company's officers, several years ago predicted, in a discussion with L. J. DeLamarter, vice president and general manager, that the one-man operated car would be the only solution of the problem, which even then was confronting the company. The prediction was made before the large Division avenue cars were purchased and it is apparent that his vision is being realized.

The local company will place orders at once for 19 of these one-man safety cars, having obtained the approval of the special committee of the city commission. They are an experiment or else the company would order more of them. The cars can be obtained in about 40 days and will be installed on such lines as the Madison, Butterworth and Carrier. If they are successful, the present equipment, on all lines will be gradually replaced by the smaller cars with a view of more rapid and more frequent service, although during peak traffic conditions the larger cars will supplement the one-man cars.

The small capacity of the car and the fact that it is operated by one man does away with the need of a large loading platform, which, in the past has invited the rider to linger and thus block the passageway to the inside of the car. With the safety car passengers are first let off before any get on. Very little confusion is said to result. Unconsciously the passengers attempt to have the exact fare ready, the percentage running about 25 per cent for they know that they are holding up the entire car by presenting large pieces of money to the conductor to change.

Car Operator Well Placed
The car operator is provided with an adjustable stool and on account of the closeness of the car body to the track he can sit down to do his work and still have a good view of the entire track ahead of him. The fare box is on his right, hung on brackets attached to a stanchion in the center of the platform. This stanchion is arranged to revolve so that the fare-box can be swung to the side to permit the operator to pass easily. The controller and brake valve are on the left side of the platform so as to allow as much space as possible for the entrance and exit of passengers. The door is 30 inches wide and gives sufficient width to permit passengers to pass in and out in single file. Cross seats are used throughout on the cars with grab handles on the seats."

No Further Roster Additions

No new streetcars were purchased in 1921. The street railway was pleased enough with the operating economies of the Birney cars to spend $56,000 to purchase eight more of the one-man safety cars in 1923. The company learned that operation of these cars had become a compromise between economy of operation and rider comfort. If not as comfortable to ride as the old cars, riders at least appreciated that their lower cost allowed for shorter headways.

The roster was in fact reduced when fifty-eight cars were destroyed in the Hall Street carbarn fire of 1924 (see Chapter 8). Among these were eight Birney cars purchased in 1920 and another Birney purchased in 1923.

Grand Rapid Begins Rebuilding Its Birney cars

The streetcar company rebuilt one of its Birney cars to make it more efficient to operate and to increase passenger comfort. The company described its achievement in its 1925 annual report:

> Another development has been the rebuilding of a "Birney" safety single truck car with spring-filled leather upholstered seats and cushions and a smoking compartment. This experiment if it proves out will be followed by the rebuilding of additional "Birney" cars.

Several Birney cars were assigned names rather than numbers when the cars went into the shops for rebuilding. This was to become a unique feature of Grand Rapids streetcar operation with cars being assigned names instead of numbers.

One of the Birney streetcar 386-393 Series. View looking northeast from the intersection of Lake Drive and Wealthy Avenue.
David Winick Collection at Grand Rapids Public Museum

Operations and Innovations (1924-1927)

Grand Rapids Railway Conducts a Traffic Survey

In order to determine the amount of street space used by automobiles compared to streetcars in downtown Grand Rapids, the Grand Rapids Railway made a survey of traffic in the downtown loop district on July 16, 1924. The survey was conducted during peak rush hours from an observation point on Monroe Avenue. During the morning and afternoon rush hours, 102 street cars and 1,052 automobiles passed by the survey point.

The company reported its findings in the September 1924 issue of its *Trolley Topics,* the company newsletter distributed free to streetcar riders. The total capacity of the 102 streetcars was 4,032 riders and actual count was 3,628. The total capacity of 1,052 autos was 4,532 with the actual count being 1,918 passengers.

The streetcars carried 98.9 per cent capacity loads while the autos carried loads at 42.5 per cent capacity. The average capacity of the 102 streetcars was 39.5 passengers per car with 35.5 actually carried; only four seats were empty on each streetcar. The average capacity of the 1,052 autos was 4.3 passengers while the actual count for each auto was 1.8.

Of the overall traffic, 8.83 per cent were streetcars, 91.17 per cent were autos. The 102 streetcars carried 63.8 per cent of the passengers while the 1,052 autos carried 36.2 per cent. The street space occupied by the street cars was 4,692 lineal feet while the autos occupied 14,728 lineal feet, or 75.8 per cent of street space—more than three times the amount occupied by the streetcars.

Finally, the street railway company summarized its traffic survey results as follows: The autos used seven times as much street space per passenger as used by the streetcars.

The company repeated the traffic survey of autos and streetcars a year later on October 25, 1925, and the results were virtually the same. The autos still carried an average of 1.8 passengers per auto and it required 28 autos to carry the same number of passengers that the average streetcar carried.

These two traffic surveys provided evidence that streetcars provided an important service by dramatically reducing street congestion in downtown areas such as Campau Square in Grand Rapids.

Ride the Street Car, Chat with Friends, Read, or Relax and Have No Worries.

HELPING SAVE STREET SPACE

All cities are trying to obtain the best and greatest use of the limited street space at their disposal. Surveys in many cities show street cars carry as high as 90 per cent of the traffic while using less than 10 per cent of the street space.

On October 5, 1925, a check of autos and street cars was made at a point in Monroe avenue. Summary of that check shows autos carried 1.7 passengers per auto. Thus 28 AUTOS would be required to carry the same number of passengers as carried by ONE STREET CAR.

The street space occupied by 28 autos, bumper to bumper, is 392 lineal feet, or illustrated, from Division and Monroe avenues to Ionia and Monroe avenues.

A street car occupies 46 lineal feet of street space.

The area space occupied by 28 autos is 2,078 square feet per passenger carried.

The area space occupied by one street car is 377 square feet or 8 square feet per passenger carried.

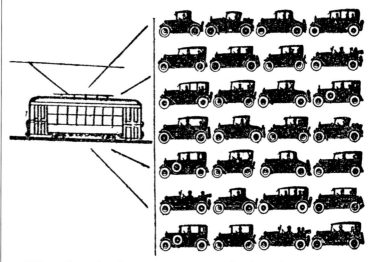

The sketch shows, comparatively, that one street car requires but a small fraction of the street space necessary for the operation of 28 autos.

This proves one of the greatest services rendered by the electric street railway—the conservation of street space, which is at a decided premium in all

Chart showing the relative amount of space occupied by one streetcar with 48 passengers and 28 automobiles with the same number of passengers at the rate of 1.8 passengers per auto based on a traffic survey done on July 16, 1924.

Trolley Topics, July 1924

New Bus Service

On May 5, 1924, a new feeder bus line began operating from Valley Avenue up the steep Bridge Street hill to the city limit at Bristol Avenue, connecting with the Bridge Street-Grandville Avenue streetcar line.

Buses began running on several streetcar routes to fill schedules after the July 1924, Hall Street carbarn fire destroyed sixty streetcars. Buses replaced all streetcar service on the Madison Avenue line on July 19. The company did not resume streetcar operations on Madison Avenue until September when it received a shipment of old cars from Akron, Ohio.

The Godfrey Avenue bus line began operating on its namesake between Hall Street and Campau Square on September 2, 1924. This bus line provided transportation for the residents of the Black Hills-Kensington community, and for workers employed in the factories in the Godfrey Avenue district, known as Pleasant Valley.

Bus service also began operating on the College–Lafayette Avenue line going as far north from Michigan Avenue as East Leonard Street. The buses connected with the Michigan Avenue streetcar line at both Lafayette and College avenues.

Using Electricity Economy Meters

Each streetcar had an economy meter installed in August 1924. The meter recorded the volume of electricity each motorman used to operate his car. A competitive campaign encouraged motormen to decrease the amount of energy used in service. A blind test at the beginning provided a basis for comparison. The Grand Rapids Railway Company was able to reduce the number of kilowatt-hours of electric power used per car-mile by 15.5 per cent.

"Read While You Ride" Campaign

Grand Rapids Railway began offering "Read as You Ride" service on all its morning streetcars effective October 15, 1924, a service that a few other street railways offered. Copies of the morning newspaper were placed in a box inside each streetcar. A passenger could deposit three cents and take a copy of the newspaper to read while riding the car.

Company Publications Help Keep Employees and Riders Informed

The Grand Rapids Railway began publishing two monthly newsletters during the 1920s. *Trolley Topics* was a newsletter published for riders. The first issue appeared in November 1923. Riders could pick up a free copy in a streetcar and read about streetcar line re-routings due to construction, how much the company was spending on specific construction projects, including those that benefited motorists who crowded the downtown streets with their automobiles. The riders read what movies and shows were playing at the downtown theaters. They even received a breakdown of what became of their streetcar fares. Riders were told forty-six cents out of every dollar went toward wages but other factors had to be considered in determining a proper fare.

The streetcar company also published a newsletter, *The Token,* for distribution among the company's employees and came with "a message of greater service and co-operation." Its mission was to help employees gain a better appreciation of what each of them did along with information of the various departments. Employees were encouraged to find ways to improve their performances and uphold service standards.

Passenger buying a copy of a Grand Rapids Herald newspaper inside the Minnesota streetcar.

Grand Rapids Public Museum

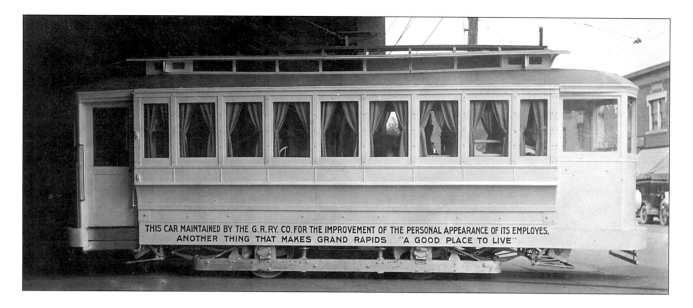

THIS CAR MAINTAINED BY THE G.R. RY. CO. FOR THE IMPROVEMENT OF THE PERSONAL APPEARANCE OF ITS EMPLOYEES. ANOTHER THING THAT MAKES GRAND RAPIDS "A GOOD PLACE TO LIVE"

Pure white Valet Personal Appearance car.

Grand Rapids Public Library

Employee Personal Appearance Car

L. J. DeLamarter issued an order that the uniforms of the "platform men" must be neat and clean. DeLamarter had the company's car shops provide a valet car painted pure white that traveled to each carbarn at least twice a week to keep the men "spic and span." This employee personal appearance car had two compartments: one for the tailor to do clothing repairs and the other where uniforms were pressed and shoes shined.

A Disaster Stimulates Innovations and Leads to a National Award

A cry of "Fire!" was heard at 3:50 A.M. on Saturday, July 19, 1924, at the worst possible location for the Grand Rapids Railway and at the worst possible time. The fire occurred at its car house on Hall Street at night when the barn was packed with streetcars awaiting their morning runs.

The result: Fifty-eight streetcars and two maintenance-of-way cars destroyed—nearly

Hall Street carbarn ruins with young spectators in the foreground.

Dave Winick Collection, Grand Rapids Public Museum

half of all the streetcars in town!

Most of the fifty-eight cars destroyed cars had been used in daily service. They included eight big heavyweight steel cars, nine newly purchased one-man Birney cars, ten Franklin-West Leonard "hill" cars equipped with special motors, a couple of maintenance-of-way cars and the *Honolulu*, the excursion car. The company had 136 streetcars prior to the fire and operated 102 of those cars during rush hours six days a week. The fire left the company with 76 street cars, not all of which were ready for service.

More than ten streetcars survived the fire because they were in the repair and paint shop which was adjacent to the burned out car house, but protected by a fire wall. Nine steel streetcars were among the survivors. All these cars were dragged out of the shops and hauled to points on the system where overhead power was still on. Seeking to profit from the catastrophe while the embers were still smoldering, the company put signs on the Division Avenue streetcars passing near the scene that read "This Car to the Fire."

Restoring Service

Grand Rapids Railway Company immediately pressed eight of its buses into service on the streetcar lines. One each was borrowed from the West Bridge Street and Alpine Avenue bus lines. Six other buses that had been in storage were also put into service. The company's repair shops began working double shifts to complete

Ruins of streetcar no. 340 after Hall Street carbarn fire, July 19, 1924.

Dave Winick Collection, Grand Rapids

Ruins of cars at Hall Street carbarn after fire on July 19, 1924.

Dave Winick Collection, Grand Rapids Public Museum

Chapter 8: Operations and Innovations (1924-1927)

Chimney still stands behind several steel frames of streetcars destroyed in Hall Street carbarn fire. View looking south towards Hall Street.

Dave Winick Collection, Grand Rapids Public Museum

streetcars in for overhaul at the time of the fire.

The company also leased three cars from the Muskegon Traction and Light Company in Michigan. Twelve additional double-truck cars were leased from Saginaw Transit Company. The twelve streetcars were shipped from Saginaw via a special Pere Marquette railway train. These streetcars had last operated in Bay City on August 10, 1921. The fifteen streetcars and the eight buses enabled the company to provide adequate service, but it was going to be a while before old headways were restored.

Finally, ten large streetcars from the Northern Ohio Traction and Light Company in Akron, Ohio, were borrowed. These cars arrived at the beginning of September and enabled the company to increase the service frequency.

The twelve Bay City-Saginaw cars and ten Akron, Ohio, cars came from streetcar companies owned by the Commonwealth Power, Railway and Light Company, the same holding company that owned the Grand Rapids Railway Company.*Most of these leased cars were still running in Grand Rapids at the end of 1924.

Converting Disaster into Opportunity

A group of employees watched their general manager poke through the ruins left after the July 19 carbarn fire. Given the circumstances they were surprised to see him in such high spirits. One employee reported General Manager Louis DeLamarter had a grin on his face the whole day. Another employee added DeLamarter had said that this was not a disaster but rather an opportunity.

Why did DeLamarter have that opinion? He knew the streetcars burned in the fire were insured. He also knew he could use the insurance money to buy new streetcars far better than the ones currently built by the various manufacturers. DeLamarter envisioned new streetcars that were much more economically efficient to operate, more comfortable to ride, more convenient, and more attractive to the riding public.

DeLamarter had met with one of the leading car builders in Chicago in 1924 before the disastrous fire. DeLamarter recalled

---

*The Commonwealth Power, Railway and Light Company was divided into two holding companies in January 1924: the Electric Railway Securities Company and the Commonwealth Power Corporation. This division placed the financially ailing traction properties and the very profitable power and light utility companies into separate holding companies. George Bush concluded in his book on the history of power companies in Michigan that the Electric Railway Securities Company was created for the sole purpose of the liquidation of the unprofitable electric transportation properties.

The Street Railways of Grand Rapids

the question he asked:

What have you that is new in car design?" I asked, after explaining my wants. The car builder reluctantly confessed that he had nothing new to offer. Still my idea, which seemed so simple, so natural and logical, obsessed me. It seemed to me that desirable changes in construction could be made comparatively easy.

Shortly after the meeting in Chicago, fire visited our Hall Street car house and destroyed more than 50 of our best cars. Our misfortune and adversity offered the opportunity for the new car design idea to be worked out.

Company Organizes Competition to Build Twenty-seven Streetcars

General Manager DeLamarter was unhappy with many of the features of the streetcars car builders offered in 1924. He disliked, "the average streetcars with the same color scheme, the same flat wheels, same old slat or cane seats, same clangy gongs, same old more or less dirty blue uniforms, same old dirty windows, same old advertising signs and same old hundred and one things our fathers and grandfathers looked at." He thought improvement was possible in both performance and appearance.

DeLamarter consulted his own engineers and then conferred with car builders, explaining the kind of new electric rail coach he wanted. He decided to organize a competition to achieve his goal of purchasing new streetcars based on his ideas. He succeeded in convincing three car manufacturers to enter the competition and build a sample test car of the kind he envisioned.

Research as a Management Tool

Louis J. DeLamarter became one of the first to use research as a major management tool in an attempt to revitalize electric street railways. He announced in the fall of 1924 that Grand Rapids was going to be the testing ground for developing a new type of streetcar. Three car manufacturers—Kuhlman Car Company in Cleveland, St. Louis Car Company in St. Louis, and the Lightweight Noiseless Electric Street Car Company in Minneapolis—agreed to participate in the competition by sending an experimental sample car each company believed was the kind of new streetcar DeLamarter wanted to purchase.

The cars built by these three competing companies were to be evaluated by employees, riders, traction experts, and others before the company made its decision to place an order for twenty-seven more cars that incorporated the best designs for efficiency, comfort, and appearance. The stage was set for Grand Rapids to become a leader in modern streetcar design.

Train of gondola cars carrying Akron street cars that have arrived at the Grand Rapids & Indiana interchange track adjacent to the streetcar track on the Taylor Street line at the west Michigan fairgrounds in Comstock Park. An accident investigator is pointing at the spot on the tracks where an accident had occurred earlier.

Dave Winick Collection, Grand Rapids Public Museum

Above: *"Minnesota" car on Lyon Street line. View of entrance into car and exit.*
Right: *Front view of "Minnesota" car.*
Minnesota Railroad Museum

Group photo of 21 men in front of the "Minnesota" street car on March 24, 1925 when the "Minnesota" made its first inspection trip on Grand Rapids streets. The motorman on the far left is Miles McDonald.
Grand Rapids Public Library

1924 Ends with Bad News and Hope for the Future

The number of fare-paying passengers riding on Grand Rapids Railway lines dropped dramatically by 13.07 per cent from 28,558,857 in 1923 to 24,825,018 in 1924. This meant less money available for any significant renovations.

The company had lost fifty-eight streetcars and two maintenance-of-way cars when the Hall Street car house burned down in July 1924. The company survived the loss by renting twenty-five streetcars, most of which were still running in Grand Rapids at the end of 1924. Service was augmented by the use of eight buses on streetcar routes.

Among the features that can be seen in this exterior view of the "Minnesota" electric coach is the step which was as easy to ascend as the first step on a flight of stairs, the doors which closed automatically, the large windows and the wheels which were bored to lighten the car and eliminate vibration.

David V. Tinder Collection, Clements Library

The Three Test Streetcars Make Their Debut

The *Minnesota* streetcar built by the Light Weight Noiseless Electric Street Car Company was the first of the three test cars to be delivered to Grand Rapids. The *Minnesota* car with railway officials as passengers, made its first trip in Grand Rapids on Tuesday, March 24. The *Minnesota* was painted in old gold and maroon, the University of Minnesota colors, and had the state name painted on each side of the car.

The street railway company took a group of technical experts, transportation men and city officials on an inspection trip so that they could evaluate how the *Minnesota* performed on city streets. The new car was then taken to the shops where meters were installed to measure the rate of electric power usage, accelera-tion, noise, vibration, and braking.

Grand Rapids Railway General Manager DeLamarter described some of the character-istics of the *Minnesota* car when he spoke to a reporter. "The new car rides like a Pullman car or a parlor car and weighs only 24,500 pounds, less than half the weight of the big steel Divi-sion Avenue cars of 57,000 pounds. It carries 43 passengers, the seating capacity of the Di-vision Avenue cars." DeLamarter went on to say that, "The vehicle is so different from the old type streetcar that it will not be called a street-car, but instead an 'electric motor coach.'"

The car was equipped with unusual safety features such as the brakes on each axle and an automatic brake that would not allow the car to move until the doors were closed. The *Minnesota* had a number of design features visible in this photograph of the car's exterior.

"Ohio" car entering loop on the end of the Wealthy street car line adjacent Ramona Park.

Washington University Library

The *Ohio* electric coach, built by the G. C. Kuhlman Car Company of Cleveland, Ohio, arrived in Grand Rapids on May 2. The car was named *Ohio* in honor of the builder's home state. Its colors of gray and scarlet were the same as those of Ohio State University whose name was painted on both sides of the streetcar.

The *Grand Rapids Herald* reported the Kuhlman Car Company had produced an electric railway coach, "that embodied the newest comfort-giving, time-saving, speed-producing and safety requirements." It added the *Ohio* car had a number of important and outstanding features including a "new type of rubber cushion wheel, roller bearings; anti-friction bearing motors; drum type, clasp shoe, eight wheel brakes; plush seats of the Pullman type; automatic rear exit emergency door."

The *St. Louis* electric coach built by the St. Louis Car Company of St. Louis, Missouri, ar-

rived in Grand Rapids on May 3 a day after the arrival of the *Ohio*. The builder had painted the *St. Louis* car in the blue and white colors of St. Louis University and lettered the name "St. Louis" on each side.

According to the *Grand Rapids Herald*, the *St. Louis* electric coach "has many features not embodied in the others. It carries a sheet steel skirt which partly hides the trucks and wheels and which is carried under the bumpers at the front and rear. This is aimed to reduce noise." The newspaper listed other features including "brass window hardware, Pantasote leather curtains, half-inch plate glass in front of the operator designed to prevent fogging and frosting, specially designed trucks, porcelain enameled stanchions, rear spotlight, five light display at the front of the coach and a loudspeaker for street announcing."

"St. Louis" sample competition car in inspection line up in Grand Rapids, May 9, 1925.

Washington University Library

Traction Officials and the Public Inspect the Test Cars

The Grand Rapids Railway company organized a night inspection trip to exhibit all three streetcars on the evening of May 5, 1925, for more than a hundred visiting traction officials and engineers. Their designs and performances elicited enthusiastic comments about the improved lighting arrangements, rapid acceleration, and automobile-style brakes. More traction company officials traveled to Grand Rapids to inspect the three new electric rail coaches during the summer of 1925.

The *Grand Rapids Herald* noted that all three of the test cars possessed smooth riding and noiseless qualities that marked a significant advance in traction engineering. The light weight of the cars meant that streetcar companies would save a significant amount of money in track maintenance and power consumption. The Grand Rapids Railway Company estimated to save about $125,000 annually.

On May 9 approximately 3,000 people visited the three new electric coaches when they were put on display on the Lyon Street siding adjacent to the Pantlind Hotel in downtown Grand Rapids. The three test cars began running on the Cherry line the very next day. Each of the test cars ultimately ran on several lines equipped with a loop or wye at the ends. Experiencing the cars in actual service enabled riders to make more informed decisions about what they liked most when given three choices.

Imagination's Streetcars

The *Grand Rapids Herald* on May 10 praised the "Imagination's Streetcars" that were on display in Grand Rapids. The editor wrote that:

Because ponderous, noisy cars had been the rule in the past was not, imagination reasoned, good cause for their continuance. Why not lighter, quieter cars with quicker acceleration and with lower operating costs?

The *Minnesota*, *Ohio* and *St. Louis* with their hitherto untried designs, are the results of that entrance of imagination into the public utility field. Already their value has been demonstrated. They move with a new quietude over the rails. They "pick up" speed more readily. Their operation cost is only about half that of the old models. When the riding public finally decides which of the new types it prefers, Grand Rapids will benefit in the decreased cost of street railway operation, in the absence of rattle and clatter and in greater riding comfort. Indirectly all street railways will benefit because, through the laboratory experiment in Grand Rapids, an improved electric coach will be made available and its value proven.

It remained for Louis C. DeLamarter, vice-president and general manager of the Grand Rapids Railway Company, to awaken the engineers of the car building companies by its suggestions for all companies to enter the local contest. The engineers caught the spirit of the automotive world and three coaches on exhibition here contain more new features than have been placed on street cars before in the last 25 years.

The eyes of car builders, motor manufacturers, traction experts and all of the allied lines have been turned toward Grand Rapids during the last week. Nearly 50 executives and specialists have journeyed here, many of them from long distances to see the new cars. Scores of others will come here during the next few weeks.

Above — The "St. Louis" Car of the General Type Adopted for New Equipment.

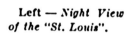

Left — Night View of the "St. Louis".

Above—Interior of the "St. Louis" Showing Improved Design.

Above — Interior of the "Ramona" — Birney Car Rebuilt According to Plans of G. R. Railway Co.

Photo of "Ramona" Birney street car.

Annual Report for 1925

The "Ramona"—The Grand Rapids Rebuilt Birney Car.

The Street Railways of Grand Rapids

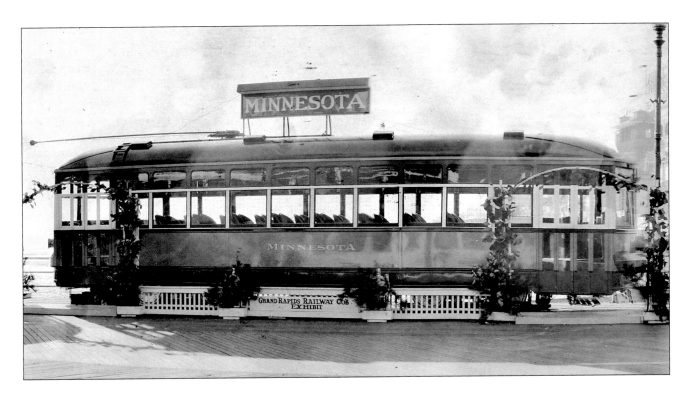

Rebuilding a Birney Streetcar

The Grand Rapids Railway Company described what the company had done while overhauling streetcars in their shops during 1925 in the company's Annual Report for that year: "Another development has been the rebuilding of a 'Birney' safety single truck car with spring-filled leather upholstered seats and cushions and a smoking compartment. This experiment, if it proves out, will be followed by the rebuilding of additional 'Birney' cars." The first Birney streetcar rebuilt according to the Grand Rapids Railway Company's plans was named *Ramona* in honor of Ramona Park, the streetcar company's most popular resort on Reed's Lake.

The *Ramona* had a "modish color scheme of katydid green and forget-me-not blue." The *Ramona* was the first Grand Rapids streetcar to be rebuilt with a skirt low enough to reduce the level of the noise made by the motors and gears, as well as the sounds made by the wheels.

The *Ramona* was equipped with a twelve-inch band skirt around the bottom of the car body covering the wheels and trucks to within six to eight inches of the ground. The skirt was made of a synthetic material that absorbed sound instead of reflecting it. The *Ramona* also had a smoking compartment. The *Ramona* was the first of a series of Birney cars the company owned modified to the new standard for Birneys operating in Grand Rapids.

L. J. DeLamarter made certain the twenty-seven cars the company planned to purchase would be equipped with the noise absorbing skirts.

Four Grand Rapids Streetcars Displayed on the Boardwalk at Atlantic City

The three test sample electric coaches and the Birney car, rebuilt to DeLamarter's specifications, had attracted nationwide attention by the summer of 1925. The three electric coaches had proven so quiet, comfortable and efficient that traction experts throughout the United States wanted to see the cars for themselves.

The committee in charge of the American Electric Railway Association Convention requested the new Grand Rapids-style cars be sent as a special feature within the exhibit of the latest development in streetcars at its annual convention held in Atlantic City, New Jersey, on October 5-9, 1925. The Grand Rapids Railway Company was happy to oblige.

By the fall of 1925 the three test cars had made Grand Rapids a "spark plug," known nationally and internationally, for the modern streetcars the three car manufacturing companies had built and tested in Grand Rapids.

The November 5, 1925, *Grand Rapids Press* editorial on streetcars drew attention to an important component of the success in Grand Rapids when it stated, "Among many electric railway men, accustomed to save on every item of paint and repairs during the recent lean years, the Grand Rapids company's idea that traction firms might successfully employ showmanship and sell their services to the public via comfort, snappy uniforms and attractive silent cars came as a revelation."

"Minnesota" car on exhibit on Young's Million Dollar Boardwalk Pier at Atlantic City during the American Street Railway Association Convention, October 5-9, 1925.

Sam Ashendorf Collection

Top to bottom: The "Ohio" car, the "St. Louis" car and the "Ramona" Birney Car, on exhibit on Young's Million Dollar Boardwalk Pier at Atlantic City during the American Street Railway Association Convention, October 5-9, 1925. The "Ramona" Birney Car, had been modified in Grand Rapids car shops.

Sam Ashendorf Collection

Panoramic view of 4 different streetcars in the Grand Rapids Railway exhibition the Boardwalk during the American Street Railway Association convention, October 5-9, 1925 at Atlantic City.

Sam Ashendorf Collection

Miles McDonald stands between two other Grand Rapids Railway Chauffeurs at Atlantic City.

Grand Rapids Public Library

Painting and Naming Streetcars

The first Grand Rapids streetcar to be given a name instead of a number had been the streetcar company's party and excursion car, which was named the *Honolulu* when it began running in Grand Rapids in 1906. DeLamarter liked the idea of personalizing streetcars with names and saw no need for numbers. He began the tradition when he directed the builders of the three test cars to have the names "Minnesota," "Ohio," and "St. Louis" already painted on the cars when they arrived in 1925.

The company held contests in public and parochial schools for the best color designs for a streetcar that would also bear the name of the school. The school's pennant was painted in its colors on both sides of the streetcar. Central High school's colors were yellow and white; Union High, red and white; South High, red and blue; Vocational school, white and green; Creston High's, gold and blue. When a car went to the shop for repainting, the car could be assigned the unique name of a school, neighborhood, a local pioneer, or person prominent in the development of Grand Rapids.

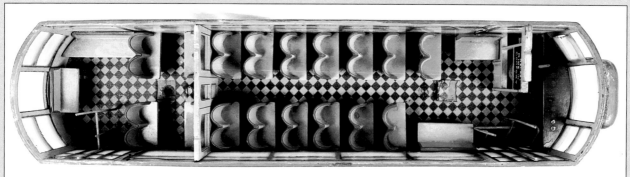

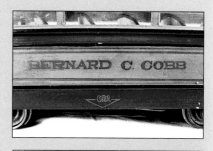

New Hall Street carbarn, View looking northwest.
Annual Report for 1925, p. 6

The Final Design of the Grand Rapids Electric Coach

The Grand Rapids Railway built two different wooden scale models of the *St. Louis* car to determine how different window sizes and color patterns would affect the appearance of the car. The company decided upon nine smaller side windows with wrap-around painted narrow bands. These accentuated a wide painted panel that produced the long flowing lines being sought by car designers as having the greatest appeal to the riding public.

External features on the front of the car were functional and aesthetic, such as the two headlights and a new style bumper. One front window was designed so a large sign displaying the route number could easily be changed.

Continued Trackwork and Expanding Bus Service

A loop was built adjacent to Walker Avenue on the western end of the West Leonard Street line in 1925. This improved safety as the cars no longer had to stop in the middle of West Leonard Street to change the trolley poles. Since a wye was built at the east end of the Franklin Street line during 1924, the addition of a loop at the west end enabled the company to save money by assigning one-man cars to the West Leonard-Franklin Street line.

The company replaced a little over two miles of old track on the Wealthy Street car line, and also installed new rails and a concrete foundation on Michigan Avenue between Ottawa and Monroe avenues.

A new bus feeder line on Kalamazoo Avenue was instituted and the bus service headway on Godfrey Avenue was shortened.

Left: *Interior and exterior photos of one of the paint color scheme models.*
Grand Rapids Public Museum

Hall Street Carbarn Rebuilt

The rebuilding of the Hall Street facility was completed in 1925 on the site of the old carbarn. The new car inspection house was enlarged and now contained three tracks, a car wash room, a boiler room, and substation. This was a one-story building 38 feet by 234 feet in size while the substation was 16 feet by 65 feet in size. There were nine tracks outside in the open for streetcars not in need of attention.

A two-story brick building, sixteen feet by thirty feet in dimensions was built for office purposes. The general office and cashier's office were on the first floor while the foremen's office and men's quarters were located on the second floor. The old substation was converted into a sand and salt storage facility.

The fire spared the carpenter and paint shops on the west end of the old car barn so they were salvaged.

"Don't Worry! Relax! Ride the Street Car—It's the Safest Place in Town"

L. J. DeLamarter promoted the fact that it was safer to ride in a streetcar than to ride in an automobile in a safety campaign during July 1925. *Forbes Magazine* described DeLamarter's publicity stunt used during this safety campaign. Streetcars suddenly appeared on the streets with a comely young woman perched nonchalantly on the roof of the car holding up a newspaper displaying a huge headline "DON'T WORRY—RELAX—RIDE THE STREET CAR—IT IS THE SAFEST PLACE IN TOWN."

The company reported that 23,947,305 passengers rode the streetcars in 1925 which represented a decrease of 877,713 in comparison with 24,825,018 in 1924 and an even larger decrease from the 28,558,857 passengers in 1923. Streetcar fares were ten cents cash or six tickets for fifty cents.

"Girl" on roof of streetcar reading a newspaper
with the "Don't Worry" headline.
Grand Rapids Public Library

"Girl" perched on Pantlind Hotel window sill reading a
newspaper with the "Don't Worry" headline.
Electric Railway Journal, 01 Aug 1925, p. 164

Newspaper advertisement.
Grand Rapids Herald, July 1925

Dawn of New Era in Street Car
Service for Grand Rapids Arrives—

GRAND RAPIDS bids fair to gain more nation-wide distinction in street railway progress, in 1926, through the achievement of a new type of de luxe electric rail coach.

From Maine to Oregon, from Texas to Minnesota, and even to foreign countries, has spread the fame of Grand Rapids and its modern coaches, the "St. Louis," the "Minnesota" and the "Ohio." These test coaches, pioneered and sponsored by the Grand Rapids Railway Company, have helped establish a new standard for vehicles for the street railway industry.

1876

With these coaches and their many refinements as a basis, the Grand Rapids Railway Company will soon offer a more advanced type of coach that is expected to set a still higher standard for American street railways. The new design of these coaches was inaugurated only after months of careful checking of operating data, mechanical performance and comparative maintenance costs of the three test coaches. The Grand Rapids Railway Company is buying a car for the future—one that will offer the utmost in comforts, luxury of appointments, combined with low operating and maintenance costs—which explains the seeming delay in equipping the system with new and necessary cars.

The Grand Rapids Railway Company has given an initial order for the early delivery of 27 of these unexcelled and beautiful coaches. Their comforts and refinements leave nothing for the street car patron to desire. These include more cheerful car interiors—spring-filled leather upholstered twin bucket type seats and cushions (to conform to the recent popular vote taken by Grand Rapids' residents during the test of the new coaches), automatic door treadles to facilitate rapid and safe exit, adoption of the step-well and rubber-tiled floors to insure cleanliness. Other appointments place these coaches in the same class with the privately owned automobile.

The time has arrived when the public, apparently tiring of its fling with automobile luxury, is returning to the street car which offers the only dependable, economical and safe method of modern transportation. Increasing traffic congestion, parking difficulties, auto accidents and fatalities are causing the people to ride the street car to and from their work and to use their autos more for pleasure purposes with their families. So these new coaches will offer the same comforts and refinements to which the autoists have become accustomed.

1926

The Grand Rapids Railway Company has planned a very comprehensive program of improvement and service that, with the sanction of the city commission, is expected to soon place the railway company at the very front of the industry. Included in this efficiency program are:

1—Modern De Luxe Coaches.

2—Improvement and reconstruction of rails and roadbed so far as finances will permit.

3—Track extension where patronage assures a service-at-cost return, according to the franchise.

4—New routing of cars to give greater efficiency.

5—Revision of schedules to speed up service, making average headway throughout the city of about 8 minutes.

6—Rapid and adequate bus feeder service for new or growing districts.

7—Improved safety zones.

8—More courtesy and greater attention to patrons' needs and comforts.

9—Replacement of old rails with standard "T" rails.

10—Safety organization and fire prevention education among employes.

11—Name system instead of numbers for cars, using names of pioneers and prominent citizens.

12—De luxe smoking compartments in many of the new coaches.

13—Rebuilding and redecorating available cars now in service to conform to the new order of things.

14—Recent adoption of chauffeur uniforms to improve appearance of the platform men.

15—Employment of traffic, electrical and engineering experts to establish and maintain high standard of efficiency set for the company.

ALL THESE AND MORE—

When the Railway Company's system has been completely equipped with the new coaches, and the above program of efficiency and service has become operative, it is believed Grand Rapids residents then may truthfully say that they have one of the best, if not the best, street railway systems in the United States.

The Grand Rapids Railway Company reaffirms its faith in Grand Rapids. The city is growing rapidly, yet normally. Business and industries are thriving. People are returning to the street car.

With this assurance for the future, and because the Railway Company has passed its dividends since 1918, because it spent $850,000 last year in wages and improvements, is planning to spend another large sum this year for similar purposes and contemplating a continued annual improvement campaign, the Grand Rapids Railway Company hopes to fulfill its pre-franchise promises by being a worthy public utility honorably maintained and providing the ultimate in service at cost.

Appreciating the good will and support of Grand Rapids residents the management and employes of the Grand Rapids Railway Company sincerely wish you and yours a Happy and Prosperous New Year.

Grand Rapids Railway Company
L. J. DeLamarter,
Vice President and General Manager.

Full page newspaper ad on New Year's Day by the Grand Rapids Railway Company announcing new and improved services to expect in 1926.

Grand Rapid Press, January 1, 1926, page 34.

New Era in Streetcar Service Begins

The Grand Rapids Railway Company published an advertisement in both the *Grand Rapids Herald* and *Grand Rapids Press* in early January 1926 heralding the dawn of a new era in streetcar service for Grand Rapids. The company announced it planned to carry out a comprehensive list of fifteen improvements in service that would ultimately provide Grand Rapids with one of the best streetcar systems in the United States.

"Grand Rapids Leads the Way"

The headline on the front page of the May 22, 1926, *Electric Railway Journal* read "Grand Rapids Leads the Way." The editor was referring to the twenty-seven new streetcars built by the St. Louis Car Company in the spring of 1926. These electric rail coaches were the product of the 1925 competition held by the Grand Rapids Railway in an attempt to design and build new streetcars that met new standards for efficiency, economy, comfort, reduced noise, and overall attractiveness to the rider. Although the St. Louis Car Company's test car won the contest, the twenty-seven Grand Rapids electric rail coaches they built combined selected features of all three test cars.

The new Grand Rapids electric rail coaches were reviewed in the May 29, 1926, *Electric Railway Journal.* The *Journal* drew attention to the attractive streamlined appearance of the cars, accentuated by the skirt around the bottom of each car that hid the wheels and trucks, and by solid horizontal bands of colors wrapped around the car.

All twenty-seven cars had a broad four-inch red belt line set off by half oval molding that ran continuously around the streetcar. This red band blended into a cowl across the top of the front dash which contained five lamps for illumination at night. (The company planned to paint such a band on all the cars in the system when each car went into the shops for repainting.) The window posts between the belt rail and letter board were painted cream.

One group of thirteen cars featured blue side panels with a light green skirt, a blue letter board and a gray roof. Another group of nine cars had pigskin-colored panels, desert sand skirts and letter boards, combined with a red roof and belt rail bands. The remaining five cars had desert sand-colored side panels with a red skirt, letter board and belt band, and a gray roof. The different sets of color patterns were to be used to help designate the streetcar line each car was assigned to operate on.

These new cars were 37 feet, 3/8 inches long and had a seating capacity of 42. Ten of the 42 seats were in a smoking compartment located

Far left: *View of front door of new 1926 Grand Rapids Electric Rail Coach showing exit and entrance.*

Washington University

Left: *View of motorman's compartment in the front of a new Grand Rapids Electric Railway Coach.*

Washington University

Below and next two pages: *Article includes list of details of Specifications for the New Grand Rapids cars, p. 917, and includes diagrams of floor plan, front & rear end external views, p.915.*

Electric Railway Journal, 29 May, 1926

in the rear that was partitioned off from the rest of the car. Each car weighed 29,500 pounds when completely equipped for operation, a great saving in weight over previous models.

While the cars were intended for one-man operation, each car was arranged so it could be used in either one- or two-man service. Four GE-264 motors were installed in each car. The platform controller was dropped down in the floor so the top of the controller was at a convenient height for the seated operator. Each car was designed for single-end operation but a back-up controller was installed in the rear so that the car could be temporarily operated from the rear for turning the car on a wye.

New Cars for Grand Rapids Being Delivered

An effort to incorporate beauty and smoothness of line into car design was made in the new Grand Rapids cars. Horizontal bands of color are carried continuously across the doors.

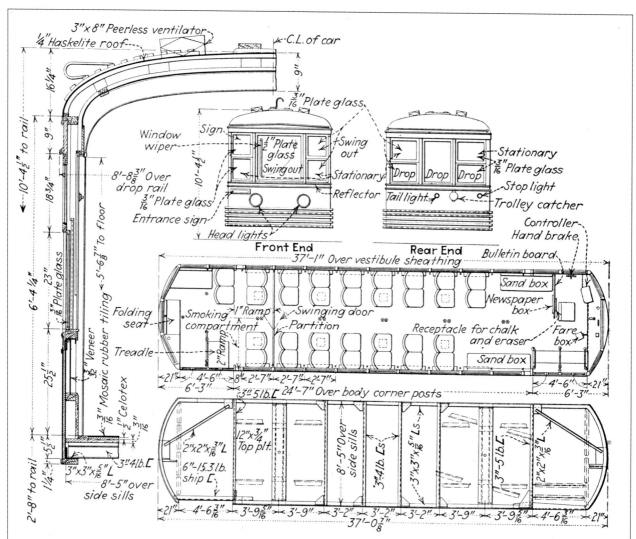

Plymetl Side Panels Are Used Outside of the Fourteen-Gage Steel Side Girder Plate on the Grand
Rapids Cars. One-half Inch Thick Celotex, Both in the Sides and Floor, Is Intended to Deaden
Noise and Provide Heat Insulation. Arrangement of Sash at Front and Rear Ends Is Shown
in the Upper Views.

Electric Railway Journal

Pleasant Surroundings and an Air of Comfort in the Interior Are
Designed to Attract Riders. View Looking Forward Toward
Operator's Position

Looking Back Toward the Smoking Compartment at the Rear
End. Preliminary Experiments Proved the Popularity of This
Arrangement

At the Rear End Is an Automatic-Treadle-Operated Exit with Folding Step. For Two-Man Operation an Entrance Door Controlled from a Conductor's Valve on the Platform Is Provided

Inside Step Construction Is Used at the Front End. Apparatus Is Inclosed in a Special Control Cabinet and the Operator Is Provided with a Comfortable Seat

Electric Railway Journal

Automobile Type Bumpers and Double Headlights Give the Front of the Grand Rapids Cars a Novel Appearance. The Cowl at the Top of the Dash Incloses Five Lamps for Illumination

Modern Electric Rail Coaches Arrive

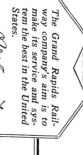

G R R

The *Grand Rapids Rail-way company's aim is to make its service and system the best in the United States.*

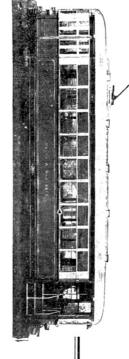

G R R

"Safety
coupled with
Service
and
Efficiency"

Announcing a New Era of Service and Efficiency

Your street railway system is a vital and tremendous factor in the life and continued growth and prosperity of Grand Rapids. It is an efficient partner in business, the dependable servant of the individual. It carries customers to the merchants, pupils to school, people to and from work, patrons to and from theaters and public gatherings. It helps develop the revenues of the city and increases property values. It helps the revenues of the city by paying taxes, spends large sums for goods purchased from local houses, and distributes millions of dollars in wages to employes through its payrolls. The street car is the safest and cheapest mode of travel and helps reduce traffic congestion by economizing street space.

The Grand Rapids Railway company takes pleasure in announcing that the 27 modern electric rail coaches, costing $360,000, and which will help replace the cars destroyed by fire, have been received from the St. Louis Car company.

These deluxe coaches mark an epoch of achievement for the city and company, and also the street railway industry—the beginning of a new era in the modernization of city transportation.

After necessary tests and adjustments these coaches will be placed in regular service Sunday, June 13, on the Cherry, Division-Plainfield and the Franklin-West Leonard lines.

On Saturday, June 12, at 1 p. m., an exhibition and parade of these coaches will be made through Monroe avenue and on the different lines upon which they will operate to show their marked improvement over the old style equipment.

These new types of lightweight, semi-noiseless coaches mark the dawn of a new era in street railway service in Grand Rapids. They represent the utmost in design, refinements, comforts and speed commensurate with safety and are the only ones of their kind in the world.

Designed and built after months of careful test, these coaches are already setting a new standard for the street railway industry in the United States. They are expected to meet every transportation need of Grand Rapids residents, in accordance with the popular vote recently taken.

The Railway company's aim is to make its service and system the best of any city in the United States. It believes these coaches will help fulfill the company's promise to give Grand Rapids an invincible service at cost. They are a noteworthy achievement, and have brought Grand Rapids nationwide publicity.

An important feature are the three different combinations of exterior color, harmonious and pleasing, and a radical departure from the old yellow used in past years.

In these coaches are incorporated many new refinements and specially designed comfort and safety devices. Smoking compartments are an innovation. In keeping with all these are the new chauffeur type of uniform for the platform men.

Coaches have been named for early Grand Rapids residents, merchants, manufacturer or citizen, who, during their lifetime, helped promote the civic and industrial progress of the village or city. Thus it is hoped to pay these pioneers worthy tribute and help perpetuate their deeds and memory.

Four of the coaches are named for city high schools.

The Railway company, through these new coaches, further proves its faith in Grand Rapids' future and we trust that residents will support that faith, and their own, by a greater patronage.

With the placing of these new coaches in service we hope to merit the continued good will of Grand Rapids residents and to aid still further in promoting the city's growth and prosperity.

Grand Rapids Railway Company

L. J. DE LAMARTER, VICE PRESIDENT AND GENERAL MANAGER.

Steel rails and electricity are without equal for city transportation.	We have faith in Grand Rapids' future. We backed that faith by spending $1,303,906 during the past five years—and we have expended $360,000 for new coaches to further prove it.	These coaches are the latest development in luxurious, economical transportation.
The comforts of these coaches are unequaled in any city in the U. S.—Grand Rapids leads the way.	One of the first important questions a home buyer or renter asks is: "How far is this house from the car line?"	

"Modern Electric Rail Coaches Arrive" advertisement. Grand Rapids Herald, 10 Jun 1926

Collage of newspaper articles praising the new streetcars operating in Grand Rapids.

Electric Railway Journal, Vol 68, No. 13, 25 Sep 1926, pg. 538

Horse-drawn streetcar no. 11 carried on the back of an auto truck during the June 12, 1926, parade of the new Grand Rapids electric coaches.

Pomarius Collection

Far right: Thousands cheer as streetcars parade in Grand Rapids - General Electric advertisement.

Saturday Evening Post, 01 Oct 1927

Rail Coaches Win Their Way in Grand Rapids

Louis DeLamarter described what he had accomplished in his paper "Rail Coaches Win Their way in Grand Rapids" published in *Electric Railway Journal* on September 25, 1926. He wrote:

> Our purpose has been so to popularize the street railway as to make it easy for public officials to lend that co-operation which is so essential to progress . . .
>
> The new cars which we recently obtained are important means to that end. In addition they have in the short period of approximately three months demonstrated that they are a profitable investment, both from the standpoint of revenue and operating expense . . .
>
> Many innovations in these cars have proved popular. They are featured by attractive appearance, interior comfort and quiet operation.

DeLamarter commented that the public relations accomplishments these new cars had brought about were particularly impressive given the fact these cars were only 30 new cars out of a total of 127 streetcars that the company operated. DeLamarter also pointed out that now "The street railway had become something to be proud of—not a disreputable necessary nuisance to be kicked about as a political football."

Thousands View Parade of Streetcars

The new Grand Rapids electric rail coaches began arriving in Grand Rapids in April 1926 but the cars did not enter service until June 13, 1926.

Thousands of Grand Rapids citizens turned out on Saturday, June 12, 1926, to watch the new streetcars parade through downtown Grand Rapids. They witnessed the evolution of streetcar operation in their city as illustrated by the first three cars in the parade which represented the "old." The first car in the parade, No. 11, an old horsecar dating back to the 1880s, was carried on an auto truck.

The second car in the parade was the *Saginaw*-type car representing the 1900 time period. The third type of "old" car was known as the Akron and Grand Rapids style streetcar designed by Hodenpyl & Hardy, and built for these two cities by the St. Louis Car Company in 1917. The Hodenpyl-Hardy car was large, heavy, and inconvenient to riders throughout the car, beginning with its high steps.

Then, the "new" was featured when the Grand Rapids-designed rail coaches (all with names but no numbers) began to pass in review. The three sample cars rolled by amid the twenty-seven new cars.

The last car in the parade was the *Ramona*, a Birney streetcar recently refurbished by the Grand Rapids Railway.

THOUSANDS CHEER
as street cars parade in Grand Rapids

GRAND RAPIDS caught the spirit of modern service when twenty-seven new trolley cars, light, speedy, and with comfortable seats, rolled smoothly, almost noiselessly, up the street.

Best of all, these cars saved 40% in power consumption, maintained faster schedules, and increased the number of passengers carried per car mile.

Grand Rapids, like scores of other cities today, is helping people to realize more and more

—that the public *must* be served.

> The electric railways carry forty-four million people daily and are forced to take care of nearly one-half of these people during four hours of the day. This, too, although there are today forty-two times as many automobiles in the country as there were in 1912.

—that the demand for such a service will continue.

> In 1925 the electric lines carried about seventeen times as many persons as all the steam roads in the United States (sixteen billion for the former as against nine hundred and two million for the latter).

—that more passengers can be carried by the trolleys with less traffic congestion.

> In Baltimore the street cars carry 89% of the passenger traffic and consist of but 12% of the vehicles on the streets. In Chicago 75% of the people are carried in this way, while trolleys constitute but 10% of the traffic.

—that extensive improvements are being made.

> In 1925 the electric railways spent over three hundred million dollars for new equipment, maintenance, and supplies.

Thousands cheered in Grand Rapids. Why? Because they appreciated the expression of service.

Ever since the inauguration of the first complete electric street railway system, in Richmond, Va., in 1888, General Electric engineers have continually contributed to the industry. G-E designed motors are used on Grand Rapids cars, and on subway cars, city and interurban lines, and electrified divisions of steam railways. G-E safety devices, brakes, and control are also a part of this complete, modern transportation service.

GENERAL ELECTRIC

Parade of 27 new street cars built to Grand Rapids Railway Company's specifications. View looking southeast up Monroe Avenue from Campau Square in downtown Grand Rapids.

Grand Rapids Public Library

The Street Railway's Big Bonfire

Less than two weeks after thousands of citizens watched the twenty-seven new rail coaches parade down the major streets in Grand Rapids, the streetcar company sentenced twenty antiquated trolleys to a fiery death. The company advertised it was going to burn a line of twenty obsolete streetcars in one big bonfire at the West Michigan fairgrounds on Thursday night, June 24. An estimated 50,000 people attended the free event which began with a band concert at 8:30 P.M. followed by an illuminated balloon ascension. Next was a major fireworks display that included a large blazing sign with the company's slogan "Don't

Worry—Relax! Ride the Street Car—It is the Safest Place in Town," and ended with a pyrotechnic reproduction of one of the new rail coaches.

Mayor Elvin Swarthout and street railway manager L. J. DeLamarter then used torches to set fire to opposite ends of the long line of streetcars which had been primed with kerosene-soaked hay and straw. The huge bonfire could be seen for miles.

The burning of so many worn-out streetcars in front of thousands was a momentous event. Movie-goers throughout the United States soon viewed the parade, the fireworks and the streetcar funeral pyre in newsreels by Pathe News Weekly, Universal Studios, and other movie makers.

Line of old street cars at West Michigan Fairground to be burned on June 24, 1926.

Grand Rapids Public Library

Marketing Grand Rapids Streetcars

The October 15, 1926, issue of *Forbes Magazine* published an article describing Louis J. DeLamarter's numerous successes in marketing the services of the Grand Rapids Street Railway. For the article's title the author chose one sentence with which DeLamarter summarized the principle underlying his marketing methods: "You Can Sell Anything if You Make It Salable." That DeLamarter was deemed successful was confirmed by the article's sub-title: "L. J. DeLamarter, Vice-President and General Manager of the Grand Rapids Railway Proved This by Getting Half the Population to Turn Out for Parade of New Stream-Lined Street Cars."

Steel Wheels Replace Iron Wheels on Streetcars

The company began replacing worn out iron wheels with cast steel wheels in 1926. The lighter weight of the steel wheels reduced the amount of energy needed to accelerate the streetcar. This change would only be advantageous if the motormen were cautious not to brake too quickly, especially when sand was needed, as the steel wheels were susceptible to developing flat spots. The company published an article in *The Token*, its publication for employees, requesting motormen to "Watch Your Wheels".

Watch Your Wheels

Company Adopts Cast Steel Wheels— Requests Greater Care by Operators in Brake Applications.

The railway company, after thorough investigation, has adopted cast steel wheels for its cars. Chilled iron wheels have long been in use . . .

The cast steel wheels cost more than double that of the chilled iron type, the prices being: 33-inch steel wheel, $28; 22-inch chilled iron, $14; 33-inch steel wheel, $26; 26-inch chilled iron, $11.

The company desires to emphasize the fact that the life of these steel wheels will depend entirely upon their usage by operators and motormen. Being cast steel they cannot be turned down like a rolled steel wheel and for that reason if they are made "flat" by being slid, become useless and must be scrapped and replaced with new wheels. Because both wheels on each axle are flatted at the same time, operators and motormen will quickly see that it costs $56 to replace a pair of "flat" wheels. This does not include the cost of machining or loss of service while new wheels are being put on.

"Flat" wheels are caused by improper application of brakes and sand. Therefore the company requests all operators and motormen make an effort to employ the right method by using the sand before making air application on the brakes when sand is required.

Old streetcars intentionally set on fire on June 24, 1926.

Grand Rapids Public Library

Exterior view of snow plow car with 10-foot side flanger open outside the Hall Street carbarn.
Electric Railway Journal, 26 Feb 1927

Interior view of snow plow car.
Electric Railway Journal, 26 Feb 1927

Grand Rapids Railway Company Reorganized as Grand Rapids Railroad Company

The company succeeded in lowering the cost of streetcar operation in 1926 by replacing old heavy cars, many requiring two-man crews, with the new lightweight streetcars that used less electricity and could be operated by just one man. Unfortunately it did not lower costs enough to meet all of its financial obligations. The Grand Rapids Railway Company petitioned the City Commission to approve a reorganization of the Grand Rapids Railway Company into the Grand Rapids Rail*road* Company for the purpose of reducing its capitalization and debt by $600,000. The City Commission approved the reorganization plan on June 13. The Grand Rapids Railway Company ceased to exist on that day and the Grand Rapids Railroad Company began operating the streetcar system. There was no change in the board of directors and the officers.

Other 1926 Events

The company extended the East Fulton track one-third of a mile from Carlton Avenue to the eastern city limits with a reversing loop between Carlton and Arthur Avenue. Numerous track replacement projects were undertaken in 1926.

The company rebuilt three streetcars into maintenance-of-way cars in 1926 to replace three similar cars that were destroyed in the 1924 Hall Street car barn fire. Old car No. 99 was rebuilt into a sand car to replace sand car No. 92 lost in the fire. The company rebuilt two

old heavy streetcars originally built by the Cincinnati Car Company into two combination snow scraper and plow work cars to replace similar equipment destroyed in the fire. Also, seven two-man cars were rebuilt for one-man operation during 1926.

The St. Louis Car Company sent *Springfield,* a new streetcar, to Grand Rapids to publicize its most modern Birney-type car as a demonstration model.

The number of revenue passengers carried by the street railway in 1926 was, 19,542,290, a slight increase of 209,612 over that of 1925. While the increase was slight, DeLamarter and his associates could take comfort in the fact that they had at least arrested a long-term downward trend. Time would tell if their efforts were to be rewarded in the long run.

John C. Madigan retired after serving twenty years as the superintendent of the street railway. John W. Knecht became the new superintendent.

Street Railway Still Paying for "Mythical Hoofbeats"

In the horsecar era, cities usually required streetcar companies to pay for the paving between the rails and for about a foot outside the two outer rails. This was considered to be fair because the hoofs of the horses pulling streetcars made ruts in the pavement between the rails.

Electric motors had been moving streetcars in Grand Rapids since 1891. Automobiles

Mishap involving "Rindge" Birney car and an auto on the Fulton Street bridge on 03 Dec 1925.

Sam Ashendorf Collection

Portrait of John C. Madigan.

Michigan Tradesman

and trucks now used the pavement between the rails and the electric streetcars did not. But the street railway ordinance still contained the requirement that the streetcar company must either construct or pay for the pavement between and around the rails. The street railway was spending approximately $50,000 a year to pay for the "mythical damage" that electric street cars did to the pavement between the rails. An amendment to the charter was proposed to have allowed the city, at its discretion, to relieve the street railway of the expense of paving between the rails. This proposed amendment was rejected by the voters in a special election on March 7, 1927.

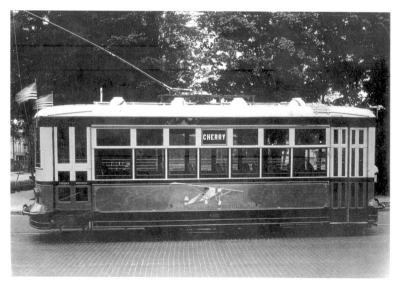

1927: Optimism and Uncertainty

The Grand Rapids Railway entered 1927 with 114 streetcars including the 27 new light-weight Grand Rapids rail coaches and the 3 test rail coaches. It had 68 miles of track and 450 employees. The company also had a small fleet of buses. The outlook for business was favorable at the beginning of 1927 but changed a few months later when the furniture industry began to lay off workers. This recession had an adverse effect on the number of individuals who rode the streetcars.

The Grand Rapids Street Railway celebrated Charles Lindbergh's successful 1927 flight across the Atlantic Ocean by naming a remodeled streetcar the *Col. Charles Lindbergh* and painted a picture of Colonel Lindbergh's *The Spirit of St. Louis* airplane on the sides of the car. Lindbergh flew *The Spirit of St. Louis* into the Grand Rapids airport on August 13, 1927, as part of a nationwide seventy-five-city "Good Will Tour". Although there is no record that he rode in his namesake car, it's likely that he saw it.

Secondhand Cars and New Track

The street railway purchased ten second-hand Birney Safety Cars and modified them to meet the Grand Rapids standard for cars in service. The major modifications involved installing new skirting and remodeling the inside of each car to provide a smoking compartment. The purchase of these cars helped offset the loss of nine Birney cars in the Hall Street carbarn fire three years earlier.

The company built 700 feet of double track on the new Fulton Street Bridge in 1927. Approximately 650 feet of worn out double track on Jefferson Avenue and 1,380 feet of single track on Plainfield Avenue were replaced. All these rail construction projects utilized 100-pound T-rail. No changes in the motor bus services took place during 1927.

Col. Charles Lindbergh flew The Spirit of St. Louis into the Grand Rapids airport on August 13, 1927, as part of a nationwide "Good Will Tour." A promotional film was made of the parade. It has been digitized and is available for viewing online at https://youtube.com.

Grand Rapids Spectator, 02 July 1927

Two views of the remodeled Lindbergh streetcar.

Grand Rapids Pubic Library

The Street Railways of Grand Rapids

PRESENT ROUTING OF
TRANSIT LINES IN BUSINESS DISTRICT
GRAND RAPIDS – MICHIGAN
SCALE 1INCH = 200 FEET

PROPOSED REROUTING OF
TRANSIT LINES IN BUSINESS DISTRICT
GRAND RAPIDS – MICHIGAN
CITY PLANNING DEPARTMENT

Present Routes and Proposed Rerouting of Transit Lines in Business District of Downtown Grand Rapids.
Grand Rapids City Planning Department, 1927

Passengers Carried in 1927

The number of revenue passengers carried by the system in 1927 was 18,378,036, a decrease of 5.96 % when compared to the 19,582,920 passengers who rode the streetcars in 1926. Fortunately, the 1926 and 1927 efforts helped to significantly lower operating costs. Yet the rider loss continued as L.J. DeLamarter and others in the company attempted to stabilize or reverse the downward trend.

Grand Rapids City Plan for Future Streetcar Service

City planners assigned a major role for the Grand Rapids streetcar system in their *The Grand Rapids City Plan* for future transportation in the city. Topics reviewed with proposals for the future included "Street Railway Company is Working Closely with City Commission to Improve Service" and "Future Street Railway System Here Proposed is Planned for a City of 300,000 by 1975." As it turned out, most of the increase in population in the Grand Rapids area by 1975 occurred *outside* the city limits.

Four of the proposed route changes were designed to relieve the congestion on Monroe Avenue, especially the Campau Square intersection. The planners proposed abandoning the tracks on Pearl Street across the bridge and on Shawmut Boulevard. A second proposal involved extending the lines on Ottawa Street from Lyon north to Trowbridge while a third proposal involved the withdrawal of lines from Monroe Avenue north of Michigan Avenue. A fourth proposal involved extending the streetcar tracks on north Division from Monroe to Lyon Street.

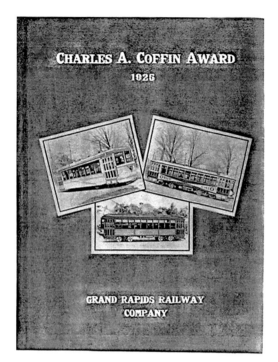

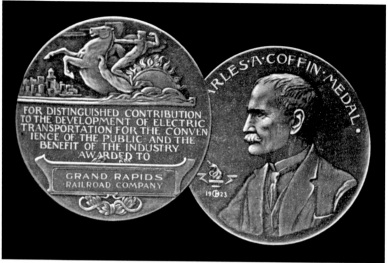

Front and Back Sides of the 1927 Charles A. Coffin Foundation Gold Medal Award.

Grand Rapids Public Library

Front cover of Coffin Award Presentation brief submitted by Grand Rapids Railway in 1926.

Electric Railway Journal, Vol. 66, Nov 1925

The Grand Rapids Railroad Wins the Charles A. Coffin Award

The American Electric Railway Association announced at its annual convention in Cleveland on October 4, 1927, that the newly reorganized Grand Rapids Railroad Company was the 1927 recipient of the Charles A. Coffin Award. This annual foundation gold medal award had been established in 1922 by the General Electric Company in honor of the co-founder and first president of General Electric. The award was to honor an electric railway company "in recognition of its distinguished contribution during the past year to the development of electric transportation for the convenience of the public and the benefit of the industry."

The Grand Rapids Railroad Company was the fifth recipient of the Charles A. Coffin Award. The traction companies that had received the Coffin award and medal prior to Grand Rapids in 1927 included Chicago North Shore and Milwaukee Railroad, 1923; Northern Texas Traction Company, 1924; Pittsburgh Railways Company, 1925; and Pennsylvania-Ohio Electric company, 1926. The Grand Rapids Railroad Company was one of thirteen of the leading and most progressive electric railways in the country that competed for the 1927 Coffin award.

The Grand Rapids Railroad Company had submitted a 150-page typewritten brief accompanied by many photographs, newspaper, and magazine clippings, commendatory letters, among other supporting items, in competition with the twelve other companies in 1927, most of which were larger.

The Charles A. Coffin Prize Committee report stated why the committee chose the Grand Rapids Railroad Company to receive the 1927 award, stating that Grand Rapids

. . . is a comparatively small city property in an industrial community of about 160,000 population, the class of city in which the effects of automobile competition are felt the strongest. It is among railway properties of this size that there is shown a serious dropping off of revenues in many cities. For them, the average of the operating figures gathered by the Association shows the gloomiest outlook. Nevertheless, this property has received national and even international attention by railway men, by the technical press and by newspapers, not only of its own city, but in many very much larger cities throughout the country.

The practices and accomplishments of this property have had a widespread influence on the entire industry and have done much to awaken the present almost universal interest in the improvement of electric railway service. With limited facilities, on its own initiative, and largely with its own resources, this comparatively small railway property, which was scarcely known outside of its own city a few years ago, undertook to demonstrate to the world the process of popularizing electric railway by the improvement of equipment and service. So radical were its methods, that when it filed its brief in this competition two years ago, there was grave doubt as to the outcome of the experiment. The present

1. Fred W. Olds
2. George Kerwin
3. R. Retan
4. J. W. Knecht
5. W. E. Livingston
6. J. Winks
7. Paul Rust
8. E. Lunda
9. S. Dubee
10. F. Heath
11. Simon Glerum
12. Ray Poteracki
13. L. J. De Lamarter

Officers and key men on prize-winning property

awakened interest in the improvement of cars, which has permeated to all the manufacturers and to almost every operating company in the country, was given strong impetus by the pioneering of this comparatively small company.

Its accomplishments have not all been in the direction of spectacular innovations and showmanship. Combined with this there has been a consistent program of increasing operating efficiency and reducing costs. With no change in the rate of fare, revenues in 1926 showed an increase of 1.04 per cent over 1925, and in 1927, when the average figures for the properties of its size showed a heavy decrease, it held its revenue slightly above what it had been in 1926, despite a reduction in the activity of the basic industry in its city. For the year ending May 31, 1927, there was a reduction of 9.88 per

cent in operating expenses and an increase of 20.83 per cent in net revenue in comparison with the year 1926. After charging off depreciation amounting to approximately 10 per cent of its gross, there was available after taxes a balance equal to 6.40 per cent of its rate base of $6,000,000. This was an increase for the year ending May 31, 1927, of over 41 per cent over the corresponding period of 1926. There had likewise been an increase in this figure for 1926 over 1925 of over 15 per cent.

In recognition of the accomplishments of this property, in 'the development of electric railway transportation for the convenience of the public and for the benefit of the industry,' your Committee takes great pleasure in awarding the Charles A. Coffin medal for 1927 to the Grand Rapids Railroad Company, Grand Rapids, Michigan.'

Portraits of men who were influential in Grand Rapids receiving the Coffin Award.

Electric Railway Journal, Vol. 69, 08 Oct 1927, p. 627

End of the Line for the Streetcar System (1927-1935)

The Ultimate Lightweight Streetcar?

General Manager DeLamarter continued his search for the ultimate lightweight streetcar. The new Versare experimental coach, the lightest-weight streetcar in the world, was developed by the Versare Corporation of Albany, New York, in cooperation with Westinghouse Company and the Grand Rapids Railroad Company engineers. It began running on the Cherry Street line in Grand Rapids during the fall of 1927. The 26-foot long Versare streetcar weighed only 13,500 pounds, and had a seating capacity for 32 passengers or approximately 422 pounds per passenger when full. The Versare car was constructed entirely of "Duralumin" (commonly used in the aircraft industry) and light alloy steel.

The running gear and drive of the Versare car also was unique. The car ran on only six wheels and was driven by two 25-horsepower Westinghouse motors. The front truck had just one axle while the rear and larger truck had two axles. This arrangement did away with the problem of lightweight single truck cars bobbing. Power was transmitted to the axle by means of automotive type transmissions which eliminated the noisy gears and made the car comparatively quiet.

It would be interesting to speculate how well such a lightweight car stood up in everyday service. As it was, the Versare car became an interesting if short-lived footnote in Grand Rapids transportation history.

Company Continues to Assign Names to Streetcars

Creston and Ottawa Hills high schools had streetcars named for them. The Grand Rapids Railroad Company put into service a new electric rail coach named *American Legion*. It was painted in the Legion's colors and bore the Legion's emblem on the sides of the car.

Dispatcher Controls Street Car Traffic on Fulton Street Bridge

As the Fulton Street bridge was being rebuilt in 1927, the West Fulton and Butterworth lines were served by buses. When the bridge was reopened in January of 1928, a street railway dispatcher in a small pagoda-like booth located in the center began controlling the use of the single track by both newly re-opened lines. The dispatcher used a system of red and white lights regulated by switches to control which streetcar could go on the one track across the new bridge.

1928 in Review

The 1928 Division Avenue widening project forced the streetcars on the following six lines to begin running between Monroe Avenue and Cherry Street by way of the Union Railroad Station until the Division Avenue widening project was completed in mid-August. The six lines affected by this were Division-Plainfield; Lafayette-Stocking; Franklin-West Leonard; Madison-Butterworth; Wealthy-Taylor and Wealthy-Scribner. The northbound streetcars were rerouted back to Division Avenue on June 12 and southbound streetcars were rerouted back in mid-August.

Pagoda style dispatcher's house in the center of the new West Fulton Street Bridge in 1928.

The Token, February 1928, p. 6 published by the Grand Rapids Railway Co., Carl Bajema Collection

Streetcars on the Wealthy-Scribner, Wealthy-Taylor, and Fulton Street lines were rerouted on November 5 to reduce downtown traffic congestion. The Wealthy-Scribner line was split and the Wealthy cars operated as Wealthy No. 5, a downtown loop line. The Scribner line was coupled with the Fulton Street line as Scribner-Fulton No. 11. The Comstock Park or Taylor line, under the new rerouting plan, was to be known as Comstock Park No. 4.

Twelve more Birney cars were refurbished in conformity with the standard Grand Rapids type of cars in service. Buses were operating on five different routes supplementing the streetcar service.

The street railway carried 17,483,996 passengers in 1928, a 31.6 per cent decrease compared to the number of passengers carried in 1917, and most, if not all, of the decrease was due to the growing use of private automobiles. The decrease of riders in 1929 was not as dramatic as the previous year as ridership decreased by 1.66 per cent to 17,193,849. Still, ridership continued to plummet in comparison to the levels of only a few years ago.

View of Pere Marquette RR and Pennsylvania RR rails at the street railway crossing on West Leonard Street in 1928, View looking east.

Grand Rapids City Archives

Grand Rapids Railway Alpine Avenue auto bus.

Richard Andrews Collection

1929: Streetcars, Buses, and Now Taxis

The Grand Rapids Railroad Company continued its Birney refurbishment program. An effort was made to maintain equipment to a high standard so the streetcars would remain an attractive travel option for the riding public.

The company purchased two new motor buses during 1929. The City Commission recommended that the street railway company conduct experiments with a number of bus routes to serve as feeder lines to streetcar lines. Continued operation of these feeder routes would depend on whether the patronage was there to make them viable.

The company also purchased five taxi companies that operated modern taxis with privileges at the principal hotels as well as at Union Station. The City Commission urged the streetcar company to purchase the taxicab companies so the company could provide a complete multi-modal system of transportation in the city.

The double track stretching south 1,759 feet between Dickinson Street and Burton Street on south Division Avenue was rebuilt during 1929.

The company decided it was becoming too costly to paint its streetcars in a variety of colors. The *Grand Rapids Herald* on September 29 commented on the decision to standardize streetcar livery:

THE END OF THE RAINBOW

Grand Rapids streetcars are taking on a standard color scheme. The change from the distinctive coloring for each line has been made so gradually that the public has failed to take note. Now that the secret is out our guess is that the public will approve. The experimenting with a variety of hues which followed the introduction of new cars locally served its purpose as advertising. But on second thought a streetcar line isn't a rainbow. The public may talk about cars which are painted liver-red, gall-bladder green, orange, blue and pink, but it would rather ride in vehicle of more harmonious coloring. The standard paint now adopted is a pig-skin brown with maroon and cream trim. It is better than the old tan and yellow, of the merry medley of later days.

1930: Hard Times Come to Grand Rapids Railroad

The Grand Rapids Railroad made plans to spend $941,000 for improvement of service on its system in 1930. The company wanted to purchase twenty single-truck Birney cars, upgrade ten double-truck cars with modern safety devices, and scrap thirteen double-truck

P.A.Y.E. streetcars. However, worsening business conditions in 1930 prevented the purchase any streetcars. The company did meet its goal to refurbish ten streetcars in1930, but in other respects the heady days of the June 1926 modernization were over.

The great financial depression, triggered by the stock market crash of October 1929, was a major cause of the company's 1930 earnings to drop from ten to twenty per cent compared with corresponding periods in the first five months in 1929. City Manager Walsh suggested that the city consider relieving the street railway of paying taxes of more than $137,000 annually. Grand Rapids Railroad Superintendent Knecht drew attention to several economies the street railway had made to lower operating costs such as replacing two-man cars with one-man cars ($20,000 per year) and clos-

ing the Wealthy Street carbarn ($12,000 a year). However, citizens were opposed to any kind of tax relief for the street railway system.

Grand Rapids suffered in 1930 due to the unfavorable business conditions prevailing during the year. Revenue passengers in 1930 were down twenty-one percent from the previous year. Riding in 1931 again plummeted by another twenty-one per cent. *(See Appendix 2 to study annual changes in the number of passengers carried by the Grand Rapids street railways.)*

The Grand Rapids Railroad Company was unable to meet all of its financial obligations in 1930 and the company lacked $97,353 to pay the seven per cent interest on its first mortgage bonds due November 1, 1931. The bondholders organized a bondholders' protective committee in late October, 1931.

South Division Avenue widening and reconstruction. View looking north from Oakes Street intersection.

Grand Rapids Spectator, 02 Jun 1928

Receivership

The U.S. District Court in Grand Rapids declared the Grand Rapids Railroad to be in default of interest on the first mortgage bonds on February 29, 1932. The judge ordered continuation of operations and appointed Louis J. DeLamarter, vice-president and general manager of the Grand Rapids Railroad, as receiver to manage Grand Rapids Railroad's streetcar and bus operations.

As receiver, DeLamarter first dealt with labor costs. He approved reducing the hourly wage of streetcar operators and bus drivers from fifty-one cents to forty-five cents an hour effective March 16, 1932. In early June he eliminated two bus lines that had been in service since 1924: the West Bridge Street buses going westward from the end of the West Bridge streetcar line to Bristol Avenue and the Godfrey Avenue buses running between Campau Square and the industrial district to Hall Street.

The Grand Rapids Railroad Company had considered the option of running trolley buses on South Division Avenue. DeLamarter decided not to pursue the experiment with trackless trolleys as good used buses were available at exceptionally favorable prices. The city wanted to repave South Division Avenue between Wealthy and Hall streets, but the street railway was unable to participate in the project

due to a paucity of funds.

DeLamarter began substituting buses for streetcars on June 15, 1932, on two streetcar lines: the Scribner Avenue line north from West Leonard Street and the Madison Avenue line.

The U. S. District Court approved DeLamarter's request to purchase ten or more buses, the cost not to exceed $16,000, on November 8. These buses were to run on South Division Avenue in place of streetcars.

The Writing on the Wall

Receiver DeLamarter was able to purchase twenty-four additional buses to replace all streetcar service on Franklin Street and on south Division Avenue south of Wealthy Street. The Plainfield Avenue streetcar end of the Division-Plainfield line was to operate via Campau Square and Cherry Street. The company published an advertisement in the July 29, 1933, *Grand Rapids Herald* notifying streetcar riders that all electric car operation on Division Avenue was to be discontinued on July 31, 1933. Buses began running north on Division Avenue from Detroit Street to downtown with every other bus going downtown heading west at Hall to Ionia, to Monroe, on Ottawa to Crescent, to Monroe and return. The next bus going downtown turned on Hall to Sheldon, thence to Wealthy, to Division, to Monroe and

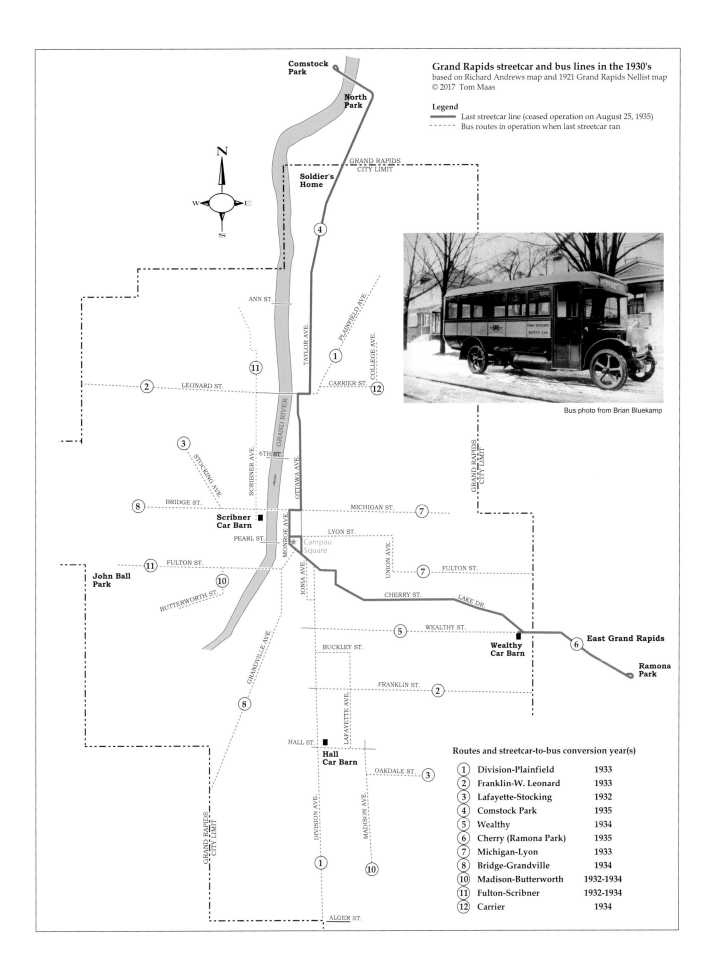

Grand Rapids streetcar and bus lines in the 1930's
based on Richard Andrews map and 1921 Grand Rapids Nellist map
© 2017 Tom Maas

Legend
——— Last streetcar line (ceased operation on August 25, 1935)
- - - - Bus routes in operation when last streetcar ran

Comstock Park

North Park

GRAND RAPIDS CITY LIMIT

Soldier's Home

N
W E
S

ANN ST.

TAYLOR AVE.

PLAINFIELD AVE.

COLLEGE AVE.

④

①

LEONARD ST.

CARRIER ST.

⑫

②

⑪

GRAND RIVER

SCRIBNER AVE.

6TH ST.

OTTAWA AVE.

③

STOCKING AVE.

GRAND RAPIDS CITY LIMIT

Bus photo from Brian Bluekamp

BRIDGE ST.

⑧

MICHIGAN ST.

⑦

Scribner Car Barn ■

LYON ST.

MONROE AVE.

PEARL ST.

★ Campau Square

UNION AVE.

⑪

FULTON ST.

⑦

FULTON ST.

John Ball Park

⑩

IONIA AVE.

CHERRY ST.

LAKE DR.

BUTTERWORTH ST.

⑤

WEALTHY ST.

Wealthy Car Barn ■

⑥

East Grand Rapids

GRANDVILLE AVE.

BUCKLEY ST.

Ramona Park

FRANKLIN ST.

②

LAFAYETTE AVE.

⑧

HALL ST. ■
Hall Car Barn

OAKDALE ST.

③

Routes and streetcar-to-bus conversion year(s)

①	Division-Plainfield	1933
②	Franklin-W. Leonard	1933
③	Lafayette-Stocking	1932
④	Comstock Park	1935
⑤	Wealthy	1934
⑥	Cherry (Ramona Park)	1935
⑦	Michigan-Lyon	1933
⑧	Bridge-Grandville	1934
⑩	Madison-Butterworth	1932-1934
⑪	Fulton-Scribner	1932-1934
⑫	Carrier	1934

DIVISION AVE.

MADISON AVE.

①

⑩

GRAND RAPIDS CITY LIMIT

ALGER ST.

Ottawa, to Crescent, to Monroe, and returning same route.

Franklin Street line streetcars were replaced by buses on August 7, 1933. One citizen complained about the unsightly, horrible-riding buses contending that the buses were third-hand when the street railway began running them, having been sold from New York to Detroit and then to Grand Rapids.

Receiver DeLamarter concluded in a report that, "It is the opinion of your receiver that gradual replacement of buses for rail service will be in order in various parts of the city as fast as it becomes necessary either to re-lay rails in streets to be repaved, or substitute bus service . . . and there seems to be a popular demand for bus service rather than rail service."

The company published an important notice to streetcar and bus patrons on November 2, 1933. The West Leonard-Wealthy Street car line was being split into two lines with each line using the downtown loop. The Eastern avenue bus line's route also was changed. These changes took effect on November 2.

DeLamarter made four more revisions in bus routes and one in a streetcar line in December. The Wealthy Street car line was to originate at the carbarn at Lake Drive and Wealthy Street, go downtown and return, starting on December 18.

The old Norwood Avenue stable adjacent the old Wealthy Street car barn was torn down in December 1933.

Streetcar Service Reduced

Buses replaced streetcars on the Carrier Street line on March 28. Another four lines were converted on July 26, 1934: the West Bridge Street-Grandville Avenue line; the Wealthy Street-Stocking Avenue line; the West Fulton Street line; and the Butterworth Avenue line.

Only four streetcar lines were still operating at the beginning of 1935: Cherry Street-Plainfield Avenue; West Leonard Street; Michigan Avenue-Lyon Street; and Comstock Park. All of these streetcar lines used lower Monroe Avenue when going through downtown Grand Rapids. If the state of Michigan approved the city's request for state funds to improve lower Monroe Avenue in 1935, then 1935 would be the end of the line for all streetcars in Grand Rapids.

On April 15, the U.S. District Court approved the request of receiver DeLamarter to abandon all streetcar lines with the exception of the Cherry-Plainfield route. The court also approved abandonment of rails in lower Monroe Avenue between Pearl Street and Michigan Avenue as requested by the City Commission and removal of the track in upper Monroe from Pearl Street to Ottawa as well. The court further granted abandonment of the track in West Leonard Street west of Scribner Avenue.

Eight new buses were expected to arrive by late April and these buses were to replace the Michigan-Lyon streetcars. Another twelve or more buses were ordered for arrival in July

Grand Rapids streetcar is being readied for relocation about 1936.

Shawn Wigant

or August to be placed in service on the Division and West Leonard Street car lines.

Four new buses, painted green with maroon trim, participated in the "Safety Parade" on Saturday, April 27, 1935. These buses gave Grand Rapids citizens their first look at the new color scheme the company planned to be standard for all buses in the future. The twenty-three-seat General Motor buses were equipped with special gear ratios, powerful motors and brakes for service on the Michigan and Lyon Street hills.

The End of the Streetcar Era

Receiver Louis J. DeLamarter planned to complete the motorization of all streetcar lines in 1935 which meant ". . . the tearing up of all streetcar tracks and removal of all trolley wire and poles in the city." A newspaper editorial dwelt on "The New Day" that had arrived for mass transportation in Grand Rapids. The editorial praised the efforts DeLamarter had made to provide as excellent a streetcar service as possible when faced with declining ridership and revenue.

On Thursday, May 20, 1935, the "Goin' to Town" day pageant picturing progress in transportation was the last time electric streetcars representing the 1890, 1900, 1910, and 1925 eras paraded on the streets of Grand Rapids.

DeLamarter sounded the final death knell for the trolley era early in August when he submitted a plan to the City Commission for the conversion of the last streetcar line to a bus line. This was to occur on Monday, August 26, one week before September 1 when the resurfacing of Monroe Avenue was scheduled to begin. An advertisement describing the routes the twelve bus lines would begin operating on

effective Monday, August 26, was published in the August 22 issue of the *Grand Rapids Herald*. The Grand Rapids Railroad Company had 100 buses to serve the 12 bus lines on August 26.

Motorman Miles McDonald took the *J. Boyd Pantlind* 1926 rail coach on the last run of a streetcar in Grand Rapids, leaving Campau Square for Ramona Park at midnight, August 26, 1935, ending seventy years of streetcar operation in Grand Rapids. With the passing of the last streetcar line, Grand Rapids became one of the largest cities in the U.S. to rely solely on motor buses for public transportation.

The passing of the streetcar era brought great sadness to a group of ten motormen who were retiring rather than stay to drive buses. The ten men had clanged the bells of streetcars while traveling more than twelve million miles during the total of 370 years they ran the cars.

Afterword

By the spring of 1935, the city of Grand Rapids with the assistance of federal money through the Works Progress Administration (W.P.A.) began removing rails from abandoned streetcar lines. More than a thousand men were employed to tear up the tracks in Grand Rapids in that year. Workers also began taking the trolley wire down and removing line poles by early September. Grand Rapids Railroad left few reminders of what only a decade previously had been one of the country's most innovative streetcar systems.

DeLamarter became president of the Grand Rapids Railroad Company when it emerged from receivership in 1938. He continued as president of the Grand Rapids Motor Coach Company when the former company changed its legal name in 1939. The switch from streetcars to buses in Grand Rapids was now complete.

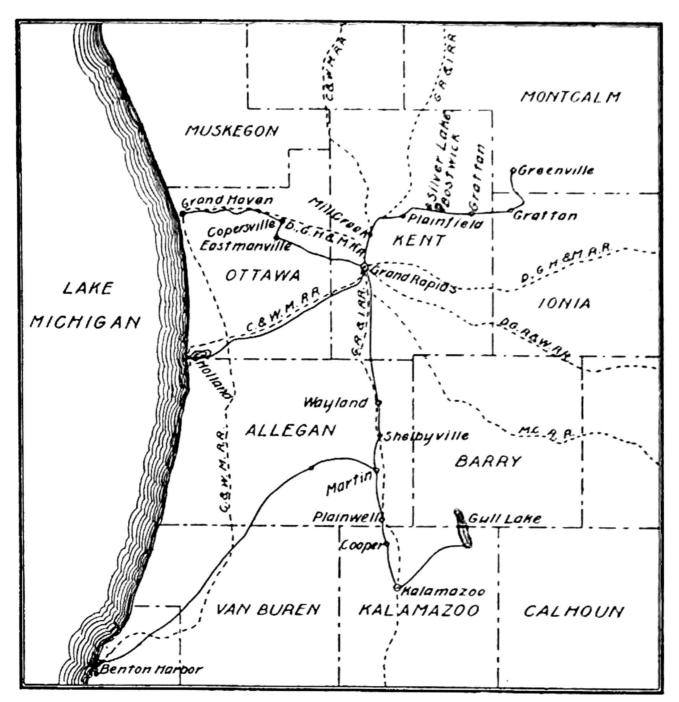

10 The Grand Rapids Interurbans (1900-1928)

An 1899 illustration gives Grand Rapids readers an idea of how all the proposed electric railways would look in the future. Dashed lines represent existing steam railroads and solid lines represent proposed electric lines.

Street Railway Review, 15 Apr 1899

The Electric Interurban Railway Era Begins in West Michigan

Technological advances in more powerful electric motors during the 1890s made travel aboard electric interurbans between suburbs, villages, rural farms and cities such as Grand Rapids a very fast and convenient way to go. Traveling via interurban had two major advantages over steam railroads. First, interurban companies were able to provide more frequent service at a lower cost. Second, interurban cars could stop at virtually every street or road crossing, start up again and accelerate far faster steam passenger trains could.

The Street Railways of Grand Rapids

Interurbans and the Development of Suburbs

So many electric interurban railway projects were proposed for west Michigan at the turn of the century that a *Grand Rapids Press* reporter wrote:

> Grand Rapids just now resembles nothing so much as a big thunder cloud. The air is heavily charged with electricity, and every moment a discharge may be expected of the zigzag lines so familiar in pictures of summer storms reaching out in every direction. In this instance, however, the lines will represent electric railways, and the discharge, instead of carrying terror and destruction, will add life and prosperity to the city and the surrounding country.

Only three of the many proposed interurban lines were ever built. The first interurban line in the area began operating in 1901 and connected Holland with Grand Rapids. The Holland interurban cars entered Grand Rapids via the Grandville Avenue streetcar line.

The next line was built to connect Muskegon and Grand Haven to Grand Rapids. It began operating in 1902. The Muskegon interurban utilized the West Leonard Street city car line for its entry into Grand Rapids. The third and last line, built thirteen years later, connected Kalamazoo and Battle Creek with Grand Rapids in 1915. The Kalamazoo interurban gained entry into Grand Rapids on its own private right-of-way to its station in downtown Grand Rapids.

The "Holland Interurban"

The Grand Rapids, Holland and Lake Michigan Rapid Railway (GRH&LMRRy) became the first interurban electric railway to run into Grand Rapids. The "Holland Interurban," as it became known, was incorporated February 24, 1900, to build an interurban railway between Grand Rapids and Holland. Benjamin S. Hanchett became vice-president of the new electric line.

The Holland interurban company purchased the Holland and Lake Michigan Railway and the Saugatuck, Douglas and Lake Shore Railway Company in June 1900. This purchase enabled the Holland interurban company to build a line between Grand Rapids and Holland that went beyond Holland all the way to Macatawa Park adjacent to Lake Michigan.

The Grand Rapids Common Council passed an ordinance on June 25, 1900, allowing the street railway company to build an extension of its Grandville Avenue city car line from Hall Street southwest, a mile to the city limit at Clyde Park Avenue. The Holland interurban cars could enter and leave the city via the streetcar line on Grandville Avenue.

Benjamin S. Hanchett. His biography appears in Chapter 12.

Construction of the new line began at Jenison, six miles southwest of Grand Rapids. The first ceremonial shovelful of dirt was thrown in Jenison on October 20, 1900, by vice-president Benjamin S. Hanchett, who was also secretary and treasurer of the Grand Rapids Railway.

Grand Rapids Streetcar First to Operate on Holland Interurban Line

The Grand Rapids-Jenison section of the Holland interurban was informally opened on July 09, 1901, when Hanchett took a group of guests on Grand Rapids Railway car No. 263 from Grand Rapids to Jenison, the end of the line at that time. Motorman Michael Fallon and conductor Adrian Blois had the honor of piloting the car as it left downtown Grand Rapids and headed southwest on the Grandville Avenue streetcar line to the city limit at Clyde Park Avenue, where it started running on the interurban line in Wyoming township. The streetcar then ran southwest on its private right-of-way (Lee Street was built later and ran parallel to the interurban tracks) for about three miles and passed through what was to become the young Wyoming Park suburb. The car proceeded southwest to the 750-foot long trestle over the Lake Shore and Michigan Southern railroad track and Byron Center Road. This trestle was twenty-four feet high at its apex and with grades of one and one half and three per cent. The streetcar stopped on the trestle and photographer Jackson took various views of No. 263 and its passengers.

The streetcar continued running southwest to Grandville where it ran on Main Street through the village and then crossed the

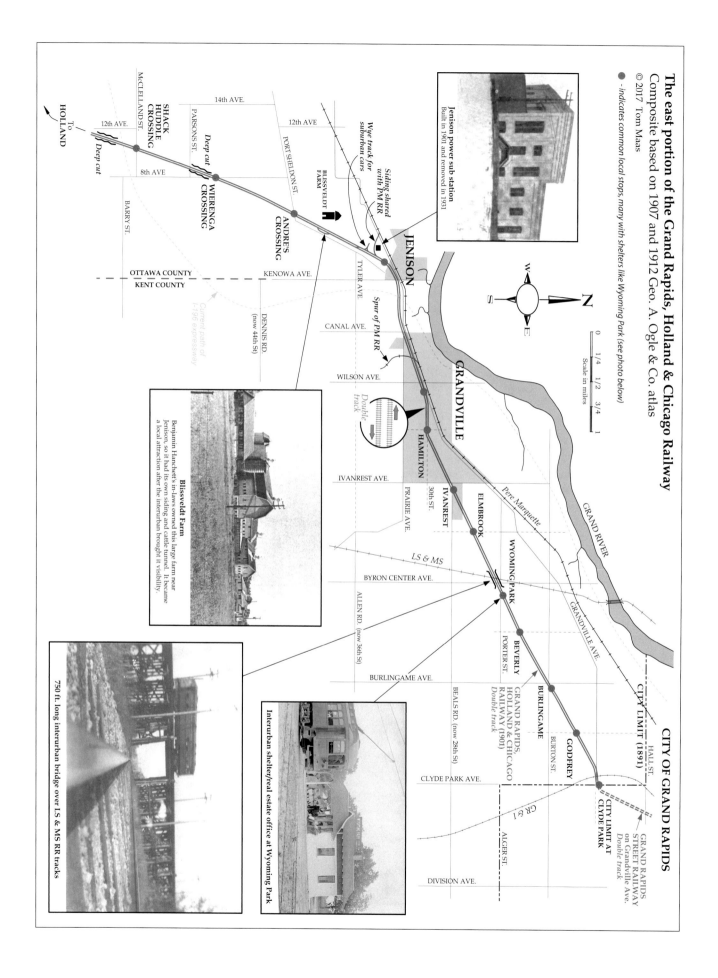

Jenison power sub station
Built in 1901 and removed in 1931

CITY OF GRAND RAPIDS

GRAND RIVER

GRANDVILLE

Pere Marquette

N

Scale in miles
0   1/4   1/2   3/4   1

To
HOLLAND

Deep cut

12th AVE.

McCLELLAND ST.

SHACK
HUDDLE
CROSSING

PARSONS ST.

14th AVE.

Deep cut

8th AVE

WIERENGA
CROSSING

BARRY ST.

12th AVE

PORT SHELDON ST.

ANDRE'S
CROSSING

Wye track for
suburban cars

BLISSVELDT
FARM

Siding shared
with PM RR

JENISON

OTTAWA COUNTY
KENT COUNTY

KENOWA AVE.

DENNIS RD.
(now 4th St)

Current path of
I-196 expressway

TYLER AVE.

Spur of PM RR

CANAL AVE.

WILSON AVE.

Double
track

HAMILTON

IVANREST AVE.

PRAIRIE AVE.

30th ST.

IVANREST

ELMBROOK

BYRON CENTER AVE.

LS & MS

ALLEN RD. (now 36th St)

BURLINGAME AVE.

BEALS RD. (now 28th St)

WYOMING
PARK

BEVERLY

PORTER ST.

GRAND RAPIDS,
HOLLAND & CHICAGO
RAILWAY (1901)
Double track

BURLINGAME

GODFREY

BURTON ST.

CLYDE PARK AVE.

ALGER ST.

DIVISION AVE.

GRANDVILLE AVE.

GR 81

CITY LIMIT AT
CLYDE PARK

CITY LIMIT (1891)

HALL ST.

GRAND RAPIDS
STREET RAILWAY
on Grandville Ave.
Double track

Blissveldt Farm
Benjamin Hanchett's in-laws owned this large farm near
Jenison, so it had its own siding and cattle tunnel. It became
a local attraction after the interurban brought it visibility.

750 ft. long interurban bridge over LS & MS RR tracks

Interurban shelter/real estate office at Wyoming Park

Change in Time Schedule of Grandville-Jenison Interurban Cars.

Beginning this morning cars will leave corner Lyon and Canal streets for Grandville, Jenison and intermediate points as follows:

First Car Leaves Corner Lyon and Canal Streets.

5:30 a. m.	2:40 p.m.
6:40 a. m.	4:00 p. m.
8:00 a. m.	5:20 p. m.
9:20 a. m.	6:40 p. m.
10:40 a. m.	8:00 p. m.
12:00 noon.	9:20 p. m.
1:20 p. m.	10:40 p. p. Last car.

First Car Leaves Jenison.

6:00 a. m.	3:20 p. m.
7:20 a. m.	4:40 p. m.
8:40 a. m.	6:00 p. m.
10:00 a. m.	7:20 p. m.
11:20 a. m.	8:40 p. m.
12:40 p. m.	10:00 p. m.
2:00 p. m.	11:20 p. m. Last car.

The round trip to Jenison and return is made in one hour and twenty minutes. This time will be lessened as soon as the new interurban cars are placed in commission, which will be in a few days.

INTERURBAN TRANSFERS.

Passengers from the Interurban line from Grandville, Jenison and intermediate points will receive free transfers upon Grand Rapids railway to any part of the city. The performance at Ramona will be over in time for passengers to catch the 10:40 car each evening at corner of Monroe and Market streets for points on interurban line.

Top: *Car traverses the long wooden trestle over the Lake Shore & Michigan Southern Railroad track on the west side of Wyoming Park.*

Wyoming Historical Commission

Above: *Car no. 263 stopped in Grandville on July 9, 1901, for a "photo op." This was the first car with passengers to make the trip from Grand Rapids on the newly laid Holland Interurban tracks. Benjamin Hanchett is the fourth person from the right, standing proudly in front. Note that this car was a new double-ended car assigned to the North Park line, but was chosen to run on the Grandville Avenue track and interurban line all the way to Jenison and back.*

Grand Rapids Public Library

Kent-Ottawa county line, finally arriving at the Jenison House in Jenison. After dinner at the Jenison House, the group re-boarded the streetcar and returned to Grand Rapids, stopping in Grandville to pick up a group of local citizens. Hanchett and his guests rode back to downtown Grand Rapids and on to Ramona Park at Reed's Lake.

The GRH&LMRRy's plan was to build a double-track system so cars would not be delayed on sidings while waiting for an opposing car to pass. However, it was not able to achieve the double track goal until 1903.

Time schedule for Grand Rapids—Jenison effective July 13, 1901.

Grand Rapids Evening Press, 13 Jul 1901

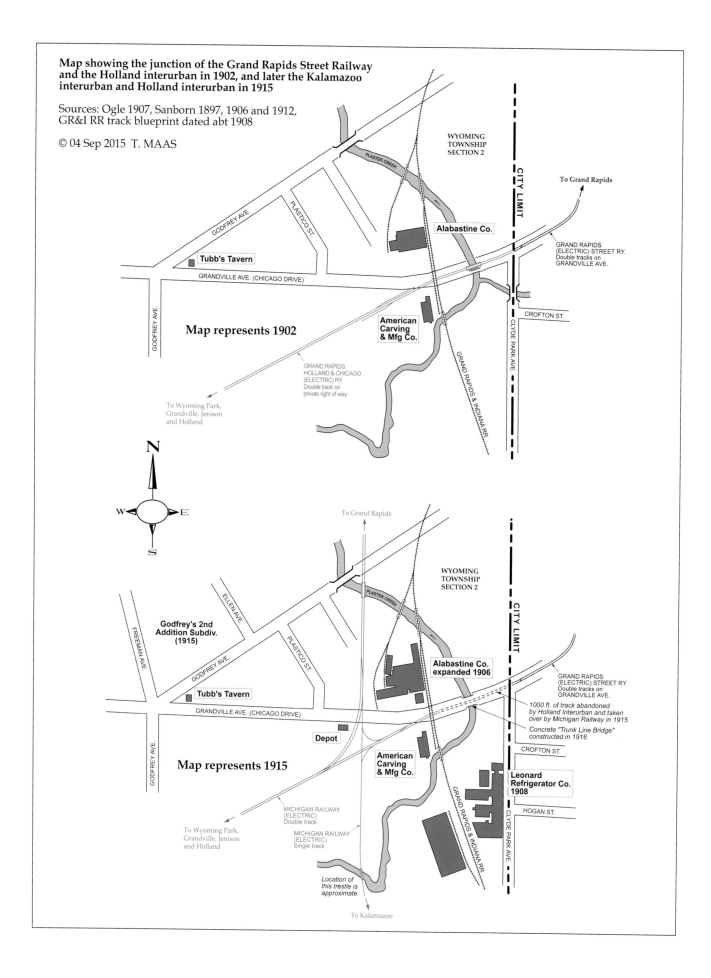

Map showing the junction of the Grand Rapids Street Railway and the Holland interurban in 1902, and later the Kalamazoo interurban and Holland interurban in 1915

Sources: Ogle 1907, Sanborn 1897, 1906 and 1912, GR&I RR track blueprint dated abt 1908

© 04 Sep 2015 T. MAAS

WYOMING TOWNSHIP SECTION 2

CITY LIMIT

PLASTER CREEK

Alabastine Co.

GODFREY AVE.

PLASTICO ST.

Tubb's Tavern

GRANDVILLE AVE. (CHICAGO DRIVE)

GODFREY AVE.

Map represents 1902

American Carving & Mfg Co.

To Grand Rapids

GRAND RAPIDS (ELECTRIC) STREET RY. Double tracks on GRANDVILLE AVE.

CROFTON ST.

CLYDE PARK AVE.

GRAND RAPIDS, HOLLAND & CHICAGO (ELECTRIC) RY. Double track on private right of way

GRAND RAPIDS & INDIANA RR

To Wyoming Park, Grandville, Jenison and Holland

N
W E
S

To Grand Rapids

WYOMING TOWNSHIP SECTION 2

CITY LIMIT

PLASTER CREEK

ELLEN AVE.

FREEMAN AVE.

Godfrey's 2nd Addition Subdiv. (1915)

GODFREY AVE.

PLASTICO ST.

Alabastine Co. expanded 1906

GRAND RAPIDS (ELECTRIC) STREET RY. Double tracks on GRANDVILLE AVE.

Tubb's Tavern

GRANDVILLE AVE. (CHICAGO DRIVE)

Depot

American Carving & Mfg Co.

1000 ft. of track abandoned by Holland Interurban and taken over by Michigan Railway in 1915

Concrete "Trunk Line Bridge" constructed in 1916

CROFTON ST.

Leonard Refrigerator Co. 1908

GODFREY AVE.

Map represents 1915

GRAND RAPIDS & INDIANA RR

HOGAN ST.

CLYDE PARK AVE.

MICHIGAN RAILWAY (ELECTRIC) Double track

MICHIGAN RAILWAY (ELECTRIC) Single track

To Wyoming Park, Grandville, Jenison and Holland

Location of this trestle is approximate

To Kalamazoo

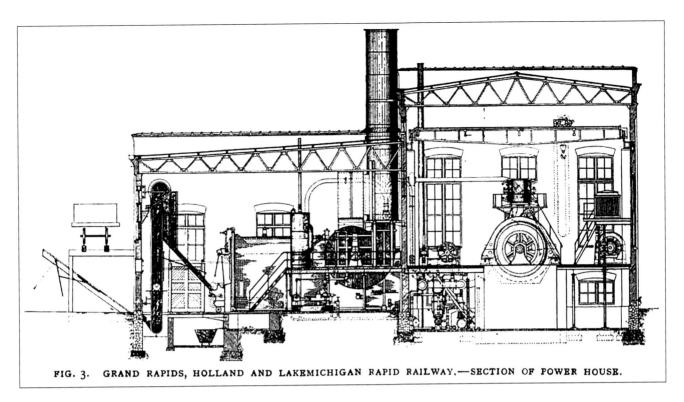

FIG. 3. GRAND RAPIDS, HOLLAND AND LAKEMICHIGAN RAPID RAILWAY.—SECTION OF POWER HOUSE.

Architectural drawings of the Holland Interurban substation in Jenison.
Western Electrician, Vol. 30, 15 Mar 1902, pgs 174-175

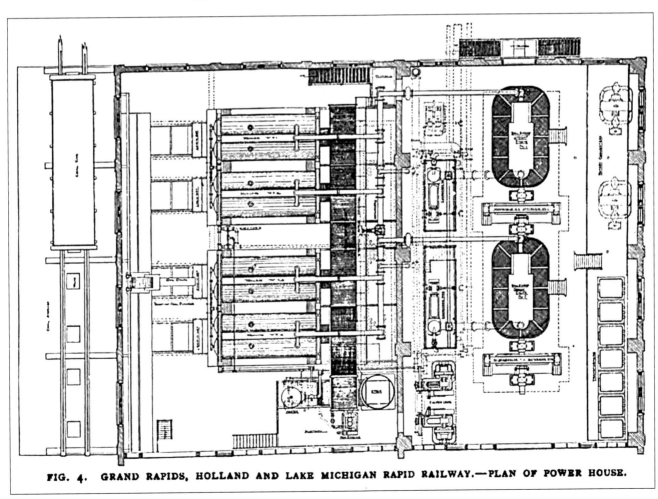

FIG. 4. GRAND RAPIDS, HOLLAND AND LAKE MICHIGAN RAPID RAILWAY.—PLAN OF POWER HOUSE.

Chapter 10: The Grand Rapids Interurbans (1900-1928)

This Holland interurban car is stuck in a deep snow drift.

Chris Byron and Tom Wilson

Building a Downtown Loop for Interurban Cars

The new interurbans were built as single-end cars. Therefore, the Holland Interurban leased double-ended Grand Rapids streetcars so that they could reverse direction without need of a loop or wye. These cars were assigned to the Grand Rapids-Jenison interurban route until the downtown loop via Monroe, Ottawa, Lyon, and Canal streets was completed. Wider curves were built at the Monroe-Ottawa and Market-Monroe intersections so the longer interurban cars could negotiate the turns without derailing. This enabled the interurban cars to reverse direction and leave downtown Grand Rapids on the same street on which they had entered downtown.

First Interurban Car Runs in Grand Rapids

Passenger coach No. 14 of the Grand Rapids, Holland & Lake Michigan Rapid Railway arrived via a freight train on July 25, 1901. The car was towed by a street railway motor car from the Detroit, Grand Haven and Milwaukee Railroad freight depot through downtown Grand Rapids to the Hall Street carbarn where it was equipped for service between Grand Rapids and Jenison starting the very next day.

Car No. 14 was distinctly different and larger than city car No. 263, one of the largest double-truck double-ended streetcars in Grand Rapids (which had made the very first trip to Jenison). A Grand Rapids newspaper described interurban car No. 14 as built like a Pullman railroad passenger car, weighing twenty-five tons and was thirty-five feet in length overall.

The car's seating capacity was slightly more than fifty passengers including twelve in the smoking compartment. The car was painted a deep red with silver lettering and decoration. The motorman had a large brake wheel and a valve for controlling the McGann air brakes next to him. He also had a Lorain Steel Company controller for regulating the speed of the car and appliances for controlling the release of sand and for striking a steel alarm bell if needed. Four Lorain motors were mounted on two steel trucks, each truck carrying two of the fifty-horse power motors geared to the thirty-three-inch wheels.

Car No. 14 was the only interurban car to operate between Grand Rapids and Jenison for several weeks because the powerhouse in Jenison was still under construction. The street railway company had only enough surplus power at that time to run one car between the two cities.

Sinkhole Devours Interurban Rails and Grade

The Holland interurban company encountered its version of the "mother of all sinkholes" in the spring of 1901 when it began to construct the line through a large swampy marsh just east of Holland. Week after week the contractors had dumped sand on what was to become the grade across the marsh. Unfortunately the prospect of getting a solid roadbed was no closer to realization than before the work began. Every night the sand sank into the marsh "until a microscope is required to find traces of it in the morning." The contractors resorted to dumping logs into the sinkhole to serve as a foundation for the sand.

The contractors were surprised on June 3 when they found that one hundred feet of the grade, ties, rails and a dump car were under six feet of water in what seemed to be a bottomless pit. The sinkhole continued to exhibit what one reporter called "an insatiable appetite." The reporter used a degree of artistic license when he penned the following news on June 18:

> The electric railway to connect Holland and Grand Rapids is nearer to China than the former city. The grade and rails took another fall towards the celestial kingdom last night and grade builders are taking soundings to determine the depth to which the tracks have sunk. At least 500 feet of grade lies buried beneath a conglomeration of mud and water. The earth seems to have parted and swallowed up all the sand that has been delivered on the grounds since last spring. Great banks of earth have risen on either side of the grade and between them lies submerged tracks.

The contractors continued to try to fill the sinkhole. The interurban devised a temporary solution to enable the company to meet an important August 31 deadline for running an interurban car between Holland and Grand Rapids.

First Run from Holland to Grand Rapids

The Grand Rapids, Holland and Lake Michigan Railway ran an interurban car from Holland east to Jenison for the first time on August 31, 1901. The last rail of the single-track line was laid during the morning, and the first car left Holland for Grand Rapids that afternoon. The interurban car rode on a temporary pontoon bridge in order to cross the notorious sinkhole east of Holland.

The Holland powerhouse provided electricity for the line's first fifteen miles. The car was unable to use electric power all the way to Grand Rapids because overhead trolley wire had not yet been erected for the entire distance. A steam locomotive pulled the interurban car over a non-electrified gap between Zeeland and Jenison. Then the interurban resumed its run to complete the journey between Jenison and Grand Rapids.

There was an important reason for making such an effort to begin service between Holland and Grand Rapids by August 31.The interurban company had signed an agreement promising to operate its cars between Zeeland and Grand Rapids by Saturday, August 31, 1901. If the deadline was missed, the company would forfeit the $1000 franchise guarantee it had deposited with Zeeland township.

The generator at the Jenison powerhouse started up for the first time on August 20 and provided the electric power that finally enabled one interurban car to travel all the way from Holland to Grand Rapids in September. By late September, the big generator was producing enough electricity to run several cars on the line between Grand Rapids and Holland simultaneously.

Passenger Cars

Interurban cars began running between Grand Rapids and Holland on Monday, October 14, 1901. By March 1902 the company had six closed passenger cars that were forty-seven feet long and four closed passenger cars that were forty-one feet long overall in length. These cars, fully equipped with motors, trucks and brakes, weighed twenty-three tons and twenty-five tons respectively and another four tons when fully loaded with passengers. The cars were built by Jewett Car Company and G. C. Kuhlman Car Company. The new interurban cars certainly stood out on the Grand Rapids streets being much larger and heavier than Grand Rapids city cars.

Five New Stations

The Holland interurban contracted for five new stations, built in late 1901 at Grandville, Jenison, Hanley, Jamestown and Forest Grove. Each station was a one-story building twenty by forty feet with two compartments—a waiting room and a freight depot painted white and brown. Other stations and waiting shelters were built later, some of which were built by realty companies that wanted to lure folks out to their new subdivisions such as Wyoming Park (1908) and Elmbrook (1913).

Interurban cars were required to operate as city streetcars, collecting local fares when picking up passengers inside city limits of Grand Rapids. They even provided passengers with free transfers.

The Holland interurban company opened a ticket office and waiting room in Grand Rapids at 76 Ottawa Avenue, just north of Monroe Avenue on the downtown loop, until the freight house opened in 1902. The company opened a new passenger station in October 1902 in a store front in the Eagle Hotel at 71 North Market Street, just south of Monroe Avenue that served the Holland interurban passengers until 1915 when the Holland interurban cars began using the private right-of-way of the Michigan Railway into Grand Rapids. Holland interurban passengers now had a faster route into downtown Grand Rapids and use of a new terminal.

West bound Holland Interurban car No. 20 and east bound Grand Rapids Street Railway car No. 96 on Grandville Avenue at Clyde Park Avenue, the city limit of Grand Rapids.

Bill Volkmer Collection

Steamer Puritan at G. & M. Dock,
Macatawa, Mich.

Holland Intererban Train
Leaves Grand Rapids 8 P. M

EVERY NIGHT $2.00

Colorized postcard of the Holland interurban at the Macatawa Graham & Morton Dock from 1911. The Steamer Puritan is about to depart for Chicago.

Ed Bawden

The "cozy" Holland Interurban station at Elmbrook as seen in this newspaper ad to attract city dwellers to the newly formed suburbs along the tracks.

Grand Rapids Press, 03 May 1913

A beautiful home for home people. $4,000. Bell Main 1128

ELMBROOK

The beautiful weather we are now having is best appreciated here at ELMBROOK. Fresh air—pure water—attractive trees—the welcome spring flowers everywhere.

The streets are now being graded—over two miles of sidewalks will be laid—attractive, cozy cottages and bungalows are being rushed to completion.

Right now, we have several bungalows ready for your immediate occupancy—you don't have to wait—shade—furnaces—electric lights—bath—fine wells—fireplace—oak trim and floors—cement porch—just the kind of a home you are proud to have your friends see.

This attractive bungalow shown above—lot 60x206 feet—surrounded with trees—all conveniences—oak trim and floors—your choice of wall paper and electric fixtures—only $2,500. Suitable terms if you desire.

The cut below shows another of our exceptional bungalows. Trimmed in oak—modern—large cobblestone fireplace with built-in seats on each side of it—cypress flower boxes built in porch—one of the nicest bungalows imaginable—only $2,650. Terms to suit.

Cozy electric lighted station at ELMBROOK. Grounds are now being "landscaped." Only twenty minutes to Monroe avenue—thirty minute service.

Take the Holland interurban Sunday—get off at ELMBROOK—and spend a little time investigating this fast growing, classy little suburb. Building restrictions to eliminate the undesirable—all lots on terms so attractive you cannot resist—every street to be graded and cement walks built in front of every lot. Come down—see for yourself—we will be glad to see you and you won't regret it.

LEON T. CLOSTERHOUSE

CITZ. 5004. 206 WIDDICOMB BLDG. BELL 1304

Realtor Sam Wilson used this small office building to help sell bungalow homes in the Wyoming Park area. He provided the large roof and benches for the comfort of local residents (and potential buyers) waiting for the next interurban car.

Wyoming Historical Commission

Freight Operations

A warehouse on the northwest corner of Oakes Street and Ellsworth Avenue was leased by the Holland interurban company to serve as a freight house in April 1902. The building was well located, being on the Grandville Avenue streetcar line used by Holland interurban cars, and being near the City Market where farmers and other merchants bought and sold fruit and farm produce. The Grand Rapids Street Railway built a side track on the Oakes Street side of the freight house.

The street railway built a branch from the Grandville Avenue streetcar line into the City Market in June 1902. The short branch line left Ellsworth Avenue and went west on Oakes Street, then south on Market Street and finally west on Cherry Street and into the City Market. This enabled both the Holland and Muskegon interurban cars to enter the market to deliver and pick up fruit, vegetables, meat, and fish. A wye at Ellsworth and Oakes streets was built to permit the interurban cars to turn around. The company also built a spur to the Holland interurban property on Oakes Street, but the street railway was forced to remove this track because the ordinance did not include permission to build it.

Double-Track Mainline

The Holland interurban finally achieved its goal of building a double-track mainline in the spring of 1903. On May 24, twelve carloads of used rail arrived from the abandoned Iron Range and Huron Bay Railroad in Michigan's Upper Peninsula. This rail enabled the company to complete construction of the second track resulting in a double-track mainline from Holland to Grand Rapids. The Holland interurban advertised service between Holland and Grand Rapids every half hour by August 1902.

The company also advertised three resort specials leaving Holland every morning: the Early Morning Flyer at 5:35, the Business Men's Special at 6:35, and the Banker's Special at 7:35 A.M.

The Holland interurban often advertised its double-track mainline. This sounded safer than the Muskegon interurban which was a single track mainline with passing sidings.

Holland Interurban Increases Its Fleet

The interurban company began 1902 with an express motor on its freight run. By March 1903, the Grand Rapids, Holland & Lake Michigan Railway had three express motors, seven box trailer cars, six flat cars and one switch motor in addition to nineteen passenger cars.

A year later in April 1904 the company's roster had increased to four express motors, ten boxcar trailers, ten flat cars, and two switch motor cars in addition to twenty-four passenger cars. The roster was the same in 1907 except for two more boxcar trailers. Many, if not all, of the trailers were built in the Holland Interurban company's shops at Virginia Park, west of Holland.

Interurban Hauls Logs and Other Freight

In 1903, the Holland interurban railway cars carried hardwood logs into Grand Rapids on streetcar tracks for use by the Grand Rapids Veneer Works and other furniture industries in the city. Citizens complained about these log cars on the Grandville Avenue streetcar line in early March of that year.

A single Holland interurban freight motor often pulled one or trailers. Citizens also complained in 1908 that the heavy weight of the freight cars was causing the Grandville Avenue streetcar rails to sink. The condition of the streetcar line continued to deteriorate until the Grand Rapids Board of Public Works investigated the Grandville Avenue track in 1915. The Board reported that the heavy interurban cars had caused the rails to sink three inches below street level.

Interurban Company Reorganized

The financial affairs of the Grand Rapids, Holland and Lake Michigan Railway Company had deteriorated so badly by 1904 that it required an infusion of capital. The Grand Rapids, Holland and Chicago Railway Company purchased the GRH&LMRy on July 21, 1904. The company was reorganized using the latter name. This name was kept until 1926 when the line ceased operation

Limited Crashes into Milk Car

Holland Interurban limited car No. 32 was running eastbound at sixty miles an hour past Shack Huddle Crossing on the evening of August 15, 1904. The limited car, with motorman Powers at the controls, had just started going down the hill toward Wierenga crossing on what was known to be one of the speediest sections of track on the entire line. Motorman Powers was shocked to see the red warning lights on the rear of an interurban car ahead of him. It was a freight motor that had been delayed while on the milk run.

The August 16, 1904, *Grand Rapids Press* published the following detailed account of the accident:

The milk car, in charge of Conductor Lord, had halted at the Wierenga crossing to take on freight and was just getting underway when the limited pitched over the brow of the hill. In a moment those in the freight car heard Powers' whistle acknowledging that he had seen the rear signals. Powers found he could not check his car in time and began blowing his whistle in a frantic signal for the milk car to pull ahead.

The signal was complied with and the milk car accelerated rapidly but almost six rods east of the crossing the limited, with motors grinding in the reverse motion and brakes latched in the emergency notch, caught up and crashed into the freight. Conductor Lord left the rear platform almost as it crumpled up, but Powers had remained at his levers and was buried in the wreckage.

The crash shattered the brake controlling mechanism and the controller box. Brakes were released on the limited and the power shut off the reversed motors. Under these conditions the two cars coasted along for some six hundred yards before the freight car brakes brought them to a standstill. Then it was Powers that surprised those who were looking for his remains by creeping out of the front end and walking unassisted to the freight car.

There were seven passengers on board. One was an infant, which was thrown violently from its mother's arms to the floor, but was not injured. The whistle had prepared those in the car for the shock and they were not injured. Motorman Powers was brought to Grand Rapids and placed under the care of a physician. His injuries consisted of lacerations of the face and head and severe bruises.

"Cable Car" Used to Transport Passengers

The Grand River overflowed its banks in 1904 and 1905. The June 1905 flood created a lake more than a half-mile long covering the Holland interurban tracks up to three feet deep in places between Jenison and Grandville. Interurban cars trying to run through the rising flood waters could not avoid getting their electric motors wet which caused them to short out. The Holland interurban company employees quickly devised a novel solution to the problem. Passengers rode on a flat car which was pulled through the floodwaters on the rails of the interurban track by two long cables. At each end of this car was a cable that regular interurban cars used to pull the flat car "ferrying" passengers back and forth across the "lake." When the flat car arrived at the end of the lake a gangplank was placed from the flat car to the door of the waiting passenger car so the passengers did not even get their shoes wet.

Competition with Muskegon Interurban for Chicago Passengers

Both the Holland and the Muskegon interurban lines competed for passengers bound to Chicago. The Holland interurban did not have steamboat connections with Chicago during winter months because Lake Macatawa froze over. There were no steam railroad car ferries to break the ice in the lake to allow steamboats to pass through a channel in Lake Macatawa and on to Lake Michigan. The Muskegon interurban, however, was able to connect with steamboats going to Chicago year-round because the Grand Trunk car ferries broke the ice coming out of Grand Haven on their way to and from Milwaukee.

The Holland interurban made two-foot-square colored signs in August 1905 that were displayed on the front and sides of each car to help passengers identify the classes of cars. Limited cars, Steamboat Limited cars, Flyer cars to particular resorts, as well as cars that stopped upon signal were classes where each had its own colored sign.

Pleasure Seekers Ride on Flat Cars to Jenison Park

In order to transport all who were expected to attend the annual Zeeland and Holland businessmen's picnic at the Jenison Amusement Park (located on Lake Macatawa west of Holland) on July 18, 1906, general passenger agent Floyd converted flat cars into passenger cars. This was accomplished by fitting them with benches, decorating them with flags, and

Flood in 1905 covers the Holland interurban tracks on Main Street on the western edge of Grandville. View is looking westward towards Jenison.

Grandville Historical Commission

Grand Rapids, Holland & Chicago Railway 1905 advertisement to attract passengers on its Grand Rapids-Chicago line via Graham & Morton.

Grand Rapids Evening Press, 30 Jun 1905

The Holland Interurban freight house on Market Street, view looking south.

Electric Traction, August 1908

providing guard rails to keep the riders on board. These converted "passenger cars for a day" had no overhead covering but the accommodating good weather allowed riders to relish riding in the open air.

The Holland interurban company built two express motors in 1907 to handle the expanding freight and express business.

The *Honolulu* open summer car that the Grand Rapids Railway purchased in 1906 for parties and excursions took a party to Macatawa Park adjacent to Lake Michigan in early August 1907.

Freight House Built in Grand Rapids

The Common Council passed an ordinance on November 4, 1907, giving the Grand Rapids Railway Company the right to build a line from Ellsworth Avenue west through Island Street to the west side of Market Street where the Holland interurban planned to build a freight house. The freight house the Holland interurban was leasing at the northwest corner of Oakes Street and Ellsworth Avenue was abandoned when the new facility was completed. The new freight house had three side tracks and a wye for turning the freight motors. This warehouse handled freight and express until 1915. Thereafter freight to be carried by the Grand Rapids, Holland and Chicago Railway was delivered to the new Kalamazoo interurban (Michigan Railway) freight house located on the west side of the Grand River just south of west Fulton Street.

Cars Built and Rebuilt

Benjamin Hanchett, president and general manager of the Grand Rapids Railway organized a group to purchase the Grand Rapids, Holland and Chicago Railway in January 1912. Hanchett then arranged for the Hall Street car

house shops to begin building two new passenger cars for the Holland interurban line. The two cars ran as a vestibuled pair. These two passenger cars could carry up to 106 passengers on the steamboat service that ran from downtown Grand Rapids southwest on Grandville Avenue and then on the Holland interurban track all the way to the Graham and Morton steamboat docks at Holland and Macatawa Park. Although the two cars were designed to run as a pair, each car had its own motors so they could be operated separately.

The Holland interurban company had virtually all of its rolling stock rebuilt at the Grand Rapids Railway Company's Hall Street car shops during the 1912-1913 winter months. Nineteen passenger coaches were extensively rebuilt with new seats, automatic air brakes and couplers and left the Hall Street shops with a new coat of paint. Seven Holland interurban express cars and thirty-one freight cars were also rebuilt at this time.

The roster of the GRH&CRy at the end of 1912 consisted of nineteen passenger cars, five express cars, fourteen box cars, fourteen flat cars, and three freight motors. At the end of 1913 the roster had grown to twenty-one passenger cars, twenty box cars, fourteen flat cars, four freight motors and one line car as well as three electric locomotives.

Collision at Wyoming Park Station

Interurban car No. 12, running as a westbound limited car, plunged into the rear of No. 26, which had been running as a westbound Jenison local car, but had been stopped due to electrical problems. The accident occurred at 6 P.M. on January 10, 1913, southwest of the city limit, just opposite the interurban station in Wyoming Park. The westbound limited car smashed into and partially telescoped the rear of the westbound local car which was stand-

Two-car steamboat train of two passenger cars at Macatawa Park steamboat pier.

Ed Bawden Collection

The Eagle Hotel at the corner of North Market Ave. and Louis St. housed the ticket office for the Holland interurban.

Thomas Dilley Collection, Grand Rapids Public Library

ing on the westbound track.

Motorman John DeGroot had climbed on top of his stalled local car in an attempt to fix the trolley pole. Conductor Don Pettis waited a while and then took a red lantern and started walking back to signal the limited car to stop. Pettis had gone back a few hundred feet when the limited car appeared coming around a long curve and moving at a rate of fifty miles an hour toward the rear of the local car.

Motorman Fred Shaw spotted the local car standing ahead on the same track. He set the brakes and reversed the motors of the limited car but it was still traveling at about thirty-five miles an hour when it plowed into the rear of the local car destroying vestibules of both cars as well as the smoking compartment of the limited car. The limited car shoved the local car more than two hundred feet down the track. Motorman DeGroot, still was on the roof of his car, was catapulted into the air. Miraculously he landed in a snow bank practically uninjured.

Motorman Shaw, however, was trapped in the front vestibule of his car. It took nearly half an hour before enough of the crushed wooden framework around him was chopped so that he could be taken out of the car before a fire that had started would have reached him. Eight passengers were hospitalized in addition to the motorman; W. J. Hubbard, who had been sitting in the smoking compartment near the front of the limited car, died of his injuries on January 26. The coroner's jury blamed the conductor and motorman of the local run for not immediately going back far enough to warn the limited car in time for it to stop.

Composite screenshot from "The Blissveldt Romance" 1915 movie of Jenison station and freight house – entire digitized 23 minute long movie is online: https://www.youtube.com/

Holland Interurban Line Sold

The Commonwealth Railway, Light and Power Company, owner of Grand Rapids Railway, and numerous other traction properties, gained control of Grand Rapids, Holland and Chicago Railway in early April 1913 through a stock trade with Benjamin Hanchett and other stockholders in the interurban line. The investors received Commonwealth stock in exchange for their Holland interurban stock. No changes were made in the management. Benjamin Hanchett remained as president of the railway.

The new owners placed an order for four new sixty-foot all-steel passenger interurban cars which were heavier and also fifteen feet longer than the existing Holland interurbans.

Grand Rapids Railway Streetcars Operate on Holland Interurban Track

In May 1915, the Michigan Railway began running into Grand Rapids on its own private right-of-way. The Holland interurban cars no longer entered Grand Rapids via Grandville Avenue but instead switched onto the Michigan Railway at its new junction just

west of the city limit. This junction was 1,000 feet beyond the west end of the Grandville Avenue streetcar line at Clyde Park Avenue. The street railway company extended its suburban service on July 6, 1915, by running on the newly vacated Holland interurban track. Passengers could now ride rather than walk the 1,000 feet when transferring between the Grandville Avenue streetcars and the Holland interurban cars.

Michigan Railway Leases the Holland Interurban

Michigan Railway leased the Grand Rapids, Holland and Chicago Railway on January 1, 1916. Michigan Railway operated the Holland interurban as part of its northwestern division. One of the most visible changes that the Michigan Railway made was to repaint the Holland interurban cars. The cars, which had been a fire engine red, were repainted green with a dark red roof.

Michigan Railway was reorganized as the Michigan Railroad in 1919. It continued to operate the Holland interurban until the lease was terminated on December 31, 1923, by the Commonwealth Power, Railway and Light Company. This holding company reorganized in January 1924 and was divided into the Electric Railway Securities Company and the Commonwealth Power Corporation. This enabled the holding company to demonstrate that its public power utilities companies were very profitable while beginning the liquidation of its financially failing transportation properties.

NO SALOONS
OR UNDESIRABLES

Every lot carries the agreement that no liquors can be manufactured or sold on the property. Other restrictions insure pleasant living conditions.

I will help you own a home place in BURLINGAME

I want to see every resident of Grand Rapids a home owner, especially every young couple. You know, as well as I, that you can be happier and save more money by owning instead of renting. You make yourself a better citizen and Grand Rapids a better city when you own.

1915 newspaper ad for the Burlingame subdivision, where the Holland Interurban was a prominent feature. Note the emphasis on distances to nearby industries.

Grand Rapids Herald, 1915

A July 1916 collision between a Holland Interurban car and a steam switch engine in Grandville was covered on the front page.

Grand Rapids Press, 17 Jul 1916

Chapter 10: The Grand Rapids Interurbans (1900-1928)

State St. looking East, Grandville, Mich.
64003-R

Postcard view of downtown Grandville on State Street with a streetcar on one set of tracks.

Grandville Historical Commission

Battle Over Street Paving Costs in Grandville

The village of Grandville tried to compel the Holland interurban company and its lessor, the Michigan Railroad, to comply with the terms of the Grandville Village franchise for operation over its streets in 1919. The interurban was responsible for paving between its rails in Grandville. After three years, the village finally filed a petition in Kent County Circuit Court for an injunction to prohibit the railway from running cars through Grandville until the interurban complied with the terms of its franchise.

The double track of the interurban company occupied a twenty-foot-wide strip of rough gravel that stretched for a half mile down the middle of the otherwise concrete-paved main street in Grandville. Michigan Railroad declared it could not keep its promise to Grandville because it lacked the money to pay for paving. The circuit court finally ruled in December 1922 that the interurban company must pay for paving the center of Main Street occupied by its tracks. The verdict was appealed all the way to the Michigan Supreme Court which ruled in December 1923 that the company had to pay the paving costs in Grandville by May 1, 1924, or the franchise could be forfeited. Further negotiations between the village of Grandville and the financially strapped Holland interurban company failed.

Grandville authorities placed temporary barriers across the interurban tracks on State Street at both the east and west village limits prohibiting Holland interurban cars from entering the village, thus severing the line on Saturday, June 14, 1924. The *Grand Rapids Herald* published the following headline on its Monday front page: "Flivvers Help in Grandville's Row on Paving: Sight of Women Passengers Trudging through Deluge Softens Hearts of Sturdy Grandville Fathers." The newspaper went on to report that Grandville citizens rose to the occasion when a heavy rainstorm began and drove enough automobiles to carry interurban passengers the mile inside the city so that very few had to walk during the rainstorm.

One interurban car was able to pass through the blockade on Monday but only because it was carrying U.S. mail in addition to passengers.

The blockade ended after four days on Wednesday, June 18, 1924, when a receiver was appointed by U.S. District Court Judge C.W. Sessions. He stated he would authorize the receiver to issue receiver's certificates at once so the tracks in Grandville would be paved during the summer. A gang of workers began tearing up one of the two tracks on Main Street in late July 1924 so the street could be completely paved by summer's end.

Holland Interurban car and automobile collision at Nagel Avenue crossing claims one fatality.

Grand Rapids Public Library

Grade Crossing Fatalities

Sixteen-year-old Harry Bos drove his auto carrying him and his fifteen-year-old friend Albert Boone onto the Holland interurban tracks at the Nagel Avenue crossing in Wyoming Township southwest of the city limit on July 11, 1925. An interurban car crosed Nagel Avenue at the same time hitting Harry's auto pushing it over 200 feet down the tracks before the motorman could stop the interurban car. The wrecked auto became wedged beneath the trucks of the Interurban killing Harry Bos instantly and causing Albert Boone to later die of internal injuries.

Andre's Crossing, in the countryside between Jenison and Shack Huddle Crossing, was one of the most dangerous rail crossings in Ottawa County. It had been the scene of several accidents including one which took the lives of five persons in 1920. Two more deaths were added to its long list of tragedies on Saturday afternoon, September 11, 1926, when a fast-moving westbound limited Holland interurban car demolished a Dodge touring car driven by Lewis Mosher. Both Mosher and his passenger Martin Van Oost were killed. The Dodge auto was hurled against a milk loading platform, which also was wrecked.*

Sale and Final Abandonment

The financial condition of the Holland interurban continued to deteriorate. The federal court finally ordered that the bankrupt Grand Rapids, Holland and Chicago Railway be sold at auction, which occurred on October 20, 1926. The Hyman-Michaels Company of Chicago, a salvage company, bought all the property and equipment of the interurban company for $227,500. The line continued to operate under receivership until Monday, November 15 (or shortly after midnight, Tuesday, November 16) when the last interurban cars ran.

The wrecking company sold most of the Holland interurban company's private right-of-way to the Consumers Power Company. The scrapper kept six miles of track and right-of-way between Jenison and Grand Rapids intact hoping to find a buyer for that part of the line.

The Safety Motor Coach Company, operators of Greyhound buses, obtained the franchise to run buses between Holland and Grand Rapids.

A group of local citizens believed the line out to Jenison was still a viable operation. They organized the United Suburban Railway Company, purchased the portion of the line between Grand Rapids and Jenison, and began service in 1927.

The Shortest Railroad with the Most Stockholders

The United Suburban Railway (USRy) was organized in early 1927 to restore electric railway service between downtown Grand Rapids and Jenison. The company purchased the former track and property of the Grand Rapids, Holland and Chicago Railway for $30,000.

---

*This September 11, 1926, accident was erroneously listed by Carl Bajema as a fatal accident that killed two men at a crossing on the Muskegon interurban line in *The Lake Line: The Grand Rapids, Grand Haven & Muskegon* Railway book.

United Suburban Acquires Used Equipment

The USRy spent $15,000 to buy and paint five former Kennebunk, Maine, electric cars from a New York City equipment broker. These cars were reconditioned and painted a somber battleship gray with blue trim at the Michigan Railway's small shops in Grand Rapids after the cars arrived. The double-ended cars were equipped for one-man operation and had a seating capacity for forty-eight passengers. The USRy's initial roster also included one additional car, Grand Rapids Railway city car No. 278 which was an ex-Muskegon Traction streetcar.

USRy Begins Service Between Jenison and Grand Rapids

The USRy cars began regular service between Jenison and Grand Rapids on Wednesday morning, July 20, 1927, three days before the formal reopening of the line. Jacob Brock, who was the motorman on the first and last interurban passenger car to run over the old line between Grand Rapids and Holland, was now the first motorman to operate a car on the new United Suburban Railway.

United Suburban Railway cars left Jenison eastbound through Grandville, then northeast through Hamilton Park, Ivanrest, Elmbrook, Wyoming Park, Galewood, and Beverly before reaching the Grandville Avenue Junction (formerly the Holland interurban Junction with the Kalamazoo interurban). The electric cars then headed north on the Michigan Railway's Kalamazoo interurban private right-of-way and immediately crossed the city limits of Grand Rapids. The USRy cars continued running north across Godfrey Avenue, Curve Street (Hall Street) along the eastern edge of the Black Hills and then headed northwest to go across the Grand River on the Michigan Railway swing bridge to the west side. The cars then ran north-northeast on the west side before crossing Fulton Street, Pearl Street and finally turned east over the West Side Canal to cross the Grand River on the interurban bridge. The cars terminated at a downtown station on Lyon Street just north of the Pantlind Hotel.

Round-trip passenger fares to downtown Grand Rapids were set at twenty-five cents from Jenison and Grandville, ten cents from Wyoming Park and Beverly, and eight cents from Galewood. Cars ran every half hour during morning and afternoon rush hours and every hour for the remainder of the day and evening. An electrical storm on the second day disrupted the schedule by causing the motors of three of the five cars to short out. The motors on two of the three disabled cars were re-

Motorman Jacob Brock is standing next to his United Suburban Railway car which features a sign on the front indicating the names of some of the suburbs that the car will be traveling through.
Grandville Historical Commission

Passengers might expect a bump upon arrival at the former Michigan Railway station in downtown Grand Rapids.
Electric Traction, 1915

The new suburban line became known as the "shortest railroad with the longest list of stockholders in the United States;" the company owned a mere seven miles of double track between Jenison and the Grand Rapids city limits and had 700 stockholders. The company spent $7,500 to purchase and install new trolley wire.

paired enabling four of the five cars to resume service two days later for the formal opening of the line. Minor changes were made in the second timetable effective July 31, 1927, to allow for more cars in service during rush hours.

Traffic on the United Suburban Railway increased during the first seven months of operation so much that the company purchased two more ex-Kennebunk cars in April. The company went a step further in October when it purchased the rival bus company for $20,000, which had been operating six motor buses between Grand Rapids and Jenison. This enabled the company to eliminate duplicate (and competing) service and better coordinate the suburban rail and bus operations.

Route Changes
into Grand Rapids

United Suburban Railway cars used the Michigan Railway company's interurban line from Grandville Avenue junction to downtown Grand Rapids for almost two years before the interurban line into Grand Rapids was sold by order of the federal district court effective March 7, 1929. The USRy petitioned the Grand Rapids City Commission in 1928 to allow its cars to enter Grand Rapids on the Grandville Avenue streetcar line, travel downtown where the cars could turn on the loop and leave via the same line.

Mayor Swarthout of Grand Rapids pro-

United Suburban Railway Timetable effective July 31, 1927.

Richard Andrews

US Ry Car Nos. 4 & 1 adjacent Front Street in Grand Rapids in 1927.
Grand Rapids Herald, 19 Jul 27 pg 3

United Suburban Railway car in downtown Grand Rapids.

Roger Monk Collection

tested against allowing the operation of United over city streets. The Mayor declared that "Some of the suburban cars are the worst looking contraptions ever devised," and concluded by saying, "I dislike to see them downtown alongside our decent streetcars." The USRy was in the process of painting its cars a dark green with a red stripe except for the one car that belonged to the Grand Rapids street railway. The City Commission voted on December 27 to allow the USRy to travel on Grandville Avenue and on a downtown loop, but did not include the Mayor's "aesthetic suggestion" to require repainting of the suburban electric cars to match the colors of the city streetcars.

The United Suburban Railway began operation of its cars on Grand Rapids streetcar tracks via a new physical connection at the Clyde Park-Grandville Avenue intersection on March 7, 1929. The USRy obtained permission to change its terminal to the Eagle Hotel and to change its downtown loop route in order to eliminate two left-hand turns; this was to help relieve downtown automobile congestion.

The Great Depression Takes Its Toll

The United Suburban Railway ceased operation on June 25, 1932. The *Grandville Star* newspaper reported in its July 14 issue that the United Suburban Railway Company abandoned electric suburban car service due to the area's high factory unemployment. The newspaper went on to state:

> The experiment which the officials of the U. S. Railway carried on for the past several months using buses in place of electric cars has proven conclusively that buses are less expensive and therefore in view of the lack of present business conditions, the cars on this, the last suburban electric line in west Michigan has been discontinued.
>
> Unless the factories resume on an extensive scale it is doubtful that the electrics will ever again operate. Buses are now taking over the entire electric rail schedule.

The last vestige of interurban operation in Grand Rapids had come to an end.

The Grand Rapids, Grand Haven and Muskegon Railway

The Grand Rapids, Grand Haven and Muskegon Railway (GRGH&MRy), locally known in Grand Rapids as the "Muskegon interurban," was built to carry passengers and freight to Chicago via Goodrich Line steamboats as well as between Grand Rapids, Grand Haven, and Muskegon. The GRGH&MRy began regular service between Grand Rapids and Muskegon and on a branch line toward Grand Haven on February 9, 1902. The new interurban was operated by third rail in the countryside and via overhead wire in cities and villages. These points were Grand Rapids, Muskegon, from the east side of Spring Lake village through Grand Haven all the way to Lake Michigan, in Coopersville, and Fruitport where the interurban company had its shops and major resort.

The Grand Rapids Railway Company, in preparation for connecting to the coming interurban line, extended its West Leonard Street car line farther west going up the steep hill between two cemeteries and down to the city limit at the Bristol Avenue-Walker Avenue-West Leonard Street intersection in the fall 1901.

The Muskegon interurban line traveled east toward Grand Rapids using third rail power to run southeast on its private right-of-way (now Remembrance Road). The electric cars then traveled east on the north side of West Leonard Street until they approached the toll gate at Covell Road. The eastbound cars stopped at the Leonard Gravel Road Company's toll gate to enable the conductor to raise the trolley pole, switching to overhead wire from third rail. The eastbound cars then left the private right-of-way and entered trackage on West Leonard Street for one-half mile to the Grand Rapids city limit at the Bristol and Walker avenues.

WHY THIRD RAIL?

The Grand Rapids, Grand Haven & Muskegon Railway used overhead trolley wire to deliver electric power to operate its cars when traveling on the streets of Grand Rapids, Grand Haven, Muskegon and Coopersville as well as in Fruitport. The GRGH&M interurban was built to handle heavy traffic—numerous passenger cars running as sections on a schedule and numerous freight cars operating as extras on the line at the same time. More electric power is required to operate the motors of many cars running on the line and at faster speeds at the same time. The interurban solved this problem by using power from a third rail to operate cars on its private right of ways in the countryside.

The outside third rail power distribution system first used to electrify the Chicago elevated system in the 1890s provided a way to deliver the extra power that is needed to operate many cars simultaneously on the same power grid. Third rail power has been used and is still being widely used by many of the subways, elevated urban railways and other electric railroads in the United States and the rest of the world.

While the copper in a trolley wire is a much better conductor of electricity than iron, the much larger size of the iron rail enables it to conduct up to more than 500 times the amount of electricity than what can be transmitted via the much smaller overhead trolley wire.

Overhead trolley wire power systems were more expensive to maintain than third rail power systems. Attempting to run a car at high speeds was also a problem with the overhead trolley wire power system. Winds generated by higher speed tended to push the trolley pole away from the overhead power wire causing the power pick up wheel to lose contact.

Each GRGH&M Ry interurban car was equipped with four third rail power pick up shoes. There were two shoes on each side of the car attached to the outside of the trucks. This enabled a car to use the same third rail going westbound or eastbound.

Which was more expensive to build-Third rail systems or overhead trolley wire systems? An economic analysis by Edgar Van Deusen (1907, p. 150) concluded that the extra poles and wires made overhead trolley systems cost approximately $4,000 to $5,000 per mile to construct which was one-fifth to one-fourth more than the cost of the third rail system per mile. However, William Bancroft Potter, writing on the "Economics of Railway Electrification" in Electric Traction Weekly (1910, vol. 6, 963-968) estimated that the overhead trolley system cost from $3,500 to $5,000 per mile to install while constructing a third rail system would require $5,000 to $7,500 per mile (cited in Hilton & Due, 1960, p. 57).

Third rail power systems were potentially more dangerous. While trolley wires could break dropping a live wire to the ground the third rail was already adjacent the ground and could deliver 600 volts DC to an intruder. Fences had to be erected along the private right of way and cattle guards installed at road crossings to keep trespassers—humans or domestic animals—out.

There were gaps in the third rail at all road crossings. Cars were equipped with power pickup shoes on both the front and rear trucks (31 feet apart on the 52 ft long cars) so that the car could still receive power via one of the shoes as it crossed the road. The two ends of the third rails at a crossing were connected by two large 250,000 C.M. copper cables carried beneath the crossing in a creosoted wood-pipe conduit filled with pitch.

Two of the three interurban railways that operated out of Grand Rapids were powered by the third rail on private right of way in the countryside. Michigan Railway built a third rail interurban from Kalamazoo to Grand Rapids in 1915 to be able to handle heavy freight and passenger traffic that never materialized.

While third rail power systems were more expensive to build they were cheaper to maintain with one major exception-sleet and snow could greatly decrease the flow of electricity between the third rail and the pickup shoes attached to the car's trucks. This was a significant problem because the interurban was operating in west Michigan's lake effect snow-belt region. The ingenuity of the employees was put to the test during the first winter.

Reprinted from **The Lake Line** • *Bulletin 144 of the Central Electric Railfans' Association* • *Bajema, Kindem & Budzynski* • *(2011)*

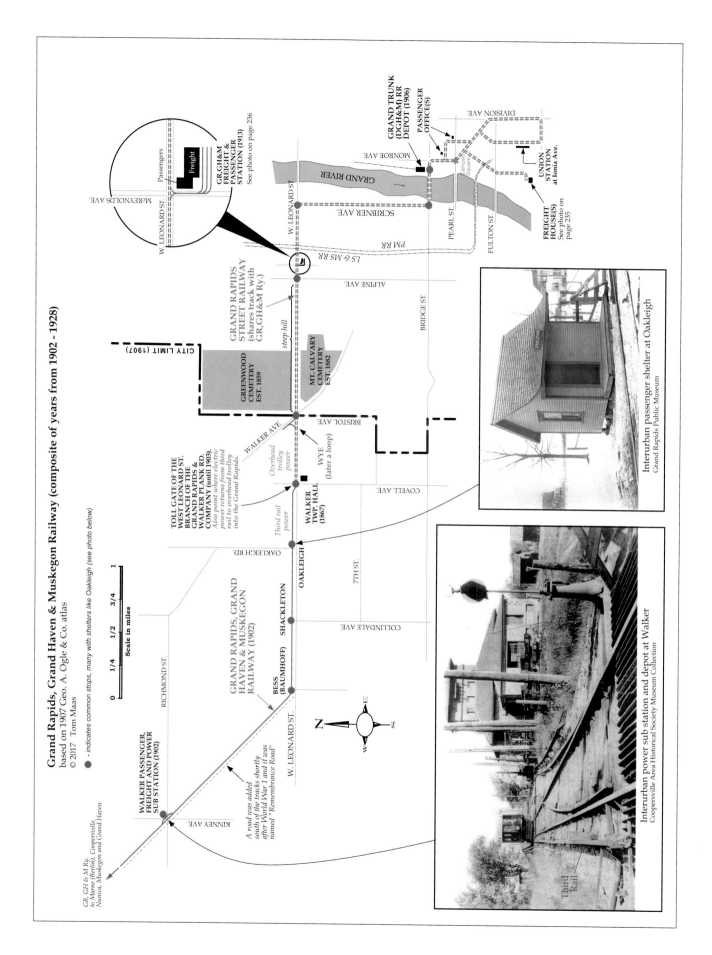

Grand Rapids, Grand Haven & Muskegon Railway (composite of years from 1902 - 1928)

based on 1907 Geo. A. Ogle & Co. atlas

© 2017 Tom Maas

● - indicates common stops, many with shelters like Oakleigh (see photo below)

Scale in miles

0   1/4   1/2   3/4   1

N

RICHMOND ST.

KINNEY AVE.

W. LEONARD ST.

GR, GH & M Ry.,
to Marne (Berlin), Coopersville,
Nunica, Muskegon and Grand Haven

WALKER PASSENGER,
FREIGHT AND POWER
SUB STATION (1902)

GRAND RAPIDS, GRAND
HAVEN & MUSKEGON
RAILWAY (1902)

BESS
(BAUMHOFF)

SHACKLETON

COLLINDALE AVE.

A road was added
south of the tracks shortly
after World War 1 and it was
named "Remembrance Road"

OAKLEIGH RD.

OAKLEIGH

7TH ST.

COVELL AVE.

TOLL GATE OF THE
WEST LEONARD ST.
BRANCH OF THE
GRAND RAPIDS &
WALKER PLANK RD.
COMPANY (until 1903).
Also point where electric
power returns from third
rail to overhead trolley
into the Grand Rapids.

Overhead
trolley power

Third rail power

WALKER
TWP. HALL
(1867)

WYE
(later a loop)

BRISTOL AVE.

WALKER AVE.

MT. CALVARY
CEMETERY
EST. 1882

GREENWOOD
CEMETERY
EST. 1859

CITY LIMIT (1907)

steep hill

GRAND RAPIDS
STREET RAILWAY
(shares track with
GR,GH&M Ry.)

BRIDGE ST.

ALPINE AVE.

LS & MS RR

PM RR

SCRIBNER AVE.

W. LEONARD ST.

GRAND RIVER

PEARL ST.

FULTON ST.

MONROE AVE.

GRAND TRUNK
(DGH&M) RR
DEPOT (1906)

PASSENGER
OFFICE(S)

DIVISION AVE.

UNION
STATION
at Ionia Ave.

FREIGHT
HOUSE(S)
See photo on
page 235

GR,GH&M
FREIGHT &
PASSENGER
STATION (1913)
See photo on page 236

Passengers

Freight

McREYNOLDS AVE.

W. LEONARD ST.

Interurban passenger shelter at Oakleigh
Grand Rapids Public Museum

Interurban power sub station and depot at Walker
Coopersville Area Historical Society Museum Collection

Third
Rail

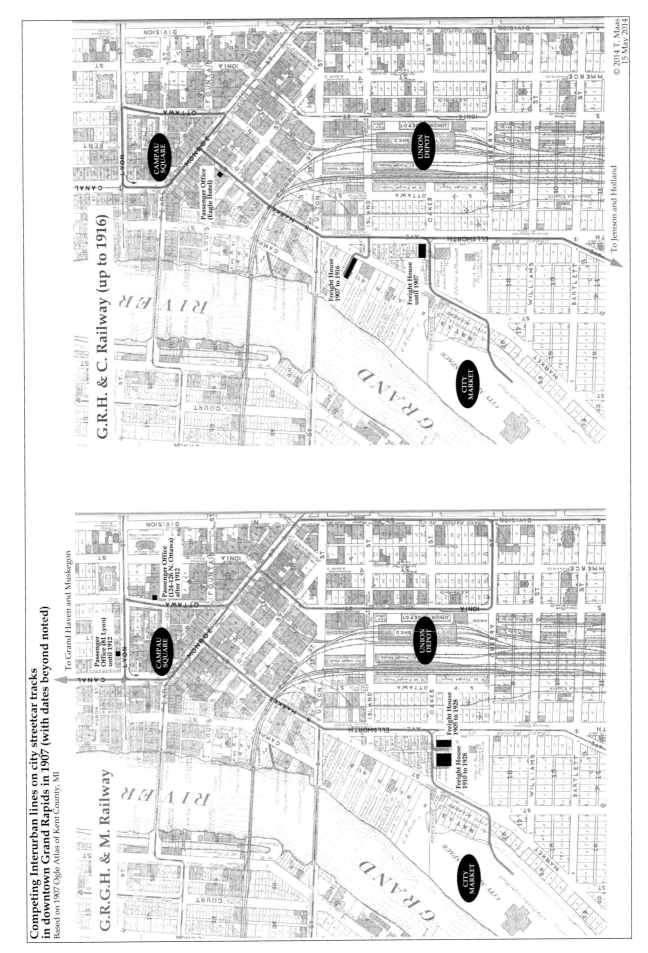

Competing Interurban lines on city streetcar tracks in downtown Grand Rapids in 1907 (with dates beyond noted)
Based on 1907 Ogle Atlas of Kent County, MI

G.R.H. & C. Railway (up to 1916)

G.R.G.H. & M. Railway

231

© 2014 T. Maas
15 May 2014

Rear view of Muskegon interurban car no. 19 alongside a much smaller streetcar on Ottawa Ave. near Pearl St. in Grand Rapids. The Houseman Building on the right (off camera) was the location of the GRGH&M downtown station. View looking north. The Waters Building as seen on the left still stands in 2016, but the Houseman Building was razed.

Coopersville Area

The interurban cars continued east over the steep cemetery hill via the West Leonard Street car line tracks on their way to downtown Grand Rapids. The Grand Rapids Common Council required that the interurban cars provide what was essentially a streetcar service inside the city by picking up local passengers, collecting the streetcar fares, and dropping them off at local car line stops.

The cars continued toward downtown Grand Rapids on the West Leonard Street line turning south on Scribner Avenue and turning east on West Bridge Street to cross the Grand River on the Bridge Street Bridge. They continued south on Canal Street passing through Campau Square in downtown Grand Rapids and then went southeast on Monroe Avenue to Ottawa Avenue where they turned left to go south on Ottawa Street. The cars then turned west and stopped at the interurban waiting room at 81 Lyon Street which served as the GRGH&MRy downtown station until 1912. The cars started on their return trip out of the city by going west a short distance on Lyon Street, completing the downtown loop (required by the single-ended cars) as they turned right to head north on Canal Street.

Some of the GRGH&MRy cars began running past the Grand Rapids and Indiana steam railroad station on Ionia Avenue in 1903 on what became known as the depot loop. Freight motors and trailers began running to their new freight house on the southwest corner of the Ellsworth Avenue-Oakes Street intersection in 1905.

Interurban Cars Attract Attention

The Muskegon interurban cars were painted yellow and were different from the Grand Rapids streetcars in a several ways. The passenger cars were fifty-two feet long, more than twenty feet longer than most, if not all, of the streetcars then running in Grand Rapids; they were also higher than the city cars. A local reporter wrote (with some artistic license) that he could lean out of a window of an interurban car and tap the roof of an adjacent streetcar with his hands.

The first Muskegon interurban cars to run in Grand Rapids differed from the streetcars in a third way. Each of the fifteen yellow interurban passenger cars that made up the backbone of the Muskegon passenger car fleet initially had unique names painted in gold leaf on the sides of the cars. The interurban cars were numbered from 1 to 15 and their names followed the numbers in alphabetical order. They were *Circe*, *Dolphin*, *Dryad*, *Katherine C.*, *Kelpie*, *Lorelie*, *Mermaid*, *Merlin*, *Nautilus*, *Nymph*, *Nereid*, *Siren*, *Sprite*, *Triten*, and *Undine*. Fourteen of the fifteen passenger cars had names associated with some fabulous myth while *Katherine C.* was named after the little daughter of Thomas F. Carroll, one of the directors of the road. The first combination passenger and baggage coach (car No. 16) was named *Nanticoke* while the first three freight motors carried the names *Puritan* (car No. 101), *Cannon Ball* (car No. 102), and *Whistle Wings* (car No. 103).

Walker combination passenger, freight, and electric power substation, 3.5 miles west of the Grand Rapids city limits, view looking northwest.

Coopersville Area Historical Society Museum

Westbound out of Grand Rapids

The Muskegon interurbans faced a weighty problem when heading westbound up the West Leonard Street hill. The voltage was so low in this area that the heavy cars could do no more than just creep laboriously up the grade. Finally in April 1912 the street railway company installed a feeder line that supplied enough power to enable the interurbans to easily make their way up and over. The streetcars also benefitted because they were no longer delayed by the Muskegon interurbans that had been reduced to a crawl while ascending the hill because of low voltage.

The Muskegon interurban cars headed west when leaving the Grand Rapids city limit on West Leonard Street at the Walker Avenue-Bristol Avenue intersection. The cars continued to use overhead wire for one-half mile on West Leonard Street until the changeover to third rail was made at Covell Road. The cars then entered private-right-of-way along the north side of West Leonard Street. The cars traveled one and one-half miles beyond Covell Road and then turned northwest on private right-of-way to Walker Station on the way to Berlin (now Marne).

When the westbound cars reached the east side of Coopersville the third rail ended and the conductors raised the trolley poles for over-

head wire pickup on the main street. The cars resumed running on third rail on the west side of Coopersville through Nunica before swinging northwest until Grand Haven Junction was reached. Passengers could cross the station platform at the junction and board a car to Spring Lake, Grand Haven, or all the way out to the sandy beaches of Lake Michigan during the resort season.

The Muskegon-bound interurban cars continued northwest on the mainline until the

Passenger waiting shelter on West Leonard Street at Oakleigh Avenue one mile west of city limits. View looking north.

Grand Rapids Public Museum Photo Collection 54 Courtesy Jack Eno

GRAND RAPIDS, GRAND HAVEN & MUSKEGON RAILWAY
and GOODRICH STEAMSHIPS

ALABAMA   CAROLINA   VIRGINIA

$2.50 Grand Rapids to Chicago, $4.75 Round Trip.   Car with Electric Star

Lv. Grand Rapids Waiting Room	8 20 p.m.	
Union Depot and Crathmore Hotel	8 25 ..	
Livingston and Cody Hotels	8 30 ..	
Morton House and Goodrich Office	8 32 ..	
Pantlind Hotel	8 35 ..	
Grand Trunk Depot	8 36 ..	
Ar. Grand Haven	9 52 ..	
Lv. Grand Haven	10 15 ..	
Ar. Chicago	6 00 a.m.	

Lv. Chicago	7 45 p.m.
Ar. Grand Rapids	6 35 a.m.

TRAIN PASSES

Grand Trunk Depot
G. R. I.   ..
M. C.   ..
P. M.   ..

Connections with
all Morning Trains

Ticket Offices:– 162 Ottawa Ave. and 80 Monroe Avenue

1913 card advertising "Take the Car with the Electric Star" from your hotel or union railroad station in Grand Rapids to board the overnight Goodrich steamboats in Grand Haven for the overnight voyage to Chicago.

Carl Bajema Collection

Close up view of the electric star with 36 incandescent light bulbs.

Carl Bajema Collection

Ride the Interurban Car with the Electric Star

In the summer of 1904 the GRGH&M Railway inaugurated a new and unique scheme for advertising its Chicago Flyer interurban car as it picked up passengers on its way to Chicago from the Grand Rapids hotels and Union Station while traveling around the downtown area. A brightly lit star glowing with thirty-six incandescent lamps was attached to the front of the car. The star had a hole in the middle for the headlight. The electric star was removed at Walker Station just west of Grand Rapids to prevent damage to the light bulbs. This star, which was over three feet in diameter, attracted so much attention that the interurban and the Goodrich Steamboat Company featured variations of the phrase "Ride the Car with the Electric Star" in its advertisements for more than twenty years.

Freight Service

The Muskegon interurban freight cars began using a different route than the passenger cars in 1905. After passing through Campau Square, the freight cars went one block southeast on Monroe Avenue before turning south-southwest onto Market Avenue. They then headed south on Ellsworth Avenue to the Muskegon interurban company's new freight house. The Grand Rapids, Grand Haven and Muskegon Railway built the two-story brick freight house that year on the southwest cor-

cars reached Fruitport where trolley poles were once again used. After going past the Muskegon interurban company's big Pomona daytime and evening resort at the head of Spring Lake and past the interurban company's extensive car shops trolley poles were again lowered as third rail pickup resumed. The cars continued northwest past the head of Mona Lake and changed over again to trolley operation for the ride over the streets of Muskegon Heights and Muskegon. The interurban cars reached the downtown interurban station on the corner of Western Avenue and Seventh Street, a couple blocks west of the steam railroad Muskegon Union Station.

The inbound and outbound freight houses on Oakes St. and Ellsworth Ave. in downtown Grand Rapids near the Union Station. View looking southeast.

Coopersville Area Historical Society Museum

THE GRAND RAPIDS, GRAND HAVEN & MUSKEGON RAILWAY COMPANY

TIME TABLE No. 19.

IN EFFECT
JULY 15, 1906
Subject to Change Without Notice.

STEAMBOAT LIMITED

GOODRICH BOATS

Leaves Grand Rapids

DAILY

AS FOLLOWS :

Lv. Waiting Room ⎰ 81 Lyon St. **7.45 pm**
" Baggage Room ⎱
" Union Depot......... ....7 50 pm
" The Livingston ⎰ ....7 55 pm
" Hotel Cody .... ⎱
" Morton House...............7.57 pm
" Hotel Pantlind ....8 00 pm
Ar. Goodrich Dock ⎰ ....9.10 pm
" Grand Haven.. ⎱
" Chicago ....6.00 am

Look for the Car with the Electric Star

Baggage checked at 81 Lyon Street any time before 7:45 p.m.

Through tickets and berths on sale at 81 Lyon St , and Goodrich office, Morton House.

FARE $2.00 one way ; **$3.75** round trip—Boat leaves Chicago Daily at 7:45 p.m , connecting with Interurban train at Grand Haven at 5:25 a m. arriving at Grand Rapids at 6:35 a.m.

Milwaukee Passengers via Crosby Boats—take the Steamboat Limited to Grand Haven, and avoid omnibus transfer in Grand Rapids.

Front cover of pocket size time table No. 19 advertising "Look for the Car with the Electric Star."
Carl Bajema Collection

ner of Ellsworth Avenue and Oakes Street, a block east of the City Market. The freight house was forty by one hundred feet in size and had three side tracks on the west side of the building. Express freight service was expedited in 1908 when a dock was added to the freight house enabling teams to unload directly into the freight cars.

The Muskegon interurban built a second freight house in 1910 just west of the first one on Oakes Street. Five side tracks were added and the new facility became the inbound freight house while the first location handled outbound freight and express. As many as fourteen freight cars could be handled at the same time by these two facilities.

The freight business continued to grow. The GRGH&M Ry built a combination freight house and passenger station on the west side of Grand Rapids in 1913. This west side terminal was located at the southeast corner of West Leonard Street and McReynolds Avenue.

Service Disrupted by Grand River Flood

The Grand River overflowed its banks and flooded a large section of the West Leonard Street car line on March 25, 1903. The streetcar tracks on lower West Leonard Street and Scribner Avenue soon were beneath three to four feet of water. The flood waters totally blocked streetcar and interurban service on these west side streets for five days. The Grand River flooded the west side of Grand Rapids again the very next year.

Runaway Accidents

Cemetery Hill on West Leonard Street was the steepest grade the interurban cars encountered and always presented operating problems for the trains. At least two eastbound Muskegon

Above: *Colorized postcard showing tracks on West Leonard St. shared by Grand Rapids streetcars and Muskegon interurban cars. View looking northwest towards Greenwood Cemetery near the peak of the Mt. Calvary hill.*

Ed Bawden

Below: *West Leonard Street freight and passenger Station, view looking south.*

Coopersville Area Historical Society Museum

interurban cars became runaways after cresting Cemetery Hill in separate incidents.

Motorman Andrew Redding discovered that the pressure in the air tank was exhausted and that the air compressor was not working on car No. 3 while heading toward Grand Rapids on September 15, 1903. Redding stopped the car at the crest of Cemetery Hill and then started the interurban car down the hill. Redding thought he could control the speed of the interurban with just the hand brakes.

Unfortunately the hand brakes themselves were not adequate for this purpose as the car headed down the steepest grade on the line. The car began accelerating so fast that motorman Redding threw the motor in reverse hoping to slow the speeding car. The asbestos in the controller box burned out and the friction produced flames in the box that for a moment filled the motorman's cab with smoke. The passengers panicked and rushed out onto the rear platform of the car. Two passengers jumped off the speeding car before the conductor could stop them. Fortunately the reversed motor stopped the wheels from turning which caused the car to come to a halt about a block further, preventing what could have been a serious runaway interurban wreck.

In another incident a streetcar began its eastbound trip down Cemetery Hill on April 1, 1915. As the eastbound city car was descending the hill, a following eastbound interurban express motor crested the hill and began picking up speed as it began its descent.

Conductor Thomas Hamilton on the rear platform of the streetcar noticed that the freight motor racing down the hill toward him had not stopped at the top of the hill where the motorman was required to test the air brakes before descending. The conductor quickly rang the bell notifying his motorman who was able to accelerate the streetcar to a speed of about thirty miles an hour before the runaway interurban, reported to be going sixty miles an hour, slammed into the rear of the streetcar. Both the conductor and the lone passenger on the streetcar jumped from the car just before the crash. Both men sustained minor injuries when they hit the street.

Holland Interurban Car Crashes into Muskegon Interurban Car

Holland Interurban car No. 23 split a defective switch as it rounded the curve at Lyon Street and Ottawa Avenue in downtown Grand Rapids on August 7, 1914. Motorman Edward Bowen was unable to get his Holland car under control before it crashed into the rear of a Muskegon interurban car as it readied to depart from the Muskegon interurban station on Ottawa Avenue. The Muskegon car was hit so hard that it was torn from its trucks. Passengers scrambled to get out via the doors and windows as the car was rocking so badly they thought it would "turn turtle." Fortunately the Muskegon car stopped its dangerous rocking and stayed upright. Six passengers were injured.

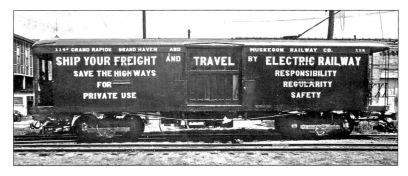

SHIP YOUR FREIGHT *billboard on the side of Muskegon Interurban freight car No. 114.*
Coopersville Area Historical Society Museum

OVERNIGHT FREIGHT *billboard on the side of Muskegon Interurban freight car No. 107.*
Coopersville Area Historical Society Museum

FREIGHT SERVICE TO DETROIT *billboard on side of Muskegon Interurban freight car No. 113.*
Don Ross Collection

Billboards on Rails

The Muskegon interurban company began a major campaign in 1925 to advertise its passenger and freight services. Thirty-two billboards were created using both sides of sixteen freight motors at the cost of paint and labor. There were four different billboard advertisements, each of which was painted on both sides of four freight motors.

L. A. Goodrich, traffic manager for the interurban, pointed out that a single freight motor traveled 120 to 160 miles a day close to well-traveled highways in the country- side and on city streets. Thousands of people were thus able to view this unique form of advertising.

Passenger car at the Michigan Railway Monteith Junction station, one mile south of Martin.

Karl Heckman Collection

1928: End of the Line for the Muskegon Interurban

Better roads and mechanical improvements enabled buses, trucks, and automobiles to more effectively compete with the interurbans for business. The Muskegon interurban began replacing some of its rail schedules with buses between the same towns in September 1927. The buses were cheaper to operate in large part because it only required a driver while the interurban cars required a motorman and a conductor. Also, the bus ran over publicly-funded and maintained highways while the interurban bore maintenance costs and paid taxes on its right-of-way. The last scheduled GRGH&MRy interurban to depart from downtown Grand Rapids left at 7:35 P.M., Saturday night, April 7, 1928.

A much more detailed history of the fascinating rise and fall of the Grand Rapids, Grand Haven & Muskegon Railway can be found in the 224-page book *The Lake Line: The Grand Rapids, Grand Haven & Muskegon Railway* by Carl Bajema, Dave Kindem and Jim Budzynski published by Central Electric Railfans' Association.

1915: Michigan Railway Expands

The Michigan Railway Company built the last of the three interurban lines that connected Grand Rapids to other cities. It began running interurban cars between Grand Rapids and Kalamazoo, Battle Creek and Allegan in 1915. This company was also known as the Michigan United Traction Company's Western Division, which in turn was a subsidiary of the Commonwealth Power, Railway and Light Company. The section of Michigan Railway Company's rail system between Grand Rapids and Kalamazoo became widely known locally as the "Kalamazoo Interurban."

The First 2,400-Volt DC Third Rail Interurban in America

Michigan Railway's interurban line that included the fifty-mile Kalamazoo to Grand Rapids line was a milestone in the history of high-speed electric interurban railroads because it was the first 2,400-volt DC third rail interurban line in America to be built. This Grand Rapids to Kalamazoo interurban line was built to enable interurban cars to travel at speeds exceeding seventy miles an hour.

Safety reasons dictated that only 600 volts DC were available in the towns for the Kalamazoo interurban cars to use. The interurban cars used trolley poles or pantographs to tap the overhead wires that provided the lower voltage.

Unfortunately, the interurban motors had major problems with electric arcing when running on the 2,400-volt line in the country. Electric arcing caused damage to electric motors, thus the Michigan Railway was forced to reduce the third rail voltage to 1,200 volts DC by the end of 1915.

The "Kalamazoo Interurban"

The "Kalamazoo interurban" was built as a north-south fifty-mile long line between downtown Kalamazoo and downtown Grand Rapids. A southeast-northwest forty-four and one half-mile newly-electrified railway line connecting Battle Creek with Allegan crossed the Kalamazoo-Grand Rapids line at Monteith Junction thirty-two miles south of Grand Rapids and eighteen miles north of Kalamazoo.

Passengers could board the big dark green interurban cars in downtown Grand Rapids for a fast fifty-mile ride to Kalamazoo or change cars at Monteith Junction to ride twelve more

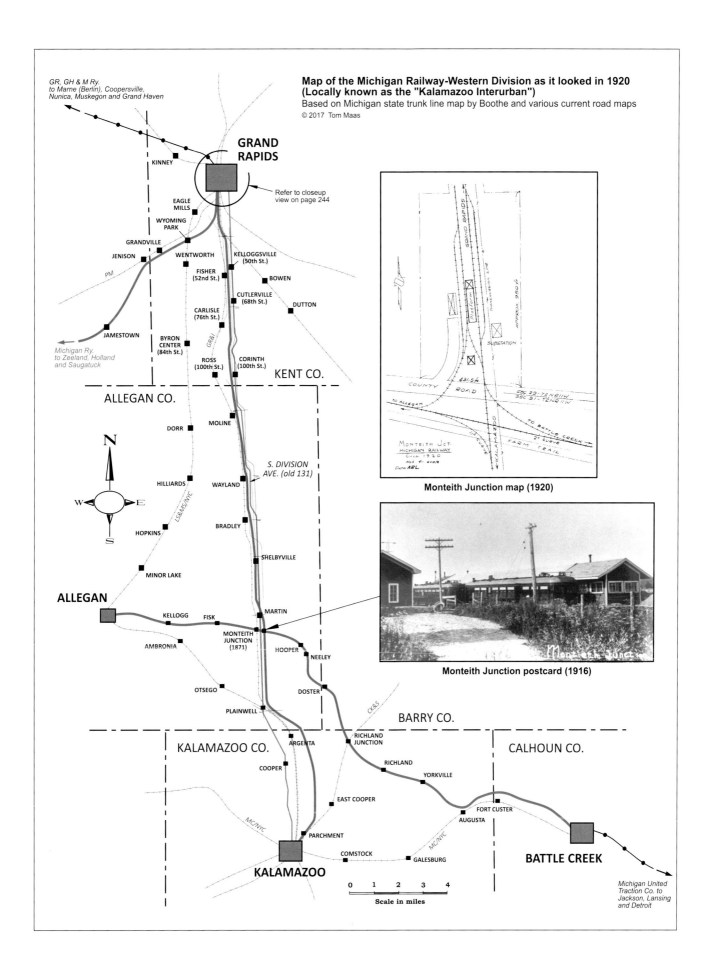

**Map of the Michigan Railway-Western Division as it looked in 1920
(Locally known as the "Kalamazoo Interurban")**
Based on Michigan state trunk line map by Boothe and various current road maps
© 2017 Tom Maas

GR, GH & M Ry.
to Marne (Berlin), Coopersville,
Nunica, Muskegon and Grand Haven

GRAND RAPIDS

KINNEY

Refer to closeup
view on page 244

EAGLE MILLS

WYOMING PARK

GRANDVILLE

JENISON

WENTWORTH

KELLOGGSVILLE
(50th St.)

FISHER
(52nd St.)

BOWEN

PM

CUTLERVILLE
(68th St.)

DUTTON

CARLISLE
(76th St.)

GR&I

JAMESTOWN

BYRON CENTER
(84th St.)

ROSS
(100th St.)

CORINTH
(100th St.)

*Michigan Ry.
to Zeeland, Holland
and Saugatuck*

KENT CO.

ALLEGAN CO.

DORR

MOLINE

S. DIVISION
AVE. (old 131)

N
W   E
S

HILLIARDS

WAYLAND

LS&MS/NYC

HOPKINS

BRADLEY

MINOR LAKE

SHELBYVILLE

ALLEGAN

MARTIN

KELLOGG   FISK

MONTEITH
JUNCTION
(1871)

HOOPER

NEELEY

AMBRONIA

DOSTER

OTSEGO

PLAINWELL

CK&S

BARRY CO.

ARGENTA

RICHLAND
JUNCTION

KALAMAZOO CO.

CALHOUN CO.

COOPER

RICHLAND

YORKVILLE

EAST COOPER

FORT CUSTER

MC/NYC

AUGUSTA

PARCHMENT

BATTLE CREEK

COMSTOCK

MC/NYC

GALESBURG

KALAMAZOO

*Michigan United
Traction Co. to
Jackson, Lansing
and Detroit*

0   1   2   3   4
Scale in miles

Monteith Jct.
Michigan Railway
Circa 1920
Not to scale
Data ARL

Monteith Junction map (1920)

Monteith Junction postcard (1916)

Chapter 10: The Grand Rapids Interurbans (1900-1928)

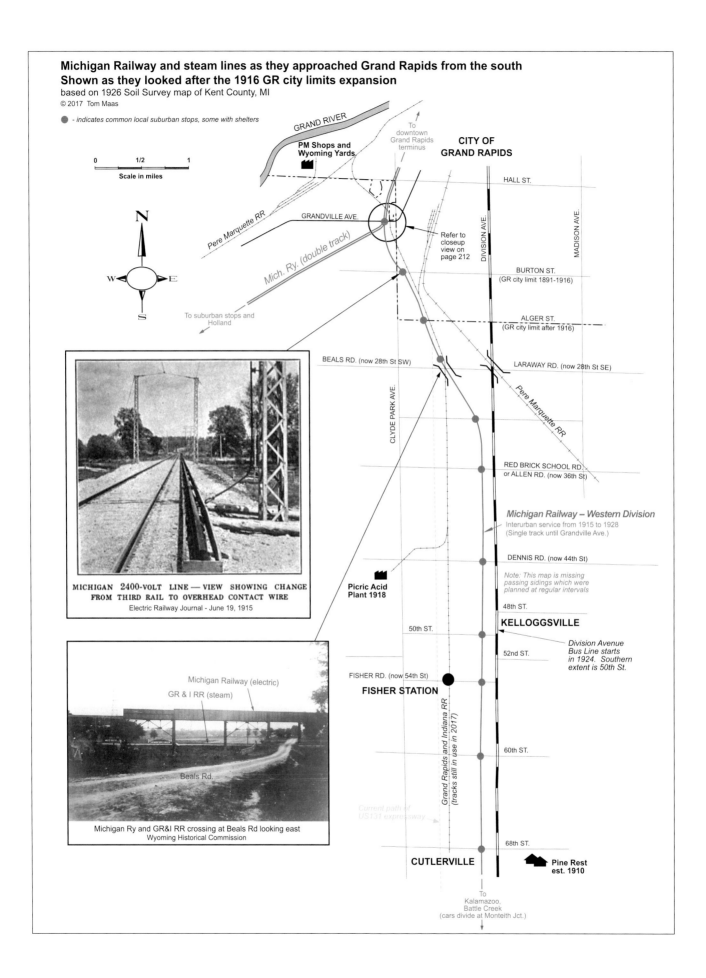

Michigan Railway and steam lines as they approached Grand Rapids from the south
Shown as they looked after the 1916 GR city limits expansion
based on 1926 Soil Survey map of Kent County, MI
© 2017 Tom Maas

● - indicates common local suburban stops, some with shelters

GRAND RIVER

To downtown Grand Rapids terminus

CITY OF GRAND RAPIDS

PM Shops and Wyoming Yards

HALL ST.

Pere Marquette RR

GRANDVILLE AVE.

Refer to closeup view on page 212

Mich. Ry. (double track)

BURTON ST.
(GR city limit 1891-1916)

DIVISION AVE.

MADISON AVE.

To suburban stops and Holland

ALGER ST.
(GR city limit after 1916)

BEALS RD. (now 28th St SW)

LARAWAY RD. (now 28th St SE)

CLYDE PARK AVE.

Pere Marquette RR

RED BRICK SCHOOL RD. or ALLEN RD. (now 36th St)

Michigan Railway – Western Division
Interurban service from 1915 to 1928
(Single track until Grandville Ave.)

DENNIS RD. (now 44th St)

Note: This map is missing passing sidings which were planned at regular intervals

Picric Acid Plant 1918

48th ST.

KELLOGGSVILLE

50th ST.

Division Avenue Bus Line starts in 1924. Southern extent is 50th St.

52nd ST.

FISHER RD. (now 54th St)

FISHER STATION

Grand Rapids and Indiana RR (tracks still in use in 2017)

60th ST.

Current path of US131 expressway

68th ST.

CUTLERVILLE

Pine Rest est. 1910

To Kalamazoo, Battle Creek (cars divide at Monteith Jct.)

MICHIGAN 2400-VOLT LINE — VIEW SHOWING CHANGE FROM THIRD RAIL TO OVERHEAD CONTACT WIRE
Electric Railway Journal - June 19, 1915

Michigan Railway (electric)
GR & I RR (steam)
Beals Rd.

Michigan Ry and GR&I RR crossing at Beals Rd looking east
Wyoming Historical Commission

N
W E
S

0   1/2   1
Scale in miles

The Kalamazoo Interurban cars crossed over Beals Road (now 28th Street) and the Grand Rapids & Indiana Railroad track (now known as Norfolk Southern Railway) on a long bridge.

Wyoming Historical Commission

miles west to Allegan or the thirty-two miles east to reach Battle Creek.

The completion of the interurban line from Kalamazoo to Grand Rapids was delayed while local politicians fought over the Kalamazoo interurban running on Grand Rapids streetcar tracks into downtown. Mayor Ellis of Grand Rapids and others opposed the interurbans running on city streets. They were concerned over the larger size and length of the interurban cars which they believed could easily block intersections. They were also afraid that the greater weight of the big Kalamazoo interurban cars would damage the streetcar track as some of the cars weighed more than 100,000 pounds while the heaviest streetcars weighed only half as much.

The Michigan Railway Company finally decided to build its line inside the city of Grand Rapids on private right-of-way all the way into downtown Grand Rapids. This was a costly but necessary decision as it was the only way the Kalamazoo interurban could reach the downtown area. Building two concrete railway bridges over the Grand River cost approximately $170,000 in addition to the costs of the private right-of-way and track construction. Nationwide it was rare for an interurban line to enter a major city without street running, especially over its own private right-of-way.

Operations Begin

Forty-seven miles in forty-four minutes! That was how long it took Kalamazoo interurban car No. 800 to travel the distance from the city limits of Kalamazoo to the city limits of Grand Rapids on May 5, 1915. The Michigan Railway Company carried two dozen newsmen on board the car to demonstrate that modern interurban cars were capable of speeds exceeding seventy miles an hour over the new 2,400-volt DC rail line designed and built with gentle curves and minimum grades. It took another four and one-half minutes for car No. 800, now

traveling at half-speed inside Grand Rapids but still on the company's private right-of-way, to reach the Michigan Railway's new downtown Grand Rapids interurban terminal.

The company advertised its new line to Grand Rapids by organizing excursions for businessmen and politicians from Kalamazoo, Battle Creek, and Jackson before May 17, 1915, the first day paying passengers rode between Grand Rapids and Kalamazoo..

Trains heading north from Kalamazoo ran on the interurban company's private right-of-way from Kalamazoo reaching Corinth, the first station on the line inside Kent County. The northbound trains continued running on private right-of-way by third rail while crossing Cutlerville road and reaching Fisher Road (now 54th Street), the site of another small interurban station. The northbound trains continued toward Grand Rapids going across Kelloggsville Road (now 52nd Street), Dennis Road (now 44th Street) and Allen Road (now known as 36th Street and as Godwin Heights) before heading northwest on a long bridge over both Beal's Road (now 28th Street) and the Grand Rapids and Indiana Railroad mainline track.

The people living on the east side of Division Avenue wanted the Kalamazoo interurban Stop 55 named Barendsen after the name of their suburban plat while residents living on the west side of Division Avenue wanted the company to adopt the name Kelloggsville for Stop 55. The Michigan Railway company tried to resolve the controversy by choosing the name Barendsen Road for the stop.

The big Grand Rapids-bound Kalamazoo interurban cars shifted from third rail to overhead pickup just south of Burton Street, the Grand Rapids city limit. The cars continued northwest crossing Burton Street and Clyde Park Avenue and reached the junction with the Holland interurban just south of Grandville Avenue (now Chicago Drive) and west of Clyde Park Avenue.

Holland interurban cars switched onto the

Northern approach to the Michigan Railway gauntlet swing bridge over Grand River showing how the two tracks start to overlap the closer the two tracks approach the bridge. View looking east.

Karl Heckman Collection

View of the two overlapping tracks on the Michigan Railway gauntlet swing bridge over the Grand River. View looking southeast.

Winslow Collection, Grand Rapids Public Library

Kalamazoo interurban track at the junction on May 27, 1915, and headed north on the Kalamazoo interurban company's private right-of-way all the way to Michigan Railway's new interurban station in downtown Grand Rapids.*

After leaving the combination passenger and freight station at the Holland interurban

Junction, the northwest-bound interurban cars immediately crossed Grandville Avenue and went north across a bridge over Plaster Creek, and then northeast across Godfrey Avenue. The cars continued north skirting the east side of the Black Hills back of the factories in the Godfrey Avenue district before they turned toward the northwest and crossed over both the Pere Marquette steam railroad tracks and Market Street on two short concrete bridges. The interurban cars then crossed the Grand River on a 600-foot long bridge just south of west Wealthy Street. The track on the bridge was supported on two parallel steel girders mounted on concrete piers and abutments.

The Kalamazoo interurban bridge south of West Wealthy Street was different than most interurban bridges. The bridge was and is still unusual in that it had a turntable that swung the bridge section parallel to the river to allow steam boats to pass through. The last time the turntable was used was in the early 1920s.

The bridge also was unusual in another way-it was a "gauntlet" bridge, that is, the two tracks of the double-track interurban partially merged becoming two overlapping tracks. Only one train could cross the bridge at a time.

Concrete bridges were expensive to build. The Michigan Railway Company was able to lower the cost by building a narrower bridge.

The three additional rails in the photograph of the gauntlet bridge served as safety rails. Two of these three guard rails were on the outside of the tracks the cars ran on. The third guard rail was on the inside of the two running rails. These three rails were designed to prevent a car from tumbling down the steep embankment if a derailment occurred.

*See map of this routing in the Holland interurban section.

215—Interurban Bridge, Grand Rapids, Mich.

Michigan Railway Interurban Bridge in downtown Grand Rapids.

Carl Bajema Collection

View looking east-northeast at the Michigan Railway trestle and bridge across Grand River and at the downtown Grand Rapids interurban passenger depot located on the east bank of the river at the foot of Lyon Street.

Winslow Collection, Grand Rapids Public Library

After crossing the gauntlet swing bridge the interurban cars turned northeast, going across West Wealthy Street, past the Hart Mirror Plate factory, diagonally across the Converse property to the corner of West Fulton Street and Front Avenue, N.W. and headed across Pearl Street. The cars went a short distance north before turning northeast on a wye and going on a trestle crossing the former west side power canal. The cars finally crossed the big concrete bridge (now known as the Gillett Bridge) over the Grand River and entered the newly-built interurban terminal on the east bank of the river.

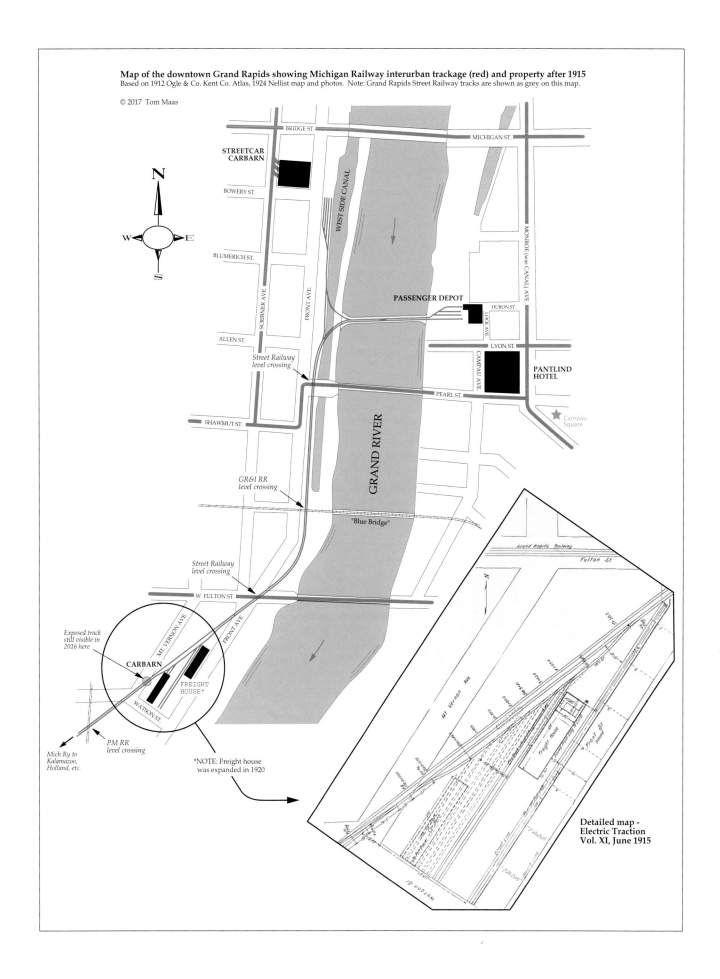

Map of the downtown Grand Rapids showing Michigan Railway interurban trackage (red) and property after 1915
Based on 1912 Ogle & Co. Kent Co. Atlas, 1924 Nellist map and photos. Note: Grand Rapids Street Railway tracks are shown as grey on this map.

© 2017 Tom Maas

N
W E
S

BRIDGE ST.

MICHIGAN ST.

**STREETCAR
CARBARN**

BOWERY ST.

WEST SIDE CANAL

BLUMERICH ST.

MONROE (was CANAL) AVE.

SCRIBNER AVE.

FRONT AVE.

PASSENGER DEPOT

HURON ST.

LOCK AVE.

ALLEN ST.

LYON ST.

CAMPAU AVE.

**PANTLIND
HOTEL**

Street Railway
level crossing

PEARL ST.

Campau
Square

SHAWMUT ST.

GRAND RIVER

GR&I RR
level crossing

"Blue Bridge"

Street Railway
level crossing

W. FULTON ST.

Exposed track
still visible in
2016 here

MT. VERNON AVE.

FRONT AVE.

CARBARN

FREIGHT
HOUSE*

WATSON ST.

PM RR
level crossing

Mich Ry to
Kalamazoo,
Holland, etc.

*NOTE: Freight house
was expanded in 1920

Grand Rapids Railway

Fulton St.

N

Mt Vernon Ave

Freight House

Front St.

Watson St

**Detailed map -
Electric Traction
Vol. XI, June 1915**

Four interurban cars adjacent covered platforms in Michigan Railway's station in downtown Grand Rapids.

CERA Bulletin 103

Passenger Service Commences

The Michigan Railway Company issued a picturesque red-and-black timecard to inaugurate service on May 17, 1915. All eighteen daily trains arrived and departed from the new Grand Rapids terminal.

The Grand Rapids-to-Kalamazoo schedule included a local at 5:10 A.M. (daily except Sunday) and locals daily at 6:10 A.M., 8:30 A.M., 10:30 A.M., 12:30 P.M., 2:30 p.m., 4:30 p.m., 6:30 P.M., 9:10 P.M., 10 P.M. , and 11:15 P.M. The limited trains left daily at 7:30 and 11:30 A.M., 3:30 and 7:30 P.M., and the Flyers departed at 9:30 A.M., 1:30 P.M. and 5:30 P.M.

Passengers eastbound for Battle Creek, Jackson, Detroit, and intermediate points and passengers westbound for Allegan transferred at Monteith Junction.Michigan Railway Company planned to expand service in the future by operating two-car trains out of Grand Rapids, while a single-car train departed Kalamazoo at the same time. The two trains would then meet at Monteith Junction, where the two- car train was to split into two sections, one car going on to Kalamazoo and the other car to Battle Creek while the single-car train from Kalamazoo continued to Grand Rapids. Passengers traveling to and from Allegan could transfer to one of the shuttle trains. Covered platforms were provided at Monteith Junction for loading purposes. Michigan Railway interurban cars began running on a new schedule effective July 1, 1915.

Examples of what local stations along the Kalamazoo Interurban route looked like.

Electric Traction 1915

Station at Bradley—Michigan Railway

Station at Wayland—Michigan Railway

GENERAL INFORMATION

LIMITED TRAINS—No extra charge on limited trains except in chair apartment.

CHAIR CAR—Chair apartment on all limited trains, seats 25c. Reservations will be made by Ticket Agent.

BAGGAGE—150 pounds of baggage checked free with each full fare ticket.

PURCHASE TICKETS—Passengers can purchase tickets to all local points and to points on connecting lines. Baggage will be checked through to destination.

TO FLAG A TRAIN—Local cars will stop at all stations and at other points designated by number. Passengers wishing to stop a car will signal motorman in time so stop can be made. Use a light at night and at all times stand clear of train after giving signal.

INFORMATION—Agents will furnish all information desired regarding connecting trains, tickets, baggage, hotels, etc.

UNION STATIONS

Grand Rapids—Foot Lyon Street.
Union with Grand Rapids, Holland and Chicago.

Kalamazoo—Corner Rose and Water Streets.
Union with Michigan United Traction Co.

Allegan—Monroe Street.
Union with Pere Marquette Railway.

Battle Creek—Corner Main and McCamly Streets.
Union with Michigan United Traction Co.

SUBJECT TO CHANGE WITHOUT NOTICE

Michigan Railway Company

TIME TABLE
In Effect July 1st, 1915
CENTRAL STANDARD TIME

Grand Rapids, Kalamazoo Allegan, Battle Creek

and Connections to Jackson, Detroit, Holland, Grand Haven, Muskegon, Chicago

CHAIR CAR ON ALL LIMITED TRAINS

F. W. BROWN, Traffic Manager
KALAMAZOO
TELEPHONE BELL 4345

GRAND RAPIDS TO KALAMAZOO

	LOC A.M	LOC A.M	LIM A.M	LOC A.M	Flyer A.M	LOC A.M	LIM A.M	LOC P.M	Flyer P.M	LOC P.M	LIM P.M	LOC P.M	Flyer P.M	LOC P.M	LIM P.M	LOC P.M	LIM P.M	LOC P.M
GRAND RAPIDS ...Lv.	5 10	5 50	7 30	8 30	9 30	10 30	11 30	12 30	1 30	2 30	3 30	4 30	5 30	6 30	7 30	9 10	10 00	11 20
Fisher	5 30	6 14		10 55			12 55		2 55		4 55		6 55		9 36		11 45	
Corinth	5 39	6 25		9 07		11 07		1 07		3 05		5 07		7 07		9 47		11 55
Moline	5 43	6 30	7 55	9 12		11 12	11 55	1 12		3 55	5 12		7 12	7 55	9 52	10 28	12 00	
Wayland	5 52	6 39	8 01	9 23		11 22	12 01	1 23		4 01	5 23		8 01	10 02	10 35	12 09		
Bradley	5 57	6 46	8 05	9 29		11 29	12 05	1 30		4 05	5 30	7 35	8 05	10 08	10 39	12 12		
Shelbyville	6 02	6 52	8 08	9 36		11 35	12 09	1 36		3 35	5 36	7 35	8 10	10 14	10 42	12 18		
Martin	6 09	6 59	8 13	9 45		11 42	12 13	1 45		3 42	5 42	7 42	8 13	10 10	10 47	12 25		
Monteith Jct.	6 12	7 02	8 18	10 12	11 48	12 18	1 48		3 45	4 18	5 48	6 12	7 45	8 18	10 23	10 50	12 27	
Plainwell	6 23	7 13	8 26	10 00	11 56	12 25	2 00		4 25	6 00		8 02		10 37		12 41		
Argenta	6 28	7 18		10 05	12 00		2 05		4 02	6 05		8 02		10 37		12 41		
Cooper	6 36	7 27		10 13	12 12		2 13		4 12			8 12		10 43		12 47		
KALAMAZOO ...Ar.	6 55	7 50	8 50	10 35	10 40	12 35	12 50	2 35	2 40	4 35	4 50	6 35	6 40	8 35	8 50	11 02		1 05

Daily except Sunday — other trains daily. F Stops on signal. Light Figures A. M. — Dark Figures P. M.

Chair Car on all limited trains. Kalamazoo Flyer leaves Grand Rapids at 9:30 a. m., 1:30 p. m. and 5:30 p. m.

KALAMAZOO TO GRAND RAPIDS

	LOC A.M	LOC A.M	LIM A.M	LOC A.M	Flyer A.M	LOC A.M	LIM A.M	LOC Noon	Flyer P.M	LOC P.M	LIM P.M	LOC P.M	Flyer P.M	LOC P.M	LIM P.M	LOC P.M	LOC P.M
KALAMAZOO ...Lv.	5 10	5 55	7 30	8 00	9 30	10 00	11 30	12 00	1 30	2 00	3 30	4 00	5 30	6 00	7 30	9 15	11 10
Cooper	5 29	6 15		8 24		10 25		12 24		2 25		4 24		6 25		9 38	11 31
Argenta	5 34	6 22		8 33		10 32		12 32		2 32		4 32		6 32		9 45	11 38
Plainwell	5 40	6 29	7 55	8 41		10 40	11 56	12 40		2 01	3 56	4 40		6 40	7 58	9 51	11 44
Monteith Jct.	5 50	6 40	8 05	8 52	10 10	10 52	12 05	12 52	2 01	2 52	4 05	4 52	6 01	6 52	8 05	10 05	11 55
Martin	5 52	6 43	8 07	8 55		10 55	12 07	12 55		2 55	4 07	4 55		6 55	8 07	10 07	11 57
Shelbyville	5 59	6 50	8 12	9 04		11 04	12 12	1 04		3 04	4 12	5 04		7 04	8 12	10 14	12 05
Bradley	6 05	6 56	8 16	9 10		11 10	12 16	1 10		3 10	4 16	5 10		7 10	8 16	10 19	12 10
Wayland	6 10	7 03	8 21	9 17		11 16	12 21	1 17		3 16	4 21	5 17		7 16	8 21	10 24	12 15
Moline	6 19	7 14	8 27	9 28		11 28	12 27	1 28		3 28	4 27	5 28		7 28	8 27	10 34	12 25
Corinth	6 23	7 21		9 33		11 33		1 33		3 33		5 33		7 33		10 39	12 29
Fisher	6 34	7 35		9 45		11 45		1 45		3 45		5 45		7 45		10 48	12 39
GRAND RAPIDS ...Ar.	6 58	8 00	8 50	10 10	10 40	12 10	12 52	2 10	2 40	4 00	4 50	6 00	6 40	8 00	8 50	11 10	1 00

† Daily except Sunday — all other trains daily. F Stops on signal. Light Figures A. M. — Dark Figures P. M.

Chair Car on all limited trains. Grand Rapids Flyer leaves Kalamazoo at 9:30 a. m., 1:30 p. m. and 5:30 p. m.

GRAND RAPIDS TO BATTLE CREEK

	A.M	A.M	A.M	A.M	A.M	P.M	P.M	P.M	P.M	P.M
GRAND RAPIDS ...Lv.	†5 10	7 30	9 30	11 30	1 30	3 30	5 30	7 30	10 00	
Monteith Junction	6 13	8 18	10 12	12 18	2 12	4 18	6 12	8 18	10 50	
Hooper	6 21	8 25	10 21	12 25	2 21	4 25	6 21	8 25	10 59	
Neeley	6 23	8 27	10 23	12 27	2 23	4 27	6 23	8 27	11 01	
Doster	6 30	8 33	10 30	12 33	2 30	4 33	6 30	8 33	11 08	
Richland Junction	6 41	8 44	10 41	12 44	2 41	4 44	6 42	8 43	11 20	
Richland	6 48	8 44	10 48	12 44	2 48	4 44	6 49	8 49	11 26	
Yorkville	6 54	8 56	10 54	12 54	2 54	4 56	6 55	8 55	11 32	
Gull Lake Junction	5 57	7 06	9 07	11 07	1 07	3 07	5 07	7 07	9 04	11 45
BATTLE CREEK Via M.U.T.	6 28	7 35	9 40	11 40	1 40	3 40	5 40	7 40	9 38	12 10
Marshall		8 05	9 58	11 58	1 58	3 58	5 58	8 43	12 40	
Jackson Via D.J.&C.Ry.		9 00	11 00	1 00	3 00	5 00	7 00	9 51		
Ann Arbor		10 10	12 10	2 10	4 10	6 10	8 10			
Detroit		11 55	1 55	3 55	5 55	7 55	9 55			

F Stops on signal only.

† Trains daily except Sunday — all other trains daily.

Chair Car on all trains. Seats 25c each.

Passengers for Marshall, Albion, Jackson and Detroit, change cars at Gull Lake Jct.

BATTLE CREEK TO GRAND RAPIDS

	A.M	A.M	A.M	A.M	A.M	P.M	P.M	P.M	P.M
Detroit (D. J. & C.)		6 00	8 00	10 00	12 00	2 00	4 00		
Jackson (M. U. T.)		7 00	9 00	11 00	1 00	3 00	5 00	7 00	8 00
Marshall (M. U. T.)		7 58	9 58	11 58	1 58	3 58	5 58	7 58	9 07
BATTLE CREEK	6 35	8 35	10 35	12 35	2 35	4 35	6 35	8 40	10 10
Gull Lake Junction	7 08	9 08	11 08	1 08	3 08	5 08	7 08	9 16	10 44
Yorkville	7 17	9 16	11 17	1 16	3 17	5 16	7 17	9 24	11 03
Richland	7 23	9 22	11 23	1 22	3 22	5 22	7 23	9 30	11 10
Richland Junction	7 30	9 29	11 30	1 29	3 29	5 28	7 30	9 36	11 16
Doster	7 42	9 39	11 42	1 39	3 42	5 39	7 42	9 47	11 29
Neeley	7 49	9 45	11 48	1 45	3 48	5 45	7 48	9 53	11 35
Hooper	7 51	9 47	11 50	1 47	3 50	5 47	7 50	9 55	11 37
Monteith Junction	8 05	10 01	12 05	2 01	4 05	6 01	8 05	10 05	11 55
Martin	8 07				4 07		8 07	10 07	11 57
Shelbyville	8 12		12 12		4 12		8 12	10 14	12 05
Bradley	8 16		12 16		4 16		8 16	10 19	12 10
Wayland	8 21		12 21		4 21		8 21	10 24	12 15
Moline	8 27		12 27		4 27		8 27	10 34	12 25
GRAND RAPIDS ...Ar.	8 50	10 40	12 50	2 40	4 50	6 40	8 50	11 10	1 00

Connections at Monteith Junction for Plainwell, Allegan and Kalamazoo.

150 pounds of baggage checked free with each full fare ticket.

Through tickets to points on Grand Rapids, Holland & Chicago, Grand Rapids, Grand Haven & Muskegon, Michigan United Traction and Detroit United Ry.

F Stops on signal.

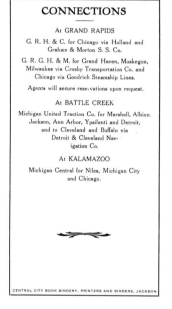

CONNECTIONS

At GRAND RAPIDS

G. R. H. & C. for Chicago via Holland and Graham & Morton S. S. Co.

G. R. G. H. & M. for Grand Haven, Muskegon, Milwaukee via Crosby Transportation Co. and Chicago via Goodrich Steamship Lines.

Agents will secure reservations upon request.

At BATTLE CREEK

Michigan United Traction Co. for Marshall, Albion, Jackson, Ann Arbor, Ypsilanti and Detroit, and to Cleveland and Buffalo via Detroit & Cleveland Navigation Co.

At KALAMAZOO

Michigan Central for Niles, Michigan City and Chicago.

CENTRAL CITY BOOK BINDERY, PRINTERS AND BINDERS, JACKSON

Michigan Railway timetable for Grand Rapids, Kalamazoo, Allegan and Battle Creek effective July 1st, 1915.

Carl Bajema Collection

Interurban Cars Operate as Streetcars in Grand Rapids

While Michigan Railway operated on its own private right-of-way into Grand Rapids, the big interurban cars were required to provide a local streetcar-type service picking up and charging the five-cent fare for travel between any of three locations: Grandville Avenue crossing station, Curve Street crossing, and the Michigan Railway's downtown terminal at the foot of Lyon Street.

Michigan Railway connected with the Michigan United Traction company at Battle Creek enabling passengers to ride all the way to Detroit and beyond by interurban. One

Michigan Railway interurban freight car carried a load of Grand Rapids furniture as far east as Akron, Ohio, in 1917.

Different Passenger Cars for Different Services

The Michigan Railway purchased two types of passenger cars from the St. Louis Car Company for service out of Grand Rapids. The Flyer and Limited passenger cars were the fastest and largest of the two car models. The Flyer could make the fifty-mile trip to Kalamazoo in seventy minutes because it stopped only at Monteith Junction. The Limited cars, stopping at every village station, made the same trip in

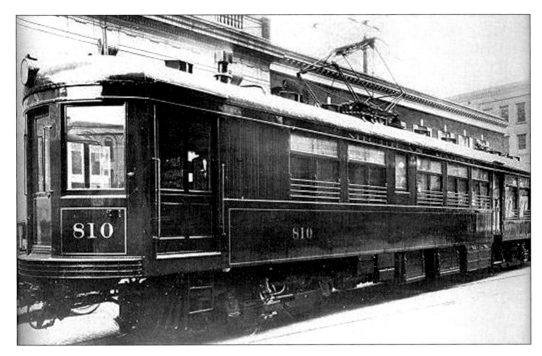

Michigan Railway Limited Passenger Car No. 810.

James Miller

Floor plan of local service Michigan Railway car.

Electric Railway Journal, Vol. 46, 1915

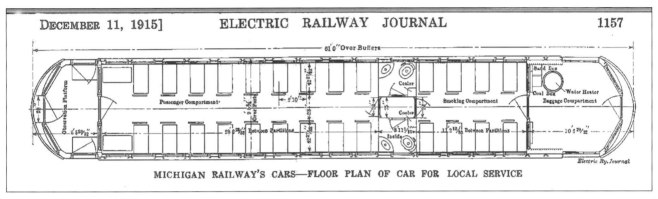

DECEMBER 11, 1915]   ELECTRIC RAILWAY JOURNAL   1157

MICHIGAN RAILWAY'S CARS—FLOOR PLAN OF CAR FOR LOCAL SERVICE

one hour and twenty minutes. The Limited and Flyer interurban cars were constructed of steel and were sixty-seven and a half feet long with scribed steel siding. Each Limited and Flyer car had a motorman's compartment, followed by baggage, passenger, smoking, and parlor compartments, and could seat fifty-one passengers. Passengers entered at a side door two-thirds of the way down the length of the length of the car. The total weight of these Limited cars including electrical equipment and trucks was an imposing 142,600 pounds.

The Local cars could accommodate passengers at many more stops, but generally stopped only when a passenger had notified the conductor or where the motorman saw a person signaling that he wanted to board. Initially locals made eleven round trips daily between Grand Rapids and Kalamazoo with the trip taking one hour and forty minutes.

The Local interurban cars were also constructed of steel but differed from the Limited cars as they had end platform entrances and lacked parlor sections. This made the Local cars over six feet shorter than the Limited cars.

Freight Service

Michigan Railway was an aggressive solicitor of freight traffic and provided fast and frequent service. The railway received four new large steel freight motors (Nos. 900-903) and ten freight trailers by the middle of July. At 61 feet 6 inches long with a width of 9 feet 6 inches, the new freight motors had ample carrying capacity. Michigan Railway began handling freight by September 1915.

In 1916 Michigan Railway opened a freight house at West Fulton Street and Front Avenue on the west side of the Grand River. The one-story freight station was 185 feet long by 50 feet wide. Freight business grew so fast that the company built a 100 foot-long dock on the south side of the freight station so a number of freight cars could be loaded and unloaded at the same time. The freight house had 600 feet of track for transferring freight directly to or from cars without passing through the freight house. In 1920 the company built an addition to the Grand Rapids freight house doubling its size.

Above: *Photo of a 61 ft. long Michigan freight motor car.*

Winslow Collection, Grand Rapids Public Library

Below: *Michigan Railway Freight and Passenger Station at Grandville Avenue (now Chicago Drive). View looking northwest.*

Winslow Collection, Grand Rapids Public Library

Above: *Michigan Railway train at the freight station. View is looking south. This is the freight house shown on the map on page 244.*

Karl Heckman Collection

Below: *Michigan Railway Freight Station in Grand Rapids located south of west Fulton Street and west of Front Avenue.*

Winslow collection, Grand Rapids Public Library

Grand Rapids newspaper ad touts special limited cars for visiting dough boys at Camp Custer, seven miles west of Battle Creek.

Grand Rapids Press, 1917

Michigan Railway Does Its Part for the War Effort

The industry periodical *Electric Traction* featured a front page article in their December 1917 edition which described in detail the efforts to build a spur off the Michigan Railway main line between Monteith Junction and Battle Creek into the newly built army training center then known as Camp Custer. Friends and relatives were encouraged to visit their "doughboys" while they were being trained to do future battle in France.

Deadly Bridge Crossings

Michigan Railway's gauntlet bridge over the Grand River south of Wealthy Street was a popular route for pedestrians who were in a hurry to cross the river. At least six hikers paid with their lives between 1915 and 1928 when trying to save a few minutes by attempting to cross the concrete gauntlet bridge and the adjoining trestle that spanned the Pere Marquette Railroad tracks and Market Street.

The big electric cars making up a second section of train 49 from Battle Creek began to cross the gauntlet bridge on January 2, 1927. A man crossing the bridge either jumped or was hit and fell to the river below where he drowned.

Floyd Fisher, the Michigan Railway accident investigator, recorded the number of pedestrians crossing the bridge the next day. He counted sixteen men attempting to cross the bridge at one time, five of whom had to cling to the outside of the towers on the bridge, the only protection against being run down by oncoming trains.

Interurban Cars Repainted to Prevent Accidents

The Michigan Railway Company's passenger cars were repainted by 1924 in an attempt to make them more visible to motorists when cars approached grade crossings. They were painted a bright orange color from the belt rail up while the original green color was retained below the windows. Unfortunately this was not enough to prevent automobile drivers from the temptation of trying to beat interurban cars at grade crossings.

The Worst Grade Crossing Tragedy in Grand Rapids History

On November 28, 1925, Herbert Jakeway, motorman of the Grand Rapids-bound Michigan Railway car, was in the process of slowing down for the Burton Street crossing just east of Clyde Park Avenue because he knew there was no signal at this location. He sounded the whistle twice and did not expect a problem because he saw a westbound auto already waiting at the crossing. At the last moment, another westbound auto sped around the waiting auto and attempted to race across the track ahead of the northbound interurban car but failed.

The heavy interurban car crashed into the side of the auto wedging it tightly under the front vestibule which severed the electric car's air pipes; this rendered the interurban car's air brakes useless. The motorman frantically reversed the interurban's powerful motors but was unable to bring the big car, with the automobile still firmly wedged under the front of it, to a stop until it had traveled another 700 feet. All seven youthful occupants of the auto were killed in what was the most tragic railroad grade crossing accident in the history of Grand Rapids.

The Beginning of the End of Grand Rapids' Interurbans

The number of people driving private automobiles, riding buses, and shipping by truck grew rapidly after World War I. The state of Michigan built 3,400 miles of surfaced highways including 1,195 miles of concrete highways making it feasible to travel reliably by road between cities. The all-weather roads caused a rapid decrease in the number of passengers carried by the three interurban lines serving Grand Rapids and prevented interurban freight revenue from growing as quickly as expected. Consequently all three interurban companies serving Grand Rapids found themselves in financial difficulties. The Holland interurban went bankrupt and ceased operation on No-

vember 15, 1926. The Muskegon interurban also went into bankruptcy and ran its last scheduled car on Saturday, April 7, 1928.

The Michigan Railroad Company, operator of the Michigan Railway Company's Kalamazoo interurban line as well as other interurban lines, could not meet its financial obligations. The U.S. District Court for the Eastern District of Michigan-Southern Division therefore appointed a receiver on October 28, 1924. The Michigan Public Utilities Commission authorized the Michigan Railroad to begin bus operation between Grand Rapids and Kalamazoo. The Rapid Transit Company, a subsidiary of the Michigan Railroad Company, began running five daily round trips by bus in place of five interurban runs on October 29, 1925. A few interurban cars continued running between Grand Rapids and Kalamazoo until the evening of August 15, 1928, when mounting financial losses forced the termination of

Kalamazoo interurban right-of-way, view looking northwest at Burton Street Crossing. Clyde Park Avenue is in background. This is where the third rail power changed to overhead power as the interurban cars entered the city limits.
Grand Rapids Public Museum

all interurban passenger service on the Kalamazoo line. Freight service continued to operate on the line until the fall of 1928.

A suburban service from Grand Rapids to Jenison continued a few years longer, but the abandonment of Michigan Railway truly signaled the end of the interurban era in Grand Rapids.

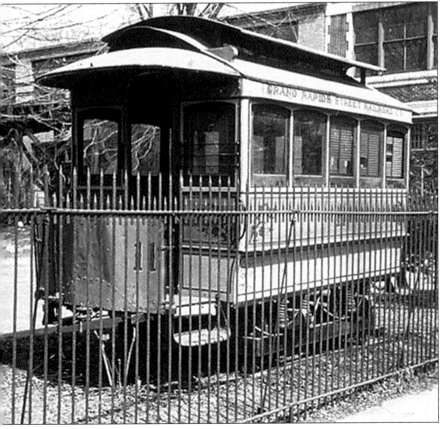

11 Remnants

Streetcars began running in Grand Rapids over 150 years ago on May 10, 1865. The last streetcar to carry passengers in the city ran over 80 years ago on August 26, 1935. What streetcars have survived? What physical evidence still exists of the streetcars and interurban cars that once ran in Grand Rapids and its suburbs?

Streetcars and Interurban Cars

If you were wondering "Can I take a streetcar ride around Grand Rapids today"? The answer would be "Only if you ride a bus disguised as a streetcar"!

Horse-drawn streetcar No. 11 (now Car No. 54) on public display outside the old Grand Rapids Public Museum at 54 Jefferson Avenue, and then later moved indoors to become part of the "Gaslight Village" exhibit.
Grand Rapids Public Museum

Left and below:
Brownell & Wight Car No. 11 "poetically" renumbered as Car No. 54 and on display in the Grand Rapids Public Museum.

Photo by Tom Maas, 2013.

Streetcar No. 11

The oldest true surviving Grand Rapids streetcar began as a horse-drawn streetcar built in 1884. The Grand Rapids Public Museum exhibit staff restored this car during the 1990s and it is on display as car No. 54 inside the Grand Rapids Public Museum.

Car No. 11 was short, only twelve feet long inside the interior of the car and sixteen feet long when the length of the front and rear platforms are included. The car had two long longitudinal seats with an aisle down the middle of the car. When the Grand Rapids streetcar system was electrified in 1891 this horse-drawn streetcar became a trailer and was pulled by electric trolley cars.

The name of this horsecar's manufacturer, Brownell & Wight Car Company of St. Louis, Missouri, was found in several places including ribbons above both interior doors, on metal plaques on the doors themselves and in the beautiful etched ruby glass in the clerestory roof of the car.

Car No. 11 was painted a yellow-orange color when it was donated to the Grand Rapids Public Museum in 1947. James R.Chapman, manager of the street railway

Car No. 11 when it was in the process of being moved from the old museum.
Grand Rapids Public Museum

the Pearl Street Bridge.

The new museum exhibit staff wanted to restore car No. 11 to its original 1884 colors when the horse-drawn streetcar began running on the streets in Grand Rapids. The paint scheme the exhibit staff chose for the car was based on samples found on different parts of the car body which matched written descriptions in Brownell & Wight's 1891 book *The Car Buyer's Helper.* The exhibit staff concluded that the major body colors used to paint the different parts of the car in 1884 were cadmium yellow with Paris green, vermillion glazed with number 49 carmine red and ultramarine blue.

Why did the museum exhibit staff choose to have the car number 54 to be painted on the side of the restored car rather than car No. 11? The number 54 was the street address of the old Grand Rapids Public Museum on Jefferson Avenue. Car No. 11 was parked outside the museum at 54 Jefferson Avenue. The exhibit staff that had worked so long at 54 Jefferson Avenue may have decided that they wanted to keep the old museum address alive by renaming car No. 11 as car No. 54!

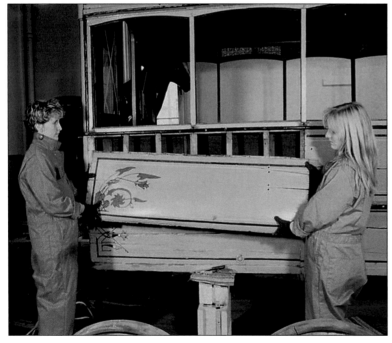

in1892, ordered that all cars were to be painted this color. It was later painted a yellow color when it was moved from the old museum on Jefferson Avenue to the new museum locatedon the west bank of the Grand River on Front Avenue just south of

View looking east at the Hodenpyl-Hardy "pay-within" street car equipped with 12 windows near Lake Michigan, as it looked in the mid-1930's shortly after it was placed on the site.

Photo by current owner

A current view of the former Hodenpyl-Hardy streetcar, fully converted into a cabin, looking west.

Photo by Tom Maas, October 2014

A Grand Rapids Electric Streetcar Survives as a Cabin along Lake Michigan

"There is an old streetcar still being used as a cabin along Lake Michigan!" Carl Bajema had heard this story several times during the past twenty-five years. Unfortunately, none of the individuals were able to tell him exactly where the car was located, nor did they know anyone who could assist with finding the car. Carl had hiked the beach along Lake Michigan for more than ten miles in the region where the old streetcar cabin was supposed to be but had no luck in finding it.

In October 2014 Carl received a telephone call from an employee in the City of Grand Rapids engineering department. She wanted information concerning an old railroad crossing watch tower that the city was interested in preserving as a historical monument. While

providing information about the history of the tower, Carl told her that he was still looking for information about streetcars for this book. She responded saying that she had spent a day at Lake Michigan and that the cabin on the property in Ottawa County was an old Grand Rapids streetcar. The priest in her parish had taken a group of individuals that had served as parish volunteers to this property on Lake Michigan. Her priest was delighted to take Tom Maas and Carl Bajema to the cabin a week later.

The streetcar could not be seen from the Lake Michigan beach Carl had previously walked in his search. The truck that hauled the streetcar onto the property in 1949 was unable to get to the sandy ridge overlooking Lake Michigan because it became stuck in the sand-filled valley just east of the ridge. The streetcar was unloaded where it could not be seen from the Lake Michigan beach. Nor was it visible from the public road that Carl had traveled along near the lake because several hundred feet of

Interior shot of cabin kitchen.
Photo by Tom Maas, October 2014

The Hodenpyl-Hardy standard streetcar was forty-six feet four inches long and had a seating capacity of forty-eight. The body of the single-end car was thirty-three feet long and designed for a two man crew, and was equipped with doors for closed vestibule operation. More information about the construction of the cars, the electric motors, and similar information can be found in the roster in Chapter 13.

Other "Survivors"

As many as thirty Grand Rapids streetcars survived to run on other transit properties in the United States and South America for a decade after 1935. More than twenty-five of the classic 1926 Grand Rapids electric rail coaches were shipped to Santiago, Chile, where they ran until after World War II.

The American Car Company built a demonstration Birney streetcar in 1926 that was sent to Grand Rapids. This double ended Birney car was named *Springfield* and operated in Grand Rapids until 1935 when the car was sold to the Hershey Transit Company in Pennsylvania. It ran for a number of years in Pennsylvania before it was sold to the transit company in Marion, Indiana.

Some local cars had a second life as sta-

Creston, the Grand Rapids neighborhood the car was named in honor of, was easy to read on the wooden bulkhead inside the Hodenpyl-Hardy streetcar near Lake Michigan in 2014.

Photo by Tom Maas

forest stood between the road and the streetcar.

Tom Maas and CarI were astounded when they saw the streetcar for the first time. The car not only was in excellent condition, it was obvious which car company had built it because the owners of the car before 1949 and the current owners after 1949 had only made minimal changes to the exterior. The streetcar is a classic example of the Hodenpyl-Hardy "pay-within" streetcar. Fifteen of these cars were built for Grand Rapids by the St. Louis Car Company in 1917.

An ex-Grand Rapids street railway coach in Santiago Chile.
Allen Morrison Collection

tionary roadside diners. One example was "Wimpy's" which occupied 3961 South Division Avenue for years.

The Grand Rapids Railway Company purchased ten Pay-As-You-Enter streetcars from the Cincinnati Car Company in 1912. These cars were assigned the numbers 342-351.

Car Nos. 343 and 346 have survived because they were used to build a cabin on Hess Lake, forty-five miles north of Grand Rapids.

When the owners wanted to build a house on the property they searched for museums and individuals who would save the two streetcars for posterity. Ed Metka who had one of the largest private collections of streetcars came from Pennsylvania and hauled these two cars to Pennsylvania where they still exist today.

A local double-truck car converted to a Pay-As-You-Enter car was still being used as a cabin on a lake in northern Kent County in 2014-2015.

This ex-Grand Rapids streetcar became Wimpy's Diner on South Division Avenue as shown here as it appeared in a South Kent News ad in 1937.
Wyoming Historical Commission

Muskegon interurban car, Merlin under the Coopersville Historical Museum's canopy in Coopersville, Michigan.

Photo by Tom Maas, 2016

Ex-Grand Rapids electric streetcar being used as a cabin overlooking a lake in northern Kent County, Michigan.

Photo by Carl Bajema

Other sightings of former cars being used as living quarters include two Grand Rapids streetcars joined side-by-side near Lake City (last seen in 2000). The authors are confident that there are more yet to be found!

Grand Rapids, Grand Haven & Muskegon interurban car No. 8, one of the many Muskegon interurban cars that provided streetcar-type service within the city of Grand Rapids, also assigned the name *Merlin*, has been restored and is on display at the

1:20 scale model car in the GR Public Museum Collection. (See page 180.)

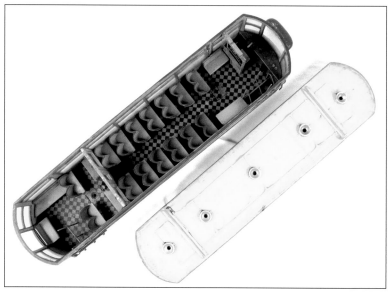

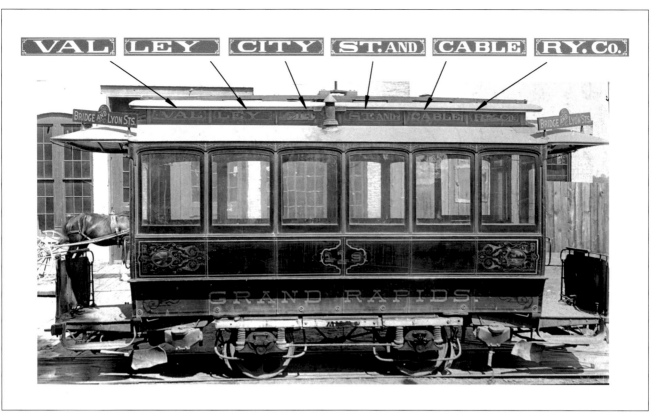

Etched windows superimposed on Car #119.

Collection of Mr. and Mrs. Tim Bultman

Coopersville Area Historical Society Museum at 363 Main Street in Coopersville, Michigan. The car is displayed under a canopy outside of the former Coopersville depot and substation, which is a Michigan Historic Site and is on the National Register of Historic Places.

For further information, readers are referred to *The Lake Line* (CERA Bulletin 144) by Carl Bajema, Dave Kindem, and James Budzynski, also *Grand Rapids, Grand Haven and Muskegon Railway* by Dave Kindem and James Budzynski.

Two scale model streetcars built in 1926 were used to demonstrate proposed new color schemes. *(See page 180.)* The models are about 1:20 scale and once featured working interior and exterior lights. The models were featured in an article about streetcar aesthetics in the *Electric Railway Journal* in the May 8, 1926, issue.

Etched glass windows were saved from the clerestory of a Valley City Street and Cable Railway Car. Images of these windows have been superimposed onto a photo to show their location.

Several headlights salvaged from local interurban cars are on display at the Grandville Historical Museum. The museum is located on the lower level of Grandville City Hall.

Interurban headlights on display at Grandville Museum.

Photo by Tom Maas, 2013

Exterior of former Wealthy Street carbarn building in 2013, view looking southeast.

Photo by Tom Maas

Remnants of Streetcar Buildings

Wealthy Street Carbarn

Address: 1530 Wealthy Street SE, Grand Rapids, MI

The building known for decades as the old Wealthy Street carbarn still stands. The facility housed motor buses at the end of the streetcar era. Its big doors were replaced with glass when Peck's Drug Store and other businesses occupied the front of the building.

The former carbarn survived a major fire in June 1954.

Wolfgang's Restaurant is one of the tenants that currently occupies the remodeled structure. While the big carbarn doors have been replaced by brick, the brick-arched frame of the doors is obvious when one looks at the front exterior of the building. The pinnacle still features a 1906 decoration.

1906 decoration at pinnacle of former Wealthy Street carbarn in 2013.

Photo by Tom Maas

Closeup view of 1906 pinnacle decoration for comparison.

Grand Rapids Public Library

The Street Railways of Grand Rapids

Hall Street Carbarn

Address: 1151 Sheldon Avenue SE, Grand
Rapids, MI

Parts of both the 1902 and the 1924-25 Hall
Street carbarns still exist. The chimney is the
most visible part of the barn. It was built just
after the turn of the century. The brick frame
of the front doors of the Hall Street carbarn,
built following the disastrous July 19, 1924, fire
is physical evidence of the doors through which
the streetcars entered and left the structure.

*Chimney of the 1902 Hall Street carbarn that
still stands upright and tall in 2016. View
looking west from Sheldon Ave.*
Photo by Tom Maas

*Former Hall Street carbarn looking northeast
from Hall Street in 2015. The west half of the
building built in 1902 which survived the 1924
fire still features its original large rounded top
windows, although they are bricked in today.*
Photo by Tom Maas

Scribner Avenue Carbarn

Former address: 336 Scribner Avenue NW,
Grand Rapids, MI

The building was listed as a Grand Rapids
Motor Coach Co. bus fleet garage in the city
directories from 1939 to 1949. It was purchased
by the nearby Attwood Brass Works as a foundry
around 1953, and then was razed about seven
years later to make room for US-131 expressway.
The site is currently occupied by the Gerald R.
Ford Presidential Library and Museum.

*Men inside the Scribner carbarn
pulling up tracks in 1942 for scrap.*

Robinson Collection,
Grand Rapids Public Library

Part of the interurban West Side freight house and passenger station that survived the 2009 fire and is occupied by Arnie's Restaurant, view looking southeast.

Photo by Tom Maas, 2016

Remnants of Interurban Buildings

West Side Passenger Station

Address: 710 West Leonard Street NW, Grand Rapids, MI

Part of the combination West Side freight house and passenger station built by the Grand Rapids, Grand Haven and Muskegon Railway in 1913 still stands. Unfortunately, most of the freight house burned down in 2009. Arnie's Restaurant still occupies most of what was the passenger station at the corner of McReynolds Avenue and west Leonard Street.

Former substation on Remembrance Road, view looking north.

Photo by Tom Maas, 2016

Walker Passenger Station and Substation

Address: 4011 Remembrance Road, Walker, MI

The Walker passenger station and substation, where high voltage AC was converted to lower DC voltage, occupies the northeast corner of Remembrance Road and Kinney Avenue. The station faced southwest toward where the GRGH&MRy interurban tracks were and what is now occupied by Remembrance Road. Kelley's Animal Clinic currently occupies the building which has been extensively remodeled. The tower of the substation makes it easy to identify both the location of the building and that the structure was a substation in addition to being a passenger station.

The Parks

Nothing significant survives of the two street railway parks. The North Park Pavilion was dismantled and salvaged in 1930. Ramona Park survived well beyond the streetcar era, closing permanently in 1955.

Often listed as one of the "Big Three" Grand Rapids resorts, the sole surviving 125-year old John Ball Park still thrives on the hilly west side of Grand Rapids. A recent addition to this park is the electric funicular, installed in 2012 to help visitors climb the steep hill to the upper regions of the zoo and city overlook. As of the writing of this book, it's the only operating electric-powered railway in West Michigan.

Funicular cars going up steep hill at John Ball Park.

Photo by Tom Maas, 2015

Bridges

The abutments on the eastern bank of the Grand River are all that are left of the Grand Rapids Railway's toll bridge that crossed the Grand River between North Park and Mill Creek (now Comstock Park) just north of the highway bridge connecting the two communities.

All three street bridges in Grand Rapids which carried streetcar traffic between the west and east side of the Grand River still exist, although the tracks are long gone and all have been upgraded or rebuilt. These include the Fulton Street, Pearl Street, and Michigan Street bridges.

The Michigan Railway known locally in Grand Rapids as the "Kalamazoo Interurban," had built two bridges across the Grand River in Grand Rapids in order to reach downtown on private-right-of-way. This was done after the Grand Rapids Common Council refused to allow them to run their heavy interurban cars on Grandville Avenue to reach downtown Grand Rapids. Both of these bridges over Grand River still stand and are being used daily by pedestrians.

The North Park railway bridge abutment remnants can still be seen on the east bank of the Grand River, north of the current bridge there.

Photos by Tom Maas, 2015

The downtown interurban bridge, now known as the Gillett Bridge.
Photos by Tom Maas, 2013

The Michigan Railway's concrete bridge located just north of the Pearl Street bridge was completed in 1915 and still spans the Grand River. The bridge is in the form of five arches that rest on four large piers and a concrete foundation at each end. This bridge enabled Kalamazoo interurban cars (1915-1928), Holland interurban cars (1915-1926), and the United Suburban Railway suburban cars (1927-1929) to reach their downtown depot. Both of the flared approaches to this bridge have been replaced. The interurban bridge was rededicated in 1988 as the Richard M. Gillett Bridge. It currently serves pedestrian traffic between the Gerald R. Ford Presidential Museum and the DeVos Place Convention Center (former Civic Auditorium).

The former Michigan Railway Bridge, now part of the Oxford Street Trail, view looking north.

Drone photos by Dan Farkas, 2016

The Michigan Railway's gauntlet style double-track swing bridge over the Grand River south of Wealthy Street in Grand Rapids was completed in 1915. The New York Central Railroad acquired this bridge in 1930 and used it as late as the 1970s. This bridge is now part of the "Rails to Trails" Oxford Street Trail which is accessible on the west side of the river via the West Wealthy Street-Straight Avenue intersection and on the southeast side of the river at Oxford Street just west of Godfrey Avenue.

This bridge has four spans resting on concrete piers and abutments. The southeastern span that crosses Market Street and extends into the Grand River is 200 feet long. The next span is about 100 feet long. The next span after that is 200 feet long and still contains the turntable that was used for swinging the span open to allow steamboats to pass through between 1915 and the early 1920s. The span that reaches the west bank of the Grand River is 180 feet in length.

Chapter 11: Remnants

Street Railway Rights-of-Way

It is easy to locate and ride on the same streets the streetcars did between 1865 and 1935. The maps published in this book are excellent field trip map guides. The major exception is the former private right-of-way that was the Sweet Street Taylor-North Park-Mill Creek (now Comstock Park) car line. Power lines follow the abandoned right-of-way to the east (back) side of Michigan Soldiers' Home (currently known as the Grand Rapids Home for Veterans).

This right-of-way curves toward the northwest, crossing Lamberton Creek on the dam and begins curving slightly northeast and then back northwest going along a two and one-half foot concrete retaining wall. This marks the eastern boundary of the streetcar right-of-way along the western boundary of the veteran's cemetery.

The right-of-way continues swinging to-ward the west crossing Monroe Avenue, North Park Street and then enters the Grand Rapids Boat and Canoe Club property. The streetcar company's toll bridge has been gone for decades but the abutments on the east bank of the river that supported the bridge are evidence as to where the bridge crossed on the north side of the North Park Street bridge. All of the abandoned right-of-way on the west side of the Grand River in the former fairground has been obliterated over time.

Unfortunately, nothing notable remains of these street lines, even in the streets where the paving bricks have been re-exposed in the Eastown district. The routes are easy to follow by using the maps published in this book, as the streets remain relatively unchanged with some renaming noted.

Panoramic view of former right-of-way north of the Michigan Soldier's Home looking towards the cemetery - view spans north-east-south.

Photo by Tom Maas, 2015

Interurban Rights-of-Way

Concrete abutment of the former Michigan Railway bridge over Plaster Creek as seen from the Godfrey Avenue bridge, view looking south.

Photo by Tom Maas, 2015

The "Holland Interurban"

This double-track interurban left the Grandville Avenue-Clyde Park intersection where it crossed the city limit, then crossed Plaster Creek, and went a short distance on what is now Chicago Drive. The current concrete arch bridge over Plaster Creek replaced a wooden structure in 1916. It was built for vehicular traffic only, since Michigan Railway no longer needed city street routes. When the Suburban Railway lost its rights to run on the private right-of-way to downtown Grand Rapids, tracks were laid on this bridge. The bridge was placed on the National Register of Historic Places in 1999 and bears a plaque to commemorate this.

Electric power lines travel along the former right-of-way southwest between Godfrey Avenue and Burlingame Avenue where it crossed Burton Street and continued southwest on Beverly Avenue. The power lines are an excellent clue as to where the tracks ran.

The old interurban right-of-way continues southwest on Lee Street going through the small Wyoming Park business district. Note the building on the south side of Lee Street in the Business district. While the building is on the same site as the Wyoming Park depot, it was built in 1928 as a small office and is not the original building.

Many bungalow-style homes in the Galewood-Urbandale-Beverly and Wyoming Park area which were so popular in the era of the interurban still exist along the right-of-way. Some homeowners have marked their 100-plus year-old homes with Wyoming centennial home plaques.

The right-of-way continues southwest. This is where the 750-foot long trestle was built to go up and over Byron Center Avenue and the Lake Shore & Michigan Southern-Michigan Central railroad tracks. Some of the right-of-way here is maintained as green space with walking paths and a playground.

The right-of-way continues southwest on Lee Street going through Elmbrook and then crosses what is now the 28th Street-Ivanrest Avenue intersection. The power line provides an excellent clue that the line was still going in the southwest direction.

Pick up the right-of-way on Peck Street-Wallace Avenue intersection, now on Peck Street to Hamilton 30th Street and west on 30th Street to Chicago Drive at Wilson Ave-the center of Grandville. The tracks went through the center of Grandville, heading southwest on Chicago Drive to the Ottawa county line where the right-of-way continues on Chicago Drive as it swings west and then farther heads back southwest.

The right-of-way at Jenison is very difficult to discern, as the area has been heavily impacted by the I-196 expressway interchange and the Rush Creek drain. Remnants of the old power substation and the Blissveldt Farm near here are no longer visible, although Benjamin S. Hanchett's summer home still exists near the right-of-way at 358 Port Sheldon Street SW in Jenison.

Beyond this, the right-of-way heads southwest to Andre's Crossing, 44th Street, 8th Avenue, Wierenga's Cut, and Shack Huddle Cut at McClelland Street before the I-196 expressway. If one wants to continue westward, some interesting interurban remnants can be found. An intact, well-maintained depot is currently located east of the church at the northeast corner of 22nd Ave and Quincy Street. A small waiting shed is also maintained at the Patmos Library in Jamestown.

This view of long-abandoned streetcar tracks in Grandville Avenue is dated 1953. View is looking southwest, with the power transmission towers visible ahead indicating the north/south Michigan Railway right-of-way.

Robinson Collection - Grand Rapids Public Library

The "Muskegon Interurban"

Since this line ran solely on existing streets until it left West Leonard Street at a northwest angle at Remembrance Road, no discernible evidence exists of the route of the Muskegon Interurban until we arrive at the current western city limits of Grand Rapids. The right-of-way at Remembrance Road pre-dates the road itself. The road was built in 1918 to parallel the tracks, eventually being widened to include the right-of-way.

Upon leaving Kent County, Remembrance Road becomes Ironwood Drive. At Hayes Street, the right-of-way turns west and continues towards the small town of Marne (known as Berlin until WWI), where the original brick interurban depot still stands, though the tracks are long gone. The building at 1580 Arch Street currently serves as a restaurant.

The next depot to the northwest on this right-of-way is also intact. The depot and substation at Coopersville currently houses a museum. The restored *Merlin* car is on display outside (see previous section on cars).

Michigan Railway rails still exposed in Mt. Vernon Ave. near the Watson St. southwest intersection.

Photo by Tom Maas, 2013

The "Kalamazoo Interurban" (Michigan Railway)

The downtown Grand Rapids depot is long gone, but the adjacent Richard M. Gillett Bridge is well-maintained and is a busy pedestrian bridge as mentioned earlier. Much of the right-of-way south of this bridge currently runs through private property; however a small section of angled track is currently exposed as of this writing in the Grand Valley State University campus on Mt. Vernon Avenue near where it stops at Watson Street.

The right-of-way becomes evident again at the northern end of the Oxford Street Trail, a short extension of the Millennium Park Trail which begins on the west bank of the Grand River, just south of Wealthy St. The former gauntlet bridge is safe for pedestrian traffic today, with guardrails on both sides, though it is fairly narrow. The bridge extends southeastward over Market Avenue and active CSX railroad tracks before ending roughly a half mile south at Oxford Street.

The Michigan Railway right-of-way on the east side of the Grand River is maintained by the Consumers Power Company, so it can be easily followed as it winds its way southward. If one looks closely at some of the steel power line towers and compares them with photos from the early days, it's possible that some current towers date back to when they were originally installed in 1914-1915.

Remnants of bridges over Plaster Creek are sometimes mistaken as part of this right-of-way, but further investigation indicates that most belonged to the GR&IRR, which ran nearly parallel in this area and serviced many of the industries located here. Remains of the interurban bridge's concrete abutments can be seen from the south side of the Godfrey Avenue bridge however.

The junction of the Holland Interurban with the Kalamazoo Interurban was located near where Chicago Drive and Clyde Park Avenue intersect.

Michigan Railway's private right-of-way continues southeast, crossing Clyde Park Avenue just north of Burton Street, and then crossing Burton Street just east of Clyde Park Avenue. This is the site of the horrendous crash in 1925 which killed seven teenagers.

The Michigan Railway changed its power source from fenced-in third rail to overhead high voltage before entering the Clyde Park-Burton street intersection.

The right-of-way once crossed Beals Road (now 28th Street) and GR&I track (now Norfolk & Southern RR) track on a large bridge, which no longer remains, due to extensive work on the US-131 expressway here.

The City of Wyoming maintains a nearly two-mile section of the right-of-way as a paved linear park aptly named "Interurban Trail." It begins on the north end at Coolidge Street SW and ends at Murray Street SW on the south end.

Remnants of concrete structures, such as signal bases, cattle crossing underpasses, and trestles still exist along the Michigan Railway right-of-way, although most are on private property, although some remnants can be seen from a car. Traveling south on US-131 today, especially between 92nd Street and the 100th Street exit, one can still clearly see the remnants of the raised roadbed of the right-of-way following the power lines on the passenger side of an auto. As you travel south from 100th Street, the power lines cross over the expressway. The right-of-way now continues southward roughly parallel to the expressway, but on the east side of the highway. Very little physical evidence remains of the once thriving junction at Monteith in Allegan County.

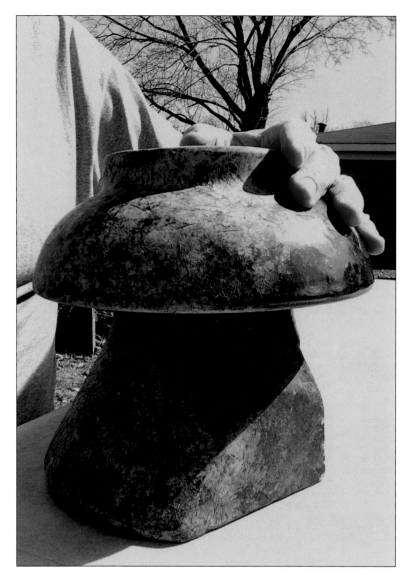

Large high voltage ceramic insulator found along Michigan Railway ROW near Plaster Creek.

Photo by Tom Maas, 2013

*Group photo of 38
street employees on
the west side of the
Hall Street car
barn in 1896.*

The Token,
January 1929, pg. 5

*Group Photo of 38
streetcar employees
taken in 1905 in front
of a Wealthy-Taylor
Line street car.
Front row, extreme left,
1st = J. Quinn,
2nd = W. O. Bates,
8th = Peter McGarry.
Backdrop is the
Wealthy carbarn
before it was
remodeled.*

Carl Bajema collection

12 Employees, Promoters and Managers

Conductors and Motormen

It took a large number of individuals performing a number of tasks to operate a street railway. The motormen that operated the streetcars and the conductors that collected the fares were the most visible employees that made the streetcars run. Each had to purchase his own uniform.

Motorman Miles McDonald identified 36 of the 38 men in this group photo (above) in 1929 as follows:

- First bottom row, left to right-Art Barns, James Cass.
- Second row-Fred Brown, James Vanderbout, Elmer Way, Jean Blodgett, Jim McCarty, unknown, Truman Daniels, Andrew Brandson, Cornelius Van Dam.
- Third Row—Elmer Cole, Jim Wright, Alva Greenbaugh, Miles McDonald, Mike McCarty, Will Allen, Will Brown, Neil Morrison, Chub Lane, Adam Sharp.
- Fourth Row-unknown, Tom Culligan, Taylor Daniels Will McIntyre, Michael Fallon, Pat Lynch, Johnny Murphy, Fred Morrison, Mike White.
- Fifth Row-Mr. Rodgers, Nels Hamblin, Mr. Yeakey, John Maloney, Joe O'Hara, George Johnson, Dan McNamara.
- Top Row-Morris Caverly.

Group of employees in front of the Wealthy Street carbarn in 1905.

Dave Tinder

"In the old Days at Wealthy Car House"

A group of street railway employees took a break to pose for a photo in front of the Wealthy carbarn in 1905 (above). These were the days when "flat-top derbies were the style, mustaches were considered things of beauty, and chin whiskers were supposed to be a facial adornment and also useful for motormen during cold weather."

The name of the employees still in the employ of the company at the end of 1926 included:
- Bottom row: left to right, No. 1, Peter McGarry, operator on Cherry line No. 3, John Quinn, Cherry line operator; No. 5, George Poland, Operator Cherry night run; 9, William Bradfield, night foreman Wealthy car house.
- Center row: No. 2 Jake Haney; until recently day janitor at Hall street; No. 4, D. W. Wetherby, day operator Cherry line; No. 6, W. O. Bates, now in accounting department, general offices; No. 10, now Police Lieutenant Emmett Burley; No. 11, John Gelders, extra operator at Wealthy car house.
- Top row: No. 1, Frank Brady, sweeper at Scribner car house; No. 15, Charles Lundquist, operator on Scribner line.

A group of motormen and conductors posing with a car in front of the Hall Street carbarn in 1908. Even though we don't know their names, this is an amazing image!

John A. Winks, "Gill" Aylesworth, and Matthew Nagelkirk, (left to right) members of the company's "Minute Men Crew" who played a major role in getting trolley cars to resume moving by fixing broken trolley wires.

The Token, May 1927

Grand Rapids Street Railway tower repair car No. 4.

Karl Hekman

Numerous group photos of Grand Rapids streetcar motormen and conductors exist but many of these group photos do not identify any of the employees in the photo.

Repair and Track Crews

The repair crews that maintained and repaired broken trolley wire played a very visible major role in keeping the streetcars moving.

How were street railway repairmen able to work in safety while within reach of a strong and often fatal current of electricity?

The September 12, 1905, issue of the Grand *Rapids Herald,* shown on the next page, provided its readers with an answer to this question.

The track crews built new track, replaced old track and fixed track right-of-way, especially the curves and switches.

CLOSE TO DEATH, YET NOT AFRAID

Newspaper photo of street repair crew on raised repair wagon ready for service.

Grand Rapids Herald, Sep 12, 1905

STREET RAILWAY REPAIR CREW READY FOR SERVICE.

CLOSE TO DEATH, YET NOT AFRAID

Emergency and Repair Men of Street Railway Company
Work in Safety Within Reach of a Strong and Fatal Current of Electricity.

Apparently toying with death, the repair men of the Grand Rapids Railway company working on the trolley wires high in the air are, under ordinary conditions, as safe as any laborer in the city. People who see the men at work handling the heavily charged wires with their bare hands often ask why they are not electrocuted. The answer given by Master of Transportation Madigan is simple. The wood of which the cart and elevated platform is constructed is a non-conductor. The men, while standing on the wood, are as safe from a shock as if they were not handling the wires at all.

The trolley wire of the Grand Rapids Railway Company carry about 550 volts of 'juice,' enough were a man to get the full benefit of it to cause instant death. With the wooden platform, however, there is no danger unless it is raining hard and the water which is a conductor runs all the way from the platform to the ground. This, forming a connection between the wire and the ground, will carry the fluid and cause death if the men were not otherwise insulated. The insulation is accomplished by means of rubber gloves and rubbers on the feet. It is necessary that these rubber appliances be perfectly whole, as a small hole will permit the electricity to enter and a shock will be the result.

In order that the men may safely handle the trolley wires at the same time with the cross wires, the latter are carefully insulated so there is no danger from this source

.Four men are kept constantly ready for quick runs to any part of the city where trouble is reported. Sometimes these men are not called upon for action for days at a time. At other times they may have a dozen cases of broken wires in a day. Last Sunday, for instance, the cold weather caused a sudden contraction of the wires which parted wherever they were weak and the repair men were called to attend to no less than 11 cases in that one day.

One would think that sleet would cause much breaking. This is not always the case, however. When cold weather comes on, the wires are slackened and ready to meet the extra strain caused by the cold. Unless very heavy sleet falls freezing on to the wires and breaking them because of the excessive load, the repair men are called upon for little more duty in the winter than in the summer.

At any rate, the repair man is under ordinary conditions as safe at his work as any other man. The local street railway company has never had a fatal accident because of its own wires. One or two accidents have resulted from the telephone, telegraph or light wires falling across the trolley wires, a matter which is, of course, unavoidable."

John McCloskey's Track construction crew.

The Token May 1929

More Members of the Track Department

| Bob Herdman Foreman | Frank Campbell Timekeeper | Lorenzo Sorrintino Track |
| Peter Bowman Paver | Elmer Faught Track | Bill Meyers Truckman |

Grand Rapids Railway baseball team (year unknown).

Grand Rapids Public Library

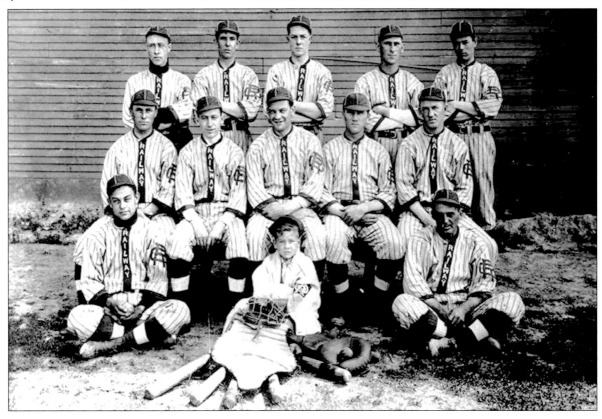

Group photo of employees of all departments of the Hall Street car shops.

The Token,
January 1929, page 2

Photo of Cromwell Batchford and William Hall, company blacksmiths.

The Token,
June 1926, page 6

Car Cleaners, Inspectors, and Car Shop Mechanics

The carbarn employees who worked during the night included those who cleaned each car during the brief hours the streetcar was in the barn overnight, and the inspectors who read the daily trip reports that each motorman and each conductor was required to fill out. The inspectors assigned those cars having minor defects that could be fixed in time for operation the next morning to the nighttime shop repair crew.

The daytime shop employees made repairs that could not be completed overnight. They replaced wheels that had gone flat, replaced burned-out motors and other electrical equipment. Shop employees included carpenters who replaced damaged wood on cars that had been in accidents, painters, and blacksmiths. These skilled workers were capable of doing more than just repairing a streetcar. They rebuilt streetcars and even constructed new ones.

Emergency Crews

How did a street railway emergency crew restore operation when part or all the system was shut down because of a broken wire, a broken rail, or some other problem? The *Grand Rapids Evening Press* on November 9, 1907, published the following description of how a three-man emergency crew of the Grand Rapids Railway worked to restore service.

(See next page.)

Always in Peril:
Street Railway Emergency Man Does His Duty.
C-r-r-rack! Flash! Siss-s-s-s-s-s! Bang!

Coiling and striking like some venomous serpent from the nether regions, spitting blue flame and sparks as each lightning-like stroke is punctuated by a detonation like the discharge of a high power rifle, the "live" trolley wire comes down from its broken hanger - and there is work in hand for the street railway emergency outfit.

While passengers surge out of cars in alarm and pedestrians press back, startled by the pyrotechnical display, there comes the wild clang of a gong, the clatter of galloping horses and the rumble of heavy wheels. In an instant cool headed, matter of fact men step into the fire zone of the spitting metallic serpent, lay deft fingers upon the death dealing instrument and draw it back into place with a temporary repair under which the calmed spectators walk safely with never a tremor and cars pass with lowered trolleys. Thus, briefly, does the emergency crew perform its duty.

Not that this alone comprises their day's work. The trio of resourceful fellows who comprise the Grand Rapids Railway company's emergency crew are just what they are termed in street railway parlance, "the trouble gang." Trouble is their specialty. Trouble, both below and aloft. They may handle a "red hot" bit of broken trolley one minute and be called upon the next to take a forty ton interurban car out of an excavation and put it back on the rails. A versatile crew, indeed, is the emergency outfit. There is no apprenticeship that fits a man for this exacting line of duty. Experience alone educates him. Hard knocks and hard work, coupled with a physical, mental make-up, peculiarly adapted to respond to emergency demands fit the repair man for his work.

Jack Winks, foreman of the crew, described how the three men viewed their work:

The men don't see anything heroic in their effort. They glory in the speed of their horses, their own ability to make repairs, and joke about the wet days when the wagon and everything they touch is 'hot' with pulsing electrical energy and they are burned and knocked down as they arrive to clear the way.

"Jack" Winks and his little band might literally be termed the veterinaries of the trolley. What the veterinary was to the street railway company of the old days of horse motive power, the emergency gang is in these days of motors, trolley circuits and high speed, only in a greater degree. All the miles of rails and wires upon which the local company depends for the proper dispatch of its cars must be maintained by the emergency crew. A break often ties up 75 percent of the service and will more than likely come when half a city is urgently demanding transportation to or from work, or the shelter of the cars from a driving rain or bitter blizzard. Without the emergency wagon, its faithful steeds and men, the city might go on waiting indefinitely. At such times traveling Grand Rapids is most dependent upon their efforts. Great five thousand horsepower engines and generators are useless. Motors are helpless. It all devolves upon the yellow tower wagon or the similar colored wrecking outfit.

Foreman Winks' word alone was all that was required to get current turned off at the powerhouse and to stay off until he said it was safe to restore electricity to the repaired part of the system.

The emergency crew had emergency wire wagon No. 2, wrecking wagon No. 3, and three horses always available for their use. The crew operated out of the centrally located Ferguson's livery barn on Kent Street.

The speed with which the crew responded to a call was so important that from 5 A.M. to 8 P.M. the horses stood already harnessed in their stalls. The crew trained so that they were able to respond as quickly as the local fire department crews did.

Tower wagon No. 2 weighed 3,400 pounds and was equipped with all the tools and parts necessary to facilitate the work of wire repairing. As the tower wagon approached the location of a broken wire:

One of the crew dons rubber gloves and the other gets out the light, but strong tackle used for pulling together broken ends. By the time the outfit has pulled up at the volleying trolley wires, this tackle is in readiness with its "come-along." The "come-along" is technically known under the trade name of Haven clamps. It is a device with an eccentric action that grips the broken end of the wire and holds it tighter and tighter as the tackle is strained to bring the ends together. If the wire breaks between two span wires and there are two loose ends, two "come-alongs" are used and the work can be done from the ground. With only one end down, one of the crew mounts the tower, taking one end of the tackle with him. The man below working with gloves attaches the "come-along" and the loose end is pulled tight. The tackle is fastened and in this position the wire is left while the blockade is raised and the cars pass with trolleys pulled down.

Once the blockade is raised, if exigencies demand it, and emergency sleeve or repair is made. This consists of a sleeve that fits over the end of the broken wire. A key is inserted and as the pull of the tackle is removed, the strain on the line causes the sleeve keying to grip the wire ends and hold them fast. If, as is often the case, the trolley wire is worn too small to be held in this sleeve, the emergency crew makes what they term a "western union" connection. This is a special variety of splice in which the ends are brought together, looped and twisted. These are only temporary repairs and are left only until the crew has time to return and make the job permanent with a solder sleeve. In this, the loose ends are inserted in a specially constructed sleeve. Molten solder is poured in and allowed to cool while the tackle holds the strain. Once the solder is set the sleeve is as strong as any portion of the line.

276 *The Street Railways of Grand Rapids*

Office Workers

Bookkeepers, accountants, and secretaries provided streetcar managers with information about income, expenses, the condition of the track and wire, and the service the company was providing.

Group photo of women office workers who are members of the company's Girls Bowling League.

The Token

Controls the Limit Switches

This would be the routine in an instance where the dropping of the trolley wire did not open the limit switches at the power house switchboard. Many times the dropping of the wire puts such an added resistance upon the circuit that the switch opens. It is the rule of the company to close a limit switch that has sprung open. If it opens again it is tried once more and upon a third opening is left and no word but the emergency crew foreman's can cause its closing. Those switches often open under an overload and in that case remain closed when they are shut.

The rule is made to protect the lives of pedestrians, horses and the crew of the emergency. They work barehanded with the wire when they find it dead, secure in the knowledge that none but their own order can cause the electrical energy again to flow through it. All emergency work in overhead construction devolves upon this crew. Occasionally there occurs some accident like the breaking of a pole which they cannot permanently repair, but no matter how serious this crew must clear things up and get cars moving. If the permanent job is too great it must be looked after by the construction gang.

Roast or Freeze

The new electro-magnetic switches are "hot" places to work about. The men of the emergency crew expect burns and heavy shocks in this work. On a rainy day, when the wagon is soaked with water, it is almost as good a conductor as the ground and the men work while the electricity from the great generators at the power house sparkles about their fingers, burning and stunning yet never warming to offset the fierce cold winds that may sweep or the sleet that cuts and freezes as it strikes.

It is a popular illusion that the live wire is warm. As a matter of fact, it is either burning hot or icy cold. When it "shorts" and there is an arc, the wire burns into human flesh like a white hot knife. It is never warning to the benumbed fingers that work it. There is no happy medium. It is a plain case of roast or freeze or be knocked down. And naturally the windy bitter cold and wet nights are the times when the emergency wagon is in greatest demand.

Of the work with the wrecker, a different story might be told. There is less danger of burning and shocks, but more chance of crushing. It is bitter cold work in the winter and disagreeable even in summer. The work must be done under the same pressure that characterizes every other branch. While the men strive to restore truant flanges to the rails, cars idle on either side and passengers frown and ridicule their service or growl as they are transferred round the wreck. The wrecking wagon No. 3 carries plates for use in restoring derailed trucks to the track, jacks of the screw, ratchet and hydraulic variety heavy cables, tackle blocking wedges and extra pieces of track. All this piled on the wagon brings its weight up to 3,800 pounds. When there is a derailment the call is sent to Ferguson's barn just as in the case of a wire break. If the crew is in, the horses are run out, hitched to No. 3 wagon and the run made at top speed. The men size up the situation at a glance and proceed to put the car back where it belongs. Often it means raising twenty to forty tons of metal and wood, six or eight feet out of an excavation or hoisting the tracks out of sand in which they are imbedded. Again, it means the gruesome task of jacking a car clear of a dead or suffering victim.

Imagine the incentive under which these men work when they drive in through a gaping throng and find crushed and bleeding under tons of metal some suffering man, woman or child, groaning and crying for mercy and assistance. They have accomplished some wonderful feats in this line. Their efforts may mean the saving of a life. There are times when the emergency crew are life as well as time savers.

The streetcar company sponsored an employee band and also an employee baseball team. Grand Rapids Streetcar Company Band in 1915.

From AERA publication

Seasonal Employees

There were many who worked in construction during the summer months and who removed the snow and ice away from the track in the winter months. Those who worked at the resorts included musicians, actors and actresses, and even policemen to keep the peace, particularly at Ramona Park.

Labor-Management Friction in the Nineteenth Century

Relations between labor and management were not always good, leading to several organized events:

- Boycott of 1884 (refer to Chapter 1)
- Strike of 1890 (refer to Chapter 4)
- Strike of 1891 (refer to Chapter 4)

An Amalgamated Street Car Men's Association union organizer came to Grand Rapids in 1898 and tried to organize the 275 streetcar men employed by the Consolidated Street Railway Company. The streetcar company discharged twenty-four street railway men who attended the union organizer's presentation at the Central Labor Union Hall. The company claimed they fired these employees because they had been "unfaithful" to the company.

Labor-Management Relations Improvement in the Twentieth Century

A group of Grand Rapids investors backed by money from Philadelphia and New York City purchased the Consolidated Street Railway early in 1900. The company owners chose Grand Rapids Railway Company to be the name of the new corporation. A year later the new owners approved raising the wage scale they paid to "every man employed on the company's cars" effective February 1, 1901, so

that the pay scale would be higher than most cities of the country." The company worked to make its employees happy in a number of ways.

1908 annual picnic button.
Gordon Hubenet

First Annual Street Railway Employee Picnic

The street railway company organized a picnic at Ramona Park in July 1903 for street railway employees and their families. About 200 employees, half the company men of all grades and classes, enjoyed the picnic on July 27 while the other half of the employees kept the streetcars running. The two groups switched roles the next day. The company's 1903 picnic was such a success that it became an annual event. In October of 1913, the American Electric Railway Association (AERA) published a six-page article with photographs in their periodical extolling the virtues of company picnics like Benjamin Hanchett held annually for his employees. The article was written by Louis DeLamarter.

Making the Carbarns a Place to Stay, Relax, and Rest

The company began equipping carbarns with modern conveniences for the comfort of the men who operated the cars. The Wealthy Street carbarn house was remodeled and had a lunch room, a well-stocked library, a billiard and pool parlor, a lounging room and six sleeping rooms each equipped with two beds *(see page 122)*.

A Mutual Protective and Benefit Association

A Mutual Protective and Benefit Association was organized and operated with the financial cooperation of the Railway Company, its object being the relief of its members in case of sickness or other disability and to provide substantial benefits in case of death. It also promoted social relationship and good fellowship and to secure such possible benefits for its members as may be obtained by cooperation.

President Hanchett announced that on July 1, 1913, the street railway company would pay 500 motormen and conductors a higher graduated pay scale that would place their pay above average for cities the size of Grand Rapids.

Grand Rapids Street Railway Men Organize a Union in 1918

The War Labor Board, created by President Wilson to deal with labor disputes during the war, declared as its first principle the right of workers to organize in trade unions and to bargain collectively through chosen representatives is recognized and affirmed. That right was not to be denied, abridged, or interfered with by the employers in any matter whatsoever. The employees of the Grand Rapids Railway Company organized Division 836 of the Amalgamated Association of Street and Electrical Railway Employees in early August 1918.*

Thousands of men worked for the street railway companies during the seventy years that streetcars rolled on the rails in Grand Rapids. The motormen and conductors had to work very long hours for low pay especially before 1900. Many of these employees enjoyed working for the company in spite of the hard conditions.

MILES A. MCDONALD: The Very Soul of the Company (1873-1959)

Miles A. McDonald worked as an electric streetcar motorman for forty-one years (1895-1935) and for the bus company for another thirteen years (1935-1948). He was one of those employees whose working "soul" became a very important part of the corporation. The reader will find several images throughout this book with Miles in them.

Miles McDonald began working as a motorman for the Consolidated Street Railway of Grand Rapids on January 7, 1895, a day he never forgot because he had to stand outside on the open front platform of what motormen called a "bald-faced" car, that is, a streetcar without an enclosed vestibule that could protect the motorman from inclement weather.

A humorous play in 1915 called A Regular Trip *featured employees in all roles. The nearly full-size prop streetcar featured a variety of typical passengers.*

Ron Strauss

---

*This is a very brief history of Grand Rapids street railway-management-labor relations. A comprehensive history of the labor-management relations is needed. That important history still needs to be written.

Miles McDonald, motorman, wearing his street railway company badge No. 204 and hat.

Descendant of Miles McDonald

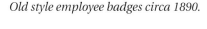

Old style employee badges circa 1890.

Miles recalled that he froze his chin, fingers, and toes one day during that first winter. The problems he and other motormen faced when operating single-truck open-front streetcars that had no air brakes led Miles to think of the 1890s as "anything but gay." Fortunately the Michigan legislature passed a law requiring street railway cars to have enclosed vestibules effective January 1, 1896.

Miles recalled the hours and shifts that they worked during the 1890s: "We worked 'swing runs,' the day run about 11 hours and the long, say about 14. The change to day and night shifts was a godsend."

Thirty years later Miles was chosen by the street railway company to serve as motorman of the *Minnesota* test car and take a carload of traction experts on a ride to demonstrate what the new car could do.

When the American Electric Railway Association asked Louis DeLamarter, the manager of the Grand Rapids street railway company, to bring its new streetcars to its 1925 convention in Atlantic City, Miles was one of the rail coach chauffeurs who went along with the new cars.

Miles was chosen by the streetcar company to be the driver of oldest Grand Rapids horsecar No. 11 in several parades.

Miles McDonald tried to retire in 1935 after operating the last streetcar to run in Grand Rapids on the night of August 25, 1935.

When asked what he would miss when he retired in August 1935, Miles responded:

"I'll miss my check every month . . . I'll miss getting up in the morning at quarter to four . . . I will miss my associates and the rattle and clang of the cars, but most of all I will mass that genial, 'Good morning Mac' from the hun-

New style employee badges 1899.

Grand Rapids Press, 01 July 1899

dreds of passengers who rode on my car, for it was this more than anything else, that made my job and my life a happy one."

Miles soon realized how much he missed working for the company. He drove a bus for a short time but he did not like having to drive his bus to a curb to pick up passengers. Miles also disliked having to shift gears on a bus while going up or down steep hills. He spent the last years of his long career working as a member of a bus maintenance crew at one of the old streetcar barns until he finally retired in 1948.

Jeremiah Boynton

JEREMIAH W. BOYNTON
Pioneer Builder and Operator
of Grand Rapids Street Railways
(1837- 1911)

Jeremiah Boynton, a Civil War veteran of limited means, was a very colorful promoter and builder of street railways in Grand Rapids during the 1870s and 1880s. Known to all in the community as "Jerry," he built and operated all three divisions of the Grand Rapids & Reed's Lake Street Railway Company. Boynton played the major role in both raising money to build the first two divisions of his street railway and in the actual construction of the line all the way east to the western end of Reed's Lake by July 4, 1875.

Jerry Boynton had contracted to pay an iron rolling mill in Cleveland to supply the strap iron for the rails he needed to continue building the Grand Rapids & Reed's Lake Railway inside the city of Grand Rapids in the spring of 1875. Time was running out because the property owners along Wealthy Street had subscribed $11,000 toward construction of the line on their street but only if it was completed by July 1, 1875. It looked as if Boynton was not going to meet the deadline required to obtain the subscribed funds needed to continue and complete the line's construction.

Legend has it that Jerry, in desperation, traveled to the iron mill in Cleveland and succeeded in getting the mill to manufacture the strap iron rails and to then load them on flat cars while he waited. Jerry, equipped with a

basket of food and a revolver, then climbed aboard one of the loaded flat cars. He ensured that the railroads also expedited the travel of the loaded flat cars to Grand Rapids. Boynton quickly shifted from guarding the rails to spending most of the next three days and nights working with his track crew laying and spiking the strap iron rail onto wood stringers. Jerry was able to meet the deadline for collecting more than $10,000 in subscriptions by running a streetcar along Wealthy Street to the eastern city limit by the end of the month.

Jerry Boynton also was able to raise just enough money and get just enough credit to build the Reed's Lake division of his Grand Rapids & Reed's Lake Railway that went east on Sherman Street from the eastern city limit all the way to Reed's Lake in 1875. He was able to complete the western division of his GR&RLRy that ran all the way from downtown Grand Rapids to the western end of West Bridge Street at the bottom of the big hill by early 1876. Passengers had to pay five cents to ride each of the three divisions of the Grand Rapids & Reed's Lake Railway Company.

Jerry Boynton was far better at building street railways than in keeping them running as the GR&RLRy went bankrupt. Others took over and were able to keep the lines in operation.

Boynton succeeded in extending the Scribner avenue streetcar line all the way north to the west side Detroit & Milwaukee Railroad depot at the Detroit, Grand Haven & Milwaukee Railroad junction by August 9, 1883.

The *Grand Rapids Evening Leader* reported a remark that a prominent citizen made on the occasion:

> Jerry Boynton, like other men, has his peculiarities, but if it had not been for Boynton, Grand Rapids would be without much of the street railway accommodation that she now enjoys.

The reporter then went on to say:

> The citizen's remarks, while not poetical, were certainly truthful, as most persons who are familiar with street railway building in this city will concede. With the exception of the Canal Street line and that in south Division and Hall streets, every foot of street railway in Grand Rapids was laid under the direction of Mr. Boynton. The Reed's Lake road, through LaGrave, Wealthy and other streets, North Division, Lyon, Kent, and Bridge streets, Scribner, Pearl and other streets to the Union depot, were all built by Mr. Boynton.

Jerry Boynton wasn't done making it more convenient for the citizens to travel by streetcar in Grand Rapids; less than half a month later Jerry played a leading role in bringing about the merging of three different Grand Rapids street railway lines in 1883.

Boynton built the first street railway in Kalamazoo in 1884. A Kalamazoo newspaper praised Boynton for building the new line in that city but the operation quickly ran into financial problems and went bankrupt. Boynton also built a steam railroad in Michigan and a streetcar line in northern Indiana.

No one in Michigan built as many railroads as Jerry Boynton did. Unfortunately almost all of them were "paper" railroads—paper maps that showed the routes of the proposed lines, and papers of incorporation and franchises. Boynton had great dreams but he had difficulties raising the necessary capital to build a proposed line or sufficient funds to keep the line running after completion. Jerry was working on his Grand Rapids Electric Railway project, which in 1907 would have connected Grand Rapids with Kalamazoo, some

eight years before Michigan Railway Company succeeded in building its branch between the two cities. Boynton's proposed Grand Rapids-Kalamazoo line was part of his much more grandiose 750-mile long electric railway that would have run from Fostoria, Ohio, going northwest to Kalamazoo, north to Grand Rapids and then northeast all the way to Alpena, Michigan.

Jerry Boynton was still promoting his "paper" Grand Rapids Electric Railway project when he died on February 18, 1911. For most of his life it seemed as if Jerry was always able to raise "just enough" to build his lines but "not enough" to keep them operating.

James R. Chapman

JAMES RUSSELL CHAPMAN
An Accomplished Civil and Electrical Engineer
(1851-1934)
By Roy G. Benedict

James R. Chapman was born and raised in Boston. He studied civil engineering. His career as a steam railroad civil engineer began in 1872 as a rodman on the Portland and Ogdensburg Railroad. He progressed becoming a division engineer on the Carolina Central Railroad (1873); with several small lines in northern Texas for the Gould system (1877) where he laid out town sites; as superintendent of bridges and buildings for the Denver & Rio Grande Railroad (1881); and building some lines for the Kansas City, Pittsburg & Gulf Railroad (1888).

Simultaneously In 1888 Chapman began

applying his engineering skills to the development of street (and interurban DC) cars at Kansas city, Missouri, where he became superintendent of a cable line, the Kansas City, Independence & Park Railway. He played a significant role in engineering the Kansas City & Independence Rapid Transit Railroad and the Chicago & Kansas City & Texas Railroad Company.

Chapman's success in converting the practically bankrupt cable line into a profitable enterprise led the owners of the newly combined Grand Rapids, Michigan horse and cable lines to invite him to visit Grand Rapids. They offered to make him superintendent of both the horse and cable car systems. Chapman initially rejected an offer to become the manager of both lines because the Grand Rapids system of street railways could not become profitable unless the company eliminated the redundant lines that served the same populations and provided faster travel to the outskirts. When the new owners of the combined streetcar system informed him that they agreed to work with him to eliminate those problems he agreed to become superintendent of the new Consolidated Street Railway Company of Grand Rapids.

Chapman was successful in converting the hodge-podge collection of horsecar lines, cable car lines, and a steam dummy line into an all-electric coordinated Grand Rapids streetcar system in less than two years. Chapman's success led him to play a major role in electrifying the street railways in Chicago. Initially he served as a consulting engineer. He began spending a "half" of each week in the summer of 1892 in the far southeast reaches of Chicago where he managed the South Chicago City Railway. He continued to spend the other half of his time managing the Consolidated Street Railway Company of Grand Rapids. Chapman was not alone in a seemingly strange relationship in two places a half day's train ride apart: Two major stockholders in the Grand Rapids company, John M. Hagar and John O'Dell, also were involved with South Chicago City Railway.

Fifteen miles north of the South Chicago City Railway, the financier Charles T. Yerkes (1837-1905) dominated local transportation on the near North and West sides of Chicago. Seven trunk lines into downtown were owned by two Yerkes companies: the North Chicago Street Railroad Company and the West Chicago Street Railroad Company. These routes were changed from horsecars to cable trains whose grip cars could pull as trailers the horsecars of outlying routes that had not been cabled. Yerkes wanted to furnish electric trolley service on those horse lines and to establish new trolley lines in other outlying areas as yet without local street transportation. He obtained a franchise to electrify these lines on May 4, 1894. For all this, he needed a man with trolley experience. Yerkes wanted the best man for the job. Immediately after being granted a franchise to put in an electric system on the north side and west side of Chicago Yerkes sent a telegram to Grand Rapids because he knew who the best man was–Chapman.

James Chapman went full time with the Yerkes organization, having severed his connections both at Grand Rapids effective May 15, 1894, and at the South Chicago City Railway. Chapman served as chief engineer for more than just the West and North side surface lines. He played a significant role in the building of approximately 430 miles of track in the Chicago area before he left the United States in 1901. Some of these lines were brand-new streetcar routes, some of them suburban. He was in charge of the electrical equipment at such locations as the Western Avenue, Cicero and Proviso, California Avenue, and Hobbie Street. The same or other power generating plants also permitted electrification of most of the horsecar lines of the North Chicago and West Chicago Street Railway companies. Working with Yerkes, Chapman also electrified other systems such as the Chicago Union Traction Co., the Suburban Railroad Co., and three of the elevated roads—the Lake Street Elevated Railway Co., the Union Elevated and the Northwestern Elevated Railroad Co.

Working for Yerkes, Chapman also used the third rail electric power system to electrify the Lake Street Elevated, the Union Elevated including the downtown Loop (theretofore using small steam locomotives) and opened the four-track Northwestern Elevated road as an electric system.

Having played such a significant role in the development of hundreds of miles of streetcar and elevated track was an impressive achievement for any man, but more was to come for Chapman.

With a population of over six million, London was the metropolis of the world. Having visited London several times, Yerkes was well aware of its "backward" local transportation.

One-fifth of the London population commuted into a square mile commercial center. There they suffered winding streets grossly overcrowded with horse-drawn omnibuses. Horsecars and electric trolleys were prohibited by Parliament. A shallow subway, competing for underground space with mains and sewers, was not the solution, especially as its locomotives burned coal in the confined space. There were electric trains in two deep tubes reached by electric elevators. But more were needed. How could English investors finance such an ambitious project? A New York brokerage company believed the answer was Yerkes.

In March 1900 Yerkes sent two of his trusted assistants to London to investigate. Their report brought Yerkes to see for himself in July 1900. On September 28 Yerkes bought the charter permitting construction of a line. In January 1901 he detailed Chapman to London, initially for three years. Chapman responded to a question from reporters stating that "he does not know in detail what his work is to be" but some of the reporters recognized that they were being put off. In any event the purpose was to develop the electrification of the underground railway. In 1904 the *Michigan Investor* called him "the foremost engineer in England." Chapman worked in London until 1910, five years after Yerkes' death.

James Chapman retired in 1910. He died on January 11, 1934, at his home in Santa Barbara, California. In the following millennium, people worldwide still know of the London Underground which he helped create, even if they do not recognize the engineer's name nor know the breadth of his accomplishments.

What remains of the American transit heritage of James R. Chapman? First, it became more economic for transportation companies to purchase electricity from utility companies than to operate their own power generating plants. Next, the general trend to convert streetcar lines to bus operation wiped out all the car lines in Grand Rapids by 1935, Kansas City by 1957, and Chicago by 1958. However, six of the eight rail rapid transit (subway-elevated) lines of the Chicago Transit Authority operate in part on elevated railway structures where the electrical power once was supplied from Chapman's power generating plants. Therefore his engineering work, though unsung today, set the stage for transportation services which remain everyday necessities for vast crowds of people both in Chicago and London.

Benjamin Hanchett

BENJAMIN HANCHETT Jr.
Errand Boy to President
(1868-1933)

Benjamin Hanchett started as an office and errand boy for the Grand Rapids Street Railway Company in 1883 when he graduated from high school in Grand Rapids. Benjamin's business skills led him to become the company assistant secretary and treasurer by 1890. He became secretary and treasurer for the Grand Rapids Railway Company when that newly formed company purchased the Consolidated Street Railway Company in 1900. Ben Hanchett's career working for the streetcar company spanned thirty-seven years and included serving as general manager in 1904 and as president of the Grand Rapids Railway Company between 1910 and 1920 when he retired.

Ben Hanchett hired Louis J. DeLamarter

Example of named car - Campfire Girls car. Refer to Roster for list of all named cars.

Grand Rapids
Public Library

in 1903 to manage the company's resorts at Ramona Park and at North Park, a decision that led the theater at Ramona Park to host many of the nation's leading performers. Hanchett and DeLamarter organized what became the first in a series of annual picnics for the streetcar company employees and their families in 1903.

Benjamin Hanchett became General Manager in 1904 succeeding the late G. Stewart Johnson and he was appointed president in 1910.

Hanchett made life easier for employees by equipping carbarns with free club rooms where they were able to play billiards and pool, checkers and chess, and read standard periodicals in addition to books in a library. Each carbarn had dormitories where crew members could sleep after ending their late night runs.

Hanchett continued to bring about a number of other changes that improved the lives of the Grand Rapids Railway employees. The establishment of the Grand Rapids Railway Company Mutual Benefit and Protective Association which was designed to help protect families in times of sickness from the clutches of "loan sharks," and to provide death benefits for employees was one of the changes that he brought about.

Benjamin Hanchett also played a major role in getting the first interurban railway built in the Grand Rapids region in 1900-1902 when he served as vice-president of the Grand Rapids, Holland and Lake Michigan Rapid Railway Company in addition to serving as secretary and treasurer of the Grand Rapids Street Railway Company. Hanchett also played another major role in the history of the Holland interurban line when he organized a group to buy the Grand Rapids, Holland and Chicago Railway in 1912 while he was working as president of the Grand Rapids Railway Company.

Benjamin Hanchett Jr. was well liked in the community as well as in the state, serving as president (mayor) of East Grand Rapids for several years and as a member of the University of Michigan's Board of Regents for eighteen years (1911-1929).

The Street Railways of Grand Rapids

Louis DeLamarter

LOUIS J. DELAMARTER
Promoter Extraordinaire
(1872-1955)

Louis DeLamarter exhibited his managerial and marketing skills working in local theaters while he was still a high school student in Grand Rapids.

DeLamarter was managing the brand new Majestic Theater in downtown Grand Rapids in 1903 when Benjamin Hanchett Jr., assistant manager of the Grand Rapids street railway system, hired him to manage the company's two summer resorts at Ramona Park and North Park in 1903. He used his showmanship and management skills to create an environment that both the public and vaudeville groups enjoyed being at Ramona Park. Will Rogers, one of the better vaudeville actors, was so impressed that he referred to Ramona Park as "DeLamarter Lake."

DeLamarter soon became President Hanchett's personal business secretary and was promoted to assistant secretary and assistant treasurer of the Grand Rapids Railway Company in 1909 while still serving as manager of Ramona Park.

Louis DeLamarter was appointed Vice President and General Manager of the streetcar company when President Hanchett retired in 1920. Ridership was beginning to decline as more citizens were using automobiles to travel in urban regions such as Grand Rapids. Delamarter immediately set about trying to reverse the ridership decline by changing the public's negative attitude toward riding streetcars by marketing them as a product. He decided to provide the public with what they were most interested in when riding streetcars—superior service and modern streetcars while he also worked at lowering the cost involved in operating them. One of the first things he did was to purchase nine new inexpensive one man Birney Safety Cars which not only reduced the cost of operating a streetcar but also gave the street railway a "new product look" in addition to providing better service.

DeLamarter played a leading role in changing how streetcar companies operated by employing marketing methods to listen to the customers (the streetcar riders) and then modifying the product (service) to better meet the wants and needs of those customers. He conducted low-cost traffic surveys in an attempt to determine the shortest, most economical, one-fare routes from residential to business areas during early 1920. He was able to identify the major problem that the riding public faced-there were not enough streetcars running on the busiest routes during the morning and evening rush hours. He changed the streetcar timetables effective June 27, 1920, so that the cars ran more frequently on the busiest routes during the rush hours. The public immediately experienced a significant improvement in service. DeLamarter also "sold" numerous business and social groups on the important role that streetcar transportation played in a city such as Grand Rapids.

DeLamarter's initiative to improve service made it easier for him when he had to negotiate a new streetcar franchise to continue to operate on the streets in Grand Rapids in 1921. He negotiated a new thirty-year street railway franchise with the city that was based on a cost of operation plus fair interest and payment on outstanding loans from the past. The new thirty-year franchise was ratified by seventy-two per cent of the voters. The future looked fairly stable except for the fact that more and more citizens were riding in private automobiles each year.

DeLamarter stressed the importance of winning public good will and summarized many of the marketing methods he employed to overcome long standing indifference and prejudice in his attempt to obtain public recognition for the Grand Rapids streetcar system in 1926. He pointed out that it was difficult to get the public to believe ". . . enthusiastically in the average streetcar with the same color scheme, the same flat wheels, the same old slat or cane seats, same clangy gongs, same old more or less dirty blue uniforms, some old dirty windows, same old advertising signs and same old hundred and one things that our fathers and some grandfathers looked at," without being considered ready to be admitted to the asylum.

What did DeLamarter do to win the public good will? He worked to cultivate good will by developing good relations with more than just those who rode the streetcars. He also targeted two other groups-the city authorities and the newspapers. Advertising future events in the newspapers kept riders, city politicians and city employees, as well as newspaper editors and reporters, up to date with what was happening. DeLamarter's optimistic advertisements appeared in more than in the local newspapers. Posters in streetcars, theater slides, motion pictures, construction signs, and in *Trolley Topics*, the company's monthly publication that it distributed free to its riders, were all ways that the company communicated good will.

The Hall Street carbarn fire on July 19, 1924, destroyed more than fifty streetcars.

The Grand Rapids Railway employees viewed the fire as a disaster. They were amazed when DeLamarter viewed that same fire not as a disaster but an opportunity. Delamarter knew that the section of the Hall Street carbarn and the cars destroyed by the fire were insured. He also knew that he could now use the fire insurance money as an incentive to get streetcar builders to construct the kind of streetcars that he wanted to purchase-new cars that could carry forty to fifty riders but weighing about half as much as that of the old heavy streetcar. The reduction in weight meant that they would require far less energy to operate. He also wanted the new streetcars to have the features desired by the local citizens. He gathered data from the streetcar riders via a marketing survey.

Louis DeLamarter succeeded in getting three streetcar builders to participate in a contest to build a forty-two to forty-five passenger streetcar that met the standards DeLamarter required with respect to efficiency—cars that were very lightweight and that required only one man to operate.

DeLamarter used the street railway company's free publication *Trolley Topics* to get riders to participate in a survey to find out what conveniences they wanted. The riders responded and he made sure that the twenty-seven Grand Rapids electric coaches that the winning streetcar manufacturer built contained the comfortable seats, the low easy steps to enter and exit the car, the smooth riding, and reduction in noise that the public wanted.

DeLamarter stressed the important role that courteous and neatly uniformed employees played in producing good will among streetcar riders. He pointed out that any platform man (conductor and motorman) met and served far more customers than virtually any salesman could do during a much longer period of time. DeLamarter went on to state that

"This being so, unless we give the platform man the right kind of atmosphere and surroundings, a new uniform, a clean attractive car, a vehicle in keeping with the quiet running automobile our patrons have become used to, a car the employee automatically takes pride

in, he will unconsciously not be very enthusiastic in his salesman's efforts and as a result the company will directly or indirectly suffer."

He even had the company's car shops provide a special personal appearance valet streetcar that traveled to each carbarn at least twice a week to help keep the platform men spic and span.

He drew national attention to the role that the twenty-seven new streetcars were playing, not only in Grand Rapids but in stimulating a general movement throughout the country for building better streetcars.

DeLamarter found that good will and pride among Grand Rapids citizens could be produced by giving names of prominent Grand Rapids citizens and schools rather than the traditional assigning numbers to streetcars. By the end of 1927 more than 75 of the company's 114 streetcars had names on the sides of the streetcar but no numbers.

Street railway managers and streetcar manufacturing representatives began to visit Grand Rapids to learn about the numerous designs that made the new cars more efficient to operate and that were also more convenient and comfortable for the riding public.

The Grand Rapids Railway Company was awarded the Charles A. Coffin national award in 1927 "In recognition of its distinguished contribution during the past year to the development of electric transportation for the convenience of the public and the benefit of the industry." Louis DeLamarter was able to use his knowledge of streetcar operations and his abilities with respect to advertising and showmanship to turn a disastrous 1924 carbarn fire into a national success story.

The street railway company had to pay for improvements on the parts of the streets used by the streetcars, which were also being improved for private automobile travel to the detriment of the company. That and the great financial depression that began in 1929 sealed the financial fate of the Grand Rapids Railway Company and led the creditors to force the street railway to file for bankruptcy in 1932. The U.S. District judge appointed Louis DeLamarter as receiver, and he began the process of replacing all the streetcar lines with buses until August 1935 when the last trolley car ran in Grand Rapids. DeLamarter became president of the Grand Rapids Railroad Company when it emerged from receivership in 1938 and continued as president of the Grand Rapids Motor Coach Company when the streetcar company changed its legal name in 1938.

Louis J. DeLamarter served as president of the Grand Rapids Motor Company for the next sixteen years until 1954 when the company was sold to the City Coach Lines of Detroit. He continued on as chairman of the company until he died in 1955 at the age of 83.

Cartoon from well-known local "Razzin' the Rapids" artist, Ray Barnes. The Coffin Award for 1927 went to Grand Rapids thanks mostly to efforts from "Louie" DeLamarter.

Street Railway Journal,
18 June 1927

Streetcars in Grand Rapids bore the front and back likenesses of the 1927 Coffin Award medal as a badge of honor in the days following the win as seen on the far right of this photo taken in February 1929.

David Winick Collection, Grand Rapids Public Museum

13 Equipment Roster

A Select Roster of Electric Railway Equipment
Purchased by or built by a
GRAND RAPIDS STREETCAR COMPANY

- Reed's Lake Electric Railway (August 6, 1890-1892)
- Consolidated Street Railway of Grand Rapids (July 1891-April 1900)
- Grand Rapids Railway Company (April 1900-April 14, 1927)
- Grand Rapids Railroad Company (April 15, 1927-1935 end of line)

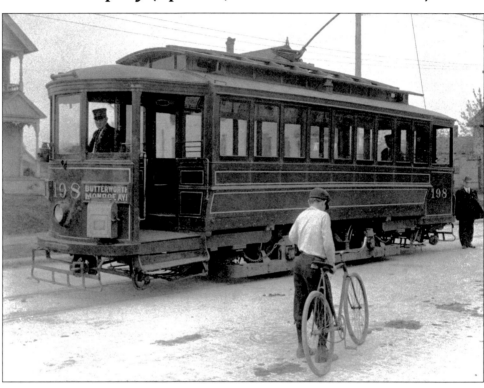

Among the earliest electric cars to run in Grand Rapids were 20 single-truck closed streetcars built by Brownell in 1892. The same company also built 20 open cars for summer service. The partially enclosed front platform afforded the motorman a modicum of protection against the elements. The 33-inch diameter wheels gave the Brownell-3E truck an unusually massive appearance.

Grand Rapids Public Museum

Instead of splitting the next large order between open and closed cars, 15 closed single-truck cars and 10 semi-convertible cars were ordered from Pullman in 1899. A car from this latter group, stopped in front of the Hotel Grand, displays the large window area that made for a breezy ride in warm weather.

Authors' Collection

A Select Roster of Electric Railway Equipment Purchased by or buil

Builder	Year	Type of Car	Car No.	Number Built	Trucks	Motors
Bodies built in MN; motors from United Electric Traction (NY)	1890	Open DE		4	Double truck	30-hp m
Brownell Car Co.	1892	Open SE		20	ST: Brownell-3E	Two WH-
Brownell Car Co.	1892	Closed SE		20	ST: Brownell-3E	Two WH-
Pullman	1895	Closed city cars SE	100-114	15	Single truck	
Pullman	1899	Semi-convertible SE	115-124	10	Single truck	
Jewett or St. Louis Car Co.	1900	City car SE		1	Double truck	
St. Louis Car Co.	1900	City car SE	125-139	15	Double truck	Two 57-h (several v 27-hp m
Jewett	1900	Convertible DE	260-series	10	DT: Brill 77E	
Grand Rapids Railway Co.	1903	U.S. Mail Cars DE		2	Single truck	
Grand Rapids Railway Co.	1904	City car SE		2	Single truck	Two 125-
Cincinnati Car Co.	1904	City car DE		6	Single truck	See rema
J.G. Brill	1904	Sprinkler	1	1	Single truck	
G.C. Kuhlman Car Co.	1905	Semi-convertible city car		10	DT: Brill 27-G1	Four 40-h
Cincinnati Car Co.	1906	Excursion car HonoluluDE		1	Single truck	
J.G. Brill	1907	Sprinkler	2	1	Double truck	
G.C. Kuhlman Car Co.	1907	Semi-convertible city car		10	DT: Brill 27G1	Four 40-h
American Car Co.	1909	P.A.Y.E. city car SE	318-329	12	DT: Brill 39E	
Cincinnati Car Co.	1912	P.A.Y.E. city car SE	342-351	10	DT: Brill 27G	Four 50-h
St. Louis Car Co.	1917	Hodenpyl-Hardy Pay-Within Car SE	352-366	15	DT: Standard 0-50-0	Four GE-
J.G. Brill	1920	Birney Safety Car DE	367-385	19	ST: Brill 79E1	Two WH
St. Louis Car Co.	1923	Birney Safety Car DE	386-392	7	ST: St. Louis	Two WH
Light Weight Noiseless Electric Street Car Co.	1925	Test car Minnesota SE		1	DT: Specially made; roller bearings	4 GE 25-h
G.C. Kuhlman Car Co.	1925	Test car Ohio SE		1	DT: Specially made	4 WH 25-
St. Louis Car Co.	1925	Test car St. Louis SE		1	DT: GR-54; roller bearings	4 GE 25-h
American Car Co.	1926	Deluxe Birney Springfield DE		1	ST: Brill 79E1	

Motors	Dimensions	Roof Type	Seating Capacity	Remarks	Photo of Car
4 GE-268F 25-hp	Length: 37'	Arch	43-44	Refer to car names at end of Roster	184, 185, 186, 187, 192, 200, 207, Roster
Two WH 25-hp motors	Length: 28'	Arch	32	Acquired secondhand in 1927 from Northern Ohio Traction & Light Co.	
Two WH 25-hp motors	Length: 26'	Arch	32	Experimental lightweight car	200

45. Ottawa Hills —
    Neighborhood
46. Page, Abel T. –
    Grand Rapids pioneer
47. Pantlind, J. Boyd —
    Pantlind Hotel owner
48. Powers, William T. –
    Grand Rapids pioneer; built West Side Power Canal
49. Ramona —
    First Birney car to be rebuilt in 1925
50. Ramsom
51. Reed
52. Rindge –
    Lester J. Rindge; shoe manufacturer
53. Riverside Gardens
54. Roosevelt Park —
    Neighborhood
55. Rumsey, James A.
56. Ryerson, Martin —
    Pioneer lumberman
57. St Louis —
    One of three test cars built in 1925
58. Scribner, James C. –
    Grand Rapids pioneer
59. Silver Creek —
    Neighborhood
60. Smith, J. Morgan –
    Grand Rapids pioneer; Pastor, First Congregational Church
61. South High School –
    A Grand Rapids Public High School
62. Spring, Henry —
    Dry goods merchant
63. Steketee, Paul —
    Retail merchant

64. Stocking, B.
65. Stone, Henry G.
66. Sunset Heights —
    Neighborhood
67. Sweet, Martin L. –
    Grand Rapids pioneer; Sweet Hotel
68. Swensburg, C.O.
69. Thayer, Georger W.
70. Turner, Eliphalit –
    Grand Rapids pioneer.
71. Uhl, Edwin —
    President, Grand Rapids National Bank
72. Union High School –
    A Grand Rapids Public High School
73. Van Buren, Oceana
74. Verdier, J.A.S
75. Waters, Daniel H
76. Winegar, William —
    Furniture Manufacturer
77. Withey, Luis H. —
    President, Michigan Trust Company
78. Wykes, George

Additional Cars Named Later:
A. Baxter —
    Pioneer Grand Rapids newspaper editor
Creston High School –
    A Grand Rapids public high school
EAST Grand Rapids High School —
    A public high school in the suburbs
Ottawa Hills High School —
    A Grand Rapids public high school

of his roster of new electric cars purchased by
arles Wrege (deceased) and others.

A Select Roster of Electric Railway Equipment Purchased b

Builder	Year	Type of Car	Car No.	Number Built	Trucks
St. Louis Car Co.	1926	Electric Rail Coaches SE	Named	27	DT: St. Louis 64EIB
J.G. Brill	1920	Birney Safety Car DE		1	ST: Brill 79E1
Versare Corp.	1927	Experimental car SE		1	3 axles/6 wheels

Names of Cars on Grand Rapids Street Railway—April 9, 1927

1. Aldrich, Moses V. –
   Grand Rapids banker and politician
2. Ball, John —
   Pioneer Grand Rapids citizen
3. Bissell, Melville R. —
   Carpet sweeper manufacturer
4. Blodgett, Delos A. —
   Lumberman
5. Boy Scouts of America –
   Illustrated in roster
6. Briggs, George G.
7. Burton Heights —
   Neighborhood
8. Butterworth — Neighborhood
9. Camp Fire Girls
10. Campau –
    Grand Rapids founder Louis Campau
11. Catholic Central High School
12. Caulfield, John
13. Central High School
14. Clay, David P.
15. Cobb, Sanford H.
16. Coit Park —
    Neighborhood
17. Comstock, Chas. G. —
    Lumberman and furniture manufacturer
18. Comstock Park—
    Suburban neighborhood
19. Creston —
    Neighborhood
20. Edgewood —
    Neighborhood
21. Fairmount — Neighborhood
22. Fisk
    (Only information available)
23. Foster, Wilder D.
24. Gay, George W.
25. Gilbert, Thomas D. –
    Grand Rapids Pioneer
26. Giddings, J. Allen.
27. Hake, William –
    Grand Rapids pioneer
28. Hall, Erastus
29. Harrison, William –
    Grand Rapids pioneer; wagon manufacturer
30. Herpolsheimer, William G. —
    Department store merchant
31. Hollister, Harvey J. —
    Pioneer Grand Rapids banker
32. Houseman, Julius –
    Grand Rapids businessman
33. Huntley, Emmons R
34. Johnson, G.S. –
    Grand Rapids streetcar manager
35. Knapp, Erastus U
36. Ledyard, William B
37. Lincoln Park —
    Neighborhood
38. Luce, Ransom
39. Lydell, Dwight
40. Lyon, Lucius –
    Grand Rapids pioneer and surveyor
41. Madison Square —
    Neighborhood
42. Minnesota —
    One of three test cars built in 1925
43. North Park—
    neighborhood
44. Ohio —
    One of three test cars built in 1925

The authors wish to thank the following individuals for the information and knowledge they shared for compilatio *the various Grand Rapids streetcar companies: Roy Benedict, Norm Krentel, Art Peterson, Gail Snow, David Winick,*

	Dimensions	Roof Type	Seating Capacity	Remarks	Photo of Car
tors			50	2 motor cars; 2 trailers	66
	Motor: 26' long; Trailer: 35 ' long				
2	Length: 25'	Deck		33-inch wheels	81, 84
2	Length: 25'	Deck		33-inch wheels	Roster
	Length: 30' + vestibules	Deck			85, 86
	Length: 30' + vestibules	Deck			Roster
	Length: 38'			Sample car	
motors ith four tors)	Length: 36'	Deck	40	Longitudinal seating	
			56		106, 110, 128, 211
	"Length: 28' 3"	Deck		Out of service August 1914	94, 111
p GE motors					
ks		Deck		Car bodies only. Cars were equipped one at a time with equipment and trucks from retired cars.	
					119
p motors	Length: 42'	Deck		"7 large "picture" windows on each side; later converted to P.A.Y.E. cars	Roster
	Interior length: 23'	Deck		Destroyed in Hall St. carbarn fire 7/19//24	117, 118
					119
p motors				"6 large "picture" windows on each side; later converted to P.A.Y.E. cars	136, 182, Roster
		Deck			158, Roster
p motors	Length: 40'	Deck			
04	"Length: 46' 4"""	Arch			"137, Roster"
5-hp motors	Length: 28'	Arch	32	One or more of series destroyed in Hall St. carbarn fire 7/19/24	162
08A	Length: 28'	Arch	32	One or more destroyed in Hall St. carbarn fire. One car remodeled in 1927 as Col. Charles Lindbergh	165
p	"Length: 37' 6"	Arch	44-46	One of 3 test cars	172, 173, Roster
p	"Length: 37' 6"""	Arch	44	One of 3 test cars	173, 178
p	"Length: 37' 11"""	Arch	44	One of 3 test cars	174, 175, 176, Roster
	"Length: 28' 6"""	Arch	32	Special deluxe demonstration Birney. Later sold to Hershey Transit	

Continued on next page.

288A

Grand Rapids had three postal streetcars used to transfer mail between the postal facilities and train stations. Known as "Ghosts" because of their white livery, the cars were in service for only 11 years before being withdrawn in 1914.

Hildebrandt Collection

Car 263 was part of the next order of streetcars to arrive including 10 fully convertible cars built by Jewett in 1900. They were practically double the length of any older Grand Rapids car. Their large capacities made them ideal for service to the local resorts and parks in the summer.

Authors' Collection

Car 260 from the same Jewett order is shown configured for cold weather operation. The mail box on the front of the car was a unique feature of the Grand Rapids system.

Hildebrandt Collection

Two groups of "picture window" cars were a distinct Grand Rapids design as was the use of single-panel swinging doors. Ten cars with 7 large picture windows were delivered from Kuhlman in 1905 with 10 additional cars, this time with 6 picture windows on each side, arrived in 1907.

Authors' Collection

By the late 1920s many of the older cars had received various upgrades, such as installation of two-panel folding doors, a new livery, and the replacement of car numbers with names. The "Emmons R. Huntley" is shown here in Campau Square in the later years of operation.

Karl Heckman

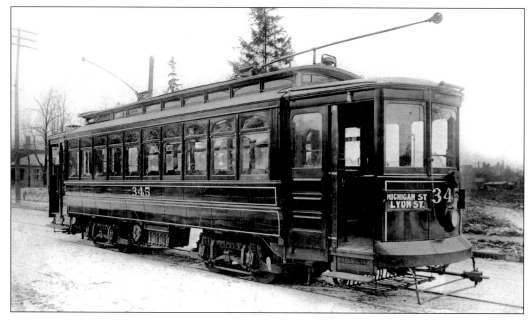

Archetypical of Grand Rapids Railway equipment in the teens and twenties were the Pay-As-You-Enter streetcars. The 10 P.A.Y.E. cars built by Cincinnati in 1912 featured curved windows in the upper sash. No. 345 pictured here was as handsome a car as could be found on any system at the time.

Grand Rapids Public Library

Motorman and conductor pose proudly in front of their Cincinnati-built P.A.Y.E. car. The size and weight of these cars, as well as the need of a two-man crew, made them increasingly costly to operate on a modestly-sized system such as Grand Rapids. Management soon began to explore designs that were kinder to the company's bottom line.

Dilley Collection

The influence of GRR's holding company, Commonwealth Power Railway and Light was made evident with the acquisition of 15 of the Hodenpyl-Hardy Pay-Within cars in 1917. Cars of similar design operated on other Commonwealth properties such as Battle Creek, Jackson, Kalamazoo, Lansing, and Saginaw.

Authors' Collection

A blind side view of the same car. Years of hard service through brutal Michigan weather contribute to its tired appearance. While not a remarkable design, the performance of these cars was deemed satisfactory enough for the Commonwealth System to use them on several other properties.
Grand Rapids
Public Library

Seeking ways to reduce labor, power, and track maintenance costs on its more lightly traveled lines, GRR received its first 19 Birney Safety Cars from Brill in 1920. Nine additional Birneys were added to the roster in the ensuing years. Tolerated at best by the riding public, loved by management for its cost efficiency, the Birney car gave many years of dependable service in the Furniture City.

Grand Rapids
Public Library

Following the arrival of the new Electric Rail Coaches from St. Louis Car Co. in 1926, efforts were made to upgrade the rest of the car fleet. The Birney pictured here received a bright new paint job and a name-"Rindge"-in place of its original number. The cars were named after prominent Grand Rapids personages or institutions. In this case "Rindge" referred to Lester J. Rindge, an early Grand Rapids shoe manufacturer.

Sam Ashendorf Collection

Several Birneys underwent extensive refurbishing to bring their appearance closer in line to the new St. Louis-built cars. Remodeled Birney "George W. Thayer" is posed for service on the Cherry-Ramona line.

Grand Rapids
Public Library

Grand Rapids received three "test" cars from three different builders in 1925. The idea was to find the best features to incorporate into a larger order. Test car "Minnesota" was the candidate submitted by the Light Weight Noiseless Car Co. It is seen here on its first day in Grand Rapids prior to an inspection run. The trucks, so white and pristine in the photo, were specially made for the car and featured roller bearings.

Erin Patrick

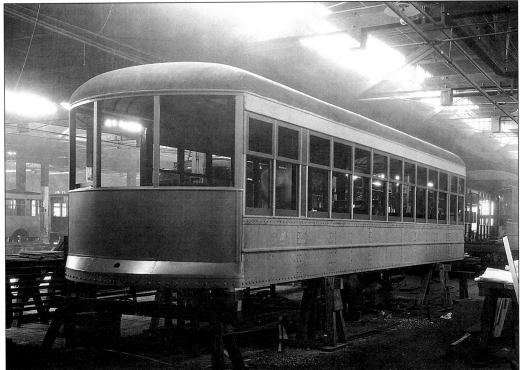

St. Louis Car Co. set about building its own entry, "St. Louis," shown here under construction at the company's plant in 1924.

Washington University Library

The finished car had many design features that were carried over into the larger order (also built by St. Louis). The "St. Louis" is shown here in service as it enters the Ramona Park loop.

Washington University Library

The prominent features of the new St. Louis cars as delivered included dual automobile-style headlights and fenders, an illuminated front dash, and full skirting to hide the trucks and reduce noise. The "David P. Clay" and its crew lay over at Ramona Park loop. This car influenced the design of subsequent new orders for Northern Texas Traction and Houston Electric in 1927.

Erin Patrick

A rear view of the same car at the same location. While there was nothing radically new in their design, the cars were popular with riders due to their attractive styling, lower steps for easier boarding, comfortable interiors, and quieter operation.

Grand Rapids Public Library

In later years the automotive-type fenders were replaced with ones of a simpler design. The full skirting was also removed for easier inspection and maintenance of the trucks and underbody equipment.

Richard Andrews

The lack of skirting on the "J. Morgan" affords a clear view of the car's St. Louis 64EIB trucks that were a standard feature of many of the builder's new city cars. Mesh screens were installed on the left side only for operation in the summer months.

Authors' Collection

Two of the Electric Rail Coaches pass each other in the later years of service. Their newness had worn off and it became apparent to management that even modern equipment and extensive marketing were unable to arrest the decline in Grand Rapids streetcar ridership.

Roger Monk

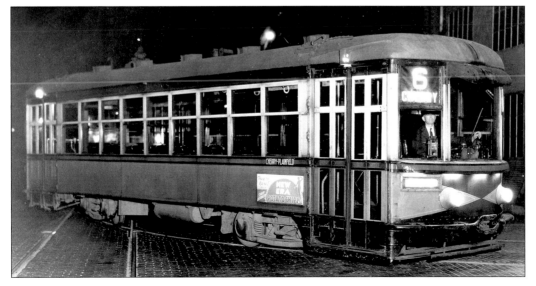

The St. Louis cars were easy for both riders and driver to spot with their various forms of illumination. The "J Boyd Pantlind" made for safer operation over city streets with its dual headlights, illuminated front dash and destination sign box along with lights over both doors to make boarding and alighting easier.

Grand Rapids
Public Museum

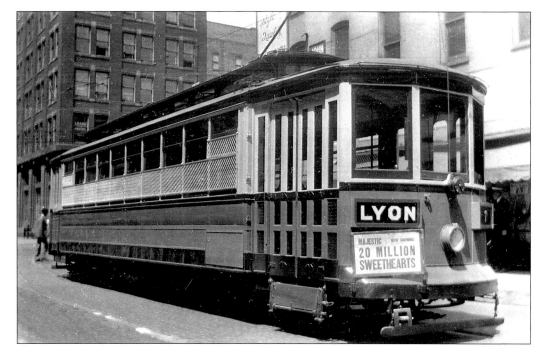

Even the old P.A.Y.E. cars were refurbished and were updated with folding (instead of sliding) front doors, end modifications, and a new paint scheme. This 1909 American Car Co. product was still providing service in 1934.

Roger Monk Collection

Grand Rapids Railway began using motor buses of rudimentary design to augment service on outlying routes, but these vehicles soon came to replace weaker streetcar lines.

David Winick Collection

The styling and comfort of Grand Rapids city buses gradually improved over time as witnessed by an ACF product from the early 1930s.

Authors' Collection

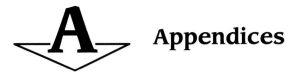

Appendices

MUST RENOUNCE THE UNION
Iron Clad Contract Promulgated by
The Street Railway Company to
Their Employees—Friends of
The Laboring Classes
Take Notice

*The following is the contract which the Street Railway
Company requires their employees to sign:*

"The undersigned, having entered the employ of the Valley City Street and Cable railway Company of Grand Rapids, a corporation, does in consideration of such employment, hereby agree to and with said corporation, that, during the entire period of said employment, what- ever the nature of the same, a day's work shall not be limited to 10 hours, but shall consist of so much time each day as the necessities or convenience of the business said corporation may seem to require, in the judgement of the proper officers, superintendents or foremen thereof; and in case such day's work shall at any time exceed ten hours, I agree to perform the same the faithfully and promptly, and for the wages agreed upon, as the case may be; and I do hereby waive any and all benefits, which I might otherwise derive from the two provisions of Act 137 of the legislature of the state of Michigan of 1885, entitled: "An act making 10 hours a legal day's work," approved June 5, 1885, or from any amendments of additions therein that may hereafter be passed.

"The foregoing and following agreement is understood to be a part of the contract of employment and is subject to no understanding, condition or modification , verbal, parol or written; and relates to work hereafter to be performed, it being expressly agreed and admitted that all other prior employment were subject to like conditions and stipulations.

"And it is further agreed, That no sum shall be at any time due and payable for my labor until the regular pay day of said corporation, next following the performance of such labor, and no demand for payment shall at any time operate to make any such sum due and payable prior to such pay day, as aforesaid.

"And it is still further agreed. That I will allow and hereby authorize to be taken out of my pay any damages for injury caused by my carelessness to the company's property; or to the property of anyone else for which the company may be liable.

"And it is further agreed, That, if any wages or monies due or to become due to me from said company shall be garnished or levied upon in the hands of said company the latter shall have a lien on such wags or monies, and such as shall thereafter become due for all costs attorney's fees, expenses, or other charges and disbursements that said company shall in anyway be put to, in, about or in connection which such garishment, and this lien shall be prior and paramount to any assignment by me, or to any garnishment, lien or claim whatsoever.

"And it is further agreed, between the parties herein, that in case the party of the second part shall join in any labor organization, he shall be at once subject to discharge from the party of the first part.

"Grand Rapids, Mich………….189. …………………………………….L. S.]"

*Those who are in sympathy with the work-
ing classes, assist us in removing this relic of
barbarism! By Order of Committee.*

Grand Rapids Morning Press,
May 13, 1891

General Description of New Electric Coaches for Benefit of Grand Rapids Residents

The *Minnesota*

Made by Light Weight Noiseless Car Co., Minneapolis

Length, 37 feet 6 inches; width, 8 feet 6 inches

Type: double trucks, specially made.

One-man or two-man operation

Weighs approximately 25,000 pounds

Seating capacity: 44 to 46

Motors are four General Electric 25-horsepower roller bearing

Brakes are drum band type, air controlled

Steps are well type, three inside

Seats are rattan

Plain wooden double floor with insulator

Windows are anti-rattle

Lighting fixtures, specially designed sidelights,

Holo-phane reflectors

Interior finish is Philippine mahogany

Exterior in Haskelite, finished in University of Minnesota's colors

Electrically heated, thermostatically controlled

Special features: Wheel development, 8 drilled holes fitted with rubber to help eliminate noise; tubular holes to reduce weight; special spring construction on trucks to assure easy riding; stoplight: bulletin board; bucket type seat for operator; attractive panel for all control levers and switches in front vestibule; newspaper vending boxes; Alemite greasing system.

The *Ohio*

Made by the Kuhlman Car Company, Cleveland, Ohio

Length: 37 feet 6 inches; width: 8 feet 6 3/4 inches

Type: double trucks, specially made.

One-man or two-men operation

Weighs approximately 25,000 pounds

Seating capacity: 44

Motors are four Westinghouse 25-horsepower

Journal bearings are Hyatt roller bearings

Brakes are drum band type, air controlled

Steps are folding type

Seats plush upholstered

Wooden floor, grooved aisle boards

Windows have special patented sash, semi-noiseless, dust-proof

Lighting fixtures in center of ceiling have opal reflectors

Interior finish, Philippine mahogany

Exterior finish, Duco, in gray and scarlet, Ohio State University colors

Electric heaters thermostatically controlled

Special features are: Extra wide, deep-seated plush upholstered seats; one half inch plate glass window in motorman's vestibule prevents fogging and frosting; automatic window wiper; exterior panels made of "Ply-metal", manufactured by Haskelite Company; stoplight; rear exit door equipped with treadle that automatically opens it; front vestibule panel that conceals all control levers and controls; motorman's bucket type seat upholstered in plush; bulletin board; newspaper vending boxes; mirrors for women at each of the entrance doors; rear warning signal device operating by battery and relay automatically when trolley trouble arises or other emergency occurs; newly patented wheel principle, a rubber cushion between core and tire.

The *St. Louis*

Made by St. Louis Car Company, St. Louis, Missouri

Length: 37 feet 11 inches; width, 8 feet 8¾ inches.

Type: double trucks, specially made, known as GR-54 "equalized roller journal bearings

Single end operation, one-man or two-men

Weighs approximately 25,000 pounds

Seating capacity: 44

Motors are four General Electric 25-horsepower with Hyatt roller armature bearings

Drum type clasp brakes, operated by compressed air on all four axles.

Steps are folding type

Seats leather upholstered, spring cushion and back.

Floor covering is mosaic inlaid rubber tiling

Windows have brass sash, are wide, dust-proof and draft-proof

Lighted by center ceiling fixtures; platforms and steps well lighted

Interior finish is natural Honduras mahogany

Exterior: steel plates done in blue and white pennant design, colors of St. Louis University, on gray background

Heaters are electric and thermostatically controlled.

Special features: Specially developed wheel that has hickory filler to help reduce noise and absorb sound; sheet steel skirt, 10 inches wide, that partly hides track and helps prevent truck rumbles; easy steps 15 ½ inches high; half inch thick plate glass in front of motorman to prevent fogging and frosting; porcelain enameled stanchions; rear end spotlight; fully enclosed instrument board; five-lamp display illumination on front dash; news bulletin board; semi-indirect lighting system; loud speaker for operator; newspaper vending box; special back-up device for emergencies; operator's seat bucket type, leather upholstered.

Grand Rapids Street Railway
Passengers Carried by Year
Service Rendered

Year	Revenue Passengers	Transfer Passengers	Total Passengers
1902	12,806,529	3,966,529	16,772,587
1909	15,045,833	5,735,167	20,780,000
1910			
1911			
1912	18,269,083	6,606,413	24,875,496
1913			
1914		at least 25%	25,484,514
1915	22,000,000	at least 25%	24,500,000*
1916			
1917	25,848,626	6,589,478	32,438,104
1918	24,884,739	5,990,443	30,875,182
1919	26,307,032	6,474,666	32,781,698
1920	27,813,220	6,627,889	34,441,109
1921	24,437,134	6,250,583	30,687,717
1922	24,058,780	6,191,023	30,249,803
1923	23,103,961		
1924	21,993,359		24,825,018
1925	19,267,331		23,947,305
1926	19,435,873		24,240,359
1927	18,378,036		
1928	17,483,996		22,089,289
1929	17,193,849		
1930	13,742,704		
1931	10,712,617		
1933			

*"The policemen, the detectives, the firemen, the agents and representatives of the city's many charities and philanthropies and others who are deserving of special favor were given limited free transportation, and the records indicate that approximately 2,500,000 million such passengers were carried during the year.

Select Bibliography of Sources

Records from City of Grand Rapids

Grand Rapids, City of (1864-1917) Proceedings, Common Council,
Grand Rapids, City of (1917-1935) Proceedings, City Commission.
Grand Rapids, City of, Plan Department (1927) The Grand Rapids City Plan.
Grand Rapids Railway Franchise Commission Records, 1912-1917.
Grand Rapids City Archives.

Contemporary News Accounts

Contemporary accounts of events in the period of Grand Rapids streetcar operation were found in the following newspapers:

Grand Rapids Daily Leader	Grand Rapids Eagle	Grand Rapids Herald	New York Times
Grand Rapids Democrat	Grand Rapids Evening Press	Grand Rapids Times	

Books

Bajema, Carl; Dave Kindem; and Jim Budzynski. *The Lake Line: The Grand Rapids, Grand Haven & Muskegon Railway Bulletin 144*. Central Electric Railfans' Association, 2012.

Baxter, Albert. *History of the City of Grand Rapids*, 1891.

Carlson, Norman. *Chicago, South Shore and South Bend Railroad: How the Medal was Won, Bulletin 124*. Central Electric Railfans' Association, 1985.

Carlson, Stephen, and Fred Schneider. *PCC: The Car That Fought Back*. Interurban Press, 1980.

Canfield, Joseph M., et al. *Electric Railways of Michigan –Bulletin 103*. Central Electric Railfans' Association, 1959.

Cox, Harold E. *The Birney Car*. Harold E. Cox, 1966.

Etten, W. J. *A Citizens' History of Grand Rapids*. A. P. Johnson, 1927.
Hilton, George W. *The Cable Car in America*, rev. ed., Howell-North Books, 1982.

Knopf, Michael. "Don't Worry, Relax! Public Policy, Franchises, and the End of Street Railways in Grand Rapids, Michigan, 1926-1935." *Grand River Valley History*, vol. 24 (2009), pp. 5-18.

Lee, Robert E. "The Streetcar Lines of Grand Rapids." *Michigan History*, vol. 46 (March 1962), pp. 15-27 and p. 24.

Middleton, William M. *The Time of the Trolley*. Golden West Books, 1987.

Miller, John A. *Fares Please!* Appleton-Century, 1960 reprint.
Rowsome, Frank Jr. *Trolley Car Treasury*. Bonanza Books, 1956.

Schramm, Jack; William Henning; and Richard Andrews. *When Eastern Michigan Rode the Rails, Book III*. Interurban Press, 1988.

Snow, Gail. *Remarkable Ramona Park: A Passionate History of a Much Beloved Place*. Color House Graphics, 2013.

Wynbeek, David. *The Dummy Line Riot—1888. 75 Years on Eastern Avenue*. Eastern Avenue Christian Reformed Church, 1954.

Periodicals

Beld, Gordon G. "Been There, Done That. A Proposed Route through Downtown is Not a New Idea. It's a 70-year Old Part of Grand Rapids History." *Grand Rapids Magazine*, (December 2008), pp. 24-25.

"Conditions Which Govern the Type of Car for City Service: Grand Rapids, Michigan". *Brill Magazine* 8 (15 May 1914), pp. 130-137.

Dunne, Forrest. "You Can Sell Anything if You Make It Salable." *Forbes Magazine*, vol. 18 (October 15, 1926), pp. 19-22.

"Freight Station at Grand Rapids [Holland interurban]." *Electric Traction Weekly*, (August 8, 1908), p. 787.

Gillespie, Robert S. "A Streetcar Named Grand Rapids." *Michigan History Magazine*, vol. 89, no. 3 (May/June 2005), pp 34-39.

Greenwood, Regina A., Charles D. Wrege, Peter J. Gordon & John Joos. "Louis J. DeLamarter: Can He Save a Dying Industry?" *Journal of Management History* 15, no. 2 (2009), pp. 134-145.

Hilton, George W. "The Cable Car in Grand Rapids." *American Railroad Journal*, 2 (1967-1968), pp. 16-30.

Jenkins, W. B. "The Human Factor. What President Hanchett Has Done for Grand Rapids Company." *Public Service Magazine*, vol. 16, no. 4 (April 1914), pp. 123-126.

Knopf, Michael. "Don't Worry, Relax! Public Policy, Franchises, and the End of Street Railways in Grand Rapids, Michigan, 1926-1935." *Grand River Valley History*, vol. 24 (2009), pp. 5-18.

Lee, Robert E. "The Streetcar Lines of Grand Rapids." *Michigan History*, vol. 46 (March 1962), pp. 15-27 and p. 24.

"New Car House for Grand Rapids Railway Company." *Electric Traction*, (August 1912), pp. 815-816.

"New [Kuhlman] Cars for Grand Rapids." *Brill's Magazine*, vol. 1, no. 11 (November 15, 1907), pp. 222-223.

"Proceedings of the Conference on Historical Analysis & Research in Marketing." *CHARM*, (April-May 2005), pp. 312-321.

Periodicals

"Street Railway History: "The Development of Half a Century in Local Transportation." *Michigan Tradesman* vol. 31, no. 1595 (April 15, 1914), pp. 64, 66-67.

"Two-Car Trains on Michigan Road [GR, H & C Holland Interurban]." *Electric Traction Weekly*, vol. 4 (June 27, 1908).

White, John H. Jr. "Horse Power [for streetcars]." *American Heritage of Invention & Technology*, vol. 8, no. 1 (Summer 1992), pp. 40-51.

White, Arthur S. "Boynton & Wesselius: Disastrous Careers of Grand Rapids Railway Promoters." *Michigan Tradesman*, (December 4, 1929), p. 114.

Street Railway Review

Articles from the *Street Railway Review* and its predecessor, the *Street Railway Journal*:

Wrege, Charles D., Regina A. Greenwood, and Carl J. Bajema. "Louis J. DeLamarter: Marketing Changed the Transit Industry: 1920-1935." *CHARM*, (April-May 2005), pp. 312-321.

"Railway Power House at Grand Rapids." vol. 2 (June 1891), pp. 373-374.

"Street Railway Mail Boxes in Grand Rapids." vol. 10, no. 1 (January 15, 1900), pp. 45-46.

"The Grand Rapids, Holland and Lake Michigan Rapid Railway." vol.19, no. 11 (March 15, 1902), pp. 330-336.

"New Car House and Club Rooms in Grand Rapids." vol. 29, no. 2 (January 11, 1908), pp.45-46.

"The New Standard Hodenpyl-Hardy Car." vol. 50 (September 15, 1917), pp. 446-447.

"C.E.R.A. Holds Two-Day Session." vol 54, vo. 21 (December 20, 1919), pp. 989-990.

"Car House in Grand Rapids Burned. Fifty-eight Cars Destroyed in a Fire Which Wiped Out Hall Street Plant." vol. 64, no. 4 (July 26, 1924), p. 141.

"Telling the Public What the Track Cost." vol. 64, no. 9 (August 30, 1924), p. 315.

"Car Order Delayed; Grand Rapids Intends to Conduct Test of Vehicles Supplied by Three Manufacturers." vol. 64, no. 21 (November 22, 1924), p. 906.

"First Grand Rapids Test Car Delivered." vol.65, no.13, (March 28, 1925), p. 529.

"Grand Rapids Car Competition Should Be Only a Beginning." vol. 65, no. 19 (May 9, 1925), pp. 719-720.

"Many Innovations in Grand Rapids Cars." vol. 65, no.19, (May 9, 1925), pp. 721-725.

"Many Innovations in Grand Rapids Cars." vol. 65, no. 20 (May 16, 1925), pp. 767-770.

"Many Innovations in Grand Rapids Cars." vol. 65, no. 21 (May 23, 1925), pp. 807-810.

"Root Lifeguard Used in Grand Rapids." vol. 65, no. 23 (June 6, 1925), p. 880.

"Style in Car Design." vol. 65, no. 24 (June 13, 1925), pp. 936-937.

"The Car Builder's Car." vol. 65, no. 24 (June 13, 1925), pp. 937-938.

"Board Ends Controversy." vol. 65, no. 24 (June 13, 1925), p. 946.

"'Don't Worry' Campaign in Grand Rapids." vol. 66, no. 5 (August 1, 1925), pp. 163-164.

"Convenient Information Office in Grand Rapids." vol. 66, no. 8 (August 22, 1925), p. 280.

"Advertising That Travels." vol. 66, no. 12 (September 19, 1925), p. 441.

"Replacement Due for 25,000 Obsolete Cars." vol. 66, no. 15 (October 10, 1925), p. 576.

"The Coffin Award for 1925 Goes to Pittsburgh." vol. 66, no. 15 (October 10, 1925), pp. 598-599.

"Grand Rapids Car Exhibit Deserves Thanks of the Industry." vol. 66, no. 17 (October 24, 1925), p. 724.

"Coffin Award Contestants Tell of Economies." vol. 66, no. 17 (October 24, 1925), pp. 733-734.

"Many Safety Methods Developed by Companies in Coffin Prize Contest." vol. 66, no.18 (October 31, 1925), p. 785.

"Promoting Better Relationship Between Employee and Employer." vol. 66, no. 19 (November 7, 1925), pp. 823-825.

"Grand Rapids Car Exhibited in Detroit." vol. 66, no. 19 (November 7, 1925), p. 841.

"Securing New Capital for Extensions and Betterments." vol. 66, no. 20 (November 14, 1925), pp. 857-860.

"Spray Cleaning Methods Are Easy and Economical." vol. 66, no. 21 (November 21, 1925), p. 893.

"Construction Practices that Reduce Maintenance and Operating Costs." vol. 66, no. 21 (November 21, 1925), pp. 898-902.

"Spray Washing for Cars." vol. 66, no. 21 (November 21, 1925), p. 910.

"Important Exhibit Made. De Luxe Coaches of Grand Rapids Railway Shown Before Convention of City Managers." vol. 66, no. 21 (November 21, 1925), p. 923.

"Service Is a Necessary Function of Successful Operation." vol. 66, no. 22 (November 28, 1925), pp. 947-948.

"Grand Rapids Railway Specifications for New Cars." vol. 66, no. 23 (December 5, 1925), p. 1020.

"Grand Rapids Railway Orders New Cars." vol. 66, no. 26 (December 26, 1925), pp. 1113-1115.

DeLamarter, L. J. "Winning Public Good Will." vol. 67, no. 6, February 6, 1926, pp. 247-249.

"Hinged Apron Permits Easy Repairs to Cars." vol. 67, no. 8 (February 20, 1926), p. 326.

"Grand Rapids Enlists Support of Boy Scouts." vol. 67, no. 14 (April 3, 1926), p. 584.

"Steel Frames Make Neat Car Signs." vol. 67, no. 16, (April 17, 1926), p. 686.

"Reels Protect Shop Hose." vol. 67, no. 17 (April 24, 1926), p. 727.

"Grand Rapids Cars Are Soon to Be Delivered." vol. 67, no. 18 (May 1, 1926), p. 786.

"Small Models Visualize Car Appearance." vol. 67, no. 19 (May 8, 1926), pp. 806-807.

"Traffic Accidents Analyzed at Grand Rapids." vol. 67, no. 20 (May 15, 1926), p. 840.

"Convenient Rack for Trolley Catchers." vol. 67, no. 21 (May 22, 1926), p. 890.

"Car Design Gets a Forward Impetus." vol. 67, no. 22 (May 29, 1926), p. 911.

"New Cars for Grand Rapids Being Delivered." vol. 67, no. 22 (May 29, 1926), pp. 914-917
.
"Turntable Speeds Sash Painting." vol. 67, no. 22 (May 29, 1926), p. 934.

"Large Wheeled Acetylene Welding Truck." vol. 67, no. 23 (June 5, 1926), p. 978.

"Waste Cans Insure Uniform Saturation." vol. 67, no. 24 (June 12, 1926), p. 1018.

"The Glory That is Grand Rapids." vol. 67,no. 25 (June 19, 1926), p. 1039.

"New Cars in Service in Grand Rapids." vol. 67, no. 25 (June 19, 1926), pp. 1069-1070
.
"Grand Rapids Has a Bonfire." vol. 68, no. 1 (July 3, 1926), pp. 36-37.

"The Grand Rapids Bonfire Was a Mistake." [Letter] vol. 68, no. 1 (July 10, 1926), p. 66.

"Grand Rapids Rides in New Cars." vol. 68, no. 7 August 14, 1926), p. 272.

"Cartoonist Uses Grand Rapids Cars to Point Moral." vol. 68, no. 8 (August 21, 1926), p. 319.

"More Praise for Grand Rapids Cars—More Patrons Carried." vol. 68, no. 10 (September 4, 1926), p. 393.

"What New Cars Are Doing for Public Relations." vol. 68, no.13 (September 25, 1926), p. 485.

DeLamarter, L. J. "Rail Coaches Win Their Way in Grand Rapids." vol. 68, no. 13 (September 25, 1926), pp. 537-540.

"World's Series News Told by Grand Rapids Cars." vol. 68, no. 17 (October 23, 1926), p. 781.

"Savings in Operating Costs With New Cars on Grand Rapids Railway." vol. 68, no. 22 (November 27, 1926), p. 972.

DeLamarter, L. J. "Courage and New Equipment Accomplish Results in Grand Rapids." vol. 68, no. 23 (December 4, 1926), pp. 1015-1016.

"Free Parking Spaces Increases Street Car Riding." col. 68, no. 24 (December 11, 1926), p. 1040.

"Excessive Noise Eliminated by Rebuilding Trucks." vol. 68, no. 25 (December 18, 1926), pp. 1087-1088
.
"Not Unfriendly, Just Indifferent." [GRH&C; Grand Rapids-Jenison] vol. 69, vo. 5 (January 29, 1927), p. 191.

"Now They Know What They Miss." [GRH&C; Grand Rapids-Jenison] vol. 69, no. 5 (January 29, 1927), p. 217.

"Campaign to Restore Michigan Suburban Line Continues." vol. 69, vo. 6, (February 5, 1927), p. 260.

"Progress in Campaign to Restore Michigan Road." vol. 69, no. 11, (March 12, 1927), p. 466.

"United Suburban Railway Takes Form." vol. 69, no. 14, (April 2, 1927), pp 624-625.

"Grandville Officers Elected." vol. 69, no. 15, (April 9, 1927), p. 675.

"Line from Grand Rapids to Jenison to Open Up." vol. 69, no.24, (June 11, 1927), p. 1060.

"Grand Rapids Makes Its [Annual] Report." vol. 69, no. 5, (January 29, 1927), p. 193.

"Good showing in Grand Rapids [Annual Report]," vol. 69, no. 5, (January 29, 1937), pp. 223-224.

"Spring Plunger Holds Tail Light in Place." vol. 69, no. 6, (February 5, 1927), p. 251.

"Welding Brake Beams to Make as Good as New." vol. 69, No. 8, (February 19, 1927), p. 344.

"Combined Snow Scraper and Sweeper." Vol. 69, no. 9, (February 26, 1927), p. 380.

"Fire Equipment Location [in car houses] Shown by Striking Colors." Vol. 69, No. 10, (March 5, 1927), p. 424.

"Handy type of Car Wheel Buggy [to use in car shops]." vol. 69, no. 12, (March 19, 1927), p. 525.

"Paving Relief Measure Lost in Grand Rapids." vol. 69, No. 13, March 26, 1927), p. 585.

"Unusual Publicity Campaign in Grand Rapids." Vol. 69, no. 14, April 2, 1927), p. 627.

Street Railway Review

"Another Coffin Contest [Entry] Announced—Grand Rapids." vol. 69, no. 15, (April 9, 1927), p, 665.

"Readjustment in Grand Rapids [reorganization]." vol. 69, no. 16, (April 16, 1927), p. 718.

"Corporate Readjustment Favorable to Future Financing." vol. 69, no. 17, (April 23, 1927), p.726.

"Convenient Truck for Armatures [in car shop]." vol. 69, no. 17, (Aril 23, 1927), p. 744.

"Suggests Eliminating Parking in Downtown Grand Rapids." vol. 69, no. 18, April 30, 1927), p. 776.

"Stockholders of Grand Rapids Railway to Meet May 25." vol. 69, no. 20, (May 14, 1927), p. 882.

"Grand Rapids Railroad Accepts Obligations." vol. 69, no. 21, (May 21, 1927), p. 929.

"Readjustment of Grand Rapids Approved." vol. 69, no. 22,(May 28, 1927), p. 978.

"Grand Rapids Sees Rail Coach Christened 'Lindy.'" vol. 70, no. 1, (July 2, 1927), p. 34.

"Col. Lindbergh Honored by the Grand Rapids Flying Club; Coach at Grand Rapids Named After Col. Charles Lindbergh." vol. 70, no. 2, (July 9, 1927), pp. 76-77.

"Rebus Contest as a Business Getter." vol. 70, No. 16, (October 15, 1927), p. 736.

"This Year's Coffin Prize Winner." Vol. 70, no. 16, (October 15, 1927), p. 726.

"Modern Coaches Important Factor in Winning Coffin Prize." vol. 70, no. 16, (October 15, 1927), pp. 727-728.

"The [Coffin] Prize Winner This Year: What It Is and Has Done; Car Named After Colonel Lindbergh; Side and End Bumpers in Grand Rapids; Seats for the Passenger and Operator Operating Costs Reduced at Grand Rapids; Winning Popular Approval in Many Ways." vol. 70, no. 16, (October 15, 1927), 728-738.

"Glorifying the Coffin Award." vol. 70, no. 24, (December 10, 1927), p. 1051.

"Capitalizing the Coffin Award." vol. 70, no. 24, (December 10, 1927), pp. 1052-1054.

"Another Sensation [Versare six-wheel streetcar] in Grand Rapids." vol 70, no.24: (December 10, 1927), p. 1079.

"Tunney Rides the Trolley in Grand Rapids." vol. 71, no. 10, (March 10, 1938), p. 413.

"Grand Rapids Solicits Suggestions [from employees via *Token,* the company magazine]." vol. 71, no. 13, (March 31, 1928), p. 557.

Unpublished Manuscripts

Knecht, John. *History of Grand Rapids Street Railways Down to the Purchase by the Commonwealth Power Co.* Unpublished, 1910.

Stuart, L. G. *History of the Grand Rapids Street Railways Down to the Purchase by the Commonwealth Power Company, 1910.* Manuscript at Grand Rapids Public Library, 1926.